THE ELUSIVE
ENEMY

THE ELUSIVE ENEMY

U.S. Naval Intelligence and the Imperial Japanese Fleet

DOUGLAS FORD

NAVAL INSTITUTE PRESS
Annapolis, Maryland

This book has been brought to publication with the
generous assistance of Marguerite and Gerry Lenfest.

Naval Institute Press
291 Wood Road
Annapolis, MD 21402

Library of Congress Cataloging-in-Publication Data
Ford, Douglas
  The elusive enemy : U.S. naval intelligence and the Imperial Japanese Fleet /
Douglas Ford.
    p. cm.
  Includes bibliographical references and index.
  ISBN 978-1-59114-280-5 (hbk. : alk. paper) — ISBN 978-1-61251-065-1 (ebook) 1.
World War, 1939–1945—Secret service—United States. 2. Japan. Kaigun—History—
20th century. 3. United States. Office of Naval Intelligence—History—20th century.
4. Military intelligence—United States—History—20th century. 5. World War,
1939–1945—Naval operations, Japanese. 6. World War, 1939–1945—Naval operations,
American. 7. World War, 1939–1945—Campaigns—Pacific Ocean. I. Title.
  D810.S7H637 2011
  940.54'8673—dc23

                                                        2011023456

♾ This paper meets the requirements of ANSI/NISO z39.48-1992
(Permanence of Paper).
Printed in the United States of America.

19 18 17 16 15 14 13 12 11   9 8 7 6 5 4 3 2 1
First printing

Contents

Maps

Acknowledgments

This book is largely a sequel to my first published monograph on British intelligence and the campaigns against Japan on the Southeast Asia front, which admittedly focused on what was a peripheral, albeit interesting, theater of World War II. The idea of producing a work that covered the much wider canvas of American intelligence and the Imperial Japanese armed forces in the Pacific Ocean areas dawned on me toward the closing phases of my tenure as a graduate student, when most aspiring scholars begin to contemplate how they envision their careers as academic researchers.

The completion of this book would not have been possible without the generous support provided by my employers at the University of Salford. During the summers of 2005 to 2007, I was able to undertake several trips to the other side of the Atlantic and spend extended lengths of time in the Washington, D.C., area, thanks to the travel allowances that were unquestioningly offered by John Keiger and the European Studies Research Institute. A good part of the finances needed to complete the research for this book were also made available through the University of Salford's research investment fund. Last but not least, I would like to thank my colleagues for letting me take a six-month sabbatical leave during the early part of 2008. Without being allowed parole from my normal teaching duties, it is most unlikely that the work could have been finished in the time frame that it was completed.

A team of archivists have gone out of their way to assist me in compiling the materials needed for this research project. I thank the staff at the National Archives in College Park. In particular, Patrick Osbourne, along with the lately departed and much missed John Taylor, was invaluable in helping me make sense out of the seemingly endless and indecipherable catalogs of the Navy Department and Office of Naval Intelligence records. The archivists at the U.S. Naval Historical Center were nothing but cooperative in tracking down the documents and private papers in their collections. During my visit to the Naval War College at Newport, Rhode Island, Evelyn Cherpak untiringly retrieved the countless boxes that I ordered on an around-the-clock basis. Last my gratitude also goes to the staff at the manuscripts collection of the Library of Congress, as well as the British National Archives in London. Every effort has been made to ensure that the necessary permissions for quotation of documentary material have been obtained, and I offer my most sincere apologies to anyone whose copyrights I have unknowingly infringed upon.

Portions of this book have already appeared in works published. Many of the documents from the British National Archives have been cited in the monograph *Britain's Secret War against Japan, 1937–45* (2006). A large part of Chapter One has been published as "U.S. Naval Intelligence and the Imperial Japanese Fleet during the Washington Treaty Era, c.1922–1936," in *Mariner's Mirror* (2007). The sections on Japanese intelligence and strategic culture also appeared in "Strategic Culture, Intelligence Assessment, and the Conduct of the Pacific War, 1941–1945: The British-Indian and Imperial Japanese Armies in Comparison," in *War in History* (2007). Finally, a small part of Chapter One, on American war planning prior to December 1941, was published in "Realistic Caution and Ambivalent Optimism: U.S. Intelligence Assessments and War Preparations against Japan, 1918–1941," in *Diplomacy and Statecraft* (2010).

Among the scholars who have offered priceless advice and ideas that helped me better my understanding of the intricacies of intelligence studies and naval affairs, as well as to follow through with the research and writing phases of this manuscript, I would like to thank Richard Aldrich, Martin Alexander, Antony Best, John Ferris, Eric Grove, Peter Jackson, Ken Kotani, Joe Maiolo, Chris Murphy, Sally Paine, Nick Sarantakes, Len Scott, Alaric

Searle, and Larry Valero. The history and security studies team at Salford is simply a wonderful group of friends, and the most congenial colleagues one can hope to work with. Finally, my students, both my former ones at the London School of Economics and Aberystwyth University as well as the current cohort at Salford, have never failed to offer fresh ideas and concepts on how to study the subject areas of military history and intelligence.

This book is dedicated to my family, for their never-ending support of my life ambitions and endless patience at having an academic in their tow.

DOUGLAS FORD
MANCHESTER, MAY 2011

Abbreviations

AAFSWPA	Allied Air Forces, Southwest Pacific Area
ABDA	American-British-Dutch-Australian Command
ASDIC	Active sound detection apparatus
BuAer	Bureau of Aeronautics
BuOrd	Bureau of Ordnance
CAP	Combat air patrol
CIC	Combat information center
CINCPAC	Commander in chief, Pacific Fleet
CINCPOA	Commander in chief, Pacific Ocean Areas
CNO	Chief of naval operations
COMAIRPAC	Commander, Air Force Pacific Fleet
COMAIRSOPAC	Commander, Aircraft South Pacific Force
COMINCH	Commander in chief, U.S. Fleet
COMSOPAC	Commander, South Pacific Force
CV	Fleet aircraft carrier
CVE	Escort aircraft carrier
CVL	Light aircraft carrier
DNI	Director of Naval Intelligence
FDO	Fighter direction officer
FTP	Fleet Tactical Publications
IFF	Identification-friend-or-foe
IJN	Imperial Japanese Navy

IJNAF	Imperial Japanese Navy Air Force
JCS	Joint Chiefs of Staff
JIC	Joint Intelligence Committee
JICPOA	Joint Intelligence Center, Pacific Ocean Areas
Op-16-V	Air Intelligence Group, ONI
Op-35	Air Information Division, Office of the CNO
PAC-10	Current Tactical Orders and Doctrine, U.S. Pacific Fleet
POW	Prisoner of war
RCM	Radio countermeasures
RMA	Revolutions in military affairs
sigint	Signals intelligence
SWPA	Southwest Pacific Area
TAIC	Technical Air Intelligence Center
USAAF	U.S. Army Air Force
VB	Bomber squadron
VF	Fighter squadron
WPD	War Plans Division

THE ELUSIVE
ENEMY

Introduction

More than sixty years have passed since the Pacific War ended, and the U.S. Navy's experience in fighting the Imperial Japanese Navy (IJN) continues to attract attention from historians. The sustained interest is due to a number of factors. The campaign in the Asia-Pacific theaters constituted one of the first occasions where the participants made extensive use of modern naval technologies, including maritime aviation and the submarine, both of which caused much greater levels of damage than previously available weapons. Personnel from the U.S. and Japanese navies faced what was often a complicated task of figuring out ways to deploy their armaments to neutralize their enemy, while at the same time providing adequate protection for friendly forces.

More significant, the Americans were engaging an opponent whose capabilities they had long tried to assess prior to the conflict, but which they had seriously underestimated. Until the Japanese launched their attack on Pearl Harbor in December 1941, the accepted belief among defense officials was that the IJN had serious weaknesses that prevented it from challenging the U.S. Navy. The destruction that the IJN and its air arm inflicted during the opening stages, including the sinking of a large portion of the U.S. fleet, along with HMS *Prince of Wales* and *Repulse* off the coast of Malaya, compelled the Americans to reconsider their views. In order to develop a more realistic evaluation, the U.S. Navy needed to undertake a substantial endeavor to obtain accurate information on its opponent, and study the material in a judicious manner. Naval intelligence played a pivotal role in shaping the conduct of the Pacific War. It helped U.S. ship crews and airmen learn how the IJN was a skillful fighting force that could be overcome only when they developed an effective means of deploying their weapons.

Three conclusions emerge from the work. First, combat experience was the most important source of intelligence that helped the Americans to understand the Japanese. Second, while first-hand encounters were vital, an equally significant catalyst was the naval establishment's organizational culture, which stated that wars were to be carried out with a good awareness of the enemy's capabilities. Because strategic plans were based on a premise that fighting the Japanese required U.S. forces to conduct a protracted campaign, intelligence efforts were subsequently geared to evaluate the IJN's capacity to do likewise. Finally, and directly related, racial perceptions did not play a significant role in shaping American opinions of the Japanese. On one hand, the ethnic divide that separated the belligerents made it difficult to ignore cultural characteristics and their effect on the enemy's performance. Nevertheless, intelligence staffs, along with naval personnel, realized that they did not have enough information to make an educated assessment. This was in line with the U.S. Navy's habit of basing its judgments of foreign armed forces on a logical analysis of the available evidence, rather than inferences.

Intelligence Studies and Pacific War Historiography

A large part of the existing literature on the Pacific War tends to overlook the intelligence dimension, mainly because intelligence studies, as an academic discipline, remains in a stage of relative infancy. Until the use of intelligence in warfare became common at the turn of the twentieth century, scholars of military affairs, along with practitioners, made minimal references to the subject. A notable exception was the Chinese theorist Sun Tzu, whose treatise, written around the sixth century BC, affirmed that knowledge of the enemy was an essential requisite for avoiding defeat. Success did not necessarily hinge on the use of weapons, but more on what he described as "measurement," or weighing the relative strengths and weaknesses of the opposing sides.[1] Yet until recently the majority of academics held an accepted view that maintained that the study of intelligence was impossible. The notion was not entirely mistaken. Intelligence activities have always been carried out with exceptional secrecy, and those involved hesitate to expose their results, whether successful or otherwise. During the early 1980s, Christopher Andrew and David Dilks described intelligence as the "missing dimension" of history, because written records available for public inspection were few and far between.[2]

In subsequent decades, as freedom of information acts enabled governments around the world to release archival materials on intelligence during World War II and, later, the Cold War period, intelligence studies became a growth industry. Today, with the plethora of documentation that is accessible, the assumption that one cannot conduct serious research in the area must be treated with utmost skepticism. Scholars, as well as practitioners, have put forward a number of definitions for the term "intelligence," all of which are key to comprehending the nature of its activities. While intelligence constitutes "information," it needs to be conceptualized as information that is handled in a certain manner. Intelligence does not necessarily need to be based on confidential sources, nor does it have to be carried out by specialized agencies.[3] Nevertheless, the main functions of the "intelligence cycle," namely, the collection, analysis, and distribution of knowledge, along with its implementation into policy, need to be undertaken by state officials, and kept secret so as to prevent the enemy from compromising the success of an organization's activities.[4] In reality, the intelligence cycle is not a smoothly integrated process, but a complex web of relations between the "producers" of intelligence and the policymakers they serve.[5] The interactions are frequently characterized by uncertainties within both parties on what types of information need to be obtained, as well as disagreements over who should have access to the material. Furthermore, when intelligence organizations are not equipped to handle information, policymakers take on a large part of the tasks, including analysis. Yet the concept of the cycle is useful for viewing intelligence as a series of discrete steps, moving from early decisions concerning data compilation to the ultimate act of using the finished product to inform decision-makers. Of equal importance, intelligence is information geared for a specific purpose. John Ferris describes it as "the collection and analysis of information by a power, to enable it to make the maximum use of its resources" against potential enemies.[6] Intelligence helps leaders understand their environment, and can offer hints on how to employ the main instruments of statecraft, namely, diplomacy and armed force, to protect national interests. Among the most popular approaches to intelligence studies are those that treat it as a way of providing new explanations as to why decision-makers have developed their perceptions of world events, and the way in which the perceptions, in turn, have led them to deal with particular crises in the manner that they have.[7] The best works have examined the relationship between collection and analysis on one hand, and the subsequent influence on the decision-making process on the other hand.

Although intelligence has proven to be an integral component of international conflicts, the scholarship still contains large gaps. Part of the reason is that intelligence archives are not always neatly organized, and hence are harder to navigate in comparison with other primary sources. The root of the problem, however, most likely stems from the fact that historians do not attempt to make use of the evidence that has become available, because they are reluctant to cast off their traditional view that intelligence studies is an esoteric and inaccessible subject area.[8]

This book fills the gap by examining how U.S. intelligence on the IJN developed during the Pacific War and explaining the subsequent influence on the Navy's conduct of its operations. The semi-official histories on U.S. naval operations during World War II provided detailed accounts of the campaigns in the Pacific theaters.[9] Attempts have also been made to determine the underlying causes for the U.S. Navy's performance. The works covering doctrine and technology suggest that the main task was to deploy the Pacific Fleet's ships and weapons in a manner that worked to overcome the Japanese.[10] The perceptions that U.S. personnel held concerning the IJN, and their views of the obstacles they faced, have been described, but the ways in which the views evolved have not been analyzed in great detail. Likewise, the literature on the key naval battles addresses the lessons learned through encounters with the Japanese navy, but tends not to describe how those lessons influenced the long-term advancement of U.S. fighting methods.[11]

In explaining the U.S. victory in the Pacific theaters, many authors have highlighted material factors such as economic prowess. John Ellis illustrated how America's abundant supply of resources and manufacturing plants enabled it to build an overwhelmingly larger quantity of ships, aircraft, and equipment than the Japanese. The outcome thus relied "heavily on industrial predominance and the enormous margins of superiority in military hardware that flowed from it."[12] At the same time, a number of historians have argued that the success did not depend solely on resources. Ronald Spector concluded that effective training and strategic planning played an equally important role.[13] More recently, Richard Overy emphasized how the statistics pointing to matériel do not tell the whole story, and argued that one needs to look at equally important features, including the comparative quality of the weapons, and how well they were used.[14] Industrial productivity made the Allied victory in World War II possible, but did not render it a foregone conclusion. Economic strength had to be harnessed to construct an effective fighting machine, whose performance was not merely determined by quantitative factors, but by a number of intangible aspects, such as doctrine and morale. The hypothesis raises questions as to how other qualitative facets, such as knowledge of the enemy, helped U.S. forces wage a successful campaign. This is not to suggest that intelligence was the primary factor that enabled the Americans to prevail. The best intelligence is "impotent" unless armed forces have sufficient strength to execute their operations.[15] Nevertheless, when commanders properly utilize intelligence, it acts as a "force multiplier" that allows for a more efficient and economical deployment of resources. Intelligence helps one identify enemy weaknesses that are open to attack, as well as the strengths one needs to guard against. The U.S. Navy's engagements against the IJN were no exception to this rule.

The majority of the works that do cover intelligence during the Pacific War focus on the traditional sub-area of signals intelligence (sigint). The literature describes how the Allied intelligence services succeeded in decoding the IJN's communications, and provided commanders with information that was vital for carrying out their operations.[16] While signals decrypts have proven useful for obtaining statistical data on force dispositions and numerical strengths, they often provide limited information on matters such as fighting methods and the quality of training. The latter are often described as *qualitative* or *non-material* features, a knowledge of which is essential in order to engage enemy forces.[17] Indeed, an officer who served extensively in Asia during the interwar period described cryptanalysis as "only one part of intelligence."[18] Intelligence staffs need to draw upon an array of evidence, including human agents, documentary sources, and photographic reconnaissance.

The particular conditions of wartime also permit the use of material that is not available in times of peace, the most important of which is observations of how enemy forces perform in battle. The term "intelligence" will encompass the full range of information the U.S. Navy drew upon. To use a term coined by practitioners, this work focuses on "all source analysis."[19]

While all military organizations need to properly gauge their adversary, the task involves substantial complications. In the early part of the nineteenth century, Carl von Clausewitz described how one of the foremost dilemmas facing any army is that the situation on the battlefield undergoes constant changes. According to Clausewitz, the value of intelligence is at best questionable, and commanders thus have to use their imagination, while relying on boldness and surprise to overcome their opponents.[20] In recent decades, scholars have drawn upon numerous historical case studies to lay out the uses and limits of intelligence. One of the most prominent works has been written by Michael Handel, who questioned Clausewitz's contention that "military genius" and intuition be used to deal with the unknown, and asserted that all leaders need "at least some sort of intelligence" to support their estimates.[21] At the same time, intelligence does not necessarily offer an insight into the enemy's intentions and capabilities. Much depends on how the material is evaluated, and the analyst's intellectual capabilities are the key assets needed for a good judgment.[22] The harsh reality that befalls any intelligence organization is that data processing remains a human activity, which is frequently prone to error. Analysts need to synthesize a wide pool of information, and make sense out of a world where the strategic and political environment consists of a multitude of unfamiliar elements that are constantly evolving. In addition, when foreign nations keep their activities secret, assessments are by definition based on incomplete knowledge. Intelligence can thus alleviate the element of uncertainty that decision-makers are persistently confronted with, but cannot be realistically expected to remove it.[23] Technological improvements, in the form of more efficient equipment for collecting, collating, and communicating information, do not offer a panacea. On the contrary, the large amounts of intelligence that become available often create a data overload and further confusion.[24]

Nevertheless, when appraised properly, intelligence does provide a more realistic image than would otherwise be the case. While the battlefield situa-

tion may be composed of complex features that preclude a crystal-clear estimate, it does not follow that calculations are futile.[25] Furthermore, predicting
the behavior of outside parties is problematic, but judgments to the effect
that certain courses of action are more or less probable in given circumstances
can often be made, and with good accuracy.[26] Leaders who use intelligence
regularly are also more likely to pursue a policy that is suited for dealing with
the situations they face than those who try to manage without it.[27] The ideal
assessment produces a coherent overall analysis for the policymaker, while at
the same time drawing attention to the aspects that remain uncertain.[28]

Intelligence and the Conduct of the Pacific War: Challenges and Benefits

The U.S. Navy's intelligence effort during the Pacific War illustrates how
evaluating an enemy presents a number of challenges, as well as benefits.
The most significant problem stems from the fact that military organizations
almost invariably embark on hostilities without fully knowing the elements
they have to face, largely because the preceding period of peace provides limited opportunities to obtain information. In comparison to other state institutions, defense establishments contend with a unique dilemma, in that they
must prepare for conflicts that may occur at an undetermined point in the
future, against an opponent whose fighting potential is uncertain, and in conditions of violence that cannot be simulated in peacetime.[29] Yet the preparatory measures taken prior to hostilities have a decisive impact on how armed
services perform in wartime conditions. The task becomes more intricate
during periods of revolutions in military affairs (RMA), when nations acquire
a significantly altered capacity to project their military potential, as a result of
various technological, economic, and social changes. The years prior to the
Pacific War witnessed a particular type of RMA, where the increased availability of the internal combustion engine, coupled with advances in aircraft
technology, led to the development of new weapons systems such as maritime
aviation and the submarine. Naval war plans had to be based on the understanding that friendly forces and potential enemies alike had opportunities
to devise new ways of fighting. Indeed, one of the key axioms emphasized in
Alfred Mahan's seminal work was that changes in naval technology do not
necessarily alter the strategies used to achieve wartime objectives, but they

inevitably affect more detailed features such as the tactics for defeating the opponent's fleet.[30] Julian Corbett also described how, throughout the centuries, naval staffs held certain theories on how to conduct operations, often without realizing that the ideas actually influenced their practices.[31] To provide an obvious example, the types of ships that constitute a fleet are the material expressions of the strategic and tactical ideas that prevail at any given time. When RMAs take place, defense establishments not only need to rethink their perceptions on how to deploy their forces. They must visualize how future wars might transpire, and discern the ways in which the innovations can render those conflicts different from their predecessors.[32] Yet the efficacy of the innovations, whether they are taking place at home or abroad, cannot be discovered until they are tested in battle.

To reduce the ambiguities, the defense communities of the Great Powers during the interwar years assigned their intelligence staffs to secure and examine data concerning the combat methods and equipment being developed by their rivals. The experiences of World War I were a helpful benchmark that enabled military officials to calculate the military capabilities of foreign powers.[33] During the conflict, a number of modern armaments made their first appearance in combat, thereby providing some indications on how they might affect the conduct of warfare.

Aside from historical precedents, the manner in which individual armed forces responded to the circumstances facing them was largely influenced by the organizational ethos, or strategic culture, that prevailed in the particular establishment.[34] Strategic culture is defined as a distinct and lasting set of behavioral and thought patterns governing the use of force, and it plays a central role in determining how officials assess the external environment and figure out possible responses to the threats with which they contend.[35] The notion that cultural factors affect military performance is derived from the premise that human actions are conditioned by the principles that prevail in their environment. Likewise, the policies followed by a particular institution are shaped by the distinct ideas that it holds. In warfare, certain attitudes are more likely to bring success than others. Organizations that show less imagination in peacetime are unlikely to adapt to the actual conditions they have to fight in.[36] On the other hand, armed services that seek to develop a knowledgeable assessment of strategic realities have better prospects of overcoming their opponents.[37]

In determining the foundations of strategic culture, one can examine a number of visible features, including a nation's geopolitical position, its past experiences with warfare, and the value systems held by its armed services. On the subject of culture and its relation to intelligence, the existing scholarship frequently explains how the functions of an organization, along with the types of information it seeks, are governed by the specific policy priorities of the parent nation.[38] Cultural factors also have an effect on the importance that leaders place on creating a realistic view of their adversaries. Less rigorously explored is the interaction between strategic culture and a defense establishment's use of intelligence to improve the performance of its own armed forces.

In all areas, the U.S. Navy enjoyed a number of advantages over the Japanese. Since the beginning of the nineteenth century, its main mission was to safeguard America's oceanic commerce and trade. Thus, the Navy had a legacy of keeping a lookout on foreign rivals, even though long-standing traditions of avoiding involvement in international conflicts prevented it from rising to the ranks of the world's leading maritime forces during the first hundred years of its existence.[39] By the 1900s, the protection of the Pacific areas became a top national security concern, owing to the growing presence of U.S. economic and imperial interests in the region, and the Japanese had been identified as the most likely opponent. War Plan Orange, originally drawn up in 1907, stated that in the event of a conflict against Japan, U.S. forces needed to undertake an extended effort in order to emasculate the IJN's capacity to fight.[40] The main aim was to secure control over the vast expanses of the Pacific Ocean, and thereafter blockade Japan's Home Islands in order to curtail its supplies of vital war materials from abroad. While in peacetime isolationist opinion within the public and government discouraged the commitment of large forces overseas, the Navy's strategic thinking dictated that wars were to be fought by optimizing the nation's industrial resources, and constructing a vast armada composed of the most modern vessels.[41] Because the Americans had a clear vision of their strategic aims and the means to achieve them, they were well-placed to recognize the types of challenges that the IJN could pose. As a matter of fact, the Orange plan has been credited with laying out the fleet's requirements in a manner that was "so sound that it could easily deal" with a wide variety of contingencies.[42] Naval intelligence policy also explicitly stated that "all preparation for war must be premised on the best available information."[43] Most important, the available intelligence on the IJN was applied to enable the Pacific Fleet to prevail in a prolonged conflict, where the efficient and widespread use of advanced armaments played a decisive role in determining the outcome.

The practices followed by the Japanese were in striking contrast to those of the U.S. Navy. In a case similar to most imperial powers, Japan's overseas expansion was driven primarily by economic concerns, namely, to provide its growing industries with a secure source of raw materials and a captive market for their manufactured goods. However, what distinguished Japan's policy was the extent to which authorities made a haphazard effort to study the problems that could arise in the event of a conflict with rival nations. Because the Japanese had purposely secluded themselves until the 1850s, their defense establishment was inexperienced in gauging foreign states.[44] Military calculations were not based on facts, but on the notion that Japan would eventually create a new Asian order where it played the dominant role, and the Western nations were to acquiesce in a fait accompli.[45] The concept originated from the Meiji era of the late nineteenth century, when the ruling elite, in an effort to forge public unity within their newly established nation, created an ideology proclaiming that the Japanese had a preordained right to become the leading power in the Far East.[46] Thus, a cornerstone of Japan's strategic thinking was a belief that its people were a superior race, and this aspect precluded an objective opinion of its adversaries.[47] Navy planners also held a muddled idea on how to defeat the United States, and presumed that wars could be won by dealing a knockout blow at the onset and waiting for Japan's enemies to offer peace, in the same way the clashes against China and Russia had been conducted at the turn of the twentieth century. Because victory hinged on the success of the initial operations, intelligence activities tended to be geared toward helping the armed forces wage a short campaign. The practice was bound to bring disaster when engaging enemies who insisted on conducting a total war. Nor did the Japanese navy's leadership carefully consider how Japan was going to compel America to give in, when the latter's industrial capacity and weapons production was far superior.[48] IJN personnel paid minimal attention to how Allied capabilities might evolve in the long run, and neglected the need to learn new ways of fighting. To make matters worse, Japan's triumphs during the commencement of the Pacific War reinforced the deep-seated faith in its ascendancy. By late 1943, when U.S. forces commenced their counteroffensive, and the Imperial Navy faced vastly superior opponents, it was too late to remedy the mistakes. The best intelligence was unlikely to compensate for the fact that Japan's leaders had decided to initiate a war for which they were ill-prepared.

The U.S. Navy did face difficulties in preparing for hostilities, among the foremost of which was a shortage of intelligence. In many areas, including the use of carrier-based air power and the development of surface warfare doctrine, naval staffs were unable to scrutinize the IJN's activities. True, one of the key problems that prevented officials from understanding their potential enemy before the Pacific War was their inclination to assume that American doctrines and weapons were superior.[49] As a result, evidence that indicated that the IJN possessed certain qualities was often ignored. U.S. naval authorities also tended to assume that the Japanese abided by the same rationale as their Western counterparts, which maintained that a weaker fleet could not afford high losses and thus had to move cautiously. Subsequently, even if the Imperial forces initiated hostilities, the prospect of an attack against key U.S. positions in the Pacific, including the Philippines and Hawaii, was considered unlikely. Yet without reliable information, a clear picture was unlikely to emerge. Tokyo carried out its rearmament program with extreme secrecy. The few pieces of data that could be secured tended to suggest that Japan did not have the resources to construct a fighting machine that could equal its Western counterparts. As a result, the Navy Department abided by its opinion that the Imperial fleet was a second-rate adversary who was not to be feared. Nor could U.S. forces adjust their combat methods and technologies in a way that was effective for confronting the Japanese.[50]

The opening months of the conflict saw the Americans continuing to deal with the obstacles arising from an inadequate knowledge of their opponent. The speed with which the IJN and its air arm achieved a complete dominance over Southeast Asia and the western Pacific regions compelled the U.S. Navy to reassess the Japanese. After all, defeat is by far the "better teacher," and critical faculties are often sharpened by experiences of failure.[51] Officials acknowledged that the Pacific Fleet needed to reform its combat methods, and confront the Imperial forces by making good use of limited resources. To achieve this end, it was essential to know which enemy strengths to avoid, and the shortcomings to exploit. Intelligence was therefore treated as an integral instrument, and the Navy Department made a substantial effort to supply the Office of Naval Intelligence (ONI), along with the organizations working alongside the Pacific Fleet, with the manpower and material resources needed to work on a wartime footing. However, the trauma of defeat meant that evaluations concerning the IJN focused almost entirely on their advantages. Indeed, the Japanese defeat at Midway in June 1942, and the failure of their Solomons campaign during the autumn, provided the first concrete signs that the Imperial fleet did not have the skill and technological resources needed to prevail. Even then, intelligence on Japanese capabilities remained scarce, because the Americans had yet to engage in extensive operations. Consequently, frontline personnel were tasked to collect information on how the IJN performed, and to analyze the data gained in combat experience.

The evolution of U.S. intelligence also demonstrates how, even in wartime with the increased availability of information, making an accurate evaluation is by no means an easy task. Organizations are not always able to secure data on the doctrines and principles that shape the opponent's ways of fighting. The question of whether the enemy is likely to reform its techniques and weaponry is open to conjecture. The uncertainty becomes especially visible when engaging an adversary with an alien cultural mindset, such as the IJN. No study of American perceptions regarding the Japanese during the Pacific War is complete unless it addresses the race issue. The ethnic divide between the belligerents had a profound effect on their views of each other. Yet few historians aside from John Dower have extensively studied the subject.[52] Dower focused mainly on the opinions held by the rank and file of the U.S. Army, as well as the general public. According to his work, racial hatred was the overriding influence, and the Japanese were portrayed as a menace that needed to be eradicated. The animosity, in turn, affected the way in which military personnel judged their enemy's martial qualities.

However, Dower tends to put forward a one-sided argument that overlooks the extent to which American strategic culture demanded concerted moves to achieve a rational understanding of the enemy. Intelligence staffs and naval commanders were wary about making generalized statements regarding the "national characteristics" of the IJN. Such statements were bound to create flawed perceptions, which in turn might lay the grounds for further setbacks. Hypotheses were based on a careful analysis of the available information, and conclusions that could not be supported by empirical evidence were avoided. An equally important factor that limited the role of racial views was that information on cultural aspects and their influence on the IJN's operations remained patchy. As the conflict progressed, the Americans were able to draw on a growing array of sources, including prisoners of war, captured documents, and specimens of Japanese weapons. The Navy established dedicated organizations to process the material and disseminate it to officers in a timely manner. Yet the material did not clearly explain the ideas that shaped the enemy's combat capabilities, and the U.S. Navy conceded that it did not have sufficient data to formulate an informed opinion. Intelligence reports focused mainly on features that could be observed, such as the way in which the Japanese performed in battle. The Imperial fleet's failings were attributed to resource shortages, rather than faulty concepts on how to conduct warfare.

The IJN's efficiency could not be determined with a good level of accuracy until the Pacific Fleet fought its opponent over an extended period. Naval crews, along with aviators, were assigned to collect information by making a thorough observation of their opponents, so that U.S. forces could develop a knowledgeable means to achieve a victory in the long run. Action reports described how the enemy demonstrated a number of weaknesses, the most important of which was a shortage of modern equipment. Yet even toward the closing stages of the conflict, after the Imperial fleet and its air arm had been depleted through attrition at the hands of the Allies, it continued to possess substantial numerical strength. The IJN also showed how it remained a resilient enemy that inflicted considerable losses on the U.S. Navy by using its limited resources skillfully. The ONI, as well as personnel in the Pacific Fleet, undertook the assessment of a wide array of conflicting characteristics, and sought to provide an evenhanded evaluation of the IJN's strengths and weaknesses.

However, the U.S. Navy faced complications in transforming its understanding of the Japanese into a workable practice. Combat experience provides military organizations with concrete indications of how their fighting methods and weapons fare. Furthermore, when wartime objectives and operational concepts are clearly articulated, and enemy forces better understood, commanders can determine the reforms needed to help them carry out their prescribed missions.[53] One of the overriding principles of U.S. naval doctrine was to minimize losses. Therefore, the intelligence that indicated that the IJN's tactics and weapons caused significant harm was treated as a sign that the Americans needed to improve their own performance. To illustrate a key example, the U.S. Navy recognized that the development of Japanese naval aviation required friendly forces to protect themselves by achieving air superiority in the areas where they operated. The intelligence obtained during the opening phases of the conflict exposed how the existing antiaircraft and fighter defenses were unsatisfactory. Nevertheless, introducing innovations in wartime is not easy, since the tempo of operations calls for quick solutions but new technologies take a long time to develop.[54] U.S. industrial and technical resources were not sufficient to produce better equipment. Intelligence on the IJN therefore did not always bring about an immediate alteration of the U.S. Navy's weaponry. Instead, naval personnel learned to deploy their available hardware more imaginatively.

To summarize, intelligence played a significant role in shaping the U.S. Navy's capabilities only after it entered the Pacific War in December 1941. Until then, information on the IJN was too limited to enable doctrines and equipment to be developed specifically to counter the Japanese. A large portion of America's naval arsenal, along with the manner of its deployment, had been devised with the broad aim of fighting a protracted war. The intelligence gained through combat experience was used to refine the techniques that the U.S. Navy had already created, in a manner that was suitable for defeating the Imperial fleet.

1

Gauging an Untested Opponent

U.S. PERCEPTIONS OF THE IMPERIAL
JAPANESE NAVY, 1918–41

Between December 1941 and spring 1942, the Americans were overwhelmed while the Imperial fleet established control over the waters of Southeast Asia and western Pacific areas. U.S. officials did not expect the Japanese to eliminate Allied forces and gain a dominant position in the region so rapidly. The main reason was that, throughout the years prior to the conflict, the naval establishment did not have the means to formulate a knowledgeable assessment of the IJN. The secrecy with which the Japanese authorities shrouded their naval construction program prevented U.S. intelligence organizations from collecting comprehensive information. Consequently, detailed aspects such as operational doctrine and weapons technologies were hard to determine. The available material also tended to put forward an unbalanced picture, which emphasized how the Japanese navy's combat potential was not equal to its Western opponents.

The shortage of information significantly affected intelligence analysis. The Office of Naval Intelligence produced a large number of reports, which opined that the IJN did not have the capacity to challenge U.S. forces, even though the Japanese had made some progress in developing a competent fighting force. Intelligence staffs also lacked a dependable benchmark for gauging Japan's forces. The IJN had only fought weaker opponents, namely, Imperial China and Tsarist Russia during the turn of the twentieth century. Its ability to confront an American or European opponent remained open to speculation.

Officials in the Navy Department held a less sanguine view, and focused on Japanese numerical strength, as well as the fact that the United States was struggling to maintain a lead. The accepted conclusion was that in the event of war, enemy forces would attempt to conquer a large portion of the Asia-Pacific region. At the same time, while the IJN was a threat to American interests, it did not have the resources to defeat enemies with greater military potential. Subsequently, naval officials surmised that the Japanese were likely to act cautiously, and avoid a confrontation with the main elements of the American fleet, at least until the latter's strength had been whittled down through attrition. U.S. forces were therefore not considered vulnerable to any significant dangers, and were deemed capable of counteracting any situation they faced.

In order to determine the effectiveness of the U.S. Navy's prewar intelligence efforts, one needs to establish a workable criterion. Theorists have argued that the key obstacle to an accurate evaluation is not the failure to collect information. While the ambiguous nature of the data causes confusion, errors more often occur when intelligence analysts, along with those involved in the policymaking process, misinterpret the material, and base their assessments on preconceived notions.[1] Having a "mindset," or fixed outlook on the outside world, is unavoidable to a degree, and even beneficial, because it helps humans process the complex array of information they receive in a more systematic manner.[2] However, prejudices can take a disproportionate control over one's judgment, to the point where it becomes difficult to accept data that seem to contradict a set conclusion.[3] The circumstances give rise to a phenomenon described as "excessive consistency," where predispositions become so deeply ingrained that people acknowledge only the types of information they expect to see, and ignore the remainder.[4] The longer the bias remains in place, the more evidence is needed to alter the existing view. Further problems arise when ethnocentric biases lead policymakers to believe that their own ideas are superior and thus bound to be followed by all others.[5] Again, the willingness to abide by preset judgments is driven largely by a desire to conduct strategic planning more rationally. Yet the result is often a failure to see the world through the eyes of different national groups, as well as a subsequent inability to understand the actions that potential enemies are capable of undertaking.

Indeed, American assessments of the IJN were affected by a number of popular misconceptions. The accepted belief was that the Japanese could not challenge the United States, on the grounds that Japanese economic and technological advancement was lagging.[6] A corollary to this notion was the assumption that the Imperial Navy would realize its own shortcomings, and remain apprehensive about attacking areas where the United States held sizeable military strengths. The latter move, from the American point of view, entailed the risk of suffering disproportionate casualties. In expecting the Japanese to be guided by the same logic, U.S. officials followed a line of thinking known as "projection," or "mirror imaging."[7] Naval leaders did not fully grasp how the presence of U.S. forces in the Asia-Pacific region, coupled with the economic reprisals that the administration of President Franklin Roosevelt imposed in response to Japan's moves into Indochina between 1940 and 1941, could incite the ruling elite in Tokyo to embark on risky ventures and attempt to eliminate American naval power. On one hand, the defense chiefs, including Admiral Harold Stark, the chief of naval operations (CNO), did not favor sanctions, on the grounds that the Japanese might construe such measures as a provocation.[8] However, even when diplomatic signals decrypts indicated that Japan had decided to commence hostilities, U.S. authorities did not think that their main bases at Hawaii and the Philippines would be endangered.[9] Another common criticism is that the service departments' complacent attitude led them to devote insufficient resources toward intelligence activities. The intelligence service was not regarded as a prestigious career path, and officers assigned to attaché posts abroad or the top positions in Washington almost invariably showed a minimal dedication toward their duties.[10] David Kahn has gone as far as to contend that intelligence organizations had a negligible impact on assessments of Japan, since military and naval officials held little respect for their work.[11]

Yet cognitive faults do not fully explain the U.S. Navy's failures. An accurate assessment was hindered because, in spite of numerous signs of the IJN's attempts to build a strong fleet, its efforts appeared unfruitful. To complicate matters, the Japanese successfully concealed their rearmament program, as well as their war plans. Aside from secrecy, U.S. intelligence faced problems that arose from the fact that neither the Japanese government nor military command had a definite plan to fight America and its allies until a few months prior to the outbreak of the Pacific War. Under the circumstances, accurate data on the IJN's operations were simply not available. Before summer 1941, Japan's main objective was to bring the war in China to a successful finish, with southward expansion being a secondary goal. Officials in Tokyo understood that the annexation of European territories in Asia could elicit U.S. intervention, and were circumspect about facing such scenarios. When Japan occupied southern Indochina in July, its leaders had not agreed on any definite policies to prepare for a confrontation with the Western powers. The aim was to place the Imperial forces in a favorable position to seize the natural resources of the East Indies if the need arose.[12] Only in August, after the United States and its allies froze Japan's overseas assets and imposed an oil embargo, did policymakers decide that an occupation of the southern regions was imperative.[13] Even in September, when the decision was made to ready the armed forces for war, Admiral Osami Nagano, the navy chief of staff, along with the civilian leaders, insisted on a last-ditch effort to negotiate a rapprochement and secure a lifting of the sanctions.[14] It was not until early November, following the accession of prime minister Hideki Tojo's hard-line government, that the final decision for commencing hostilities was ratified. As long as Japan's policies remained undecided, its war plans were by definition bound to remain unpredictable, and without good data, the Americans were inclined to rely on prevailing assumptions to clear away their uncertainties. For this reason, any judgment has to consider the results attained with the limited data that U.S. intelligence managed to gather.

Importance of Japan as an Intelligence Target

Throughout the interwar period, gauging the IJN was treated as a priority, mainly because the Navy Department considered the threat of a war against Japan to be sufficient to require an adequate defense plan. Since the late nineteenth century, the United States had established a number of important economic interests in China, along with a chain of island bases, including Hawaii, Guam, and the Philippines, to protect its sea communications in the Pacific. The developments created a strong motive to defend the area, and to monitor the activities of hostile powers. After 1905, when the IJN crushed the Russian fleet at Tsushima and confirmed its status as the strongest fleet in the region, the creation of a coordinated strategy to deal with possible Japanese aggression became a strategic priority.[15] Further apprehensions surfaced after World War I, when the IJN emerged as the third largest fleet in the world. Japan also acquired Germany's former island colonies, including Micronesia and the Carolines, thereby securing a network of bases that lay astride the trans-Pacific sea lanes. The main aim of the Washington Conference held during 1921–22 was to set up a treaty that protected the status quo in the Asia-Pacific region. The world's leading maritime powers, including the United States, Japan, and Great Britain, along with a host of European nations, agreed to limit naval construction and refrain from seeking further territorial conquests in China.

Nevertheless, the danger of Japanese encroachments did not disappear. Ongoing advances in naval technology required a careful watch on the IJN. The advent of air power, along with the introduction of new types of vessels such as the submarine, enabled Japan to attack American positions more quickly than it had hitherto been able. The defense community also voiced concerns that the Imperial forces were determined to undermine Western interests in the Far East. As early as 1923, a U.S. naval intelligence bulletin noted that the Japanese were "thoroughly imbued" with the idea that they had to seek aggrandizement.[16] The Joint Board, which provided a forum for the Army and Navy chiefs to devise a combined strategy, labeled Japan as "the most probable enemy."[17] Popular literature often portrayed the Japanese in what was bellicose language.[18] Officers at the Naval War College were also exposed to a curriculum containing a seemingly endless volume of readings and lectures that explained how the Japanese national character was shaped by a desire for eventual domination of Asia.[19] Indeed, Japan's pursuit of an aggressive policy began in earnest during 1931, when the economic effects of the Great Depression led the military to demand that their nation's problems be solved through overseas expansion. Three years later, the IJN announced it would not sign further arms limitation agreements once the Washington treaties expired in 1936. The steady deterioration in U.S.-Japanese relations produced an impetus to establish an intelligence machinery that could scrutinize the Japanese fleet.

Within the Navy Department, the main body responsible for handling information on the IJN was the ONI. The organization had existed since 1882, and underwent significant growth during World War I. By 1918, its staff consisted of 306 officers.[20] The ONI's duty was to acquire, analyze, and disseminate information pertaining to "political, military, naval, economic, and industrial policies and conditions of our own and of foreign countries."[21] The Foreign Branch was organized geographically, with the Far Eastern section coordinating all work related to Japan, and the director of Naval Intelligence (DNI) supervising the office's activities.

During the aftermath of the Great War, naval intelligence contended with a number of problems. Cutbacks in defense expenditures led to a dramatic reduction in personnel.[22] The ONI also had to disperse its efforts over separate tasks. On one hand, the office was assigned to handle intelligence on foreign powers. At the same time, it acted as a domestic security force, monitoring subversive activities that alien nationals were planning to undertake on American territory.[23]

Yet the ONI made a sizeable effort to acquire information on the Imperial fleet. Within the Navy Department, the various bureaus, including Construction as well as Repair and Ordnance (BuOrd), were keen to determine the types of vessels and naval weapons that Japan was constructing.[24] Measures were also taken to improve the ONI's collection capabilities. In 1925, the Bureau of Aeronautics (BuAer) suggested that an assistant naval attaché be appointed, whose specific job was to study the Japanese air arm.[25] U.S. officials therefore recognized the need for reliable data on the Imperial fleet, and the lack of intelligence could not be attributed to poor tasking.

Nature of the Intelligence Received

In spite of the U.S. Navy's attempts to improve its knowledge of the IJN, the intelligence service did not achieve significant results. This was largely due to the difficulties involved in obtaining good information, which "existed hardly at all" for much of the interwar period.[26] The main source was the attaché's office at the U.S. embassy in Tokyo. Between 1919 and 1936, a total of nine naval attachés served in Japan, more than half of whom held the rank of captain.[27] Insofar as their collecting skills were concerned, attachés did not receive the training necessary to identify the main innovations in the Imperial Navy's doctrine and technology. The Japanese concealed the relevant information, thus making it difficult for the ONI to specify the developments to be followed. Nevertheless, the attachés had certain important qualifications.

Most of them studied in the ONI's language instruction program, and acquired the aptitude to translate written evidence such as government documents and press sources, as well as to conduct conversations with their hosts. Private U.S. citizens, who either resided in Japan or traveled there on temporary visits, periodically obtained intelligence and supplied it to the American embassy. Information was also procured by collaborating with attachés and agents from friendly nations who had an interest in monitoring the IJN, the most important of whom was Great Britain. Last but not least, intercepts of radio communications occasionally offered a glimpse into the Japanese navy's operational plans.

The U.S. mission in Tokyo occasionally acquired useful material, especially in regard to warship construction. Opportunities to observe naval facilities were infrequent, mainly because the local authorities took great care to curtail visits. Yet inspections sometimes provided basic information on the characteristics of certain vessels. During his service as naval attaché, Lieutenant Commander Franz Melendy was invited to witness the construction of the carriers *Akagi* and *Kaga*, and secured details on the layout and measurements of their flight decks.[28] The restrictions on intelligence activities did lead to a heavy reliance on open sources. Press reports offered the most accessible data. Newspaper articles outlined the budgets that the government had allocated to the navy ministry.[29] Information was also collected by forging contacts with local officials. Although the Japanese either refused to furnish data or purposely placed delays when they considered exchanges to be inconvenient, they did occasionally cooperate. In 1921, Captain Edward Watson secured comprehensive statistics on the number of vessels the IJN was planning to build under its postwar expansion program.[30] Navy officials in Washington also cultivated contacts with the Japanese embassy. Between 1932 and 1935, the ambassador presented the particulars of several cruisers, including the *Tone*.[31] Intelligence officers operating within the United States managed to secure material via surreptitious means. In 1929, a break-in at the Japanese naval machinery inspector's office at New York's Madison Square led to the capture of a number of important photostat documents revealing information on the latest Japanese aircraft, photographs of shells, and a chart illustrating the range of individual guns.[32]

As the interwar years progressed, the Japanese government imposed a host of laws to prevent foreigners from learning about Japan's ability to wage war.[33] One of the few aspects that could be calculated with some certainty was the tonnage of the fleet. Under the Washington Naval Treaty, the U.S., British and Japanese capital ship and aircraft carrier forces had been limited to a 5-to-5-to-3 ratio, respectively. However, after the treaty expired in 1936, the only fact that could be ascertained was that the IJN aimed for parity with, if not superiority over, its U.S. and British rivals.[34] Estimates on the most basic aspects, including the number of ships under construction, were made by culling and comparing various pieces of data, the reliability of which was dubious. For example, during 1939, naval attaché Captain Harold Bemis received several reports from his British counterpart and the U.S. ambassador, suggesting that capital ships were being assembled in civilian dockyards run by the Kawasaki shipbuilding works, located at the port cities of Nagasaki and Kobe.[35] The information contradicted earlier assumptions that such vessels were built only at navy yards, and indicated that the Japanese were putting together additional ships. The rumors were partially cleared after conversations with IJN officials, who admitted that the dockyards were in fact being used to build cruisers and carriers.[36] The accuracy of such reports could be confirmed only by maintaining a vigilant lookout on Japanese activities, and even then, intelligence on naval construction remained uncertain. The ONI, along with the U.S. naval establishment, held a lack of knowledge described as "so incomplete" that, as late as 1942, the chief of naval operations confessed that he did not know whether Japan was building super-battleships over 45,000 tons in displacement.[37]

Because the Japanese severely restricted what Western observers could see, the available intelligence tended to hide the extent to which the IJN was constructing a technologically advanced fleet. One of the most visible weaknesses was that most components were copied from foreign, namely, British and German, designs. The characteristic allegedly stemmed from an endemic inability to invent new weapons. Naval attaché Captain Fred Rogers once remarked that the Japanese regarded the process of devising more modern machinery to be tedious.[38] Japan's industries were also known for producing poor replicas of foreign-built equipment. Diesel engines were "found to be greatly inferior to those turned out by European workmanship."[39] Nor were the Japanese well placed to import good quality weapons. Information supplied by British officers suggested that because Western manufacturers were advised by their governments not to sell their most advanced technologies to

Japan, and the navy could not afford high-grade material, it was reasonable to assume that the IJN's fire-control equipment was inefficient.[40]

Allegations concerning Japan's dependence on imported technology were true. However, the practice actually constituted a strength. The IJN often procured samples of the best equipment it was able to purchase from abroad, including submarines, aircraft, and optics, and thereafter adapted them in a way that suited its own operational concepts. The overriding principle behind naval policy was to overcome the disadvantages arising from the inferior ratio assigned by the Washington treaty by focusing on excellence, and constructing warships with greater firepower and endurance than their Western counterparts. By the late 1920s, technicians and engineers had developed a number of sophisticated armaments. The guns and torpedoes on board surface vessels, including the battleships *Hyuga*, *Ise*, and *Mutsu*, outranged most of their opponents.[41] The battleships of the *Nagato* class, along with the *Kongo*–class battle cruisers, were fitted with larger propulsion systems to increase their velocity and cruising radius.[42] By 1934, when the Japanese openly renounced their adherence to the Washington treaty restrictions, the naval general staff started to investigate the possibility of constructing battleships with displacements over 60,000 tons, larger than any vessel built to date.[43] Work on the super-battleships *Yamato* and *Musashi* commenced in 1937. When they entered service in 1942, both were equipped with turbine engines totaling 150,000 horsepower. Their 18-inch guns fired shells weighing over three thousand pounds, at a distance of almost 46,000 yards.[44]

The IJN also made a painstaking effort to build up its air power. In 1921, the government requested British help, and an unofficial mission, headed by Lord William Forbes-Sempill, laid the foundations for developing Japan's fleet air arm.[45] In an attempt to become less dependent on foreign technology, the navy implemented a policy to encourage the design of indigenous aircraft.[46] In 1937, the navy air staff established the specifications for the Zero fighter, which was constructed with a view to achieving a higher range, speed, and maneuverability than any rival interceptor.[47] Mitsubishi was commissioned to design and produce the new fighter, and by September 1940 the first completed machine entered service in China.

Yet U.S. intelligence personnel considered the IJN's prospects of improving its capabilities to be questionable, mainly because they could not monitor its rearmament program. Estimates were produced by comparing fragments of data. On certain aspects, such as battleship ordnance, the Americans did learn that good equipment had been produced. Information obtained from the gunnery officers at the Yokosuka and Sasebo naval bases, as well as photographs provided by the British naval attaché, suggested that the guns on board the *Mutsu* and *Nagato* had elevations of thirty degrees.[48] The performance of battery guns was estimated via a similar method of culling various pieces of information. Most battleships and battle cruisers were believed to have firing ranges of approximately 25,000 yards.[49] However, intelligence personnel were less able to examine Japanese moves to modify their weaponry. Information on other important features, such as the air arm, was also scarce. By the eve of the Pacific War, the Japanese appeared to have made some progress. The Type 97 fighter was described to be highly maneuverable, with a top speed of over 250 miles per hour.[50] Yet the majority of the evidence tended to obscure the IJN's achievements, and highlighted how aircraft had poor performance. An inspection carried out by engineers from the Douglas aircraft manufacturing company showed that the Kawanishi four-engine plane and the Type 96 light bomber flew at relatively low speeds.[51] Maintenance was also unsatisfactory, with aircraft having broken gasoline lines and being in a "general condition that could be only classified as dangerous."

Economic factors also appeared to hinder the IJN's expansion. The Japanese were noted to have an insufficient industrial base to produce aircraft in large numbers. Among the most significant defects was the shortage of machine tools. Manufacturing equipment was imported, and the Japanese could not afford the best types.[52] Locally made designs lacked the precision required to cut metals, and had poor durability. Technical research facilities were meager when compared with those of the United States.[53] The available intelligence also emphasized how resource shortages were holding back naval construction. Admiral Harry Yarnell, commander in chief of the Asiatic fleet, observed that while the Japanese had built a sizeable fleet, they did not have the productive facilities needed to replace the ships that would be lost or damaged in a protracted campaign.[54]

Naval intelligence was no more successful in figuring out how the IJN might deploy its fleet. Japanese doctrine throughout the interwar period and the Pacific War was based on the concept of "using a few to conquer many" (*ka o motte shu o sei-su*).[55] Commanders realized that a numerically inferior fleet could not be expected to win a decisive battle at the onset of a conflict, and thus opted for the "diminution operation," where the initial objective was to reduce the U.S. Navy's strength through attritional attacks.[56] As the inter-war years progressed, naval officials sought to take advantage of the benefits afforded by air power, and planned to engage the enemy fleet in areas further afield, including the mandated islands of the Carolines and Marshalls.[57] The key aim was to prevent the Americans from establishing a foothold within proximity of Japan's home waters. Air raids were to be launched against the enemy as it crossed the Pacific. The U.S. fleet was then to be defeated in an "ambush strategy" (*yogeki sakusen*); the IJN had used a similar method to sink the Russian fleet in 1905. The "decisive battle" was to be fought at a chosen point close to Japan proper, at nighttime, so that the Imperial forces could catch their opponent off guard, and prevent it from making full use of its naval power. The final confrontation was envisaged at daybreak, where the remnants of the battered and disorganized U.S. fleet were to be annihilated. Naval doctrine also focused increasingly on commencing future wars with a preemptive strike. By January 1941, Admiral Yamamoto Isoroku, the com-mander of the Combined Fleet, drew up a detailed plan that called for the use of carrier-borne aircraft to destroy a large portion of the U.S. Fleet's main base at Pearl Harbor. For the remainder of the year, extensive efforts were made to perfect the plan, and secure the navy general staff's approval for the operation.[58]

Attachés managed to collect some details on Japanese naval maneuvers, via government publications and conversations with authorities. Reports on fleet exercises showed that the IJN was preparing to carry out a variety of ambitious moves, including the use of aircraft to detect and attack surface fleets.[59] The naval attaché also reported that the Japanese regularly practiced night operations, with a view to simulating battle conditions to the great-est extent possible.[60] Shots were fired from broadside guns on board capital ships and cruisers, with gunnery practices carried out at ranges up to 10,000 yards. Star shells and searchlights were used to illuminate targets. Based on the observation, the Japanese appeared exceptionally prepared to fight under the cover of darkness. However, during the 1930s, with increased security measures in place, foreign nationals became correspondingly unable to visit the ports where the IJN conducted its exercises.[61]

Japanese signals communications, which the ONI also utilized, were equally unclear on the operations contemplated by the IJN. The U.S. Navy had maintained a sigint (signals intelligence) network in the Far East since the mid-1920s, with intercept stations at Guam and the Philippines, as well as one at the American legation in Peking.[62] During 1931–32, when Japan commenced its incursions into Manchuria, the Americans prepared to enhance their coverage. The ONI's sigint branch, OP-20-G, stepped up the training of cryptanalysts. By 1938, Japanese naval codes and ciphers consumed all of the U.S. Navy's cryptanalysis efforts, and 90 percent of its translation activities.[63] Radio intercepts occasionally provided interesting information.[64] Following the June–August 1933 grand fleet maneuvers, naval intelligence deduced that Japanese forces had simulated an attack on the Philippines, as well as moves to secure the mandated islands as bases for attacking the U.S. fleet.[65] Yet cryptanalysts did not decode the more complex systems, including the flag-officer code, which was used to transmit information on operational plans. Consequently, sigint officers were unable to read "anything but the absolutely most routine messages," such as those detailing the daily movement of individual ships.[66] Following 1939, Japanese traffic became even more inaccessible, because the IJN overhauled its communications system and set up the JN-25a code. By late 1941, progress had been made in decoding JN-25a. However, in December, the Imperial Navy again introduced a new variant, JN-25b, which remained unbroken at the time of the Pearl Harbor attack.[67] In any case, the IJN succeeded in concealing its plans, to the point where information could be collected only with the greatest difficulty. Japanese operational orders also stipulated that naval units achieve surprise by maintaining radio silence prior to an attack.[68] The Americans did attempt to compensate for their incomplete sigint by falling back on human sources, which were also unreliable. In March 1941, an attaché report by Lieutenant Commander Henri Smith-Hutton quoted a former IJN admiral, who suggested that war against the United States would commence with attacks against the Philippines and Hawaii. However, because the statement was made long before the Japanese had made concrete plans, it was more likely to appear as a boastful remark.[69]

To complicate matters, when American personnel did manage to observe the IJN's preparations for battle, the available intelligence tended to highlight troubles. The most visible shortcoming was a low standard of training.

The general staff planned its maneuvers to the last detail, and discouraged personnel from using their initiative. Subsequently, commanders appeared incapable of devising contingency plans for instances when their operations went wrong.[70] In the event of setbacks, officers preferred to return to port for discussion, rather than concoct new procedures. IJN personnel also demonstrated a poor ability to handle modern equipment. The assistant naval attaché reported that during a destroyer maneuver, messages were sent by blinker tube, and the speed of transmission was "quite slow."[71] Facilities for training aviators appeared inadequate. A visit to the Yokosuka naval air station led to the conclusion that the site was "not well suited for extensive flight activities," because it had a limited field area.[72] Under the circumstances, U.S. intelligence did not have a strong basis for expecting the IJN to execute operations that required skillful planning.

When the Japanese commenced their invasion of China in 1937, U.S. personnel gained a valuable opportunity to view concrete signs of the IJN's ability to wage combat. Amphibious operations were carried out with considerable success, and the landing boats employed in the Shanghai area impressed many observers. The Type A craft was designed with a shallow keel so it could approach within close distance to the beaches, while the hinged bow structure facilitated the unloading of troops and wheeled vehicles.[73] However, because the Japanese had fought weakly defended opponents, their capacity to achieve similar successes against American forces had yet to be tested.

The air arm also demonstrated a high level of adeptness. Attacks on the Canton-Kowloon railway often caused a complete stoppage of traffic.[74] Captain Bemis commented that Japan's naval aviation was expected to emerge from the hostilities as a "very satisfactory unit," with trained and proven personnel.[75] Indeed, experiences in China taught some valuable lessons, particularly in regard to conducting long-range air strikes.[76] The losses suffered during the initial sorties led air commanders to provide fighter protection, and eventually the Japanese were able to cause significant levels of damage. Between April and July 1938, the 12th Air Group, which was assigned to provide support for operations in southern China, cleared the skies of opposition by shooting down over a hundred enemy aircraft, while only losing a handful of planes.[77] Bombing methods also improved, and raids against urban areas laid waste to a significant portion of China's infrastructure. Nevertheless, the bulk of the intelligence reports tended to downplay Japanese feats. The Chinese failure to offer aerial resistance was attributed to their lack of effective planes, rather than the efficiency of the IJN air arm.[78] Air raids caused destruction, but considering that the Chinese did not have a strong defense, Japanese airplanes had not proved to be "a decisive a weapon as expected."[79] The IJN air service had not demonstrated its capabilities in relation to a technologically advanced opponent.

The available intelligence on the Imperial fleet therefore tended to portray a fragmentary picture on its capabilities and intentions. Furthermore, the material suggested that its performance was at best average and at times inefficient. While some of the allegations were correct, the material obscured Japanese successes in assembling the technologies needed to wage a large-scale war effort. Equally important, U.S. intelligence was unable to pick up on the fact that the IJN had devised ways of employing its forces in a manner that was to pose a significant challenge for its rivals.

Intelligence Assessments of the IJN

The ONI's evaluations of the IJN reflected how intelligence officials had to work with incomplete and misleading data. While the Japanese could be credited for a certain level of aptitude, their combat potential was considered second rate in most areas. Furthermore, intelligence that indicated the Imperial Navy had developed sophisticated pieces of weaponry was rejected, on the assumption that it was unable to achieve substantial results. However, because the available material tended to conceal the IJN's strengths, assessments of its capabilities were likely to remain negative. The lack of reliable precedents to judge the Imperial Navy's performance was also a key impediment. The last major encounter had been against a weaker opponent, namely, the Russians in 1904–05. The Japanese did not participate in any significant operations during the 1914–18 world conflict, and had not been exposed to the lessons regarding the use of new weapons such as the submarine and fleet aviation. Under the circumstances, the Imperial fleet's capacity to carry out anything aside from the most basic operations was considered doubtful.

The tendency to belittle the IJN also needs to be viewed alongside instances when the ONI praised its professionalism. The operations alongside the Royal Navy in the Mediterranean during the Great War were described to have been "carried out smoothly," with personnel and matériel being "of a high order."[80] The Japanese navy's peacetime performance also received commendation. Observations of exercises gave rise to the conclusion that the Japanese were in a constant state of battle-readiness, with maneuvers being held to determine whether the fleet was adequate to protect the home waters.[81] William Puleston, the DNI, once remarked that there was "no reason" to discredit the Japanese people's talents as seafarers.[82]

Yet the evidence pointing to the IJN's qualities was not convincing enough to compel intelligence staffs to conclude that it wielded a great danger. In regard to tactics, the prevailing view was that the Japanese faced troubles in developing procedures for using advanced technologies. This opinion arose partly from the stereotype that Western naval personnel held regarding Oriental fighting forces for a large part of the interwar period.[83] For example, the ONI alleged that the Japanese fleet was plagued by "widespread inefficiency." The shortcoming was due to a number of inherent traits, including a lack of ingenuity. As a result, the Japanese were "incapable, as yet, of being occupied with more than one matter at a time," and were thus liable to "become confused and do nothing" when faced with stressful situations.[84] The report concluded, "Physically and mentally, [Japan's] leaders would prove incapable of supporting the burdens . . . of a war conducted by a powerful, active, resourceful, and aggressive foe." A further problem was that U.S. commanders tended not to monitor foreign doctrines and weapons development in a methodical manner. Naval intelligence was subsequently not tasked to investigate ongoing innovations unless the Americans were simultaneously pursuing them.[85] The ONI's reports on naval maneuvers illustrated the dilemma. Following the 1930 exercises, the Imperial fleet was noted to be making a strenuous effort to compensate for its numerical inferiority by enhancing the efficiency of its surface units, with emphasis placed on nighttime operations and the use of limited visibility to achieve surprise.[86] However, because U.S. officers believed that such moves were too complicated, the IJN's methods were not subjected to further examination. As long as the available material provided few credible indications that the Japanese had developed the ability to carry out complex maneuvers, the naval establishment was not going to raise unfounded concerns.

Allegations regarding the IJN's inefficiency also appeared to be reinforced by tangible evidence. For example, crews were adept at conducting drills, but less skillful in managing situations that required quick action, most notably when facing enemy attack. Fire control methods tended to be labor-intensive, with a large amount of time consumed in transmitting data between the various components, including the director, command center, and finally the turret.[87] The loading of batteries was slow and haphazard, with personnel evidently not prepared to cope with the damage and casualties that could be incurred in an actual fleet engagement. Fire control appeared ineffective even against fixed targets. Reports on the operations at Shanghai during 1932 were "anything but flattering," with shore installations being missed even when the ships were anchored at harbor and bombarding at close range.[88] The ONI was largely unaware of the improvements that the Imperial Navy made during the 1930s. A report on target practices, produced in 1941, admitted that information was sketchy, and could only surmise that the Japanese had not carried out such exercises frequently, owing to the expenses involved.[89]

Insofar as naval construction and weapons development were concerned, inadequate intelligence precluded a comprehension of the principles that influenced the design of Japanese vessels. While the general impression was that the Japanese possessed a "formidable" fleet, a number of faults attracted attention. Battleships and heavy cruisers appeared to have an "excessive amount of upper works" built around the foremast, making them more discernible from extended distances.[90] There was little awareness that the perceived shortcomings actually represented strengths. The superstructures of capital ships were constructed at a higher elevation in order to maximize their gun-firing capabilities, and to house the various pieces of equipment needed for fire control, including range finders, searchlight directors, and firing calculators.[91] Officers in the control deck were also able to locate their targets from a longer range.

Likewise, indications of the IJN's success in producing high-quality equipment were frequently rebuffed, on the premise that its technical knowledge was lacking. Minimal attention was paid to the fact that the Japanese had built their guns and torpedo tubes to fire at long ranges. The perception was a by-product of the accepted belief that because the U.S. Navy was facing troubles in this realm, foreign fleets also were bound to be struggling. For example, in 1934, the ONI received a report on an oxygen-propelled torpedo that was described as "run[ning] with practically no wake," thereby rendering it "very difficult to see."[92] The officer reading the paper noted the passage with a question mark and an "X," suggesting that he judged the information to be erroneous. Again, in 1940, the naval attaché in Tokyo was fortunate enough to secure data from a local contact who described the Type-93 long-lance torpedo, which was capable of traveling 10,000 yards, at a speed of forty-five knots.[93] The information was thereafter sent to the ONI. This time around, Lieutenant Commander Arthur McCollum, director of the Far East section, was impressed by the weapon's "phenomenal" speed, range, and payload, and forwarded the report to BuOrd. Technical experts, on the other hand, concluded that the IJN was incapable of constructing better equipment than the U.S. Navy. By the late 1930s, some officers started to acknowledge the possibility that the Japanese had assembled effective weapons. The Navy Department's War Plans Division advised that because the Japanese were believed to be building cruisers with 8-inch guns that had superior firepower, the Americans needed to construct comparable vessels.[94] Student exercises at the Naval War College envisaged IJN battleships being faster than their U.S. counterparts, and fitted with longer-range guns.[95] Nevertheless, the Imperial fleet's skill at deploying its armaments remained open to question.

The naval air service received equally contemptuous remarks because, again, the available intelligence tended to highlight shortcomings. Insofar as flying skill was concerned, as early as 1920, the ONI described how "the Japanese is [sic] naturally unfitted for any mechanical pursuit."[96] Even after two years of instruction, most pilots were unable to execute complex maneuvers such as quick turns, and continued to make poor landings. The information correctly indicated that the IJN's fleet aviation had a long way to go before it could catch up with the West. The Japanese did manage to effect substantial improvements by the latter half of the decade, but assessments of their aerial combat capabilities did not show a great deal of veneration. Airmen were described as being more "alert," with accidents occurring less frequently.[97] Pilots were also doing "remarkably well," especially when considering the obstacles they had to contend with.[98] The mountainous terrain that prevailed in the Home Islands was unsuited for constructing airfields, while in flat country numerous rice plots prevented the building of emergency airstrips. Poor climatic conditions, with frequent typhoons, were another hazard. Yet in spite of its progress, the IJN's air arm was considered "mediocre," owing to the evidently backward state of its training.[99] For example, only a small number of the navy's aircraft were actually operated from carriers. Aviation personnel from the carrier *Hosho* were shore-based, and practiced on an air-drome at Oppama air station, where a wooden platform was laid out and used to simulate deck takeoffs and landings.[100] Although flight officers compared "favorably" with their American counterparts, they were rated as "somewhat inferior" because they had fewer hours of flying experience.[101]

The shortage of modern equipment was another perennial disadvantage. When manufacturers attempted to produce original aircraft designs, the quality proved to be poor, with many components, including fuselages and propellers, constructed of wood.[102] In 1934, Puleston concluded that in the event of a war, Japanese technology would be two years behind the American technology, and the gap was bound to grow if their aviation was denied help from abroad.[103] When evidence pointing to the IJN air arm's efficiency appeared, it was not readily accepted. During spring 1941, U.S. aviators received a report from China on the Zero fighter, which had been observed in action, and the information appeared in a fleet air tactical unit bulletin during the autumn.[104] The plane was described to have a performance "far superior to anything [the Americans] had," in almost every category, including maneuverability and speed. While some aircrews took the information as a telltale sign that they needed to develop adequate counter-tactics, most commanders were inclined to disparage the Japanese.[105] The prevailing opinion was articulated in an article published in the September issue of *Aviation* magazine, which concluded that Japan's aeronautical designs depended entirely on "handouts" provided by Western nations.[106] The report purportedly signified how the IJN had managed to conceal the majority of its accomplishments from foreign observers. Intelligence staffs were not fully aware of the fact that the Japanese had developed a level of performance needed to establish supremacy in the western Pacific regions. True, the ONI sometimes relied on dubious evidence such as racial characteristics, and opinions were also grounded on biases that assumed American forces were superior. At the same time, the Japanese showed visible signs that they faced difficulties in building a fighting machine that could menace the U.S. Navy.

A Formidable Adversary?
The Navy Establishment's View of the IJN

At the highest levels of the naval leadership, opinions of the IJN also reflected a number of features that obstructed U.S. intelligence efforts. The General

Board was the focal point for formulating policy and approving the propos-
als put forward by the various bureaus before securing a final decision by
the secretary of the Navy. The U.S. Navy's organizational ethos encouraged
officers to thoroughly study the challenges that they might have to contend
with in an armed conflict. Owing to the shortage of data on Japanese tactics and technology, assessments tended to concentrate on matters related to
operations and strategy. War plans were developed while bearing in mind the
substantial effort required for defeating enemy forces, and were based on the
conclusion that the IJN had the strength to seize an array of island bastions,
thereby hindering U.S. attempts to secure control over the Pacific region and
advance toward Japan's home waters. Naval officials were also aware that the
antiwar sentiments prevailing within the public and in Congress, which subsequently led to continued limits on defense spending, meant that American
forces were not able to procure all of the ships and weaponry needed to carry
out a protracted campaign. However, assessments were based on incomplete
intelligence concerning what the Japanese intended to do. The uncertainty
was compounded by preconceptions that dictated that the Pacific Fleet was
bound to prevail, owing to the quantity and quality of its armament. Despite
the difficulties facing the U.S. Navy, the IJN's ability to defend its conquests
was equally disputable. The Japanese were credited for planning their operations by paying careful attention to potential obstacles. Owing to the inferior
size of its fleet, the enemy could not risk high losses. Therefore, the Imperial
Navy was expected to execute a defensive war effort, providing the U.S. fleet
with good opportunities to wrest the initiative at an early stage.

The shortage of intelligence on the IJN's tactical capabilities meant that
war preparations were often undertaken without considering such factors.
The development of doctrine highlighted this dilemma. Instead of being tailored specifically to fight the Japanese, the U.S. Navy's combat procedures
were geared for the general purpose of engaging opponents who were able
to deploy large numbers of vessels. As a result, the Americans were oftentimes unprepared to cope with the unique challenges put up by the Imperial
fleet. In a similar manner to their equivalents in Great Britain and Japan, U.S.
naval officers anticipated a scenario laid out by the strategist Alfred Mahan,
where the outcome of all future conflicts was to be decided in a single climactic
engagement. Tactical publications prescribed the measures needed to minimize

losses, and neutralize enemy ships, in lengthy detail. Substantial efforts were made to study the Battle of Jutland, which was the only large-scale fleet action fought during World War I. The Royal Navy's failure to bring its overall numerical superiority to crush the German fleet became a subject of considerable attention at the Naval War College.[107] Successive classes arrived at three key reasons, namely, poor approach dispositions, inadequate communication between the British formations, and finally, the British fleet's reluctance to seize the initiative and thereby control the pace of the engagement. Senior U.S. naval officers considered it essential that their forces avoid the same mistakes when fighting the Japanese. A pamphlet issued in 1922 laid out the circular formation, consisting of battleships at the center, surrounded by a concentric ring of cruisers and destroyers screening the larger ships. The main idea was to enable the task force to receive early information on the approaching fleet's position, so that accurate fire could be delivered to destroy it. Fleet commanders developed the idea of the battle line formation further, and specified that ships were to be laid out in accordance with the situation existing at the time of the engagement, taking into account various contingencies such as the danger of submarine and destroyer attacks, as well as the probability of encountering enemy capital ships.[108]

Once hostilities commenced, the ultimate aim was to reduce the enemy's fighting strength as rapidly as possible, with large concentrations of fire. Battle instructions outlined meticulous procedures for directing guns at the various ranges where enemy ships were likely to be engaged, by making use of optical devices and fire-control computers to calculate the distance and location of the targets. By 1940, when advanced search devices such as radar became available, they became an integral component of the fire-direction apparatus. Due allowance was made for emergency situations such as surprise encounters under the cover of darkness, in which case evasive action was the most effective move. In particular, when faced with torpedo attacks, the battle line commander needed to decide whether to continue engaging the enemy or withdraw. Although the U.S. Navy understood the elements it was likely to face, it did not anticipate the heavy losses it would incur at the hands of the IJN's long-range torpedoes and gunfire.

Likewise, wartime experiences were necessary to teach the U.S. Navy how the proper use of the air arm was essential when fighting the Japanese.

Naval officials did consider the development of a balanced fleet, which included a sufficient number of aircraft, to be an utmost necessity. Although doctrine continued to focus on surface actions, many officers recognized how the advent of maritime aviation required preparations for aerial engagements.[109] In any conflict fought amidst large expanses of ocean such as the Pacific, the fleet had to provide its own air power, without relying on friendly bases close at hand.[110] Carrier-based aircraft were expected to perform a range of tasks, including the escort of convoys, screening against air and submarine attacks, conducting attacks against enemy fleets, and last but not least, defending friendly vessels during an engagement.[111] As early as 1919, the General Board stipulated that if the Americans wished to fight their enemies on equal terms, fleet aviation and aircraft carrier strengths had to be developed to "the fullest extent."[112] As technology became more advanced, aviation became a more prominent part of naval thinking. The 1929 version of War Plan Orange predicted that in order to defeat the IJN and destroy Japan's industrial infrastructure, U.S. forces would need to launch air offensives from advanced bases in the western Pacific regions.[113] In order to carry out such operations, carriers had to be designed to hold a sufficient complement of planes. Officers at the Naval War College carried out annual war games that envisaged both the Americans and the Japanese deploying large carrier fleets. One criticism leveled against the college is that it did not come to terms with the new developments in warfare, and failed to develop effective operational plans involving the use of aircraft.[114] In actual fact, staff exercises were carried out with attention paid to how the new weapons could affect the outcome of naval battles, and the results proved that maritime aviation could exert a "decisive influence" at all stages of the campaign.[115] Prewar doctrine also paid close attention to the need for neutralizing the opponent's striking power, and the destruction of carriers at the initial stages of an engagement was given high priority.[116]

However, the exact role that aircraft could play in aiding surface operations remained unresolved, and many officers adhered to the traditional view that battleships were the primary weapon, with aviation being an auxiliary arm. One of the unfortunate by-products of that perception was a situation where officers formulated their doctrine without a clear comprehension of how effectively the IJN could use its air arm against U.S. forces. The General

Board's 1925 special report, based on the testimony of over seventy witnesses, including fleet commanders and junior officers from BuAer, reaffirmed the supremacy of the surface fleet.[117] Carriers were purportedly the least important weapon, even when the objective was to gain control over disputed sea areas and maritime communications. As late as the 1930s, air power was considered a secondary component. The commander in chief of the U.S. Fleet pointed out how the Navy's thinking concerning fleet aviation had not advanced since the Great War.[118] Further problems arose from the continued limits placed on defense expenditure, which hindered carrier construction. Consequently, officers did not have the matériel to test their operational concepts, or to learn about the full effects of air power. By 1939, the accepted belief was that no single carrier-based air group could mount a dive-bombing strike or aerial torpedo attack intense enough to destroy large surface vessels.[119] Under the circumstances, most commanders could not anticipate the damage that the IJN air arm would inflict on surface ships. Yet while the Navy did unduly emphasize the "big-gun fleet," efforts to develop aviation entailed committing resources toward weapons whose capabilities remained undetermined.[120] Until the U.S. Navy had a direct encounter with the Japanese, combat methods could not be adjusted in accordance with the threat posed by potential enemies. As Admiral Ernest King, the wartime CNO, recalled, "Nothing could [replace] the acid test of war," and it was not until the Americans entered the conflict that they could confirm the effectiveness of their practices.[121]

Owing to the shortage of intelligence on the IJN's doctrine, prewar calculations were often based on numerical strength, which had traditionally served as the yardstick for gauging foreign navies.[122] The data frequently painted a worrying picture, and showed how the U.S. fleet was struggling to maintain its capacity to confront the Japanese. Yet ultimately, the Americans were considered capable of dealing with the IJN, owing to their greater strength in ships and aircraft. Throughout the interwar years, the underlying principle of War Plan Orange, namely, to secure the Philippines as an advance base for conducting attacks on the IJN's main fleet and Japan's sea communications, remained unaltered.[123] U.S. strategy stipulated that the Navy had to sustain an extended campaign. The 1923 survey stated that the fleet was to mobilize with a view to immediately carrying out an advance toward Manila, followed by a push, in sufficient force, to operate offensively in Japanese waters.[124]

The U.S. Navy also attached a high importance to constructing a peace-time fleet with a clear margin of superiority and a capacity to secure its inter-ests in the Pacific. For this reason, the growth of Japan's navy raised worries. As early as 1922, while the Washington naval quotas were being negotiated, the General Board warned how any arms limitation agreement was bound to "greatly lessen" America's capacity to contain Japanese aggression.[125] The War Plans Division (WPD) described the 5-to-3 ratio as "dangerously close to inadequate" for defending the Philippines.[126] Furthermore, any benefits accrued through the U.S. fleet's numerical strength were likely to diminish as it sailed across the Pacific, where it needed to operate at long distances from its main bases.[127] The limits posed by the naval agreements compelled the General Board to improve the fleet's efficiency by modernizing its capi-tal ships, and fitting them with enhanced armament and propulsion sys-tems. Yet the Navy Department was unable to secure the necessary funds, owing to congressional restrictions on defense expenditure. Robert Coontz, who served as CNO from 1919 to1923, once accused politicians of being "too niggardly and too slow in acting upon matters pertaining to the Navy."[128] In regard to carriers, even at the middle of the decade, the United States had not embarked on any postwar construction, with the exception of the *Lexing-ton* and *Saratoga*. The Japanese, meanwhile, were planning to have a total of three by 1932, in addition to the *Hosho*.[129] After the naval agreements expired in 1936, and Japan earnestly commenced its expansion program, U.S. officials became increasingly skeptical of the American fleet's ability to maintain its lead.[130] Seven of the fifteen battleships were reaching twenty years of age and a state of obsolescence. Four years were needed before the first replacement could be completed.[131] On the other hand, the IJN was expected to have up to three additional capital ships with displacements over 45,000 tons under its third replenishment program, scheduled for completion in 1942.[132] Any increase in Japanese strength was likely to considerably undermine the Pacific Fleet's lead.

To remedy the situation, the United States needed to undertake a broad program of expansion. Although the construction plans for 1940 and 1941 called for three fast capital ships, the WPD recommended that an additional vessel was necessary to maintain an edge over the IJN.[133] The drive for superior-ity was also applied to fleet auxiliaries, including cruisers, destroyers, and sub-marines. To meet the targets, shipbuilders had to extend their operating hours and make the maximum use of their labor forces.[134] Yet as late as 1941, the naval establishment was considered "not ready to meet a serious emergency."[135] Among the reasons cited were the shortage of trained personnel who could administer the construction program, and Congress's reluctance to allocate sufficient funds to enlarge the productive capacity of navy yards.

In spite of the statistics indicating that the IJN could pose a significant danger, the U.S. Navy's assessment of the situation that could arise in the event of war was shaped by ambivalence. The Naval War College played an active role in determining the moves that enemy forces could undertake. Officers admitted that they were not familiar with their adversary's practices, and the scope of Japanese operations could not be predicted. The assumption was that the IJN devised sound operational plans, with a full knowledge of the doctrines used by rival forces. The national trait of painstaking research was most likely to lead Japanese admirals to undertake "a thorough study of every book or document . . . on which [they] could get their hands."[136] Staff exercises were based on an underlying preconception that dictated that Imperial navy commanders would follow doctrines similar to those accepted by their U.S. counterparts. Conventional thinking maintained that a numerically inferior fleet could not afford losses during the early stages of a campaign, and the Imperial Japanese Navy was therefore considered more likely to avoid large-scale actions, at least until the Blue fleet's strengths had been sufficiently reduced through attritional attacks. The initial objective was to establish a protective barrier for Japan's eastern flank by capturing the Philippines, while at the same time securing the chain of islands stretching from the Aleutians to Wake Island and the Marshalls.[137] Captured outposts were to serve as bases for launching sporadic air raids on the U.S. fleet, as well as reconnaissance missions to detect the approach of enemy forces. The main battle was expected to take place when the remaining elements of the Blue armada reached the vicinity of the Home Islands, at which point it was to be destroyed through a combination of torpedo, gunfire, and carrier-based air attacks.[138]

The prediction was in line with the main features of IJN doctrine during the early part of the interwar period, and naval officers were correct in deducing that a defensive campaign provided the most sensible means to safeguard Japan's empire. Historians of Japanese wartime strategy have also convincingly argued that the navy and its air arm could have been more usefully deployed to reinforce areas closer to the Home Islands, namely, the Marianas and the Philippines.[139] The failed attempts to destroy the U.S. Fleet during 1942 at Midway and the Solomon Islands ultimately resulted in a needless expenditure of limited strengths. The main misjudgment made by U.S. officers was to assume that their own line of thinking would also be followed by the Japanese. The war games did not foresee the Imperial Navy adopting a more enterprising plan that called for a preemptive strike to damage a large portion of the U.S. Pacific Fleet.

Another presumption was that the United States had adequate strengths to attack Japanese forces during the opening stages of the conflict. Early studies suggested that Blue forces could advance directly to the Philippines, and the Japanese needed to undertake a laborious effort to interfere with such moves.[140] As the 1930s progressed, naval officers became less cavalier, and conceded that the U.S. Fleet could not extend its presence into the western Pacific without eliminating Japanese island bastions in the area.[141] Nevertheless, the war games continued to envisage operations aimed at extensively interfering with enemy operations. Within a few months after the commencement of hostilities, the Blue fleet was to seize the Marshall Islands, while at the same time neutralizing the opponent's long-range air forces based in the Carolines.[142] Thereafter, the advance toward Truk and the Philippines was to be launched once Blue had developed the necessary strength. U.S. forces were expected to possess sufficient numerical superiority to secure the waters surrounding the mandated islands. The IJN, in the meantime, was unlikely to intervene, owing to the danger of exposing its fleet.

The Navy Department held equally unclear views on the possible magnitude of Japanese operations. The IJN was not judged to be capable or willing to undertake aggressive action against areas where the U.S. Fleet could concentrate large forces. Orange (i.e., Japanese) operations were likely to be confined to minor raids on Blue vessels operating individually, in the hope of wearing down enemy strengths. Submarine raids and carrier-based air attacks had to cause more damage than they received in order to be profitable. Such moves were considered to be "not easy against an efficient Blue force."[143] Nor did the Japanese have the capacity to prevent the U.S. Fleet from using all key bases in the western Pacific. Shortly after stepping down from his post as DNI, Puleston wrote a monograph in which he opined that while the submarine and airplane had "added to the problems confronting the American commander," they had "presented even more perplexities" for the Japanese.[144] The conclusion was similar to the views held by other Navy officials. Japan's aircraft production was impeded by resource shortages, which meant that industries could not secure sufficient supplies of alloys to produce special steels.[145] With limited strengths, Orange forces could only secure a few objectives close to the Home Islands. In areas further afield, including the Marianas and Pelews, defense forces were more likely to be small enough so that they could be evacuated when subjected to a counterattack. U.S. planners correctly concluded that their forces were able to procure significantly larger numbers of ships and aircraft than the Japanese, owing to America's industrial potential. Nevertheless, the estimates did not consider scenarios where the Japanese used their forces with the aim of significantly reducing the U.S. Navy's capacity to take offensive action. Without solid information on Japan's capacity to wage war, negative opinions were unlikely to change.

The notion that U.S. forces would be immediately able to launch counteroffensives against Japan prevailed until the eve of Pearl Harbor. Although strategic planning had focused on the Pacific, by 1940 Nazi Germany became the primary concern, mainly because it was in a position to threaten the British Isles and the Atlantic sea lanes. If the Axis powers gained control of either area, the security of the Western Hemisphere and the U.S. mainland was likely to be seriously compromised. In June 1940, following Hitler's conquest of western Europe, President Roosevelt asked the Army and Navy planners to appraise the situation that could arise if Germany continued to menace Britain while Japan remained neutral.[146] Plan Dog, prepared by Admiral Stark in November, warned that a British collapse held such grave ramifications that the United States needed to provide every form of assistance, including the eventual dispatch of naval, ground, and air forces to the Atlantic Ocean and western Europe to defeat Hitler.[147] For this reason, operations in the Pacific had to be confined to the defensive.[148] Between January and March 1941, U.S. and British defense planners met to clarify Allied objectives. The final plan that emerged from the talks, ABC-1, closely resembled Plan Dog. In May, the Army and Navy planners prepared the final version of the global strategy that the United States was to follow in the event it joined the war. Rainbow 5 stipulated that the main effort was to be concentrated against Germany.[149]

At the same time, in the event the Imperial forces intervened, the Americans needed to take countermeasures aimed at weakening Japan, and to help their British and Dutch allies contain enemy advances against the East Indies and Malaya. While defense chiefs had a clear view regarding the paramount importance of the Atlantic theater, they were less realistic in their plans regarding the Pacific. The main mission was to contain Japanese aggression, but the moves for carrying out the task were overambitious. U.S. naval forces in the Far East were to divert enemy strength away from Southeast Asia and the Philippines by capturing positions in the Marshall and Caroline Islands. The Asiatic Fleet was also to "raid Japanese sea communications and destroy Axis forces," while supporting the defense of British and Dutch territories.[150] The strategy appeared to overlook the fact that U.S. forces were not adequate to hold out against a concerted attack. Equally important, defense staffs overestimated the extent to which diversionary raids against the periphery of Japan's empire could disrupt the progress of its operations.

The miscalculations made by U.S. naval authorities were inevitable, in light of their existing knowledge. Owing to the shortage of information, assessments of the IJN's operational plans were based on preconceptions that assumed that enemy forces would follow the same principles as those accepted by the U.S. Navy. Because the Japanese had an inferior numerical strength, actions that entailed the risk of significant losses at the hands of their American opponent seemed counterproductive. Any area where the Americans had a sizeable naval force, including Hawaii, was considered secure. In other far flung regions, such as the Philippines, the Japanese could be forestalled once the capital ships based at Pearl Harbor arrived in sufficient numbers. Few officers believed that the Imperial fleet was capable of mounting more than one major operation at a time. The carrier fleet was considered likely to be concentrated in the Dutch East Indies and British Malaya, which, owing to their oil and mineral resources, constituted much more important objectives for Japan.[151] In November 1941, when Stark noted that a large amphibious Japanese force had been located near Thailand, the accepted conclusion was that the entire Japanese navy was committed to protect the convoys heading for the southern regions. The IJN did not appear to have surplus forces to attack positions in the Pacific. The U.S. Fleet, on the other hand, with its superior strength, was considered more suited to undertake bold moves during the opening stages of the conflict. Only the magnitude of the IJN's operations in Southeast Asia and the western Pacific during December 1941 could convince the Americans that their perceptions were mistaken.

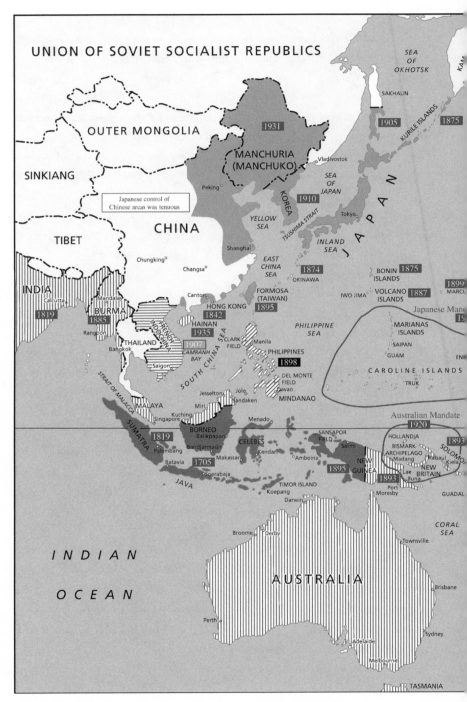

Map 1.1 The Imperial Powers in the Asia-Pacific Region, c. 1940

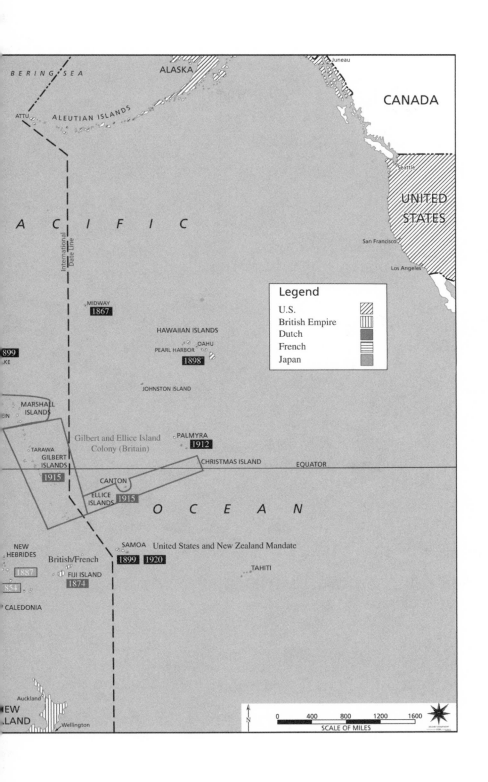

BERING SEA

ALASKA

Juneau

CANADA

ALEUTIAN ISLANDS

ATTU

UNITED
STATES

Seattle

P A C I F I C

International
Date Line

San Francisco

Los Angeles

Legend

U.S.
British Empire
Dutch
French
Japan

MIDWAY
1867

899
KE

HAWAIIAN ISLANDS

OAHU
PEARL HARBOR
1898

JOHNSTON ISLAND

MARSHALL
ISLANDS
EIN

Gilbert and Ellice Island
Colony (Britain)

PALMYRA
1912

TARAWA
GILBERT
ISLANDS
1915

CHRISTMAS ISLAND

EQUATOR

CANTON

ELLICE
ISLANDS 1915

O C E A N

NEW
HEBRIDES

1887

351

CALEDONIA

British/French

FIJI ISLAND
1874

SAMOA   United States and New Zealand Mandate
1899 1920

TAHITI

Auckland

EW
LAND

Wellington

0   400   800   1200   1600

N

SCALE OF MILES

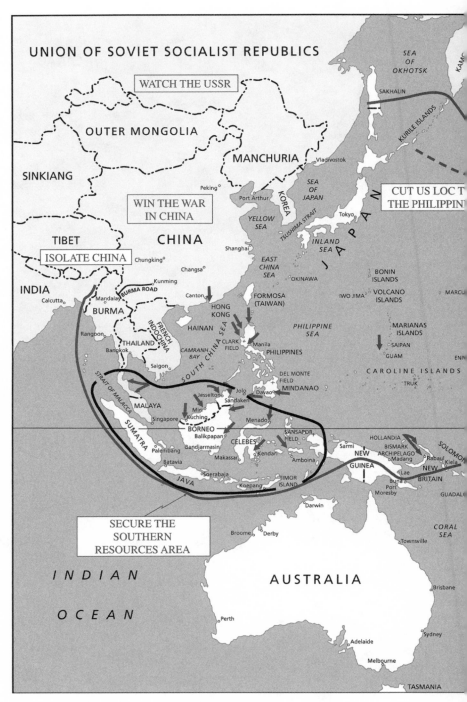

Map 1.2 Japanese War Plans, December 1941

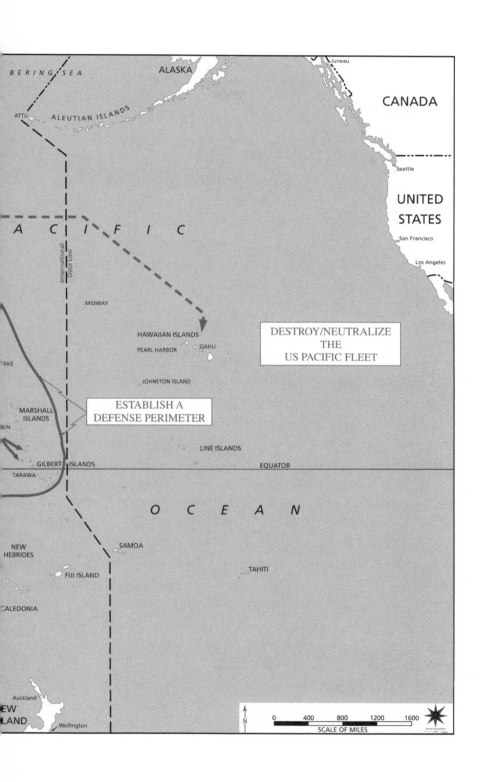

Conclusion

Flawed intelligence was not the main reason why the U.S. Navy failed to prepare for the Japanese onslaught against Pearl Harbor and Southeast Asia between December 1941 and early 1942. The Pacific Fleet simply did not have sufficient resources to contain the IJN, owing to the limited funds that the U.S. government had allocated for defense spending during the inter-war years. Instead, misperceptions of the Imperial fleet led the Americans to develop a false belief that they would be able to cope effectively with their opponent.

The Navy Department was aware that the Japanese posed a distinct menace to U.S. interests in the Far East, and its strategic thinking placed a high importance on making an effort to properly evaluate the IJN, so that a viable course of action against enemy forces could be implemented in the event of hostilities. Unfortunately, the Americans had neither the information nor intellectual assets to formulate an accurate assessment. At the level of collection, the main difficulty was the shortage of reliable intelligence. The Imperial forces managed to hide their activities behind a wall of secrecy that Western observers found difficult to surmount. To complicate matters, the Japanese did not appear to have the resources and skill to wage a war against the United States. As a result, a large portion of American personnel in the Far East reported that the IJN was not to be feared.

At the level of analysis, the ONI faced the twin problems arising from incomplete information coupled with a lack of precedents that could be used to evaluate Japan's forces. The last occasion when the Imperial Navy participated in extensive operations had been during the wars against China and Russia at the turn of the twentieth century. Even when the IJN demonstrated its aptitude in China, most U.S. observers were inclined to conclude that it had yet to confront a more efficient opponent. The ONI's opinions were therefore shaped by speculations on how the Japanese might perform, along with incomplete data that suggested they were not able to construct or operate a fleet that could rival their U.S. counterparts.

The opinions expressed by top officials in the Navy Department reflected the hindrances arising from the absence of a yardstick for gauging the Japanese. Until the Americans had a direct encounter with the Japanese, authorities were not able to determine how efficiently their own forces could cope with their adversary. To complicate matters, the Americans tended to rely on the principles followed by their own armed forces when judging the IJN. The U.S. Navy measured material strengths when evaluating its rivals, mainly because its own doctrines called for the use of mass quantities of technologically advanced weapons. Therefore, the Japanese were considered inferior, since they could not deploy equal quantities of armaments. The assessment was largely correct, and material deficiencies were the fundamental cause for the IJN's ultimate defeat in the Pacific War. The main error committed by U.S. leaders was to presume that Japan's weaknesses would prevent its forces from embarking on any ambitious expeditions. Naval doctrine stated that, in any conflict, the smaller fleet could not afford to risk losses. Therefore, it seemed irrational for the IJN to conduct a large-scale attack against the numerically superior American Navy. The U.S. Fleet, meanwhile, with its substantial force of capital ships and naval aircraft, was better placed to launch a counteroffensive. The miscalculation stemmed largely from the fact that the scope of Japanese operations could not be predicted.

In the end, one needs to be cautious in condemning the U.S. Navy establishment for its misjudgment. Defense officials had few concrete reasons to fear the Japanese. Assessments were based on conjecture, coupled with incomplete knowledge. Furthermore, the numerous indications of the shortcomings that burdened the IJN made it logical to take a complacent view. The spate of victories that the Imperial fleet achieved during the opening stages of the Pacific War was necessary to convince the Americans to change their opinions.

2

Dismantling the "Lesser Foe" and "Superior Enemy" Images
DECEMBER 1941 TO EARLY 1943

The information secured via observations of the IJN and its air arm during the early months of the Pacific War provided U.S. intelligence staffs and naval officials with infallible reasons to abandon their belief that the Japanese could not exert a serious challenge. In fact, the Imperial fleet's crushing successes gave rise to a widespread belief that it possessed a superior level of fighting ability. Following Japan's defeats at Midway and the Solomons during the latter part of 1942, the Americans developed a more rational view. Naval intelligence noted how the enemy suffered weaknesses, among the most significant of which was a shortage of resources, which in turn hindered Japan's capacity to expand its forces. However, because the U.S. Navy had minimal experience in engaging its adversary, commanders in the Pacific Fleet made the initial assessments regarding operational and tactical matters. The ONI also had yet to acquire the manpower and material resources to function under the increased demands brought about by wartime conditions. The dismantling of the "superior enemy" opinion was therefore largely achieved without the help of the intelligence services. As far as shortcomings were concerned, the Imperial forces faced troubles in overcoming opponents who had proper equipment and combat skill. Yet on many occasions, the Japanese continued to demonstrate a capacity to cause substantial damage to, and even the destruction of, Allied vessels and aircraft. The U.S. naval establishment was therefore wary not to veer into over-optimism, and maintained that the IJN was a foe whose qualities were to be noticed.

In regard to methods for fighting the Japanese, the opening phases of the conflict taught some valuable lessons. The main task was to reform the U.S. Navy's practices in a way that worked to neutralize the IJN. During the first six months following the attack on Pearl Harbor, the key hindrance that prevented U.S. forces from applying the lessons of defeat into a set of effective tactics was that they had not developed sufficient numerical strength to embark on large-scale counteroffensives against the Japanese. After summer 1942, when the Pacific Fleet commenced its first major operations, its use of intelligence was geared to fulfill its immediate mission, namely, to mobilize the Navy's limited resources to curb further enemy advances. A large portion of the existing weapons and tactics had been created without a clear understanding of Japan's armed forces, owing to the lack of intelligence. Nevertheless, the Americans were in a good position to identify the appropriate means to counter their enemy, since one of their cardinal principles was to attain their objectives without suffering excessive setbacks. Officers were therefore likely to seek evidence of enemy weaknesses, and interpret them as hints on ways to inflict losses. The IJN's failed attempt to secure Guadalcanal was a reassurance that its forces could be countered. More important, indications of the enemy's ability to disrupt the Pacific Fleet's operations were bound to compel U.S. officers to reconsider their capacity to fight successfully. Combat experiences showed how the Navy was not fully prepared to engage its opponent in an intensified campaign, and improvements were needed if the Imperial fleet was to be defeated in the long run. In surface operations, ship crews needed to develop better methods for defending against Japanese torpedo attacks, by making good use of radar and aerial reconnaissance to locate approaching vessels while establishing a system where the information could be disseminated among all units. Task forces also required greater numbers of high-performance aircraft, along with trained pilots, to protect themselves against bombardment. Equally important was to secure search devices that could accurately track the movement of planes.

Lessons of Defeat, December 1941 to Early 1942

The trauma arising from the disasters suffered by the Allies led U.S. Navy personnel to adopt a more careful method of assessing the Japanese. Prior to the outbreak of hostilities, strategic priorities had already led the Americans to attach a high importance to developing a good understanding of the IJN. A realistic calculation was precluded by the shortage of information, coupled with the fact that the few pieces of available data often suggested that the Imperial fleet suffered from a number of disadvantages. Consequently, the common tendency was to abide by preconceptions that stated the IJN was not a threat. After the war commenced, the Americans received an influx of data that facilitated their efforts to gauge their adversary. However, because Japan's forces had achieved a spate of spectacular victories, opinions took a dramatic swing, to the point where they became exaggerated. In particular, the Japanese naval air service's operations, including the attack on Pearl Harbor and the sinking of the British capital ships *Prince of Wales* and *Repulse* off the coast of Malaya, proved its capacity beyond doubt. As far as U.S. naval intelligence staffs and combat personnel were concerned, the most salient fact was that their opponent had conquered large parts of the Pacific regions with unexpected efficiency. Indications of the IJN's weaknesses therefore did not attract the attention they previously had. The manner in which racial perceptions affected assessments of the enemy also changed visibly. Whereas the accepted view before the conflict was that the Japanese were a backward people who could not build a well-organized fighting machine, the U.S. Navy began to focus on the characteristics that rendered the Imperial fleet a formidable foe. Among the most distinct aspects were dedication and an ability to devise sound combat methods. At the same time, the Americans admitted that their knowledge of Japanese martial qualities was rudimentary, and they were conscious of how making assumptions entailed the risk of encountering further setbacks. Assessments were thus based on a careful examination of the operations carried out by enemy forces.

The U.S. Navy's moves to expand its intelligence capabilities were among the key expressions of its altered outlook, and a recognition of the need to construct a more accurate evaluation of the threats that the IJN posed. In January 1942, Admiral Theodore Wilkinson, the DNI, met with Admiral Ernest King, the newly appointed commander in chief, United States Fleet (COMINCH), to discuss the ONI's wartime functions.[1] The ONI was to retain its duty of compiling, collating, and disseminating studies on enemy fleets. In an effort to redeem the damaged reputation that the office suffered after its failure to anticipate the Pearl Harbor attack, Wilkinson met with naval commanders and top intelligence officers to map out a plan whereby the ONI could operate more effectively. Under a recommendation from Vice Admiral William Pye, head of the Naval War College, King designated naval intelligence as a special division, to be headed by a rear admiral.[2] The ONI was tasked to work with fleet intelligence sections to ensure that naval crews and airmen received updated information. The weekly bulletin, which first appeared in January 1942, included photographic material, combat data, and historical background studies. Intelligence publications were also produced in conjunction with the Navy Department's main bureaus, including BuOrd, and made available to all high-ranking officials.[3] The new arrangement did not end the debate as to whether the ONI or the Pacific Fleet was the leading authority on handling intelligence.[4] A power struggle emerged between Washington and Pearl Harbor, with the division of responsibility not fully delineated until 1943.

At the apex of the defense hierarchy, the Joint Intelligence Committee (JIC) coordinated the activities of the armed services and became the chief producer of reports on the operations that enemy forces were likely to undertake.[5] Under a charter of the Joint Chiefs of Staff (JCS), established in February 1942, the JIC was composed of the DNI, the head of the War Department's military intelligence division, and the head of Air Force intelligence, as well as representatives from civilian organizations such as the State Department and Board of Economic Warfare.

In spite of these improvements, the inadequate funding that the ONI had received in peacetime meant that resources were in short supply. Commander Wilfred Holmes, an officer attached to the Fourteenth Naval District at Honolulu, recalled how his superiors regarded him as "a temporary encumbrance," and provided neither the assistance nor facilities to help intelligence personnel carry out their duties.[6] The ONI did not possess the organizational structure to operate on a war footing. In particular, an apparatus for handling information on the Japanese air service was urgently needed. At the eve of the conflict, the ONI's analysis section had consisted of a number of Far Eastern experts, but did not have any aviation specialists.[7] In January 1942, the Air Intelligence Section of BuAer was given branch status and authorized to manage the task of compiling and disseminating information on foreign air forces.[8]

Further difficulties arose from the fact that the IJN's prowess remained largely unknown, even after it completed its initial round of operations. This was especially true in regard to the surface fleet. Japanese capital ship operations were largely confined to escorting task forces heading to the Pacific islands and Southeast Asia. Their ability to conduct fleet engagements had not been tried, and intelligence summaries contained little material on the subject. A report by the commander of Destroyer Division 59, on the attack against the Japanese convoy in the Makassar Strait in the East Indies area during January 1942, appeared in an ONI bulletin.[9] The outstanding feature was that four destroyers were in close contact with the enemy for almost an hour before being fired upon, suggesting that the IJN's search equipment was not efficient. However, the document did not comment on the means which the Imperial fleet used to detect enemy vessels.

Despite the shortage of intelligence, whereas prewar assessments presumed that the Imperial fleet faced considerable troubles in conducting large-scale operations, the opening months of the conflict saw U.S. officials erring on the cautious side. Admiral Chester Nimitz, who succeeded Husband Kimmel as commander in chief, Pacific Fleet (CINCPAC), conceded, "We can certainly assume that [the IJN's] . . . efficiency is as good as ours, even though perhaps we hope it is not."[10] The wariness was apparent when the Americans tried to predict the moves the Japanese were likely to attempt. In April 1942, the JIC noted how the reverses sustained by the Allies required a sharp revision of earlier estimates.[11] The Imperial forces had secured a strategic barrier stretching from Burma to the southwest Pacific, providing them with a strong defense in depth. The IJN was also considered fully capable of embarking on further offensives. Nimitz concluded that enemy cruiser strengths were sufficient for raids on the lines of communication between Hawaii and the U.S. Navy's outlying bases at Fiji and New Caledonia.[12]

In planning the U.S. Navy's operations during the initial stages of the conflict, commanders faced the fact that the Allies were bound to remain in a precarious position until they could develop adequate strengths. Admiral King advocated forward action, and insisted that U.S. forces hold the trans-Pacific supply line to Australia, while securing the islands which lay astride.[13] However, Allied strategy was based on the premise that Germany constituted the most menacing member of the Axis coalition, and hence its defeat was the top priority. Shortly after the United States entered the war, the British and American leaders held their first summit meeting at Washington, where President Roosevelt and Winston Churchill, the British prime minister, stipulated that their forces needed to be concentrated in the European and Atlantic theaters.[14] King's Army counterparts on the JCS, including George Marshall, along with Brigadier General Dwight Eisenhower, the director of war plans, argued that offensive moves in the Pacific represented a diversion from the "Germany First" strategy. A large portion of the available ships, including cruisers and destroyers, was needed in the Atlantic. Developing forward naval bases in the Pacific also required a fleet of transports to carry troops and supplies. Again, shipping resources were committed to ferrying war materials to the European theater. In spite of his calls for going on the offensive, COMINCH King was aware of the difficulties involved in carrying out such measures, as evidenced by his January 1942 letter to the secretary of the Navy, in which he wrote, "[The year] 1942 will be a year of 'build and hold,'" during which time "the shipping situation alone will hamper aggressive operations, no matter how much we wish to press them."[15] By March, King conceded that operations against Japan needed to be restricted to "current commitments."[16] Officials at the theater level, including Nimitz, also maintained that the U.S. Navy was inferior in all categories of vessels, and could not hold out against the scale of attack that the Japanese were able to carry out.[17] Consequently, there were few options aside from awaiting a time when the Pacific Fleet could strike back successfully. In the meantime, the Americans had to protect their island positions by basing their aircraft in areas such as Hawaii, while at the same time carrying out minor raids against Japan's outlying conquests in the Marshall Islands and New Guinea, in an effort to slow down the enemy's advance. In light of the overwhelming victories that the IJN had achieved, assessments of its capabilities warned against any underestimation.

A similar alertness was exercised when gauging the Imperial Japanese Navy Air Force (IJNAF). In contrast to the surface fleet, the air services carried out a number of operations that clearly demonstrated their efficiency. Yet during the opening phase of the conflict the Americans struggled to assess the Japanese in an objective manner. Several months were needed before air intelligence could develop an adequate team of trained personnel. At the theater level, the Pacific Fleet was responsible for handling information. Its duty was

Map 2.1 The Height of Japanese Expansion, April 1942

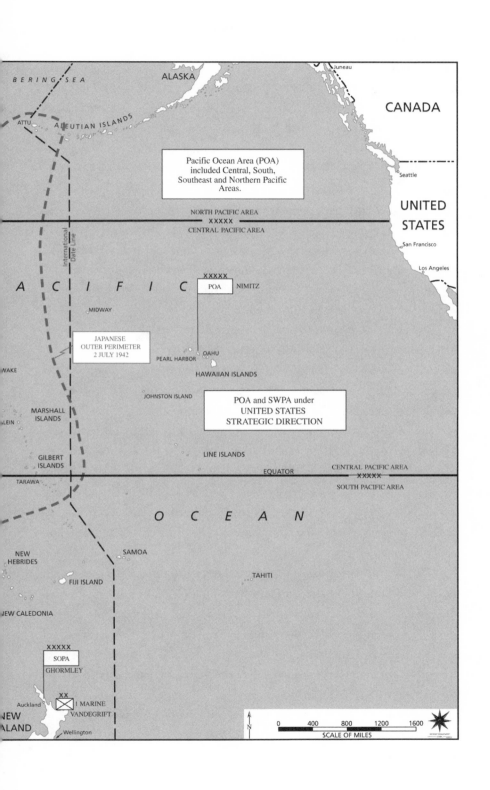

to collate the reports received from naval and air units and propagate them via a monthly bulletin. Intelligence staffs received a steady flow of accounts, which warned that the IJN air arm exerted a serious threat. Because analysts were not entirely familiar with Japanese aviation, the raw intelligence was oftentimes simply reproduced verbatim. Information summaries therefore highlighted the IJN air arm's triumphs, and did not provide an overall picture of its characteristics, including weaknesses that hindered its performance. At the same time, intelligence organizations were not culpable for formulating the unbalanced image. The data originated from U.S. personnel serving in the combat theaters, who were not familiar with their opponent and tended to show trepidation when describing the Japanese. The observations made during the opening stages provided what were only the preliminary indications concerning the enemy's fighting capabilities.

Attacks on Allied vessels inflicted crippling losses. A key contributing factor was that aircraft carried large payloads. The Mitsubishi Type 96 twin-engine plane, which sank HMS *Prince of Wales* and *Repulse*, dropped bombs weighing up to 1,800 pounds.[18] During the Battle of the Java Sea, armor-piercing ammunition achieved a direct hit on the *Houston*.[19] Aerial torpedoes functioned well, taking depth quickly, and struck ships without being detected.[20] At the same time, naval intelligence conceded that the available information was incomplete, and the uncertainty called for a close watch on future developments. An ONI report was prefaced, "It should not be overlooked that Japanese plane types are periodically improved." Aircraft described as "older" models were thus likely to be fitted with more efficient engines and enhanced weaponry.[21]

The tactical performance of bomber crews also proved to be of a high order. The damage inflicted on the U.S. battleship fleet at Pearl Harbor led Nimitz to conclude, "The mechanical excellence and resolution of [Japanese] flyers have been proven beyond doubt."[22] In high-level bombing runs and torpedo attacks, the most common feature was a straight run flown in close formation, with the planes dropping their ordnance simultaneously.[23] In order to evade antiaircraft fire, pilots released their bombs from high altitudes, between 12,000 to 18,000 feet. The Japanese also used several types of maneuvers in conjunction, in an effort to overwhelm their opponents. Horizontal bombers initiated the raid, attracting the attention of antiaircraft crews.[24]

Torpedo planes and dive-bombers followed, and were often able to operate without interference. Pilots pressed home their raids, even when they faced opposition. Although such practices made the aircraft relatively easy targets, the result was an excellent bombing pattern. Instances where U.S. vessels escaped damage were attributed to good fortune, rather than errors made by the Japanese. Reporting on opposition encountered during the U.S. Navy's carrier raids against the Marshall and Gilbert Islands, an officer on board the *Enterprise* noted how the Japanese pressed home their attacks in spite of antiaircraft fire, and remarked that the ship could have been sunk had it not been making a sharp turn.[25]

The numerous indications of the IJNAF's successes led the Americans to brush aside the fact that it had yet to defeat enemies with superior numbers and technology. The air service's operations were made easy because the Allies could not put up a strong defense. Nevertheless, the fact remained that pilots carried out their operations competently. The IJNAF was used to support amphibious operations, with good results. In the Dutch East Indies and in Malaya, landing forces relied heavily on air power to prepare the way for their assault. Flying boats conducted reconnaissance missions, while heavy air attacks took out communications facilities and coastal defense batteries.[26] Support missions were executed by carrier-borne planes, or, if the distances were not too great, by land-based aircraft.[27] Aerodromes were neutralized to help the Japanese achieve air superiority over the vicinity of the landing beaches, and to prevent the defenders from raiding the convoy. Although the Imperial forces were aided by minimal opposition, the proper use of air power was cited as a crucial factor that enabled them to prevail.

While U.S. naval personnel described the IJNAF's tactics against shipping targets in detail, on other important matters, namely, the IJNAF's capacity to wage air-to-air combat, substantial data were not available. Aside from Pearl Harbor and Java Sea, the Pacific Fleet had engaged the Japanese in peripheral areas where neither side could deploy large fighter forces. The Americans therefore had no basis for comparing the design and performance of their own aircraft vis-à-vis their counterparts.[28] As late as Midway, aircrews had little information on the capabilities of the Zero fighter or the pilots who flew them.[29] A large amount of intelligence was obtained from the U.S. Army Air Forces (USAAF), whose aviators in the Philippines and Dutch East

Indies made a number of attempts to slow down the Japanese drive to secure control of the skies over Southeast Asia. Pilots who managed to escape the forward areas without being captured described the Mitsubishi Type Zero as "an excellent plane," with a speed and maneuverability that surpassed most of its Allied counterparts.[30] However, because information on the particulars of the Zero remained rare, rumors began to spread throughout the naval air service. Aircrews who had been accustomed to believing that the words "made in Japan" implied an inferior and poorly imitated product concluded that the plane was originally an American design that had been rejected by the Navy, and thereafter purchased by the Japanese to be reproduced.[31] Others suggested that the Zero's maneuverability was due to its components being made of light materials such as plastics, which was a far-reaching achievement beyond the capacity of most Western manufacturers. In order to clear away the myths, U.S. intelligence initiated a search for an intact specimen that could provide the exact details.

The flying skills of enemy pilots were easier to discern. The Japanese demonstrated their ability to exploit the advantages possessed by their aircraft, and effected good coordination. Fighters made large circles at different altitudes. When the lower fighters were attacked, they dove to evade the gunfire. Meanwhile, aircraft flying at higher elevations closed in to attack the U.S. planes. The method optimized the Zero's ability to make abrupt dives and climbs. Aircrews were also quick to target weaknesses in Allied formations. Disabled planes flying independently were subjected to determined attacks.[32] Last but not least, the IJNAF frequently altered its methods. While frontal attacks on fighters were often avoided, when engaging bombers that were not equipped with large amounts of defensive armament, such as the B-17 Flying Fortress, Zero pilots preferred to close in from the forward areas. The Japanese were therefore not bound by any rigid rules, but used their discretion. The ability to adapt their tactics as the circumstances dictated rendered IJNAF aviators "the more formidable foe."[33]

By spring 1942, intelligence assessments of the IJN air arm demonstrated the extent to which the U.S. Navy had almost unanimously shed all traces of contempt. The ONI expressed an unquestioned veneration, and admitted that Japanese aircrews had demonstrated "to a marked degree, thorough indoctrination in sound aerial tactics."[34] Japanese successes were attributed to excellent training, coupled with the possession of aircraft designed to carry out the assigned task, namely, to sink Allied vessels and dominate the airspace over areas where task forces operated. Similarly, the Pacific Fleet disseminated a remark made in a USAAF report that "enemy tactics and technique have shown the Japanese pilot to be highly trained and to possess all the qualities that make for a good pilot."[35]

Regarding the development of tactics against the Japanese, the early encounters taught only the basic maneuvers. American aviators learned that they needed to execute moves that enabled U.S. aircraft to evade their opponent's strengths. Army pilots established a procedure where no plane was to enter a target area below 25,000 feet, since within that range, enemy fighters could conduct abrupt climbs and dives, attacking U.S. planes at will.[36]

However, the lessons were recognized to be inconclusive, and the available intelligence was not complete enough to form the basis of a solid doctrine. Aircrews did note shortcomings that could be exploited. Zero fighters were vulnerable to gunfire, owing to their lack of armor and self-sealing fuel tanks.[37] The Japanese also laid themselves open to attack. During a raid on the IJN's main air base at Rabaul in the southwest Pacific, Zero pilots often made the mistake of climbing steeply immediately after the attack, thereby losing speed and exposing the underside of their aircraft.[38] Yet many of the tactics devised were aimed at defending against enemy planes, and methods for shooting them down could be determined only through further engagements. Countermeasures were therefore prescribed on the proviso that they remained tentative. Naval intelligence deduced that the most favorable direction for attacking enemy aircraft was via the sectors where they could not deliver fire.[39] Calculations concerning the vulnerable zones were to be taken as approximate, owing to the lack of accurate information. Realizing the need for better data on the IJN's air arm and ways to engage it, BuAer ordered that all naval units be provided with combat intelligence officers, whose tasks were to interrogate pilots returning from missions, and thereafter communicate the findings to the Pacific Fleet.[40] Experts in air intelligence also had to be trained, and a special school was established at Quonset Point, Rhode Island, in April 1942.

Engagements with the IJNAF also showed that naval vessels had to be refitted with stronger antiaircraft defenses. Bulletins prepared by COMINCH contained extensive explanations. The commander of the Destroyer Battle Force pointed out that 5-inch guns with open sights were required to provide a more effective fire-control system to deal with torpedo bomber attacks.[41] Training centers were also to be established to indoctrinate crews in the proper use of automatic weapons, with all ships taking advantage of the facilities.[42] Nevertheless, without adequate combat experience and a more detailed knowledge of Japanese techniques, commanders were not in a position to recommend definite procedures on how to use the equipment.

At the higher ends of the naval command, the foremost concern was to achieve air superiority and enable the U.S. Navy to wrest the initiative. In July, the Pacific Fleet published a letter written by General George Marshall to the commander of the Hawaiian Department, which emphasized that a concerted effort was required to ensure that sufficient planes were dispatched to the Pacific theaters.[43] An adequate pool of skilled pilots was also essential. Shortly after becoming chief of BuAer, Admiral John Towers insisted that because carriers comprised the only surface striking force in the Pacific, only the most qualified officers could be placed in command of task groups.[44] To ensure that carrier operations were conducted properly, experts on the matter had to be promoted to flag rank, and Towers calculated that the Navy would require at least thirty air admirals by 1943.

The experiences of defeat not only highlighted the need to gain a comprehensive knowledge of the fighting methods and equipment used by the Japanese navy and its air services. More important, naval and air crews faced the harsh fact that U.S. forces were not prepared to confront their opponent, and substantial reforms along with increased numerical strengths were vital. At the same time, U.S. personnel acknowledged how they had a limited knowledge of the elements they faced, and the development of tactics thus hinged on a process of trial and error. Further encounters with enemy forces were needed before a sufficient understanding could be achieved.

The Turn of the Tide, June 1942 to Spring 1943

During the latter part of 1942 and winter 1943, U.S. forces conducted a number of operations aimed at containing Japanese moves toward further expansion. The Navy halted the IJN's advance against Coral Sea and Midway, thereby frustrating Japan's efforts to secure bases that could be used to threaten Allied strongholds in the central and southwest Pacific areas. Starting in July, the Japanese attempted to capture the island of Guadalcanal in the Solomon Islands. The aim was to acquire a staging point for air and submarine attacks against the trans-Pacific shipping line and thereby disrupt Allied moves to develop Australia as a base for counteroffensives against the southern perimeter of Japan's empire. Throughout the following months, the Americans conducted a series of surface and air engagements to gain control of the surrounding waters and airspace, and prevent the IJN from sending reinforcements to the island. By the closing stages of the campaign in January 1943, the U.S. Navy concluded that the casualties suffered by the Imperial fleet had led it to lose the strategic initiative, since it no longer had sufficient ships and aircraft to support large-scale invasions. Nevertheless, enemy forces showed that they still had the numerical strength to impede Allied attempts to recapture Japan's conquered territories. For this reason, the IJN's operational and tactical qualities continued to attract substantial attention.

The available information on the Japanese fleet presented a muddled picture, and U.S. naval intelligence was aware that the shortage of data continued to thwart an accurate assessment. Reliable evidence did indicate that the IJN's strengths had diminished considerably. The ONI estimated that combat losses since the start of the war amounted to over a quarter of Japan's gross tonnage.[45] Economic factors posed additional difficulties. Iron and steel output was not sufficient to produce large quantities of ships, munitions, and heavy equipment.[46] The maintenance of the war effort depended on whether the Japanese could secure adequate raw materials, including oil and strategic metals. Although the conquered territories in Southeast Asia provided most of the necessary supplies, and the merchant fleet had enough tonnage to transport supplies to the Home Islands, the shipbuilding industries did not have the capacity to replace sinkings that could be incurred as a result of Allied attacks.[47]

Nevertheless, U.S. naval intelligence was unable to determine exactly how resource shortages could affect Japan's efforts toward naval expansion. The size of the construction program remained uncertain, owing to the secrecy with which the Japanese shrouded the information. In terms of battleships, the prewar program was known to have envisaged the launching of eight new vessels, including the super-battleships *Yamato* and *Musashi*. Yet the extent to which the Imperial fleet had modified the original plan was uncertain, and the numbers due to be completed remained open to speculation. An estimate on the building program was prefaced with a warning that the figures had to be "accepted with reserve."[48]

For U.S. commanders, the uncertainty was compounded by apprehensions that arose from indications that they did not have superiority in many categories of vessels, even though the IJN's forces had been depleted. The situation necessitated a balanced assessment, which described the troubles confronting the Japanese, while at the same time paying heed to the challenges that the U.S. Navy continued to face. The victories at Coral Sea and Midway encouraged naval leaders to divert their effort away from operations against Germany and step up the tempo of operations in the Pacific. On July 2, 1942, the JCS issued a directive stating that the short-term goal was to seize and occupy the New Britain–New Ireland–New Guinea area. When reports had been received that a U.S. reconnaissance plane observed the Japanese building an airfield on Guadalcanal, the island was added to the list of objectives. However, the Americans had yet to produce a sufficient number of ships and aircraft to achieve a decisive victory. When the Guadalcanal offensive commenced in August, theater commanders, including Nimitz and Vice Admiral Robert L. Ghormley, commanding the South Pacific forces, doubted whether they could maintain their hold over the South Pacific for a significant length of time.[49] The situation partially improved when the JCS agreed to dispatch more aircraft to the area. Still, the margin was too close to reassure the Americans that they could contain their opponents. In November, after the U.S. Navy repelled the Japanese attack on Henderson field at Guadalcanal, Nimitz conceded, "Had the powerful enemy fleet succeeded in [its] mission . . . the task of preventing a major attack and [the] landing of large-scale reinforcements would have been much more difficult, if not impossible."[50] As late as December, CINCPAC concluded that while the Pacific Fleet had inflicted "disproportionate losses," he did not think that it had an edge.[51] Only a further decline in the IJN's strength, coupled with the construction of new U.S. vessels, could significantly shift the balance. As long as the Japanese retained a substantial number of capital ships, carriers, and aircraft, naval officials remained reluctant to conclude that their opponent could be easily defeated.

Lessons of Limited Victories: Encounters with the IJN's Fleet

The U.S. Navy's engagements with the IJN's surface fleet in the Solomons during autumn 1942 provided the first substantive data on the latter's combat effectiveness. Enemy weapons achieved a high standard of performance, while naval crews proved capable of carrying out moves that worked to sink Allied warships. U.S. commanders were also aware that the Pacific Fleet often had to fight with inferior numerical strength, and losses could not be afforded. Even in early 1943, when mounting losses compelled the Japanese to withdraw their main units from the Guadalcanal area, the general consensus was that the Imperial Navy remained a resilient enemy. To complicate matters, observations of the IJN's activities offered only vague indications of its weapons and doctrines. Under the circumstances, countermeasures had to be formulated with a corresponding uncertainty as to whether they were likely to work. Many American crews also continued to assume that their own forces were superior, and encountered a number of unpleasant surprises, including the setbacks at Savo Island and Tassafaronga. The difficulties were alleviated because the U.S. Navy avoided speculating on the reasons why the enemy fought the way it did. Instead, officers focused on ways by which the Pacific Fleet could introduce better countermeasures against the devastation that the Japanese were able to inflict with their torpedoes and gunfire. Task force crews had to learn how to fight effectively at nighttime, when the enemy was apt to take advantage of the limited visibility by conducting surprise attacks. Tactics were also devised on the understanding that reforms in the IJN's fighting capabilities could not be ruled out.

As late as the Guadalcanal campaign, intelligence staffs did not have a great amount of data to work with, as evidenced by the material that appeared in the ONI summaries. A statement on Axis torpedoes conceded that "very little factual information" had been received on Japanese weaponry.[52] Nor was naval intelligence able to play a large role in disseminating battle lessons, mainly because it was hampered by the long distances that separated the office from the main combat theater. The information received from the Pacific had to be sent to Washington before it could be analyzed, and the time lag was often several months. The ONI thus had to rely on alternative sources. A report on the naval battle that took place between November 11 and 15 was based on an article written by a war correspondent from the North American

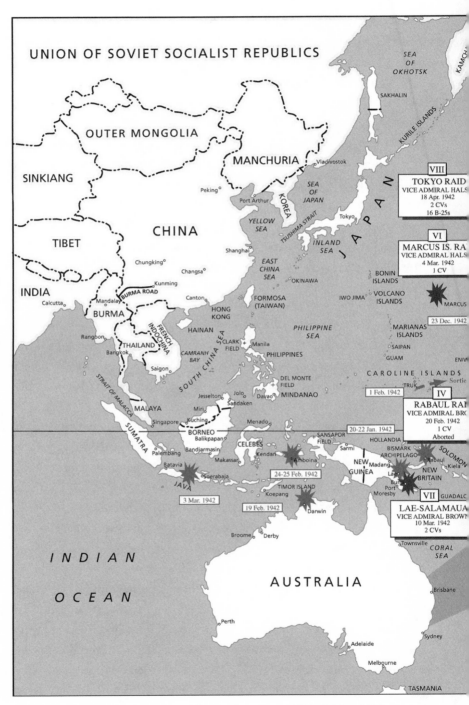

Map 2.2 U.S. Naval Operations in the Pacific, Winter 1941–Spring 1942

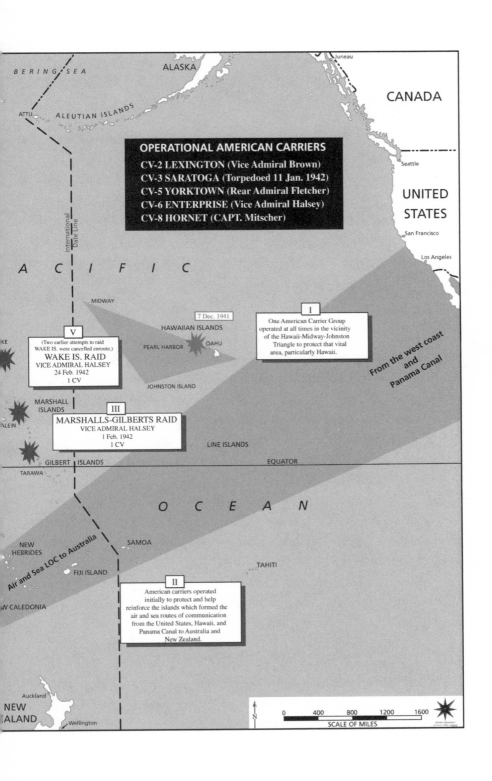

OPERATIONAL AMERICAN CARRIERS

CV-2 LEXINGTON (Vice Admiral Brown)
CV-3 SARATOGA (Torpedoed 11 Jan. 1942)
CV-5 YORKTOWN (Rear Admiral Fletcher)
CV-6 ENTERPRISE (Vice Admiral Halsey)
CV-8 HORNET (CAPT. Mitscher)

V

(Two earlier attempts to raid
WAKE IS. were cancelled enroute.)
WAKE IS. RAID
VICE ADMIRAL HALSEY
24 Feb. 1942
1 CV

III

MARSHALLS-GILBERTS RAID
VICE ADMIRAL HALSEY
1 Feb. 1942
1 CV

I

One American Carrier Group
operated at all times in the vicinity
of the Hawaii-Midway-Johnston
Triangle to protect that vital
area, particularly Hawaii.

II

American carriers operated
initially to protect and help
reinforce the islands which formed the
air and sea routes of communication
from the United States, Hawaii, and
Panama Canal to Australia and
New Zealand.

7 Dec. 1941

BERING SEA
ALASKA
CANADA
ATTU
ALEUTIAN ISLANDS
Juneau
Seattle
UNITED STATES
San Francisco
Los Angeles
International Date Line
A   C   I   F   I   C
MIDWAY
HAWAIIAN ISLANDS
PEARL HARBOR   OAHU
JOHNSTON ISLAND
From the west coast and Panama Canal
MARSHALL ISLANDS
ALEIN
LINE ISLANDS
GILBERT ISLANDS
EQUATOR
TARAWA
O   C   E   A   N
NEW HEBRIDES
Air and Sea LOC to Australia
SAMOA
FIJI ISLAND
TAHITI
N CALEDONIA
Auckland
NEW ZEALAND
Wellington

0   400   800   1200   1600
SCALE OF MILES

Newspaper Alliance.[53] The item simply narrated the engagement. It was not until early 1943 that intelligence reports began to cover the IJN's performance in the Solomons. Even then, enemy tactics were described in a vague manner. Referring to the Japanese task force, the ONI went no further than to state that the naval units had been assigned "to gain complete control of the seas."[54] Conclusions on a number of key aspects, including the way in which destroyers were used in fleet engagements, could not be made with certainty. Extensive information had not been secured, since most of the encounters had been fought at night, where limited visibility precluded an observation.[55]

The shortage of intelligence was primarily a reflection of the U.S. Navy's limited combat experience. Ship crews were therefore assigned to study the tactics that the Japanese executed. Among the notable observations was that the enemy maneuvered its vessels with a view to achieving surprise. During the Battle of Savo Island on August 7–8, the attacking force avoided detection by U.S. destroyers that had been assigned to patrol the surrounding approaches. Japanese ships were not identified, owing to the cover of darkness. The failure was also explained by the enemy's successful attempt to evade the destroyer screens.[56] The outcome was the all but complete destruction of the U.S. warships. While a number of Japanese vessels were struck, none appeared to have suffered extensive damage, and the entire enemy fleet cleared the battle area. Had the Japanese pressed ahead and attacked the transports and cargo ships, they would likely have compelled the American task force to abandon its attempt to stage a landing on Guadalcanal. Commenting on the encounter, Nimitz restated his respect for the IJN's fighting capabilities, and concluded, "The basis of the Japanese victory . . . was their bold offensive spirit and alertness."[57]

Japanese naval ordnance was also handled effectively. The commanding officer of the transport *President Jackson* described the accuracy of gunfire as "excellent."[58] Once the ship was located, enemy salvoes scored a hit virtually every time they were launched. The efficiency of the IJN's fire-control and range-keeping methods could not be dismissed, and the encounter convinced U.S. naval commanders that the Japanese were adept at carrying out nighttime operations.[59] In fact, the difference in gunnery performance was described as "so marked as to show plainly what success can be achieved by correct training," as well as the disasters that could result from the lack thereof.[60]

Nevertheless, information on the IJN's equipment and doctrine remained scarce, and naval commanders did not expend a large effort inferring on the matter. Instead, the most pertinent point was that the Japanese had performed well, and the Pacific Fleet needed to amend its procedures significantly. The Americans reflected on their own weaknesses, particularly in the areas of night fighting and close-quarter engagements, both of which had not received much attention prior to the conflict. Among the foremost faults was that the Navy expected radar to provide early warnings of approaching enemy vessels. During the early stages of the conflict, considerable efforts were made in this area. CINCPAC actively supported the establishment of a radar center at Pearl Harbor, comprised of schools dedicated to subjects such as maintenance, operations, and tactics.[61] However, top leaders, including Ghormley, noted that the encounter at Savo had exposed the Pacific Fleet's tendency to over-rely on radar, and to pay insufficient attention to other means of detecting enemy forces, including aerial search.[62] The official inquiry concluded that U.S. commanders overlooked the fact that reconnaissance missions had not been conducted for almost a day prior to the engagement.[63] The Japanese were believed to be avoiding the Savo Island area, fearing a head-on clash with the U.S. fleet. Subsequently, a minimal effort was made to track enemy movements. Admiral Richmond Turner, commanding the amphibious forces, noted how many officers maintained that, owing to U.S. technological superiority, the IJN could be easily defeated.[64] The Americans were also reported to have not established an effective system for communication, which resulted in a failure to issue timely information once the attackers had been detected.[65] Although the Navy had set up centralized combat information centers when conducting aerial engagements, officers had not recognized the need to create a similar apparatus for surface operations.

While U.S. commanders recognized the need for changes, the learning process proved slow. The problem stemmed largely from a lack of knowledge regarding the IJN, and the proper ways to combat it were hard to determine. Naval crews attempted to cope with the dilemma by developing their tactics through experimentation. The improvements in communications networks and radar, which had been implemented following Savo Island, were tested at Cape Esperance during October 11–12. All ships in Task Group 64.2 were equipped with gunnery radars, and cruisers had SC search devices to facilitate surface detection. Radar-guided fire from the cruisers *Salt Lake City*, *Boise*, and *Helena* was credited for compelling the Japanese to abandon the engagement.[66] The victory provided a confidence builder, in that it showed that the guns on board U.S. ships could counteract the IJN's vessels before the latter deployed their torpedoes. Yet the Americans were aware that they needed to enhance their own performance in nighttime engagements, by making greater use of surface-tracking radar and voice radio communications.[67] During the night actions of November 12–15, U.S. warships again used radar to deliver fire from long ranges. By doing so, they avoided having to use flares and exposing their position to enemy gunners.[68] One of the main deductions drawn from the IJN task force's failure to counterattack was that it did not have sufficiently advanced equipment to locate enemy ships.[69] At the same time, the U.S. fleet's use of radar was of "tremendous value," because it permitted the task force to deploy its overwhelming firepower with a level of accuracy "far in excess" of what could be achieved when ship crews relied on optical devices and human vision.[70]

However, the lessons were not always applied in a manner that enabled U.S. forces to develop effective moves. The organization of the Pacific Fleet's command did not help. Commanding officers were placed in charge of units for short periods, owing to the rapid pace of operations, making it difficult to implement new tactical ideas among crews, most of whom were inexperienced.[71] Ship-based personnel thus did not have opportunities to familiarize themselves with the conduct of night battles. Fire-control and fire-direction sets were primarily built to aid the use of antiaircraft batteries, and could not always detect surface vessels, owing to the interference caused by surface waves. Nor did the higher officials fully understand that their crews needed to be indoctrinated with the uses and limits of radar. For example, combat experience showed that in order to identify enemy ships, operators had to discriminate between the various blips that appeared on their screens.[72]

Resource shortages also held back the Navy's ability to apply its limited knowledge of the IJN in its tactical practices. One of the key lessons learned was the need to deploy screening vessels at longer distances from the convoy, to facilitate the detection of enemy forces. Destroyers were to sail at a distance from the carrier group equal to the estimated range of Japanese torpedoes. Following the sinking of the carrier *Wasp*, Nimitz recommended that destroyers be arranged in a complete circular vanguard.[73] However, the necessary number of vessels had yet to be dispatched. The U.S. Navy faced a more urgent need to deploy destroyers in the Atlantic, where German U-boats continued to prey on Allied convoys carrying troops and equipment to the British Isles. By late October, Admiral William Halsey, who had replaced Ghormley, was expressing grave concerns that the majority of destroyers under his command had been sunk or damaged, and the reinforcements sent to the Solomons were not enough to satisfy his requirements.[74]

The U.S. Navy's tactical and material shortcomings became apparent at the night action off Tassafaronga on November 30. During the second phase, the Japanese launched an "amazingly effective and devastating torpedo attack" that sank the heavy cruiser *Northampton*, and seriously damaged the *Minneapolis*, *New Orleans*, and *Pensacola*.[75] The commanding officer of the *New Orleans* noted how several ships were hit almost simultaneously before their crews detected the torpedoes.[76] The Imperial fleet's capabilities also remained open to debate. Enemy moves could not be monitored because engagements were fought under the cover of darkness. Admiral Carleton Wright, commander of the task force, conceded that "all attempts to determine with certainty the composition of the Japanese forces participating in the action, or the tactics employed by those forces, . . . are defeated by conditions preventing accurate observation."[77] Imperial Navy vessels were seen only at brief intervals, when they were illuminated by star shells or the fire emitted by burning ships. Conclusions on basic matters, including the types of ships employed, were based on deduction. The number of torpedoes launched, and the wide spread, seemed to rule out the possibility of a submarine attack. Yet the attackers appeared too distant, making it improbable that torpedoes with the same speed and range as the U.S. Navy's weapons could have wrought such havoc. A large number of personnel remained reluctant to concede that the Japanese produced better equipment than the Americans. At the same time, Nimitz admitted that enemy techniques were superior, even though he did not fully appreciate the long-lance's destructive power.

The only certain conclusion was that task forces needed to maintain an adequate technological lead over their opponents, and commanders were wary not to become overconfident. The chief concern was that the available resources did not offer guaranteed protection against the damage that the IJN was able to cause. U.S. and Japanese forces had a roughly equal operational capability. The Americans did not have an edge in terms of experience, skill, or quality of personnel.[78] Nimitz conceded that the possession of fire-control radar was the Pacific Fleet's only significant advantage.[79] Ship crews needed to exploit this asset, while at the same time denying enemy forces the opportunity to use their torpedoes to good effect.[80] U.S. forces were to approach without being detected, and destroy enemy ships with radar-controlled gunfire before the latter could respond. Yet search devices were of little use if the gunners were not properly trained to adjust their fire.[81] Nor did the use of radar always protect surface vessels. The Tassafaronga encounter showed that when ships operated in confined waters, the effectiveness of radar was reduced, owing to the reflections created by the surrounding islands, and the Japanese were alleged to have taken good advantage of the situation.[82] The U.S. Navy's use of advanced equipment thus had to be combined with efforts to develop more effective moves. The IJN was confident in the capabilities of its destroyers, as evidenced by their frequent employment, and the destructive capabilities of their torpedoes caused concern. U.S. naval commanders realized that a concerted effort was needed to develop night tactics, and they attempted to devise evasive moves. However, because the exact details regarding the performance of enemy ordnance remained unknown, there were few choices apart from formulating tactics through a process of trial and error.

Due allowance was made for Japanese advancements. In his contribution to Nimitz's memorandum on the countermeasures that the U.S. Navy needed to undertake, Halsey warned that while enemy ships did not appear to have fire-control radars, in the event such devices were introduced, the Americans could retain their advantages "only by continuous improvement" in their handling of search equipment.[83] Last but not least, naval crews had to deal with situations where radar suffered damage from enemy attacks. U.S. battleships were not designed or armed for close-range actions, since naval doctrine had not made proper preparations for such scenarios. In a few instances, including the attack on the *South Dakota*, intense enemy fire rendered the radio and fire-control circuits inoperative. For this reason, vessels had to be provided with a larger number of backup radar sets so that battery personnel could avoid becoming blinded.

At the finish of the Solomons campaign, the U.S. Navy's perception of its ability to engage the Imperial fleet was one of cautious confidence. The IJN's most noted flaw was the underdeveloped state of its equipment for searching and tracking enemy vessels. As a result, Japanese ships were vulnerable to surprise attacks. The Pacific Fleet, meanwhile, had discovered that the use of control systems gave it a significant advantage. At the same time, the U.S. Navy did not have a marked superiority. The Japanese held a number of strong points, the most important of which was that their torpedoes continued to sink many ships. The Americans learned that they needed to develop the tactics and technology to enable them to make good use of their assets, while minimizing the losses that the Japanese could inflict.

The experiences gained during the U.S. Navy's submarine operations were also perceived as a sign that proper tactics had to be developed before naval personnel could confidently fight the Japanese. In addition to attacking convoys carrying reinforcements to Guadalcanal, U.S. submarines were used to patrol the western Pacific and track the movements of Japanese ships, as well as to sink merchant vessels transporting raw materials from the southern regions to the Home Islands. The intelligence obtained from the missions did reveal how the enemy's defensive measures were rudimentary. As a matter of fact, the Japanese failed to develop an adequate antisubmarine warfare capacity for the duration of the conflict. At the start of the war, the Imperial Navy did not have any ships assigned for convoy tasks, and even when Japan commenced its construction of destroyer escorts, the number available was far below the minimum required. Japanese naval traditions had scorned escorting missions as mundane, and not befitting of a fighting force geared for offensive warfare.[84] Subsequently, convoy protection was unpopular among officers. Because IJN doctrine focused on the Mahanian concept of defeating the enemy in a decisive battle, its studies on antisubmarine actions were devoted to the measures most likely to be employed in fleet engagements.[85] By focusing on battle-fleet actions, the navy paid scant attention to developing the vessels, tactics, and doctrine needed for a successful merchant shipping defense.[86] Nor did the Japanese give serious thought to a situation where the U.S. Navy conducted sustained attacks on their supply lines, since the accepted conclusion was that enemy submarines operating in the western Pacific, beyond shore-based air cover, were more likely to face destruction.

Although the details concerning Japanese concepts for defending their merchantmen and transports were not available, U.S. submarine crews witnessed a number of flawed practices. One captain noted the absence of any signs that aerial patrols were conducted regularly.[87] Escort vessels were deployed only when submarines had been detected.[88] Destroyers also appeared to be using obsolete detection equipment, as evidenced by their practice of stopping periodically to listen for the sounds of approaching vessels, thereby suggesting that their development of sonar was lagging.[89]

However, the intelligence pointing to the vulnerability of Japanese shipping was considered of limited value in discrediting the IJN's capabilities in this area, mainly because the U.S. submarine fleet was in a weak state. Throughout the interwar period, American officers had entertained the idea of using submarines to conduct unrestricted warfare against Japanese maritime commerce, in a manner similar to the German attempt at strangulating Britain during the Great War.[90] Underwater vessels were designed for long-range missions into the far reaches of the Pacific, where refueling and re-supply facilities were bound to come at a premium. Nevertheless, the performance of torpedoes was the most serious shortcoming. The lack of communication between BuOrd and fleet officers meant the latter were not informed on the weapons being produced.[91] In addition, financial constraints precluded proper experimentation. Exercises were conducted without having torpedoes detonate, in an effort to preserve the limited supply of ordnance. Torpedoes were also constructed to fire at sufficient depth to pass beneath the target, to facilitate recovery. As a result, there were few opportunities to discover and remedy existing faults. When the U.S. submarine fleet embarked on its initial operations, a large proportion of torpedoes turned out to explode either prematurely or not at all. Following a mission in May 1942, when one of the *Skipjack*'s torpedoes passed directly under a transport, the captain remarked that he had "little confidence" in his weapons.[92] The defects were compounded by the uncooperative attitude shown by BuOrd, which tended to blame submarine crews for not adjusting their firing range properly. Submarine captains pressed the Navy to supply better weapons. The Westinghouse manufacturing company was assigned to develop the Mark XVIII electric torpedo that could carry larger warheads and fire at shallower depths.[93] Yet progress was hindered by numerous setbacks in the experimentation process. The continued lack of cooperation from BuOrd and the naval torpedo station at Newport, in pressing Westinghouse to speed up production, also prevented the

Pacific Fleet from acquiring the new devices in sufficient quantities well into 1943.[94] In the meantime, submarine crews were most likely to remain skeptical about their capacity to inflict significant damage.

Tactical doctrine also had adverse consequences. Commanders insisted that surface-level attacks were risky, since they exposed submarines to detection. U.S. crews thus avoided this type of maneuver. Submarines remained submerged, often waiting for targets to appear, instead of seeking them out. At Guadalcanal, submarine captains were castigated for awaiting Japanese transports and warships to enter the littoral waters, instead of attempting to interdict them in the open sea.[95] Urgent calls were raised for the development of aggressive combat methods that were more suitable for conducting large-scale attacks. The Japanese navy's shortcomings did not enable the U.S. Navy to prevail, unless the latter developed the appropriate means to exploit the former's inadequacies.

Encounters with the IJN Air Arm

The IJNAF demonstrated a conflicting array of strengths and weaknesses during the Midway and Solomons campaigns. The declining fighting skills of enemy pilots indicated that the Japanese had lost a large portion of their trained aviators. At the same time, on a number of occasions, the air services managed to damage and destroy a good number of Allied vessels. Similarly, combat experiences provided convincing reasons to conclude that Japanese aircraft were not superior to their U.S. counterparts as they were previously purported. In particular, enemy planes proved vulnerable to gunfire, owing to their lack of armor protection. Yet American aviators continued to acknowledge that aircraft such as the Zero fighter were tough opponents, owing to their maneuverability. Therefore, despite the IJNAF's visible failings, U.S. personnel were inclined to maintain a vigilant watch on their opponent. Ship crews, along with naval aviators, bore in mind that the balance of forces in the South Pacific was precarious. The situation was taken as a clear indication that the U.S. Navy and its air service needed to improve their antiaircraft protection and fighter defenses. Yet efforts toward this end were complicated because the weaponry that was suitable for combating the Japanese had yet to be produced on a large scale.

In a case similar to the IJN's surface fleet, a striking feature of assessments concerning the IJNAF was the extent to which U.S. naval and air personnel, rather than intelligence organizations, processed the information. Although a number of bodies had been established to handle intelligence on aviation matters, including the ONI's Air Intelligence Group (Op-16-V), along with the Air Information Division of the Office of the CNO (Op-35), the shortage of trained staff hindered timely analysis and dissemination. Combat narratives frequently covered actions that had been fought several months previously. For example, a report on Japanese attacks against shipping targets up to the Solomons campaign did not appear until August 1943.[96] As late as February 1944, Op-35 was circulating the lessons learned during the opening stages of the conflict. BuAer also played an active role. Pilots returning from the battlefront were asked to report on Japanese aircraft and tactics, as well as to share their views on tactics that worked to neutralize the enemy. The information was thereafter disseminated through the Technical Aviation Intelligence bulletin, under the guise of COMINCH. However, the U.S. Navy had not established a system for communicating the information to frontline units in an expeditious manner.

At the theater level, aircrews recognized that they needed to work in close conjunction with intelligence organizations, and ensure that information on the IJNAF could aid the operations of U.S. forces. The Air Force Pacific Fleet established its intelligence unit in December 1942. Vice Admiral Towers, who had taken command of the force, specified that an important task facing the unit was to "obtain, through analysis of combat experience, a sound basis for the improvement of tactical orders and procedures."[97] Naval air doctrine needed to embody the salient battle lessons if it was to offer a suitable guide for crews in action. Likewise, officers assigned to intelligence duties were to familiarize themselves with current practices, so they could identify the deficiencies in U.S. combat techniques. Yet for a large part of the Solomons campaign, theater-level intelligence organizations were not sufficiently developed to carry out their prescribed functions.

In the meantime, the Air Force and Navy commands bore the brunt of the tasks related to intelligence dissemination. In October 1942, the commander of the South Pacific Force (COMSOPAC) began to issue a summary on battle lessons. In the following month, Air Force Pacific Fleet distributed a weekly air operations memorandum. The bulletins consisted largely of reports provided by naval aviators. Pilots from the Marine Corps, who were also exten-

sively involved in operations against the Japanese, provided valuable information. The lessons learned by ship crews on enemy attacks against naval
targets were propagated by CINCPAC, as well as in publications such as the
Pacific Fleet gunnery bulletin. Owing to the influx of data, by early 1943 U.S.
personnel had developed a more extensive knowledge of how to overcome
their enemy than was the case during the opening stages of the conflict.

The IJNAF's performance showed efficiency, along with visible limitations. Among the most crucial aspects that attracted attention was the quality
of Japanese aircraft. In July 1942, the Americans gained an unprecedented
opportunity to secure raw intelligence. A Zero fighter of a modernized type,
the model 21, known as the Nagoya, crash-landed at Akutan in the Aleutian
Islands. The specimen was recovered and taken back to the naval air station
at San Diego, where it underwent repairs. U.S. pilots carried out test flights,
but the experiments were not completed until the autumn, and the first naval
intelligence report did not appear until November. Airmen in the frontlines
thus had to rely on their own observations, and, in the end, the information on
the captured Zero "merely reinforced and added to what pilots had already
learned in the school of hard knocks."[98] The intelligence was also useful for
determining the comparative performance of American fighters that had yet
to engage extensively in combat, such as the Corsair and the Hellcat.

U.S. aircrews expressed a range of opinions on how their aircraft performed against the Japanese. The F4F Wildcat, the Navy's main carrier-based
interceptor, had armor protection for its crew and carried more armament,
while the Zero was weak in this respect. A pilot who participated at Coral
Sea reported that every Zero he saw burned immediately when hit, and carried slow-firing 7.7-mm cannons that did not cause much damage when they
scored shots.[99] Lieutenant Commander James Flatley, who headed Fighter
Squadron 10 at Midway, commented, "In the Wildcat, we have a solid and
dependable machine whose armor protected us against bullets . . . and whose
engine could not be shot up" by the Zero.[100] At the same time, the Zero had
certain strengths. A pilot from the *Hornet* opined that the F4F was "vastly
inferior," in most categories, including speed, flying, and maneuverability.[101]

Although a large number of accounts passed through BuAer, the Pacific
Fleet was also privy. This was evidenced by Nimitz's attempt to resolve the
conflicting views put forward by aviators. The F4F, when properly handled,

was "more than a match for the Zero."[102] The conclusion was based on the fact that fighter losses at Midway were 3-to-1 in the U.S. Navy's favor. The maneuverability of the Zero was largely due to its light construction, but at the same time, protection for the crew and fuel tanks had been significantly sacrificed, while its guns could be considered "only fair." The F4F, on the other hand, was a "sturdy, tough plane" that provided "the best possible protection for the pilot." Likewise, Towers concluded that the Wildcat, when flown by good pilots, was "markedly superior in combat" to the Zero.[103] However, the comparisons were intended to suggest that Japanese aircraft were not as superior to their U.S. counterparts as they had appeared during the initial stages of the conflict.

The Americans remained reluctant to take evidence of their opponent's faults as a sign that they were unlikely to face problems, and the most noted fact was that U.S. aircraft did not have a decisive lead. Nimitz conceded, "We are beginning to find out that our airplanes are not, as advertised, always the best in the world."[104] At the theater level, pilots felt outclassed when fighting the Zero. One Marine lieutenant who fought at Midway noted how nobody in his squadron had ever "observed a fighter-type aircraft with as much versatility."[105] Another fighter ace told his superiors that the successes achieved by his squadron were not due to any particular features of the Wildcat but largely the result of effective teamwork.[106] If the Japanese improved their shooting techniques, U.S. units were likely to face significantly higher casualties. During subsequent encounters in the Solomons, aircrews continued to express caution. Although the Zero was vulnerable, the overall consensus was that its maneuverability rendered it difficult to intercept, and that the plane was also well equipped to pursue U.S. aircraft. One aviator recalled that his fighter was unable to dogfight the Japanese at any altitude.[107] If the Grumman failed to score a shoot-down, the standard practice was to take evasive action by getting out of the enemy plane's firing range. Otherwise, the Japanese were most likely to position themselves for another attack. Nor was the design of American aircraft entirely sufficient to allow them to take advantage of the enemy's vulnerabilities. For example, when the F4F pursued the Zero, the latter most often made a sharp turn and moved upwards.[108] This move gave U.S. pilots an opportunity to shoot the underside of enemy planes; however, the F4F engines eventually stalled when they attempted to pursue the Japanese in climbs.

The tactical finesse of Japanese pilots also continued to raise apprehensions. The defeat at Midway did result in the loss of a large number of trained Japanese aviators. Indeed, the IJN air arm started the war with a pool of highly qualified personnel, who averaged over seven hundred hours of flight time. The instruction program was designed so that only a select few could enter the service, and of the 1,500 students who enrolled at the flight training school at Kasumigaura annually, only a hundred were likely to graduate. However, the stringency of the program constituted its main drawback, because the supply of crews was too small to sustain the casualties that were likely to arise in a protracted conflict. In December 1941, the number of first-line carrier pilots stood at a mere four hundred. The remainder of the rank and file were largely non-commissioned officers, who received less than twelve months of training and required an additional year of preparation before they could be considered fit for carrier-based operations in the forward areas.[109] Prior to the Midway operation, one of the prime concerns facing Admiral Chuichi Nagumo, the task force commander, was the inadequate reserve of pilots that could fill the ranks left vacant by the losses suffered at Coral Sea.[110] The manpower toll at Midway amounted to 10 percent of the IJN's veteran aviators. A further depletion was caused when surviving pilots were recalled from frontline duty to become instructors, since the air service realized it needed to expand its supply of crews if Japan wished to continue fighting the U.S. Navy.[111] Because expert aviators could not be replaced in a timely manner, a less rigorous training scheme was introduced.[112] The new generation of pilots sometimes entered battle with less than a hundred hours of flying experience. Naval air commanders also failed to grasp the extent to which their successes during the opening months of the conflict owed themselves to Japanese forces having an overwhelming numerical superiority.[113] Instead, the victories were attributed solely to tactical skill, and by paying insufficient attention to statistical factors, the IJNAF failed to prepare for encounters with stronger opponents.

Combat experiences in the Solomons revealed how the dexterity of Japanese aircrews had declined. During the Battle of the Eastern Solomons on August 24, Zero pilots did not utilize their aircraft's ability to make rapid climbs, thus enabling the Wildcats to position themselves within range to shoot down their targets.[114] Another noted feature was poor gunnery, with frequent errors of judgment in speed and distance. Tracers were reported to have missed their targets by up to four hundred yards.[115] However, the intelligence was treated merely as an indication that some Japanese airmen were not as skilled as those that had appeared in prior encounters.

The IJN air arm did demonstrate a wide-ranging aptitude, and its operations suggested that it still possessed its share of capable aviators, albeit lower in proportion. U.S. personnel therefore hesitated to draw general conclusions. When pursued by enemy fighters, Zero pilots maneuvered their aircraft in evasive action, often carrying out tight turns and loops.[116] Allied vessels remained the targets of skillful attacks, and the Japanese fought with determination. Commenting on the Battle of the Eastern Solomons during August 24–25, the landing signal officer on board the *Enterprise* noted how enemy dive-bombers approached at such low altitudes as to be "suicidal," and the attacks were carried out with an accuracy that left many ship crews feeling helpless.[117] Reporting on the Battle of Santa Cruz, the commander of the *Hornet*, which was sunk during the engagement, noted how planes approached their targets at 45-degree angles, and made "extremely low pull-outs" after dropping their ordnance at close range.[118]

Enemy pilots also carried out their missions to achieve their desired results, namely, to disable and sink Allied vessels. Attacks were launched from several directions, thus compelling the defending vessels to direct their antiaircraft fire at different sectors simultaneously.[119] Deception and surprise were common elements. The Japanese made good use of the limited visibility caused by strong sunlight and clouds, attacking from directions where they could not be easily seen.[120] Ruses were often employed, among the most notable of which was to assign decoy aircraft to attract the attention of antiaircraft crews. In the meantime, a formation of high-level bombers approached without being noticed. The apprehensions arising from the IJN air arm's proven capacity to cause damage were compounded by concerns that it might alter its tactics. Admiral Halsey warned that enemy forces quickly adopted different methods of launching aerial torpedo attacks where old ones had failed, and for this reason, ship crews had to submit information on any new moves.[121] The U.S. Navy was aware that it was engaging an unfamiliar opponent, whose capabilities needed to be consistently monitored.

In the area of night fighting, U.S. and Japanese forces were roughly equal. The IJN's vessels were vulnerable, owing to the backward state of their radar fire control, which meant that antiaircraft guns could not hit their targets accurately.[122] At the same time, enemy planes regularly attacked under the cover of darkness. The Pacific Fleet needed to develop its own night-fighting capabilities by equipping fighters with radar, to help them detect enemy planes. On the other hand, in the event that the Japanese developed airborne radar, they were likely to gain a decisive edge.[123] Encounters in the Solomon Islands did provide ominous indications that nighttime raids would remain frequent.[124] During the bombardment of Vila airfield, pilots used float lights and flares to illuminate the position of U.S. vessels.[125] Although the task force did not suffer any losses, the encounter raised questions as to whether ships should be used against air bases, where the aircraft could strike at short notice.

Nor did the IJN air arm's defects blind the Americans to their own problems. The provision of fighters that could match the Zero's performance was treated as an urgent priority. During the opening stages of the Guadalcanal campaign, U.S. aircraft losses ran up to 50 percent, leading one squadron leader to report to Pearl Harbor that pilots were "anxiously awaiting faster and better fighters."[126] As early as spring 1942, even before the capabilities of Japanese planes were fully known, the Navy ordered the construction of new models, and by June, the Grumman F6F Hellcat was introduced. The machine was equipped with a heavier engine that allowed it to carry enhanced armor and armament, and was also able to out-dive and climb faster than the Zero. The F4U Corsair, with its ideal combination of superior armament and high maneuverability, also enabled aircrews to fight on more favorable terms. In an action over the Russell Islands, pilots agreed that the Corsair was "at least equal to and possibly superior to the Zero" in climbing ability at medium altitudes, with an equal level of maneuverability.[127] However, the U.S. Navy did not procure enough advanced fighter types to dispatch them in large numbers to the Pacific until the middle of 1943, since a sizeable proportion had to be deployed in the Mediterranean and North Africa. In the meantime, airmen were more likely to conclude that their technical capabilities were at best not markedly superior, or at worst inferior to their opponent.

U.S. personnel also realized that manpower resources, in the form of trained aircrews, were essential. Commenting on the attack against the *Enterprise*, the commanding officer went as far as to point out that the declining skill of enemy pilots provided some important lessons concerning the mistakes that U.S. forces needed to avoid.[128] While Japanese aviation was originally composed of "very expert and highly trained personnel," its performance in the Solomons indicated that the IJN was not able to produce enough good pilots to make up for its losses. This development emphasized the necessity for the Pacific Fleet to be supplied with qualified aviators. Prior to the conflict, the U.S. Navy had developed a rigorous instruction program that included up to one thousand hours of training.[129] The pressures of wartime demand led to the introduction of a less strenuous regime that included only three hundred hours, and many crews practiced in obsolescent planes. As a result, when pilots arrived at the front lines, they often did not know how to operate the U.S. Navy's more advanced machines. Airmen lamented that their gunnery and bombing techniques were unsatisfactory. Pilots also were not trained to conduct multiple missions. The weakness became apparent at Midway, where air squadrons tested a procedure where fighters were committed to fleet protection, which meant that attack groups were "completely at the mercy" of Zeros.[130] Many officers believed that greater protection might have reduced the heavy losses of torpedo bombers. Although some aviators showed a good level of skill, they were too few in number. The commander of the South Pacific Air Force complained that the situation often resulted in pilot fatigue and an inability to carry out sustained operations.[131] As a remedy to the situation, Towers recommended to Admiral King that the administration of flight schools had to be reformed, so that they were run by the most competent personnel.[132] Nimitz raised similar concerns, and reported, "New flight school graduates have done little more than balance the operational and battle losses" that had been suffered at Coral Sea and Midway.[133] Together with King, CINCPAC introduced an innovative solution where experienced pilots were periodically sent back to the United States to train new aviators. To expand the pool of combat-ready pilots, carrier replacement air groups were established, consisting of a nucleus of veterans whose job was to initiate new recruits. As a result, squadrons could be "rotated" for rest and refitting, while carrier groups received new crews. As long as the U.S. Navy suffered shortcomings, assessments of its capacity to fight the Japanese were likely to warn against complacency.

In order to develop the tactics needed to combat the Japanese, pilots endeavored to carry out extensive experiments. By late 1942, the Air Force

Pacific Fleet obtained sufficient information to recommend a basic doctrine. The Zero fighter's weaknesses, such as its light armor, had to be properly exploited. F4F pilots were to take shots when the Japanese slowed down to make climbing turns and loops.[134] Marine aviators flying the Grumman adopted a move where they dove toward enemy bomber formations until they were within firing range. The height advantage enabled U.S. planes to avoid gunfire.[135] Yet fighting methods were largely defensive, and geared to prevent Zero pilots from utilizing their maneuverability. Many pilots noted how they had little opportunity to use their aircraft in an offensive role. Teamwork was cited as one of the main reasons why U.S. pilots were able to counter the Japanese.[136] Pilots needed to make the best use of their "second-rate technology," by developing formation tactics.[137] Wildcats operated in sections of two planes, which flew in groups composed of several sections. Pilots from Fighting Squadron 10 insisted that the benefits of fighters operating in teams had to be emphasized when training new aviators.[138] One popular maneuver was the "Thach weave," named after Lieutenant Commander John Thach, a fighter ace from the Midway operation.[139] Fighters flew in pairs, at a distance where both planes could U-turn without colliding. Both pilots kept regular lookouts on each other's tail. When a Zero was seen attacking one of them, the partner plane altered course, bringing its guns onto the enemy. The pilot of the plane being attacked, upon seeing his squadron mate's maneuver, then made a similar turn. Zero pilots, upon discovering that they were being aimed at simultaneously by two opponents, often broke off the engagement. The Thach weave eventually became a standard procedure among air units.

Yet apprehensions concerning enemy capabilities were not to be dispelled unless the U.S. Navy achieved a clear ascendancy in numbers, technology, and efficiency. Neutralizing enemy planes required the coordinated use of a number of crucial components, including antiaircraft equipment and fighter cover. The guns on board U.S. vessels were not always reliable. Aircraft carriers continued to be the main targets; however, their 20-mm batteries could not stop any type of attack, including those carried out by torpedo planes, dive-bombers, and horizontal bombers.[140] The 40-mm quadruple mount was considered the only weapon that offered any promise of breaking up a dive-bombing raid at long ranges, but it was available in limited quantity. Further problems arose from the lack of an adequate means to direct flak against incoming planes. The Navy's prewar tactical instructions had called for the establishment of a director system to provide a precise method of controlling antiaircraft fire. Correct estimates of the target's position, speed, and course were deemed important to ensure its destruction.[141] However, the available radar devices were not designed to track the quick movements that the Japanese frequently executed. By November, Nimitz concluded that cruisers had little value in shooting down aircraft.[142] Until carriers were equipped with more powerful weapons such as the 5-inch, 38-caliber dual purpose gun and the 40-mm Bofors, along with better fire-control devices, the Pacific Fleet could not place a great reliance on its gunnery.

Instances where flak brought down enemy formations were attributed to ships being supplied with trained personnel, rather than errors made by Japanese pilots. During the raid on the *Enterprise*, the battleship *North Carolina* destroyed approximately half of the Japanese squadron, thus raising suggestions that it was practicable to fit enough artillery on a ship to "greatly reduce the effectiveness of a dive attack."[143] At the same time, the commanding officer noted how his crews had conducted extensive practices prior to the action, with observers trained to constantly survey the overhead area for high-altitude aircraft.[144] Indeed, the encounter exposed the deficiencies of U.S. equipment, the most visible of which was a failure to direct guns toward the targets. The instruments on board the cruiser *Atlanta* were described as "completely inadequate for the machine-gun control problems," since they were too slow to follow rapidly diving planes.[145]

Owing to the flaws demonstrated by antiaircraft weaponry, a growing number of personnel concluded that carrier-borne planes provided better protection. Air groups needed to be employed in a manner geared to destroy Japanese planes before they could be brought into action. Offensive actions, in the form of surprise attacks, had sunk enemy carriers in a number of encounters, most notably at Midway. However, pilots agreed that too many hits were needed to destroy ships, and planes had to be equipped with heavier bombs.[146] Aviators also complained that the existing aerial torpedoes did not carry enough explosive power.[147] While the Navy's first-line torpedo bomber, the TBF-1 Avenger, carried up to 1,600 pounds of ordnance, the SBD Dauntless could not carry sufficient loads. The Curtiss Wright Company was thus contracted to build a new plane, the SB2C Helldiver; however, production difficulties meant it could not be dispatched until early 1943.[148] Furthermore, preemptive strikes did not guarantee success in the long run, especially as U.S. ships began to operate in areas that were more thoroughly covered by enemy shore-based aircraft.[149]

Carrier-based fighters therefore had to intercept enemy attacks. Pilots returning from the South Pacific theaters agreed that combat air patrols (CAP) were needed to shoot down airborne targets before they could threaten friendly vessels.[150] As early as the Coral Sea engagement, U.S. commanders admitted that their air forces were not fully capable of providing security. Nimitz suggested that carriers were not provided with enough fighters, and the lack of cover had prevented the adequate protection of both the bomber groups and the ships of the task force.[151]

In addition to supplying task forces with adequate fighter complements, an equally pressing concern was to develop better systems for searching for enemy forces and directing friendly planes against the attackers. The early detection of enemy planes was especially important when dealing with the deceptive maneuvers that the Japanese frequently carried out, including the launching of attacks simultaneously from several different directions and altitudes. Even before the outbreak of the war, the U.S. Navy became acutely aware of the extent to which radar and radio communications played a vital role in intercepting aircraft. Initially, the Americans adopted their ideas concerning fighter control from the British. Prior to the conflict, the Naval Research Laboratories made substantial progress in investigating methods for using radar to detect aircraft, and had concentrated largely on developing ship-borne devices.[152] The first significant steps to establish a fighter direction doctrine were undertaken after U.S. observers returned from their attachments to the Royal Navy during the Battle of Britain. The exchange of information during the British technical mission to North America in the autumn of 1940, headed by Sir Henry Tizard, was a further catalyst.[153] The British used a system where the carrier equipped with radar was called the "fighter direction ship," and its function was to coordinate the task force's aerial defenses. Small groups of patrols were stationed above the force and controlled by the fighter direction officer (FDO) via radio or visual signs. Following the introduction of CXAM radar, the U.S. Navy started to experiment with radar-guided fighter direction. In July 1941, the secretary of the Navy approved recommendations from the CNO and the various bureaus to provide each ship with a radar plot room that acted as the "brain of the organization which protects the fleet or ships." In the following month, COMINCH issued a tentative doctrine for carrier-based fighter control. The training of FDOs was also treated as a top priority. In October 1941, a specialized program was started at the naval air station in San Diego, and the course was greatly expanded when war broke out.

Equally important was to establish a centralized unit for processing and disseminating information on the location of enemy planes, in the form of a combat information center (CIC). Again, the idea of establishing a CIC for fighter direction was adopted from the Royal Navy, who had worked out the first battle tracking system even before radar was introduced.[154] The operations were concentrated in one compartment, referred to as the visual plot, where reports received from lookouts and various stations were filtered. The installation of radar sets gave operators a greatly expanded pool of data to work with, and the CIC provided an ideal apparatus. The British handed over their specifications to American observers during 1940–41, and the U.S. Navy applied the main features of the early system to its own CIC. Combat experience provided a critical impetus for modifications. Following the Battle of Coral Sea, crews from the *Yorktown* recommended that the radar plot needed to become a separate component with enough space to allow the FDO and the plotting assistants to work without interference from other units.[155] Radar plot also needed to have its own communications circuit connected to other radar-equipped vessels, and maintain a constant liaison with the air plot unit, to ensure that fighter direction was properly maintained. The first CIC school was established at Pearl Harbor in October 1942. In the following month, Nimitz issued a radar doctrine letter, stipulating that all electronic equipment be concentrated in one room, which was assigned to handle information from all sources, including the communications center, the warning net, and lookouts.

Nevertheless, in spite of the progress, a key flaw of the U.S. Navy's fighter direction was that its ship-borne radar could not calculate the altitude of approaching enemy aircraft until they neared the task force. The CXAM was not designed to emit vertical lobes.[156] Owing to the lack of data on the position of enemy planes, defending fighters were not stationed high enough to intercept, and most enemy bombers were shot down only after they commenced their attacks. U.S. personnel found that the Japanese often sent their Zeros in at lower heights to divert the defending fighters, only to have the bombers approach at a higher elevation.[157] When FDOs fell for the ruse, planes were placed in a position where they could not intercept. The only way to ensure that enemy forces could be counteracted was to place the Wildcats at sufficient heights, without relying on radar estimates. Most pilots preferred to remain at the upper altitudes, since from that position they could launch high-speed dives.[158] However, the method required planes to be stationed over the task force for long periods and waste their fuel. Radar was also not always capable of providing timely warnings. At Santa Cruz, fighter direction was unsatisfactory because the equipment on board the *Enterprise* and *Hornet* did not pick up the attackers until they were within forty-five miles.[159] The development of a better system for detecting planes was considered urgent in order to enable U.S. air squadrons to protect surface forces against the Japanese in a more efficient way.

Further problems arose from poor liaison between control groups and air squadrons. Aviators lacked radio discipline, and often sent so many transmissions that the result was confusion among their fellow pilots. Fighter directors also issued detailed orders on where to fly, which caused further disorder. In other instances, pilots did not receive any definite vectors, and no altitude information was issued aside from "look high" or "look low."[160] In the technical area, systems were equipped with a single voice circuit, and could not handle a large volume of traffic without becoming overloaded. To remedy the situation, Nimitz insisted that training schools needed to devote more time to subjects such as communications procedure.[161] The situation was deemed serious enough to demand that "every possible step that offers improvement must be pushed to the utmost," and instruction needed to focus on radio discipline.

Owing to the unsatisfactory state of radar-guided fighter direction, naval forces had to rely on aerial reconnaissance. This was especially true in cases where the Pacific Fleet operated in areas where the Japanese could launch long-range aircraft from land bases. Again, the performance of U.S. forces was not entirely adequate. Although the Imperial Navy's reconnaissance had committed a number of errors, with the failure to locate enemy carriers at Midway being the prime example, the fact remained that American land-based scout planes also did not detect the approaching task force.[162] The IJN, on the other hand, held significant advantages. Its air units in the Solomons were aided by an effective tracking system, with planes at various stations providing a thorough "umbrella" over areas where U.S. vessels were expected to appear.[163] The advantages the Japanese enjoyed as a result of their forces being able to fly longer ranges had to be countered by employing carrier-based search aircraft in sufficient numbers, and over a wide sector.[164]

The Pacific Fleet also needed to guard against improvements that the Japanese could introduce. Nimitz's report on the Battle of the Eastern Solomons conceded the possibility that the IJN was developing radar for fighter direction, and as a result, American seaplane scouts were likely to become prone to interception.[165] The PBY Catalina, whose primary duty was reconnaissance, proved vulnerable against fighters. Reconnaissance operations thus had to be undertaken by heavy bomber aircraft. Naturally, the U.S. Army Air Force (USAAF) was reluctant to assign its B-17 Flying Fortresses on patrol missions, since such moves were likely to detract from the bomber force's main mission, namely, to destroy Japanese ground targets.[166] U.S. forces thus had to operate as effectively as possible, while contending with the troubles arising from their limited search capacity. The commander of the Aircraft South Pacific Force (COMAIRSOPAC) noted that in light of the dangers posed by attacks on Allied ships in the Guadalcanal area, daily reconnaissance was necessary.[167]

Encounters against the IJN air arm during the Solomons campaign taught ship commanders and naval aviators that significant reforms were necessary before the Pacific Fleet could engage its adversary without incurring too much attrition. The unfortunate fact was that the U.S. Navy could not immediately provide better airplanes and antiaircraft defenses, owing to the time required to produce advanced weapons in mass quantities. In the meantime, the Americans needed to employ their existing resources in the most effectual manner. For this reason, the successes achieved in neutralizing enemy planes were largely attributed to the tactics used by the U.S. Navy and its accompanying air units. Even then, the IJNAF continued to be regarded as a testing opponent. The development of technologically superior forces, coupled with their proper deployment, was seen as an essential step toward gaining a greater edge over the Japanese.

Conclusion

The U.S. Navy's evaluations of the IJN and its air arm, after the attack on Pearl Harbor and the Japanese conquest of Southeast Asia, were characterized by an arduous effort to climb an extensive and oftentimes steep learning curve. American strategic thinking had an important influence on how the lessons of defeat and limited victories during the opening year of the conflict were absorbed. The overarching priority was still underlined by an earnest desire to understand the enemy, so that U.S. forces could develop the most knowledgeable countermeasures. In addition, for a large part of 1942, the Pacific Fleet understood that it could not operate with substantial resources, and it had to avoid further losses that could diminish its capacity to launch an offensive against Japan. A substantial amount of time and effort was required before the Americans could build up the strength needed to secure a decisive superiority. For this reason, the immediate aim was to mobilize the available weapons and manpower in a cost-effective manner. Within this frame of thought, the U.S. fleet was likely to examine any indications of the dangers posed by the Japanese, as well as aspects that lay open to exploitation, and thereafter use the information to enhance its own efficiency.

However, the Americans continued to be hindered by the lack of intelligence. True, the ONI was supplied with increased resources so that it could function well in wartime conditions. Moreover, the Navy adopted a more cautious criterion for assessing the Japanese. The main objective was to identify the enemy's strong points, so that U.S. forces could comprehend the threats they had to face. In this area, considerable progress was achieved. The Navy establishment paid heed to the evidence that described how the IJN and its air arm were formidable opponents, and discarded all traces of its prewar contempt. At the same time, evidence concerning the shortcomings of the Imperial fleet and its air arm tended to be overlooked. Neither the intelligence services nor the U.S. Navy were at fault for creating the inflated opinion. The ONI did not have enough information to produce a balanced assessment. Intelligence staffs had to rely on combat personnel serving at the theater level, who reported how enemy forces had achieved numerous victories, and correctly noted that they held some decisive advantages. The emergence of the "superior enemy" image was therefore inevitable, and a more educated view could arise only after the Navy acquired further experience in fighting its opponent.

In regard to tactical methods, the U.S. Navy realized that its incomplete knowledge of the IJN meant that officers had to follow a process of trial and error. The encounter at Midway provided the first concrete signs that the Japanese could be defeated, as long as the Pacific Fleet made proper use of its carrier fleet and accompanying aircraft. During the Solomons campaign of autumn 1942, the Imperial fleet began to demonstrate a number of visible weaknesses. Surface vessels were not equipped with radar, which hindered their ability to detect enemy attacks. The air arm showed a declining level of skill after losing many of its trained pilots. Last but not least, enemy aircraft proved incapable of withstanding the attrition incurred through intensified combat. These features offered opportunities for American forces to use their material resources to neutralize their opponent. Nevertheless, the Japanese continued to cause significant damage to forces that were not properly equipped and trained. The sinking of a number of U.S. carriers and surface ships was treated as warning that Japanese naval capabilities could not be downplayed. The U.S. Navy also perceived its own performance as an indication that task forces did not have all of the equipment and skills needed to cope with the Japanese. Ship crews and aviators had to devise effective measures by exploiting their assets. Demands were made for more technologically advanced planes and better antiaircraft guns. Equally important was to reform existing methods of using radar and aerial reconnaissance to detect enemy forces. At the closing stages of the Guadalcanal campaign, officers admitted that they had only started to take the initial steps in applying their weaponry and concepts of warfare in a way that worked to overcome the elements they faced.

3

The Elusive Enemy

U.S. NAVAL INTELLIGENCE AND THE IMPERIAL JAPANESE NAVY'S FLEET, 1943–45

For a large part of the remainder of the conflict, the U.S. Navy's opinion of its Japanese counterpart was characterized by continued ambiguity, coupled with a reluctance to become complacent about the difficulties that enemy forces were able to cause. Oftentimes, naval crews were not able to thoroughly explain the maneuvers that enemy forces carried out, due to the lack of intelligence on Japanese weapons and the doctrines that governed their use. To complicate the situation, following its defeat during the Solomons campaign of late 1942 to early 1943, the IJN reverted to a defensive strategy, and withdrew its main units away from the forward areas. Consequently, crucial aspects such as the capabilities of capital ships and aircraft carriers remained vague until they reappeared at the battles of the Philippine Sea and Leyte Gulf in 1944.

Further uncertainties arose from the fact that on the few occasions when Japanese vessels did engage the Pacific Fleet, their performance showed conflicting pieces of evidence. Because the U.S. Navy adhered to its practice of conducting its campaigns while keeping material losses and holdups at an acceptable level, it hesitated to dismiss the threats that the IJN could pose, at least until enemy forces had suffered casualties to a point where they were no longer able to impede Allied operations. As the conflict progressed, the U.S. fleet's gunnery showed a marked improvement, thanks to the good use of radar to locate targets and direct fire on them. The Japanese, meanwhile, made minimal progress in this area, and the growing technological gap was one of the key factors that eventually led to their demise. Yet in spite of its weaknesses, the IJN showed a good level of fighting potential, and as late as 1944 its numerical strength remained substantial.

For U.S. naval commanders, the shortage of intelligence had some adverse effects on their efforts to develop ways of confronting the Imperial Navy. On one hand, the desultory state of Japanese search techniques and equipment greatly helped the Pacific Fleet conduct surprise attacks. Yet officers had only a sporadic knowledge of ways to exploit Japanese faults and provide adequate protection against their weapons. In particular, task forces needed to guard against enemy torpedoes, which continued to cause significant damage. Furthermore, the successes achieved in neutralizing the IJN did not blind American personnel to the fact that they still faced a resourceful opponent. Even after the Japanese defeat at Leyte Gulf in October 1944, the consensus was that enemy forces could be overcome only when the U.S. Navy deployed its armaments in a competent manner.

Evolution of the U.S. Navy's Intelligence Capabilities

After 1943, when the tide of the war in all theaters started to tilt against the Axis powers, naval officials both at the theater level and in Washington were aware that they needed to mobilize their growing material prowess in order to achieve the Allies' stated objective of dismantling Japan's overseas empire and destroying its capacity to wage war. The U.S. Navy's strategic thinking, in turn, had a decisive impact on the development of its intelligence capabilities, including the creation of an apparatus to process information, the types of data that were collected, the criteria used to gauge the IJN, and last but not least the application of intelligence into a working set of combat procedures. The ultimate aim was to understand the obstacles that the Japanese were able to put up, so that U.S. forces could build up a capacity to prevail in a large-scale confrontation.

The elimination of the Imperial Navy was a crucial step toward winning the campaigns in the Pacific. At the January 1943 conference held in Casablanca, the U.S. and British defense chiefs agreed that one of the key goals was to intensify the erosion of Japanese strength, while at the same time concentrating on bringing about the defeat of Germany.[1] The drawn-out struggles being waged in the Solomons showed that the Allies could not "allow the Japanese any pause," and Admiral King proposed that the division of resources between the Atlantic and Pacific theaters needed a corresponding adjustment.[2] Commitments for operations against Japan were to be raised from 15 to 30 percent in the coming year. In order to neutralize the Imperial armed forces, including the fleet, the U.S. Navy needed to extend its presence into the far reaches of the western Pacific regions and Japan's home waters. The specific moves to be carried out to achieve this objective were articulated by the JCS in June. After capturing Japanese outposts in the Marshall-Gilberts archipelago, the Americans were to launch operations aimed at neutralizing the IJN's main base at Truk, while at the same time intensifying attacks on the enemy's line of communications.[3] Among the main aims of U.S. strategy was to compel Japan to deploy its fleet in an effort to defend its island positions and supply lines, so that the Pacific Fleet could secure the opportunity to destroy a large portion of the Imperial Navy.[4]

Although naval doctrine increasingly focused on the use of the air arm, the surface fleet remained an integral element of maritime operations. Moreover, U.S. personnel considered the destruction of Japanese vessels to be important, and subsequently sought to understand the latter's strengths and weaknesses. Under certain conditions, such as nighttime battles, aircraft could not be relied upon to deliver accurate attacks on surface ships, owing to low visibility. Task forces had to utilize their battleships, whose large-caliber guns constituted one of the Pacific Fleet's main assets.[5] Tactical instructions continued to envisage battleships approaching within ranges that permitted them to place enemy vessels under the maximum amount of fire.[6] The idea was to crush the IJN with overwhelming strength. The concept was encapsulated in Halsey's letter to Nimitz prior to the Philippines invasion, where he stated, "In all my recommended operations, I aim to achieve superiority at the point of contact through weight of numbers, surprise, superior performance, stratagem, or other device."[7] Surface vessels continued to form important components of the fleet until the closing stages of the conflict. At Leyte Gulf, while the naval guns of the Third and Seventh Fleets were activated only to finish off crippled ships, destroyer-launched torpedoes accounted for a large proportion of enemy casualties.[8] According to Halsey, one of the most conspicuous lessons of the operation was that air strikes alone could not destroy heavy ships at sea.[9]

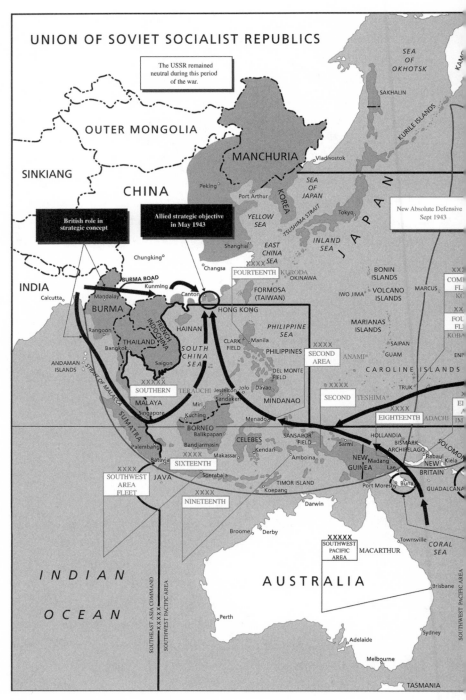

Map 3.1 General Concepts of Allied Strategy in the Pacific, 1943

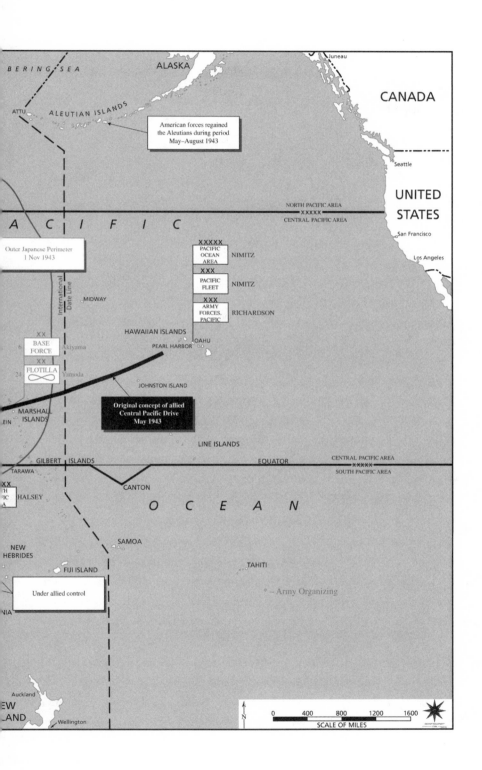

BERING SEA
ALASKA
Juneau
CANADA
ATTU
ALEUTIAN ISLANDS
American forces regained
the Aleutians during period
May–August 1943
Seattle
UNITED
STATES
NORTH PACIFIC AREA
XXXXX
CENTRAL PACIFIC AREA
P   A   C   I   F   I   C
San Francisco
Outer Japanese Perimeter
1 Nov 1943
Los Angeles

XXXXX
PACIFIC
OCEAN
AREA   NIMITZ

International Date Line
MIDWAY

XXX
PACIFIC
FLEET   NIMITZ

XXX
ARMY
FORCES,
PACIFIC   RICHARDSON

HAWAIIAN ISLANDS
OAHU
PEARL HARBOR

XX
6   BASE
FORCE   Akiyama

XX
24   FLOTILLA   Yamoda
∞

JOHNSTON ISLAND

Original concept of allied
Central Pacific Drive
May 1943

MARSHALL
EIN   ISLANDS

LINE ISLANDS

CENTRAL PACIFIC AREA
XXXXX
SOUTH PACIFIC AREA
GILBERT ISLANDS
EQUATOR
TARAWA
CANTON

XX
TH
FIC   HALSEY
A

O   C   E   A   N

NEW
HEBRIDES
SAMOA
TAHITI

– Army Organizing

FIJI ISLAND

Under allied control
NIA

Auckland
NEW
LAND
Wellington

N
0   400   800   1200   1600
SCALE OF MILES

Because naval planners strove to defeat the IJN in an extended war effort, intelligence efforts were aimed not only at determining the enemy's current capabilities—officials also paid attention to the possibility that Japanese fighting methods and weapons technologies could change, and thereby pose greater hurdles. The ONI, along with the organizations working alongside the Pacific Fleet, was tasked with processing data on a wide array of subjects. Intelligence staffs also remembered the miscalculations that had been made prior to the conflict, and were conscientious to avert further fiascos that could damage their standing. Unfortunately, the available information did not permit an accurate evaluation. In particular, the ideas that shaped the design of Japanese equipment and methods of their use remained unclear. Future trends also could not be foretold. The complications were largely mitigated by the U.S. Navy establishment's practice of not arriving at conclusions unless they could be supported by concrete evidence. When certain aspects of the IJN were unknown, a concerted move was made to recommend that a vigilant watch be maintained on its activities, so that U.S. forces could be better prepared to deal with the elements facing them.

The measures taken to promote a better understanding of the Imperial fleet also reflected the value that the U.S. Navy attached to enhancing its intelligence activities. By late 1943, the ONI was able to play an active role in analyzing and disseminating material on the IJN. Commanders in the Pacific Fleet continued to forward their reports to Washington, and the material was processed more expeditiously. As a result, information summaries contained an increasing number of accounts on the performance and characteristics of Japanese vessels. The office also produced a series of monographs that covered topics such as weapons development, tactics, and naval construction.

More important, the intelligence apparatus at the theater level became more centralized. The South Pacific Force combat intelligence unit was responsible for disseminating its findings through a weekly bulletin. After 1943, when the focus of operations shifted to the central Pacific, the Joint Intelligence Center, Pacific Ocean Areas (JICPOA), based at Honolulu, was the leading organization. The center had been established back in spring 1942, by approval from the CNO, and originally named the Intelligence Center, Pacific Ocean Areas (ICPOA).[10] Its initial duties focused on code-breaking; however, by the following year, ICPOA's functions were expanded to include

the analysis of captured equipment and document translation, as well as collating information on the particulars of enemy vessels. By September 1943,
in response to the growing scale of operations in the Pacific theater, ICPOA
was designated a joint Navy-Army-Marine organization, and given its new
name. Its mission was defined as "the collection, collation, evaluation, and
dissemination of all strategic and tactical intelligence for the CINCPOA."
In the southwest Pacific, intelligence efforts were largely under the control
of General Douglas MacArthur's command headquarters. Brigadier General
Charles Willoughby, who served as MacArthur's head intelligence officer,
jealously guarded his section's powers. Nevertheless, the commander of the
Southwest Pacific Force (COMSOWESPAC) maintained that force's own
advanced intelligence center that handled information on matters concerning
the Navy.

The results of the research carried out by JICPOA and other theater-
level bodies were distributed via the CINCPAC-CINCPOA intelligence bulletin and the Pacific Fleet's weekly summary. By the end of the war, up to
14,000 copies of each issue were produced. Naval forces received what was
described as a "prodigious quantity of periodicals, monographs, and papers."[11]
The main impediment, in terms of distribution, was the shortage of officers
afloat who could collate the volumes of material received from Pearl Harbor and Washington. The Navy did not have sufficient manpower to operate
intelligence centers in the forward areas, and consequently, ship-borne personnel spent an unbalanced amount of time on tasks such as filing, sorting,
and indexing. The setup was not conducive to ensuring that naval personnel
received the information they needed without becoming inundated with volu-
minous publications.

Moreover, the material that appeared in naval intelligence reports reflected
the difficulties involved in securing information. A large portion of the bulletins focused on statistical data such as the measurements of Japanese vessels,
as well as basic matters, including the types of ships in operation. The practice resulted from the fact that, as late as the middle stages of the conflict,
quantitative information remained incomplete, and intelligence organizations felt obliged to clear away the uncertainties. Yet estimates concerning the
particulars of key vessels were based on speculation. The displacements for
the auxiliary carriers *Otaka*, *Unyo*, and *Choyo*, which had been converted from

merchant vessels, were calculated on the basis of how much their U.S. counterparts often weighed after refitting.[12] The caliber of the guns on board the super-battleship *Yamato* also remained a mystery, and figures were derived from contradictory data.[13] A drawing captured at Tulagi in October 1942 suggested that the main batteries were sixteen inches in diameter, and the figure appeared to be confirmed by information secured via signals intercepts. On the other hand, ship-identification authorities, basing their work on photos taken over Truk, estimated the *Yamato*'s guns to be eighteen inches. Although the latter calculation proved correct, U.S. intelligence struggled to confirm the exact caliber. The efforts to acquire statistical intelligence did produce benefits, in that it enabled U.S. naval crews to identify enemy vessels when they appeared in combat. By June 1945, the ONI produced a reference manual that contained over forty pages of diagrams, and laid out the dimensions, armament, and speed of many IJN ships.[14] Nevertheless, naval intelligence had few opportunities to discover the precise characteristics of the majority of Japanese vessels, and postwar investigations revealed details "undreamed of during the conflict."[15] In fact, the ONI is alleged to have known "far less" about its wartime enemy than the general public could learn, through open-source references, about the supposedly secret Soviet Navy during the Cold War.

The concentration on quantitative matters also reflected how an equally important type of intelligence, namely, information on qualitative subjects such as the ideas that influenced the IJN's conduct of its operations, was scarce. The U.S. Navy was engaging an opponent whose thought patterns were not familiar to Western observers, yet intelligence staffs could only surmise on the relation between cultural factors and Japanese combat methods.

The principal elements of the Imperial Navy's doctrine stemmed from the idea developed in the 1920s, namely, to alleviate the disadvantages accrued by its numerical inferiority in relation to the U.S. fleet. In order to prevail, the Japanese were to optimize the high-performance weapons at their disposal, along with the tactical skills of their personnel. The concept laid the grounds for a host of advantages, as well as fatal flaws. On the liability side, the Japanese did not adequately prepare for a war against enemies with superior matériel. By 1943, following the IJN's setback at Guadalcanal, its leaders faced a situation they had not anticipated. Whereas the original plan called for establishing a strategic barrier around the islands of the Pacific, the naval command realized it did not have the resources to defend Japan's overstretched empire against the ever-growing forces that the Allies were able deploy.[16] Yet operational planning continued to be based on the idealistic expectation that the U.S. Navy could be crushed in a single decisive battle as it approached Japan's Home Islands. The scheme grew out of the experiences of the 1904–5 war, when the Russians dispatched their Baltic fleet in an attempt to relieve Port Arthur, and the IJN annihilated the armada as it sailed through the Straits of Tsushima. Thereafter, naval policy dictated that all future conflicts would replicate the success. Naval officers did not carefully consider the strong possibility that before conducting any large-scale engagement in the far reaches of the Pacific, the Americans were more likely to ensure that their forces were supported by a strong logistical network, and would be able to fight with overwhelmingly superior strength.[17] Nor was the possibility of defeat given much serious thought.

The IJN also made minimal progress in the area of advanced weaponry. While Japanese industries were not able to produce large quantities of modern armaments, the poor results also arose from the naval establishment's habit of believing that its forces were invincible. Subsequently, the importance of technological resources when engaging the U.S. Navy was not fully comprehended.[18] The lack of efficient radar devices constituted the most significant deficiency, and the Japanese saw their relative capabilities vis-à-vis the Allies undergo a steady decline, particularly in the area of fire direction.

Simultaneously, Japanese practices gave rise to some key strengths, the most important of which was that naval crews continued to show a high level of tactical skill. Sailors were imbued with strong discipline, which led them to undertake meticulous steps to perfect their procedures and carry out extensive exercises. The Imperial fleet also succeeded in developing the equipment needed to implement its ideas. Its torpedoes and ordnance enabled task forces to conduct devastating attacks on Allied vessels. The IJN was exceptionally competent in nighttime engagements. Deck crews made good use of their optical equipment to locate the enemy before the latter could detect Japanese forces with radar.[19] Furthermore, while officers tended to be complacent about improving their weaponry, on a number of occasions they were apt to realize that changes were necessary, and sought help from abroad. The Imperial Navy succeeded in securing German assistance to develop search devices, and although the efforts were too belated to enable Japan to reverse its technological inferiority, by July 1944 radar was installed on every vessel of the Combined Fleet. As a result, the efficiency of surface units saw a marked rise, and crews on board the battleship *Musashi* became confident that, at least during training maneuvers, they were able to fire their guns easily at any detected target.[20]

U.S. naval intelligence therefore had to gauge an enemy that held a mixture of characteristics. Yet the ONI conceded that an in-depth explanation could not be put forward, and made minimal references to how the IJN's practices affected its operations. The problem was illustrated in a weekly summary issued in January 1945, which contained a report prepared by the Office of War Information. The document concluded that IJN officers and crews were "excellent sailors," with exceptional dedication.[21] The hypothesis was based primarily on what was known about the training that crews had undergone in Japanese war colleges and naval academies prior to the war. Insofar as weaknesses were concerned, personnel often stuck to rigid plans and tactical moves, mainly because they had not been taught to use individual initiative. No substantial details were provided on the fleet's conduct of particular engagements.

The quality of the IJN's weapons was also not easy to determine. On this aspect, the Americans tended to make do with the limited data that were available, and avoided making detailed judgments on Japanese technical expertise. Although the ONI deduced that the enemy had made alterations in its equipment, the extent was uncertain, as demonstrated by a March 1943 report on radar-guided fire control. The paper merely stated, "It is indicated that the Japanese navy has not made any great development in its use."[22] It was not until a year later that CINCPAC surmised that the IJN was eighteen months behind its U.S. counterpart, as opposed to the twelve-month lag put forward previously.[23] The estimate was admittedly based on inconclusive evidence, in the form of radar intercepts that showed a high proportion of frequency signals that were lower than those emitted by Allied radar. Likewise, the Combined Intelligence Committee could go no further than to state that despite attempts to increase the production of instruments such as precision electrical equipment, the shortage of industrial plants and the underdeveloped state of research in Japan were likely to prevent any significant expansion.[24] The report did not provide any substantial details on the types of new equipment that the Japanese were likely to introduce. On the aspect of naval ordnance, the IJN's guns demonstrated a "somewhat lower standard of efficiency" than their U.S. equivalents.[25] However, the conclusion was based on fragmentary intelligence concerning equipment that had been produced prior to the war. In light of the possibility that the Japanese had developed new weapons, naval intelligence judged that a blanket assumption, to the effect that the Pacific Fleet had a lead, was not warranted.

Commanders in the Pacific Fleet, on the other hand, did attempt to guess how Japanese military thinking could affect the IJN's operational planning, in order to lay out the various scenarios that were likely to materialize. Some U.S. officials continued to hold the view that the Japanese were a less advanced people, and made contemptuous remarks. Admiral Halsey was notorious for his racist statements, which often referred to the Japanese as "stupid animals."[26] Opinions of Japanese martial qualities were thus occasionally tainted by the notion that the enemy was culturally inferior. At the same time, naval leaders admitted that they did not have sufficient information to create an accurate assessment of their opponent's mindset. For example, in March 1944, at a meeting of the JCS, Nimitz suggested that the IJN was unlikely to seek an engagement in the event the Allies invaded the Marianas. The estimate was based on an article that had appeared in the periodical *Foreign Affairs* a few months earlier, and had been written by Alexander Kiralfy, who had reviewed Japan's history since ancient times.[27] Kiralfy concluded that the Japanese tended to refrain from large-scale battles unless the Home Islands were directly threatened. The hypothesis was questioned by senior defense chiefs, including Admiral Ernest King, on the grounds that it had not been premised on solid evidence. By the eve of the operation, most commanders, including Nimitz, agreed that it was safer to plan the Marianas operation on the assumption that the IJN would deploy its main fleet in order to forestall U.S. moves to secure a base that was within proximity to the heart of Japan's empire. Thus, while cultural stereotyping did periodically affect assessments of the enemy, U.S. officials were aware that making unfounded conclusions, over matters on which they did not have a full knowledge, could lead to unpleasant surprises.

The shortage of evidence regarding Japanese doctrine and combat capabilities remained prevalent until the closing stages of the war, despite the concerted measures that naval intelligence undertook to systematically handle the growing amount of material it was able to draw upon. The first source of information was captured Japanese sailors. On a number of occasions, U.S. crews managed to rescue survivors from stricken vessels. The POWs (prisoners of war) were then taken ashore and handed over to one of the Navy's three main interrogation centers, at Brisbane, Noumea, and Honolulu. By 1944, over four thousand prisoners had been taken in the central Pacific.[28] POWs from the IJN showed a varying level of willingness to cooperate with U.S. intelligence officers when compared to their army counterparts. Imperial Army soldiers showed an unusual desire to divulge secrets. The phenomenon stemmed from the way in which troops were indoctrinated into believing that surrendering to the enemy was tantamount to the highest form of treason, and when soldiers did so, they had terminated all ties with their nation. Prisoners thus always endeavored to ingratiate themselves to their vanquishers, and unhesitatingly provided intelligence.

Naval personnel, on the other hand, did not appear to have lost their loyalty to the same extent. For example, survivors from the destroyer *Matsu* were described as "security conscious," and appeared reluctant to answer certain questions.[29] In the end, however, good treatment compelled them to cooperate, as evidenced by the information provided regarding the armament carried on board the ship. The data were also considered to be sound. The Seventh Fleet intelligence center concluded that the vessel's offensive potential was poor, since the main battery was "extremely light," and the velocity too slow to facilitate torpedo attacks against ships faster than thirty knots.[30] On another occasion, a POW from the carrier *Shokaku* stated that the flight deck was over two hundred meters long, with the ship's tonnage around 20,000.[31] The figures provided information that U.S. intelligence had been desperately trying to obtain since the beginning of the war.

At the same time, the information extracted from POWs was treated with reserve, since it often represented the provider's impressions. A lieutenant captured at Saipan drew pictures of the battleships *Ise* and *Hyuga*, both of which were rumored to have been converted into carriers. The prisoner had only seen the vessels from a distance when he was stationed at Kure Navy Yard, where refitting work was being done. The information was therefore considered "fairly reliable," but its authenticity had not been "conclusively demonstrated."[32] Sailors who fell into captivity also usually represented the lower ranks, and lacked knowledge of the IJN's doctrine. The information could not be used to draw firm conclusions on the operations and maneuvers that enemy forces carried out.

Intelligence obtained from the second main source, namely, reconnaissance photographs taken during search and aerial bombardment missions, provided more reliable data on Japanese ships and equipment. During a raid against Truk in February 1944, photos suggested that the carrier *Zuiho* had an overall length of 668 feet and a displacement of 15,000 tons.[33] An analysis of the turrets, guns, and hull dimensions of the *Agano*–class cruisers confirmed estimates that their armament consisted of both 6-inch and 8-inch batteries.[34] However, photographic intelligence provided only a portion of the necessary intelligence. In particular, the material did not clearly indicate how enemy weapons performed. For example, the *Kuma*–class cruisers were equipped with new 5.5-inch antiaircraft guns with a maximum elevation of twenty degrees.[35] Estimates on their range were based on what was known about the capacity of the ordnance that the Japanese used most frequently. The exact details could not be ascertained until enemy vessels were encountered in combat.

Captured documents provided the third main source. Under a Navy Department directive issued in June 1942, the ONI was assigned to administer the document processing program.[36] By 1944, naval intelligence developed a team of linguists with the skills required to translate written evidence. The achievement was creditable, given that during the start of the conflict, the Japanese language had been "a mystery to all but a mere handful of Americans."[37] Only a few universities taught the subject. Recognizing the need for a larger cohort of qualified personnel, as early as 1940 the Navy established a training program.[38] The initial course, set up with help from the University of California at Berkeley, was designed to teach officers to interpret Japanese radio communications. However, the available pool of candidates was limited because the ONI preferred to employ Americans of Caucasian rather than Japanese descent, since the latter were considered a security risk. Once the war began, the ONI realized that it needed to draw upon the skills of the Japanese community, because the training course took in a growing number of recruits who required instruction on translating written texts. However, in early 1942, the Roosevelt administration passed an executive order forbidding all Japanese

Americans of the second-generation (nisei) or younger from residing within seven hundred miles of the Pacific coast, out of fears that they were serving as fifth-columnists for an impending enemy invasion.[39] The program at Berkeley therefore could not be utilized. The legal obstacles were circumvented by setting up a specialist school at Fort Snelling, Minnesota. By the end of the conflict, the Navy Department had received a total of 65,000 applications, and several hundred students had graduated from the program.

However, deriving intelligence from captured documents presented a number of barriers, the most significant of which was that the material did not fully describe Japanese doctrine. The IJN kept the bulk of the relevant manuals, including tactical publications, on board ships, which were most often sunk in battle before the contents could be retrieved. Documents were usually secured when U.S. forces captured island garrisons and the Japanese left behind their papers. The material tended to be geared for use by shore-based personnel, and focused on subjects such as the construction of land installations and coastal fortifications. Moreover, U.S. intelligence was unable to secure information on how the IJN was likely to deploy its capital ships and carriers, because Japanese defense strategy for the far-flung territories called for using small detachments of auxiliary vessels and aircraft, and withholding the main fleet until the inner zones of the empire were attacked. A further problem was that Japanese officers appeared slow in adjusting their methods, and sources showed how the Imperial Navy did not make due allowance for scenarios where it had to operate with substantially reduced strengths. The manner in which Japanese forces could adapt their tactics remained open to speculation. For example, a document describing strike-force maneuvers emphasized the importance of outflanking and outmaneuvering the opposing fleet in order to prevent the latter from retreating.[40] Up to eighteen destroyers were assigned to screen each carrier, when in reality the IJN was severely short on escort vessels. Enemy forces also did not follow a set procedure. In one notable instance, Admiral Halsey received an officer's notebook that suggested the Japanese were giving renewed attention to using their carrier fleet for offensive action.[41] However, the document did not specify whether task groups were to be deployed on a wide front or in columns, allegedly because admirals were not able to agree on which tactic was more effective. The only certain conclusion was that a vigilant watch had to be kept for the reappearance of Japanese carriers.

Written evidence also provided information on the IJN's technology. A monograph on radio communications, based on enemy documents, concluded that the Japanese had a "complex, modern system" that was "highly flexible and efficient."[42] Although older equipment was obsolete, it was well constructed and capable of sending clear transmissions across long distances. The Japanese had also captured large quantities of Allied gear and copied the designs. As a result, it seemed probable that the IJN's equipment was approaching "reasonably close" to the quality of its Western counterparts. However, documentary material did not always provide updated information. During the latter part of 1944, a notebook on radar suggested that Japanese officers found the range and bearing accuracy to be unsatisfactory for fire-control purposes.[43] At the same time, the paper had been written back in December 1943, and the Pacific Fleet warned that the Japanese could have made "considerable progress" in developing their equipment since then.

Intelligence on Japanese weaponry was also secured through inspections of captured equipment. In one of the most notable cases, during the Guadalcanal campaign, the Navy managed to salvage a number of unexploded long-lance torpedoes, which were later shipped back to the United States. Inspections showed that the torpedo was constructed with a high level of workmanship, and possessed a range of over ten thousand yards. However, the information did not reach the Pacific Fleet until a late stage, owing to the substantial time required to finish the experiments. The torpedo station at Newport, along with BuOrd, did not report on its investigations until spring 1944.[44] As late as May, the South Pacific combat intelligence unit complained that the results had not been disseminated at the theater level.[45] A great part of the available information on enemy torpedoes had originated from POW interrogations and captured documents, and was considered neither complete nor reliable enough to reach an educated conclusion on their speed, range, and destructive capabilities. Consequently, the majority of U.S. naval officers continued to have only a rudimentary knowledge of the long-lance.

Raw intelligence, in the form of POWs, captured material, and aerial reconnaissance, therefore offered some useful data on the IJN's vessels and weapons. Nevertheless, the information often provided an incomplete picture of enemy fighting capabilities. The most important limitation was that the material did not clearly indicate the ways in which Japanese forces operated.

Furthermore, the substantial amount of time required to analyze the intelligence meant that naval crews faced delays in obtaining the necessary knowledge, with the processing of data on Japanese torpedoes being a prime example. In the end, given that the IJN had proven its combat proficiency, intelligence organizations warned against making any unfounded assumptions that the enemy was incapable of putting up a contest.

Intelligence on the IJN's Numerical Strength and Operational Plans

The intelligence pointing to the IJN's numerical strengths had an important effect on the U.S. naval establishment's threat perceptions. As long as the Japanese possessed a sizeable fleet that was able to oppose the Allied advance across the Pacific, intelligence staffs and naval officials alike felt compelled to pay close attention to the Imperial fleet's tactical and technological prowess. As the conflict progressed, the U.S. Navy received mounting indications that Japan did not have the economic capacity to replace the losses it had incurred. At the same time, the enemy continued to possess a substantial force. To complicate matters, the available intelligence did not offer clear information on operational plans, mainly because the Japanese high command formulated its strategy on an ad hoc basis. The uncertainties surrounding the IJN's moves were treated with caution, and assessments concerning the scale of opposition to be encountered at key island targets, including the Marianas and Philippines, warned that adequate preparations were required to cope with possible naval interference.

By mid-1943, the IJN had incurred a significant diminution of its strength, and Japan's industries did not have the resources to reconstitute their forces. The carriers *Aso*, *Ikoma*, and *Kasagi* were never completed, owing to shortages of raw materials and industrial plants.[46] While warships originally laid down as battleships and cruisers, including the *Unryu*, *Amagi*, and *Katsuragi*, were eventually completed as carriers, none of them carried enough planes to engage in large-scale fleet actions.

U.S. intelligence noted how the dwindling size of the Japanese merchant marine constituted the most significant obstruction against the Japanese navy's effort to build additional vessels. By mid-1943, Japan no longer had the tonnage to carry the minimum amount of raw materials that industries required to increase production.[47] American submarines and aircraft sank over 2.5 million tons of shipping, and although a concerted effort was made to produce merchantmen, losses exceeded gains by a ratio of 3-to-1.[48] By June 1944, losses had reached a critical point. With a merchant fleet whittled down to 40 percent of its prewar size, the Japanese had to prioritize on which raw materials they needed to transport back to the Home Islands.[49] Under the circumstances, a drop in output was inevitable. Reliable sources also confirmed that attacks on Japan's supply lines were having a significant effect on the tanker fleet. In February 1944, the submarine *Jack* intercepted an enemy message reporting that losses had almost doubled over the previous year, and the majority of ships returning to the Home Islands were being sunk.[50] The JIC calculated that the Japanese did not possess enough tankers to supply the IJN with oil for large-scale operations beyond the inner areas of the empire.[51] Stockpiles could last for only six months, after which the Imperial fleet was likely to face grave troubles in maintaining its operational capacity.

Yet despite its limited capacity for growth and dwindling operational capabilities, the Imperial fleet continued to possess a modest number of carriers, capital ships, and auxiliary vessels. Japanese naval strength also remained relatively close to the prewar level. To complicate matters, U.S. naval intelligence acknowledged that it could not calculate the size of the enemy fleet. In May 1943, while the IJN was known to have six carriers in operation, no reliable data were available on construction.[52] The only certain conclusion was that, owing to heavy losses, the Japanese were likely to be focusing on building this type of vessel.[53]

The available intelligence also provided what was often a vague picture of the IJN's long-term intentions, and the opposition that U.S. forces were likely to encounter remained open to deduction. The main source of data on Japanese naval movements was signals intelligence, which was provided by the radio units at Pearl Harbor and Melbourne. The unit at Hawaii, designated Fleet Radio Unit Pacific (FRUPAC), was amalgamated with JICPOA in October 1943, while the unit in Australia, designated Fleet Radio Unit Melbourne (FRUMEL), worked under MacArthur's Southwest Pacific command. Cooperation between the United States and its allies, including Australia and New Zealand, had been established as early as January 1942, when Nimitz authorized the exchange of information. Task force commanders could share intelligence directly with their Allied counterparts without rout-ing everything through their respective headquarters.[54] In October of the same year, collaboration with Great Britain was strengthened. At an Anglo-American meeting in Washington, naval representatives of both countries agreed that the British sigint headquarters at Bletchley Park was to work on the IJN's general naval cipher, and pass all decoded messages to its U.S. counterpart.[55] While the arrangement gave the Pacific Fleet a wider pool of information, the BRUSA (Britain-U.S.A.) agreement of May 1943 demarcat-ed a clear division of labor, whereby the United States was to focus on Japan, with the British working primarily on German code systems. Nevertheless, the sigint services of Australia and New Zealand continued to act as valu-able partners. Intercepts of the IJN's communications often provided valu-able information on the dispositions of enemy naval units. Signals decrypts also enabled the Americans to keep track of Japanese numerical strength, by providing information on the losses they had sustained.

Yet signals intelligence was not very useful for securing information on Japanese plans, mainly because the IJN conducted its war effort in an oppor-tunistic and secretive manner. Owing to the ambiguous nature of the data, coupled with the fact that the Japanese retained a good portion of their fleet, assessments on Japanese operational capabilities tended to pay heed to worst-case scenarios. During spring 1943, signals decrypts indicated that the Combined Fleet was conducting training exercises in the home waters. The CINCPAC diary for June 8 noted that while the maneuvers were "designed for defensive tactics," the possibility of the Japanese fleet attacking the U.S. Navy's bases in the Pacific could not be overlooked.[56] The IJN's apparent reluctance to engage in combat was not seen as a justification to lapse into complacency, and the Pacific Fleet needed to prepare for a fleet action any time it threatened a major enemy position. The JIC consistently recommend-ed that operational planning be based on the understanding that the IJN had up to five aircraft carriers, seven battleships, and eight cruisers, along with a large number of destroyers and submarines.[57] A large part of the force could be used to counter an invasion of areas such as the Marshalls, Carolines, and Marianas.

U.S. naval commanders also realized that they had to take proper actions to deal with the IJN. Admiral King warned that while the Allies were bound to prevail, owing to their material superiority, they had to prepare themselves for substantial delays before the Japanese could be vanquished.[58] The IJN was also operating on interior lines of communication, which bestowed it a great benefit in being able to attack the Pacific Fleet's widely dispersed task forces.[59] When planning the Gilbert Islands operation, one of the main concerns voiced by Admiral Raymond Spruance, commanding the Fifth Fleet, was that the Japanese might interfere with the landings by conducting a sortie from Truk.[60] For this reason, the islands were to be seized quickly, so as to avoid exposing the transports and landing craft. Encounters in situations where the Imperial fleet was able to operate in advantageous conditions were also avoided. During the invasion of Saipan, when Spruance received word that Ozawa's carriers were approaching, he decided not to seek an engagement, on the grounds that protecting the amphibious landing was a higher priority. Moreover, Spruance was wary that the Japanese could attempt to lure his task force away from its main mission, and compel him to seek an action on their own terms, in a move similar to the one that Admiral Heihachiro Togo executed against the Russians at Tsushima several decades earlier.[61] If the Americans were to fall for the trap, they had to fight without a clear knowledge of the composition and strength of the enemy fleet.

At the same time, U.S. naval commanders were eager to use available opportunities to destroy the Japanese fleet, provided that in doing so, U.S. forces would not jeopardize themselves. Vice Admiral Marc Mitscher, commanding the fast carrier force, was convinced that the appearance of the Japanese task force offered a chance to "close the enemy, . . . and perhaps score a crippling victory."[62] Naturally, Mitscher, along with Admiral Joseph "Jocko" Clark, commanding the carriers in Task Force 58, was displeased with Spruance's exercising caution by not dispatching the carriers further west, where U.S. aircraft could position themselves within range to interdict the Japanese fleet.[63] Instead, planes were launched to take out the enemy air force, and what followed was an aerial engagement where Japanese losses were so high that American aviators nicknamed it the "Great Marianas Turkey Shoot." Although the carriers *Shokaku*, *Taiho*, and *Hiyo* were sunk while the U.S. Navy pursued the enemy task force the following morning, pilots failed to carry out a sustained attack that could destroy the remaining carriers, and Spruance's decision to retain his ships in the vicinity of Saipan was cited as the main reason for the lost chance.

Oftentimes, the Japanese fleet's objectives did not become apparent until it commenced an expedition. To illustrate a key example, in July 1944, Imperial General Headquarters in Tokyo ordered preparations for the Sho (victory) operations.[64] The Combined Fleet was to forestall a U.S. invasion of the Ryukyus-Formosa-Philippines island chain. The first variation called for a decisive battle in the Philippines. However, during the following months, U.S. intelligence could only determine that most of the Japanese navy's surviving heavy ships were in the Singapore area. The opposition likely to be faced in the impending Leyte operation remained uncertain until the middle of October, a week before the scheduled landing. Seventh Fleet headquarters concluded that the IJN would not deploy its main vessels, and the enemy force would be limited to an assortment of cruisers, destroyers, and submarines.[65] Only on October 18 did radio intelligence disclose that Vice Admiral Takeo Kurita had sailed eastward from Singapore, with a task force composed of several heavy battleships.[66]

Even then, Admiral Halsey remained unsure over the position of enemy carriers. Although submarines had not spotted any carrier forces, sigint indicated that replenishment measures were under way for a planned operation.[67] The only way to locate the IJN's fleet was to conduct a thorough reconnaissance of waters surrounding the Philippines. When Halsey received word that the Japanese were approaching the Third Fleet's northern flank, he decided to divert his ships to interdict the enemy fleet, rather than support the landing, thereby leaving the San Bernardino Strait unguarded against Admiral Kurita's surface vessels. Although the latter were considered capable of inflicting some damage, their fighting ability was deemed impaired to the point where they were unable to achieve a decisive victory.[68] In actual fact, the carriers did not have full aircraft complements, and were sent as a ruse to divide the U.S. task force. Nevertheless, Halsey judged that a preemptive strike was necessary to stop the Japanese from conducting shuttle-bombing raids against the amphibious force. The admiral also wanted to avoid the criticisms leveled against Spruance following the Marianas encounter, for allowing the enemy carriers to escape. Destroying the remnants of the Japanese fleet was considered necessary to ensure that the Pacific Fleet could conduct its operations without facing the risk of damage at the hands of the enemy.

The Leyte encounter annihilated or damaged a large portion of the remainder of the Imperial Navy, and gave rise to conclusions that Japan's capacity to oppose U.S. operations had dwindled substantially. The Combined Intelligence Committee claimed that even when repairs were completed, the Imperial fleet would be "totally inadequate for the defense of the Empire."[69] By June 1945, the Japanese fleet's remaining four battleships were of old vintage, having been completed in the 1920s, and not a match for their Allied counterparts.[70] The IJN could thus be described as a "small warship" navy, with its capital ships too outnumbered to sortie against the vastly superior Pacific Fleet.

However, U.S. naval commanders remained wary of the enemy's ability to launch counterattacks. In planning the amphibious operation against Lingayen Gulf in northern Luzon, one of the chief tasks was to secure the route from the staging point at Mindoro.[71] Although the Japanese could not cut the lifeline, the assumption was that they would at least try. Halsey deduced that the converted carriers *Ise* and *Hyuga* were lurking in the South China Sea, waiting to strike the Philippines. The ships were actually stationed in Singapore, and not in a position to attack. Yet the situation was considered menacing enough to warrant a preemptive assault, and Task Force 38 was ordered to destroy all enemy naval forces in the vicinity, with the anchorage at Camranh Bay in Indochina as the main objective. The failure to detect large vessels suggested that the IJN had withdrawn its main units from the target area. Nevertheless, the Imperial Navy had to be kept at a safe distance from the Philippines, so they could not inflict damage on U.S. forces. Nimitz did not agree with MacArthur's contention that a defense force capable of meeting all heavy ships had to be kept on station, since such moves were likely to delay the launching of operations against the Japanese mainland.[72] Yet the admiral did agree that countermeasures were necessary, and suggested that the best move was to carry out air and naval attacks against the IJN's main bases in the Home Islands, so as to keep its ships at bay. Until the Japanese had lost all of their active vessels, the possibility that the Allies would face opposition could not be dismissed, and the Pacific Fleet paid close attention to the IJN's combat capabilities.

Lessons of Combat Experience

During the period following the IJN's defeat at Guadalcanal, its performance showed a range of characteristics, including declining efficiency in relation to its U.S. counterparts, coupled with a continued ability to conduct skillful maneuvers. U.S. naval officers did deduce that the Japanese were unable to match the Pacific Fleet's technological lead. In particular, the underdeveloped state of the IJN's search systems meant that its vessels could not counter the attacking forces in a timely manner. At the same time, on a number of occasions, the Imperial fleet evaded damage, and even inflicted casualties on its opponents. The destructive capabilities of enemy torpedoes caused worries until the late stages of the conflict. The Japanese also appeared to have introduced incremental improvements in their radar, and their vessels subsequently demonstrated higher performance, albeit still lagging behind their rivals. Because U.S. naval officers wished to fight a prolonged war without facing substantial casualties, they viewed with apprehension any indications of the Imperial Navy's ability to harm the Pacific Fleet. The only reason for comfort was that the Japanese were not able to deploy the same quantity or quality of ships as the Americans.

The main source of information on the IJN's combat methods was the multitude of action reports produced by U.S. commanders. The evidence gained through the Navy's operations in the South Pacific indicated that enemy capabilities were lagging. One of the most notable observations was that Japanese ships failed to locate their attackers until the latter had launched their ordnance. Yet the precise reasons could not be established, owing to the lack of information on IJN technology and tactical doctrine. During the second Solomon Islands campaign in 1943, the Japanese appeared to become bewildered and confused when faced by superior fire power. At the Battle of Kula Gulf on July 5 and 6, vessels did not increase their speed or attempt to turn away until Vice Admiral Walden Ainsworth's task force started bombarding them.[73] Once the salvoes were launched, the Japanese appeared to maneuver in a haphazard manner, with little awareness of their opponents' position. Aside from the *Helena*, which was sunk by torpedoes, no U.S. ships were hit. At Vella Lavella, Japanese gunfire was described as "slow, ineffective, and confused." Accuracy was achieved only at short ranges of 1,300 to 3,000 yards. At normal ranges, the enemy was at a "distinct disadvantage."[74] Officers admitted that they were unable to determine whether the phenomenon was due to equipment deficiencies or poorly trained personnel.

Further confusion arose from instances when Japanese gunnery functioned well. By late 1943, when the IJN had effected modest improvements
in its search devices, surface forces operated in a way that impressed U.S. personnel. At Empress Augusta Bay, Japanese salvoes missed their targets only
on a few occasions.[75] At Cape St. George, the main reason why gunfire did
not hit was because U.S. vessels conducted sharp evasive turns.[76] The observation suggested that the IJN had either perfected its methods of using optical
equipment, or fitted its vessels with better radar. Although the exact reasons
were unclear, naval commanders were inclined to acknowledge the latter possibility. Captured equipment had shown that the IJN was developing radar
sets.[77] Furthermore, since the U.S. Navy had made strenuous efforts to re-
equip its vessels, the Japanese could logically be expected to do likewise. As
a result, the Pacific Fleet's advantages were likely to decline, no matter how
great they were. Although the hypothesis was based on assumption, it signified how the Americans wished to remain alert to contingencies where they
could face a more trying adversary.

U.S. intelligence staffs used the evidence obtained from combat experience to make a prudent assessment to the effect that although Japanese vessels had demonstrated inadequacies, their quality remained high. The IJN
was judged to be in "excellent repair," with nearly every combatant unit available for deployment.[78] The apparent weaknesses of Japanese weaponry were
treated with reserve. Due attention was paid to how action reports consistently suggested that naval battles turned into duels between the U.S. Navy's
gunfire and the IJN's torpedoes. The Combined Intelligence Section summed
up the situation by stating that, while the IJN's batteries were probably of a
lower standard than their Allied counterparts, the Japanese had displayed
"outstanding skill" in using their torpedoes.[79] Yet because the Pacific Fleet did
not have access to a great deal of information on enemy ordnance and their
methods of use, the exact reasons why the Japanese caused so much damage
could not be accurately explained. The majority of engagements also still took
place at nighttime, where limited visibility precluded an accurate observation of the opponent's movements. Post-mortems on the attacks during the
Kula Gulf engagement put forward a number of conflicting interpretations.
Some crews claimed that the Japanese launched their torpedoes without being sighted by the American task force, thereby indicating that they had been

fired from long ranges. Others alleged that enemy forces scored hits by using high-speed weaponry.[80] The only certain conclusion was that during night actions, torpedo attacks were "a matter of grave concern," even in cases where U.S. ships possessed superior gunnery.[81] The situation was further complicated because future developments could not be predicted. Ship crews were therefore requested to provide their combat intelligence centers with whatever information they secured.[82] The accepted opinion was that U.S. forces needed to maintain a close watch on the quality of Japanese weapons and methods of their use.

Likewise, commanders in the Pacific Fleet based their evaluations on the knowledge that the Imperial Navy had proven to be a competent force. As late as the Battle of Leyte Gulf, personnel remained wary that Japanese cruisers and destroyers were capable of launching torpedoes at distances well beyond visual sighting range.[83] Subsequently, a show of clumsiness in one encounter was not a reason to discredit the Japanese. At Samar, the IJN's gunfire performed in a way that suggested its control methods were ineffectual. U.S. crews observed that salvoes covered an area as narrow as three hundred yards, and the commander of Carrier Division 22 concluded that the enemy had failed to learn one of the key axioms of naval gunnery, namely, that the fire needed to cover a wide arc if hits were to be achieved.[84] The commanding officer of the escort carrier *White Plains* noted how his ship "received so many straddles, that by the laws of chance it should have been hit several times."[85] Yet many officers thought that the failure was incidental, and were at a loss for explanations. Nimitz could not figure out why the large force of battleships, cruisers, and destroyers sank only one of the U.S. carriers, even after having them under fire for over two hours.[86] His report deduced, "It is quite possible that some of the Japanese ships which could still make top speed had their fire-control systems disabled." Another notable observation was that the Japanese launched torpedo attacks at ranges much longer than those that their ordnance could actually achieve.[87] The IJN appeared to be overconfident about its weapons. The evidence was viewed as an indication that in one encounter, the enemy did not carry out its operations effectively.

The Japanese were also judged to be capable of achieving much greater results than they did. The U.S. amphibious force at Leyte was not in a position to fight a drawn-out battle, since its ammunition had been depleted.[88] If Kurita had chosen to force an entrance into the gulf, his fleet had the strength to destroy most of the landing force, bombard the beach, and escape without being subjected to more than one strike from Task Group 38.1, which was on its way from the northeast. Rear Admiral Clifton Sprague, commanding the carrier division, noted how the enemy was closing in with "disconcerting rapidity" to the point where none of his ships could "survive another five minutes of the heavy-caliber fire being received."[89] The enemy's decision to abandon the operation was attributed to the fact that its strength had also been substantially reduced through prior submarine and air attacks. The IJN's ordnance also performed effectively on a number of occasions. At Surigao Strait, a large-caliber salvo that landed close to the destroyer *Claxton* was considered capable of achieving an "extremely well-placed hit."[90] The setback at Leyte did not justify a conclusion that the Japanese surface fleet's capacity to endanger its U.S. counterpart had dissipated.

Assessments concerning the IJN's antiaircraft gunnery showed a similar level of caution during the course of the Pacific War. Until the battle of the Philippine Sea in June 1944, the available information was meager. With the exception of Midway and the Solomons, most attacks were carried out on ships anchored in harbor, with little opportunity to maneuver. In fact, one of the key faults of Japanese defenses was the absence of adequate radar. The search devices installed on board aircraft carriers after the Midway disaster were "mediocre," and could detect formations at only up to sixty miles.[91] Operations in the western Pacific revealed how the IJN faced troubles in protecting its vessels in the open sea. Pilots who fought during the Marianas campaign described how, once the Japanese task force had detected the approaching planes from a distance, antiaircraft fire was "intense but inaccurate," with enemy ships throwing up a wall of fire in the hope that the attackers would fly through it.[92] Battle formations were also not positioned in an effective manner. Carriers were seen to be operating separately, in distinct contrast to the U.S. Navy's practice of sailing in single formations, which meant that the limited number of destroyers had to be divided among the groups.[93] Enemy ships retreated without coordinating their evasive tactics, and consequently, the fleet became scattered, with mutual support severely compromised.[94]

Nevertheless, U.S. naval intelligence hesitated to downplay the Imperial fleet's ability to deal with aerial attacks. Japanese ships were considered to be durable. Aircraft carriers, while not as formidable as those that had been lost at Midway, were "qualitatively at least as equal" to the forces used at Pearl Harbor and the South Pacific campaigns.[95] The *Shokaku* and *Zuikaku* were both "worthy counterparts" of the *Essex*–class carriers, with a substantial capacity to absorb bombardment.

The possibility of improvements also could not be dismissed. As early as 1943, photographs of cruisers had shown that they were fitted with curved installations that resembled fire-control radar.[96] Although Japanese technology was lagging, the IJN had been known for its attempts to catch up with the West. For this reason, enemy forces were expected to enhance the quantity and quality of their antiaircraft radar. The situation was menacing enough to give rise to recommendations that all American ships and aircraft had to be equipped with stronger jamming devices.[97] Search receivers and direction finders also needed to be fitted, so that task forces could determine which units were using electronic fire-control mechanisms. At Leyte, pilots reported antiaircraft bursts to be "surprisingly accurate."[98] U.S. aviators also reported that the Japanese were using better guns. The 25-mm Hotchkiss automatic cannon, which was installed on board every warship, was described as "the most formidable weaponry the [Japanese navy] has at present to combat low-flying aircraft."[99] Its high rate of fire and muzzle velocity and an ability to fire a flat trajectory were all desirable characteristics for an automatic weapon. Although the developments were not sufficient to enable the Japanese to match their opponent's technological capability, they were likely to entail higher attrition for U.S. forces.

In the area of antisubmarine warfare, the IJN similarly demonstrated a noticeable ineptitude, coupled with an imaginative use of limited resources. The U.S. Navy assessed the available evidence prudently, and was wary not to conclude that Japanese ships were always bound to be easy prey. By late 1943, American forces had gained a decisive edge over enemy convoys. Submarine captains adopted the wolf-pack tactics that the Germans were employing in the Atlantic, whereby groups of underwater vessels awaited in areas where merchant ships and transports were known to be traversing. When combined with the introduction of more efficient torpedoes, the tactic enabled the U.S. Navy to sink an ever-increasing amount of shipping. Cryptanalysts also deciphered the "Maru code," which provided data not only on the movements of enemy merchantmen, but also details of their cargoes, as well as the destination of the convoy. Submarine crews could be ordered to patrol at selected points and direct their attacks at specific ships, rather than sail aimlessly around the far reaches of the western Pacific in search of targets. The distribution of information was facilitated when the submarine force operations officer was designated a combat intelligence officer, and given access to all communications decrypts. Operations officers were authorized to furnish the material to all individual force commanders and submarine captains through an encrypted line.[100] The U.S. submarine fleet's operations were also facilitated by the IJN's continued failure to develop adequate countermeasures. Reports from patrol missions suggested that enemy task forces were not equipped with proper search devices. During one mission in the Truk area, the USS *Steelhead* closed within two thousand yards of a destroyer and escort carrier, but neither ship launched its ordnance until they were fired upon.[101]

Yet submarine crews often reported being subjected to skillfully executed attacks. In one instance, destroyers passed through on both sides of the *Pike*, tracked the latter, and stopped to confirm the echo range.[102] Once the position was ascertained, the enemy launched its depth charges. The encounter suggested that, even without radar, Japanese destroyers were equipped to locate underwater vessels. The captain of the *Tinosa* noted how, on one mission, airplane contacts were "irritatingly numerous," and persisted for almost the entire duration of the patrol.[103] In another instance, the *Grumpus* and *Amberjack* were patrolling off the coast of Australia when they were sunk by Japanese destroyers. Enemy forces had allegedly located the submarines' exact positions, and the conclusion was supported by previous intercepts of Japanese transmissions, which revealed that they were successful at locating the source and destination of U.S. radio signals.[104]

In spite of their inability to operate destroyer escorts on a consistent basis, the Japanese periodically managed to put up a substantial defense. Following a mission in the home waters, the *Tuna* commented that enemy antisubmarine measures represented "a very efficient employment" of the forces that the Japanese had at their disposal.[105] Destroyers and high-speed craft were stationed in groups of three at strategic points along the main shipping lanes. Small patrol craft, including motor sampans, were assigned to report on the sighting of hostile vessels, and disposed in a manner that made it "impossible to avoid contacts while on the surface."

Naval commanders were cautious not to downplay the difficulties that U.S. forces could face in sinking enemy vessels, especially when the Japanese began to modify their antisubmarine measures. Toward the end of the conflict, deceptive moves became common. Enemy ships frequently transmitted false echoes to conceal their position. Nimitz warned that an increased use of this practice was likely to "seriously complicate the problem" facing submarine crews.[106] In one instance, the *Crevalle* identified some targets, but when the attack point was reached, the only vessels present were trawlers.[107] The trick was allegedly set up after the approaching submarine had been detected with an effective type of search device. Although the Japanese were not known to possess the most advanced technology, they were believed capable of using reflectors to locate submerged vessels. Upon disseminating the report, CINC-PAC stressed that submarine commanders needed to report similar observations in a timely manner, and keep updated on new developments. Although Japanese countermeasures were not a sufficient substitute for the use of radar, the enemy had devised ways to circumvent its deficiencies. The only source of comfort was that the IJN's methods were backward, and could not inflict a great deal of damage.[108] The obstacles that submarine crews were likely to face remained open to conjecture, and the U.S. Navy tended to conclude that it needed to pay heed to its opponent's capacity to put up resistance.

Implications for the U.S. Navy's Operations

The information that pointed to the IJN's continued potential to inflict damage on Allied fleets was taken by U.S. commanders as a clear warning that they needed to adequately maintain their own combat effectiveness. The inactivity of the Japanese capital ship and carrier fleet during 1943 and the early part of 1944 meant that the Pacific Fleet focused mainly on ways to engage auxiliary vessels. The aspect that received the most attention was the need to counter Japanese torpedo attacks. However, as late as 1943 the Americans found themselves struggling to determine the most effective means to engage their opponent. The situation stemmed in no small way from the shortage of information concerning enemy tactics and weapons. Toward the closing stages of the conflict, when the Americans were conducting operations aimed at destroying the remnants of the Imperial fleet, doctrine concentrated increasingly on ways to use the U.S. Navy's technological and material resources to neutralize enemy forces. Nevertheless, the comparative performance of the opposing fleets remained uncertain, mainly because they had not extensively engaged each other for a large part of the period following Guadalcanal. The IJN also continued to possess a good number of capital ships and carriers, while at the same time having demonstrated considerable skill at deploying its fleet. U.S. officers remained conscious that in order to defeat the Japanese in the long run, they needed to conserve their resources while avoiding moves that exposed friendly forces to attrition and delays. For this reason, as late as 1945, the lessons learned through encounters with the enemy compelled a continued reassessment of American naval capabilities.

Throughout 1943, the U.S. Navy paid close attention to means for dealing with Japanese torpedoes, and countermeasures were developed through trial and error. Drawing upon the lessons learned from the Solomons campaign, commanders attempted to use the advantages accrued from their radar and detect enemy forces before the latter could attack. Operational plans were based on the premise that ship crews needed to exploit their superior firepower. The commander of Cruiser Division 9 recommended that actions be fought at ranges where 6-inch batteries were most effective, namely, at medium distance, with friendly ships maneuvering sharply to avoid being hit.[109]

The assumption was that the Japanese could be destroyed or forced to withdraw before they had the opportunity to use their ordnance. U.S. naval officers believed that by closing at a range of ten thousand yards and using radar-controlled gunfire, their ships could launch the first salvos, and thereafter sink or disable any target.[110] However, the tactic left U.S. forces vulnerable when they did not have sufficient strength to neutralize their attackers. The flaw became apparent at Kula Gulf, where Task Group 36.1 attempted to achieve surprise, and made a quick approach.[111] The enemy was then to be subjected to an intensive barrage of gunfire from six thousand yards, which was judged to be well outside the range of enemy torpedoes. Vice Admiral Ainsworth and his crews were not aware that long-lance torpedoes could reach targets at distances equal to the firing range of cruiser and destroyer guns.[112] Although the Japanese were caught off guard by the appearance of U.S. vessels, the action failed to prevent the enemy from delivering a torpedo attack.

During subsequent encounters, task forces managed to remedy their faults by using procedures that involved rapid maneuvering and retreating beyond the presumed range of the long-lance after delivering gunfire.[113] Commenting on the damage that the IJN suffered at Vella Lavella on August 6–7, the commander of Destroyer Squadron 5 noted that in future operations, ships needed to follow similar tactics of immediate withdrawal.[114] At Empress Augusta Bay, Rear Admiral Aaron Merrill, commanding Task Force 39, planned to close to the maximum effective range of Japanese torpedoes in order to protect his cruisers.[115] Destroyers were dispatched for the initial attack. Cruiser gunfire was withheld until enemy ships were hit by torpedoes, in order to avoid disclosing the position of U.S. vessels. Although Vice Admiral Sentaro Omori's cruisers evaded damage, Merrill's force was also kept at a range where enemy ordnance could not strike.[116]

However, in order to achieve a satisfactory standard of combat effectiveness, American ships not only had to evade damage—vessels also needed to be equipped and maneuvered so they could sink their opponents. War instructions stipulated that the overriding objective was to strike with maximum speed, to enable friendly forces to retain the initiative.[117] Every effort had to be made to gain surprise, which was described as "a most potent weapon," and a "factor of superiority in itself." Deck officers were confident that surface-tracking SG devices were reliable means for locating and directing fire at enemy ships.[118] Nevertheless, the equipment continued to face interference in engagements fought within range of islands and land masses, owing to the echoes created by the intervening shorelines. Under such conditions, gunfire could not be directed accurately, while the Japanese were in a favorable position to attack without being detected. CINCPAC headquarters warned that radar-controlled gunnery did not provide complete protection against destroyers that fired their torpedo ordnance at long ranges.[119] Ship crews therefore had to rely on their own vision, and not expect technology to provide a complete solution. The Pacific Fleet's cruisers also had to be fitted with torpedoes that could place them on an equal footing with the enemy.[120] U.S. naval commanders remained reluctant to seek night actions. During the Marianas campaign, Vice Admiral Willis Lee was confident that the 16-inch guns of his battleships were capable of beating the Japanese, but he was loath to engage them, owing to prior experiences that showed the level of damage enemy weapons could cause.[121]

The U.S. Navy was similarly concerned about its methods of combating Japanese submarines. The underwater fleet was not considered a grave danger. The IJN in fact rarely used its submarines for sustained attacks on convoys, mainly because the high command failed to realize that such actions could hinder the buildup of U.S. forces in the far-flung garrisons of the Pacific theater.[122] Furthermore, because the Imperial Navy was fixated on battle fleet actions, little effort was devoted toward interdicting merchant vessels and troop transports.[123] In terms of equipment, while the Japanese had received substantial assistance from German technicians and engineers, their vessels were burdened with a number of faults. A large number of submarines did not achieve the same diving and turning rates as their Western counterparts, and also had a relatively short range, owing to their limited fuel tank capacity. Once the war commenced, the naval leadership placed priority on constructing heavy ships, and the submarines bureau lacked the clout to alter existing designs. Nor did Japan use its underwater fleet extensively against Allied warships after the Solomons campaign, out of fear of incurring excessive losses. Owing to the limited menace that Japanese submarines appeared to be posing, U.S. destroyer commanders did not see a pressing need to reform their countermeasures, and the situation was described as "not sufficiently serious to maintain enthusiasm."[124]

However, the capabilities of enemy subs were not discredited, mainly because information on the subject was sketchy. The ONI did note how the Japanese possessed a number of advantages. Armaments were much heavier than those used by other navies. In a number of engagements, most notably Guadalcanal, attacks were conducted against approaching enemy vessels, as well as damaged ships that attempted to retire from the scene of the action.[125] A Naval intelligence report in 1944 warned that while the Japanese submarine fleet had not been employed in an offensive capacity, as Allied forces advanced upon the inner reaches of Japan's empire, it was likely to be used as a key defensive weapon.[126] For this reason, U.S. naval crews had to take precautions.

War instructions laid out detailed procedures that escort commanders were to follow. U.S. naval doctrine had always specified that fleet dispositions be laid out to facilitate the detection of submarines before they reached a position where they could interdict heavy ships.[127] Because Japanese torpedoes had an exceptionally long range, the Pacific Fleet needed to set up destroyer screens that could locate enemy vessels at a corresponding distance. In ideal conditions, task forces were to be protected by three separate circles, with the inner one assigned to drop depth charges to destroy approaching submarines.[128] The intermediate and outer screens, sailing at a greater distance, were to impede submarine attacks by detecting them through the use of radar. However, the battle-line formation for antisubmarine protection was not suitable in all situations, especially when task forces faced aerial attacks. When defending themselves against enemy aircraft, carrier task groups traveled too quickly to permit accurate calculations of sonar ranges and bearings.[129] Enemy submarines were thus in a good position to avoid detection. The situation became more complicated when the U.S. Navy began to operate in the western Pacific. As the Japanese were forced to abandon their outlying bases and retire to the inner positions of their empire, an increasingly large number of their submarines were released from supply assignments, and were free to interdict the Pacific Fleet's supply lines and task forces. The existing sound detection equipment did not always function properly, especially when submarines were lying low in the water or at periscope depth.[130] During the torpedo attacks on the *Reno* off Luzon, neither radar nor ASDIC (active sound detection apparatus) picked up the enemy. Task forces thus had to rely more on aerial patrols. As long as the Japanese possessed the capacity to inflict damage, U.S. naval commanders were reluctant to become complacent over the need to provide adequate countermeasures.

While U.S. doctrine focused on measures to defend ships, by mid-1944, when the Pacific Fleet had developed sufficient strength to conduct large-scale operations, commanders began to shift their attention toward ways to destroy the IJN's heavy vessels. However, the shortage of intelligence on enemy capital ships and carriers meant that the methods for combating them could not be readily determined. Naval officers adhered to the axiom that had been developed prior to the war, and reinforced during the Midway and the Solomons campaign, namely, that task forces needed to be provided with sufficient striking power. Carrier commanders, along with aircrews, contended that surface ships were to provide antiaircraft support, and capital ships were best dealt with by aerial attacks. When formulating the plans for the U.S. Navy's advance into the western Pacific regions, Admiral John Towers, serving as Nimitz's commander on aviation matters, supported the criticisms put forward by Vice Admiral John S. McCain Sr., the deputy CNO, that the majority of aircraft were geared for assaults on land targets, and only one torpedo squadron had been allocated to strike enemy surface craft.[131] The Truk operations showed how carrier-based torpedo planes equipped with radar were particularly useful for low-altitude raids. The success in sinking enemy vessels was attributed to the fact that aircraft were approaching at so many different bearings, and at irregular intervals, to the point where the Japanese could not direct their fire against all their targets.[132]

At the same time, tactical concepts were open to debate, and surface-force leaders maintained that plans needed to be formulated with a view to utilizing the firepower on board U.S. vessels. Commenting on the Marianas encounter, the commanding officer of the *South Dakota* noted how air strikes often did not cause sufficient damage, and Japanese battleships remained serviceable, with their batteries and propulsion systems largely intact. Because enemy vessels remained in action, surface units needed to operate more independently. The main aim was to pursue enemy ships and seek a fleet action, so that the IJN could be brought into range and sunk by gunfire.[133] The commander of Battleship Division 9 agreed that capital ships had to be disposed more flexibly so they could switch from antiaircraft duties to fleet actions more readily.[134] The role that aircraft were to play in neutralizing Japanese surface vessels thus remained unresolved until the late stages of the conflict.

Furthermore, while the U.S. Navy sought to continue developing its procedures, the extent to which its weapons and radar-search techniques could counter the IJN had yet to be determined. Experiences during the Philippines campaign revealed a number of deficiencies, and naval commanders were reluctant to surmise that the Japanese defeat had vindicated the Pacific Fleet's supremacy. Among the most noted observations was that enemy vessels demonstrated a high level of resilience, and for this reason continued changes were needed to enable U.S. forces to fight without over-expending their firepower. While air attacks provided a potent weapon, they were not effective against well-armed units unless they were sustained. The commander of Battleship Division 9 recalled how the afternoon raids of October 24 did not prevent the enemy from passing the San Bernardino Strait, and planes from the *Intrepid*–class CVE (escort aircraft carrier) groups needed to carry out relentless bombardments to convince the Japanese that they could not reach Leyte Gulf.[135] The results achieved by armor-piercing bombs were discouraging, since they could not penetrate anything thicker than three inches.[136] Consequently, heavy vessels often remained intact. In setting out the aircraft complements for carrier task forces, the commander, Air Force Pacific Fleet (COMAIRPAC), noted how only the heaviest bombs could destroy Japanese capital ships.[137] Naval commanders did report that the aerial torpedoes functioned well, as evidenced by the hits achieved against battleships and cruisers.[138] However, a large number of attacks did not even slow down the Japanese, and many pilots opined that the U.S. Navy thus needed to modify its equipment before enemy ships could be neutralized at an economical cost. During an attack on a *Nachi*–class cruiser in Manila Bay, nine aerial torpedo hits were launched before the ship sank, and the expenditure of weapons was considered excessive for the results obtained.[139] The commander of Task Force 38 concluded that U.S. ordnance had to be fitted with more explosives if it were to achieve the same results as its Japanese counterparts.[140]

Aircrews also faced obstacles arising from antiaircraft fire. Combat experience had provided valuable lessons on evasive maneuvers. The "sector" method, where three divisions of dive-bombers attacked from different directions and thereby dispersed the antiaircraft flak of enemy cruisers and destroyers, had worked successfully during previous bombing raids on Rabaul and Truk.[141] However, tactics were adjusted while bearing in mind the possibility that the Japanese could enhance their defenses. Commenting on the operations against the Marianas and Iwo Jima during July 1944, an air group leader opined that torpedo planes needed to attack at high altitudes and speeds in order to score direct hits.[142] Operations against Japanese capital ships also presented some challenges that U.S. airmen were not accustomed to. Although the *Yamato*–, *Kongo*–, and *Nagato*–class battleships received heavy damage, antiaircraft fire from fleet units was described by some pilots to be the heaviest yet encountered in the Pacific theater.[143] Air attacks needed to be more coordinated, and conducted at ranges that permitted the tactical command officer to deploy his forces in a more planned manner.

In regard to surface operations, among the most significant lessons learned from the Leyte campaign was that the guns on board the battleships and cruisers often did not destroy their opponents. Admiral Thomas Kinkaid, commanding the Seventh Fleet, did dub the battle of Surigao Strait a "smashing success," with several ships sunk in the main engagement.[144] Gunnery fire was reported to have hit enemy ships with "devastating accuracy," and in light of the relatively small amount of ammunition expended, U.S. naval guns were considered "highly effective."[145] Ship-launched torpedoes also slowed down and disrupted the enemy formation. The commander of Task Group 77.2 noted how none of his ships suffered battle damage, with the exception of a destroyer.

Nevertheless, the performance of torpedoes caused disappointment for a number of crews. While Task Group 38.3 did hit Japanese battleships and carriers, none were sunk. The scenario gave rise to the conclusion that the ordnance used did not have enough explosive charge.[146] One of the main points that the Leyte operation reiterated was that 21-inch torpedoes were ineffective against anything larger than a cruiser.[147] Commenting on the fighting skills of U.S. ship-borne personnel, the commander of Task Group 79.11 suggested that destroyer squadrons needed more training in carrying out torpedo attacks in conditions of low visibility, and in actual battle conditions.[148] The standard practice was considered to not take sufficient account of scenarios where both enemy and friendly vessels moved at high speeds. As a result, torpedo crews were not able to reload their ordnance in a timely manner.

Experiences from Leyte also confirmed the importance of radar in enabling battery crews to direct their fire more accurately, while at the same time highlighting the problems that emerged when ships were not fitted with adequate devices. Moreover, the success achieved against the IJN did not mitigate the concerns arising from the possibility that Japanese forces could introduce more effective equipment. Although the U.S. Navy had installed radar on virtually all of its vessels, a large number did not have the most modern types, largely because the increased tempo of the operations meant that many ships needed to remain at the battlefront, and could not be recalled to rear bases for overhauls. Ship crews that were not properly equipped faced difficulties in striking their targets. Admiral Jesse Oldendorf, commanding Task Force 38 at Leyte, conceded prior to the engagement that only half of his six older battleships had radar fire control. The advantage they enjoyed over the enemy battle line in terms of fire power was therefore "not nearly so great" as their numerical superiority suggested.[149] At Surigao Strait, the *California*, *Tennessee*, and *West Virginia*, all of which possessed long-range radars, launched a large number of salvoes, and the proper use of fire control was believed to have contributed "in no small degree" to the sinking of an enemy battleship.[150] The *Mississippi*, *Pennsylvania*, and *Maryland*, on the other hand, were late in opening fire, since they did not have the Mark 8 instrument that could provide an accurate bearing.[151] The Pacific Fleet also had to guard against Japanese technological advancements. Commenting on the reports submitted by battleship divisions, the commander of Task Force 77 concluded that ships had to be given the most efficient devices available in order to maintain the advantages they held.[152]

A reliable means to detect enemy forces was not the only essential feature. Equally important was a system where the information could be disseminated expeditiously. Following the Solomons campaign, where poor communication resulted in delayed transmission, U.S. doctrine stipulated that a combat information center (CIC) was to be established within all task forces and their component ships.[153] Their main function was to facilitate the full utilization of intelligence by collecting data from all sources, including radar, signals decrypts, and visual sightings. The idea was to provide a central organization for evaluating information, and ensure that the material was forwarded to commanding officers and control stations when necessary.[154] The information provided by the CIC was vital for determining the actions that gun crews needed to undertake. Yet when multiple fleet units operated in a battle area, naval commanders could not easily establish a centralized CIC. As a result, the sharing of data did not take place in a methodical manner. The inherent disadvantages of the setup were highlighted after the Japanese fleet passed through the San Bernardino Strait. Many units were not notified that the enemy force had appeared. The commanding officer of the escort carrier *Gambier Bay* suggested that in order to guard against a recurrence of surprise attacks, all naval units operating in the same general area needed to be served by a centralized control unit.[155] The IJN's defeat at the Battle of Leyte Gulf was therefore not taken as a sign that the U.S. Navy had perfected its fighting capabilities. On the contrary, for the first time since the Solomons campaign during 1942–43, naval crews were faced with concrete indications that they still needed to take adequate steps to cope with the Japanese.

The Pacific Fleet also paid attention to the problems of damage control. As U.S. forces approached the Japanese homeland, the IJN was more likely to seek a fight to the finish, where victory often went to the side whose gunnery was able to function even after sustaining hits. Most encounters had seen the opposing fleets retire after incurring a certain level of attrition. The Americans were fortunate to gain a lead in the use of radar search and fire direction, which gave them a significant advantage in night actions. In daylight battles, U.S. ships had no such edge. The IJN had also proved its capacity to deliver rapid fire, and shells had landed close to the targets. A confidential bulletin warned, "There is nothing in the past that should lead to underestimating the fighting capacity of the Japanese Navy in an 'all-out' engagement."[156] Naval personnel therefore had to be trained to minimize the disruption caused by enemy gunfire.

By the time of the Okinawa campaign, the IJN's strengths had been significantly reduced, to the point where it was no longer able to conduct large-scale operations. Nevertheless, the U.S. Navy still needed to take preparatory measures for actions against small portions of the enemy fleet. The attempt made by the battleship *Yamato* to interfere with the amphibious operations highlighted this aspect. Although the *Yamato* was ultimately sunk by aircraft, surface units were assigned to deal with the attempted incursion. The operational plan was based on the understanding that the Fifth Fleet's battleships did not have the capability to take the initiative against its most heavily armed Japanese counterpart, and defensive action provided the most viable solution. Upon receiving word on the approach of the *Yamato*, Spruance alerted all forces against a possible attack, and directed Vice Admiral Mitscher to permit the Japanese force to continue south, to be met by Vice Admiral Morton Deyo's surface vessels.[157] Spruance considered that the *Yamato* had a superior gun range and speed to his older battleships, but felt that his numerical superiority could overwhelm the relatively small Japanese force and thus prevent a breakthrough.

Yet surface crews had to contend with problems arising from their own lack of adequate combat skill. The commander of Battleship Squadron 1 noted how training had been geared toward providing fire support for amphibious forces, and his crews had not received significant instruction on matters related to fleet engagements.[158] Battle plans called for a small part of the squadron to counter the enemy force, with flank forces withholding their fire until the target ships were successfully fired upon. Once the engagement commenced, the flank forces were to envelop the Japanese, in an attempt to prevent them from escaping. The move was considered the most effective way to deal with an enemy force consisting of ships with high speed and long-range guns. Commanders in the Pacific Fleet remained wary not to believe that their numerical and technological superiority guaranteed an easy victory. Operational planning continued to be carried out while bearing in mind the need to ensure that U.S. forces were deployed so as to minimize losses, while at the same time defeating enemy forces in an efficient manner, until the final phases of the conflict.

Conclusion

U.S. intelligence efforts against the Japanese fleet between 1943 and 1945, and the Navy's use of the information it secured, were heavily influenced by factors related to strategic culture. The key principle that shaped American thinking was a desire to deploy the available material and technological resources in the most efficient manner, and defeat enemy forces without incurring damages that could erode the Pacific Fleet's ability to carry out its prescribed missions. War plans were based on the understanding that the destruction of the IJN was necessary to help the U.S. Navy secure control over the far reaches of the Pacific Ocean and pave the way for an eventual assault on Japan's Home Islands. Naval commanders also recognized that success hinged on conducting an extensive series of campaigns. Intelligence activities were therefore geared to determine the Imperial fleet's capacity to oppose the Allies in a prolonged war. Subsequently, the ONI, along with the bodies working at the theater level, was assigned to handle a comprehensive range of data, on matters related to the current state of Japanese combat methods and weapons technologies as well as the manner in which the IJN could refine them. In assessing the material, intelligence staffs strove to avoid miscalculations that could undermine their trustworthiness. For naval commanders, the most important task was to exploit the information in order to devise more resourceful ways of combating the IJN.

However, the available information provided what was often a limited picture. As the war progressed, naval intelligence organizations were able to secure an increasing amount of evidence, as well as to analyze and disseminate it in a more expeditious manner. The intelligence collected from sources such as POWs, photographic reconnaissance, and captured documents provided a number of details concerning Japanese vessels and the equipment they carried. However, qualitative intelligence on matters such as the way in which the Imperial fleet carried out its operations remained difficult to secure. Firsthand engagements remained the chief medium for determining the threat that the IJN could pose. Even then, because a large number of battles were fought in nighttime conditions, and at a considerable distance from enemy ships, naval crews could not accurately monitor the tactics and weapons used by their opponent. To complicate the situation, the IJN's carriers and battleships remained inactive for a large part of the intervening period between the Guadalcanal campaign and the Marianas operation of June 1944. The U.S. naval establishment admitted that it could go no further than to provide statistical data on aspects such as the layout and measurements of the IJN's ships. Assessments on matters such as tactical doctrine and combat methods were based on incomplete evidence. Because the Americans were aware that they had to remain vigilant against the challenges they faced, intelligence staffs and naval commanders were careful not to reach unsubstantiated hypotheses on what the Japanese could and could not do.

The ambiguity was compounded by apprehensions arising from evidence that provided mixed signals of the Imperial fleet's capabilities. On one hand, the IJN did not have the resources to defeat its opponents. Japan had suffered extensive naval losses during the opening year of the conflict, and its productive capacity was insufficient to replace its sunken vessels. At the battlefront level, enemy ships were not equipped with the most updated radar devices, and Japanese naval crews were consequently unable to detect their opponents in a timely manner. U.S. task force commanders recognized the weakness as a feature that enabled them to carry out surprise attacks. Nevertheless, the IJN continued to possess the ability to inflict harm. In addition, the Imperial Navy continued to possess a sizeable fleet that was capable of obstructing Allied operations. Subsequently, the U.S. Navy warned against dismissing the dangers that enemy forces exerted.

In the area of operational planning and the development of tactical doctrine, the nature of the intelligence regarding the IJN had some significant effects on the Pacific Fleet's conduct of its campaigns. The lack of information on the specifics of Japanese weapons and their employment meant that naval crews often faced complications in determining the most effective way to engage their opponent. The development of methods for countering the Imperial fleet's torpedoes clearly illustrated this dilemma. In other types of operations, most notably those involving the use of carriers and capital ships, the inactivity of the IJN's main fleet following the Solomons campaign hindered measures to devise the most effective procedures. The only certain conclusion was that the Japanese had demonstrated their proficiency on many occasions, and that proper countermeasures were needed. The problems were circumvented largely because the U.S. Navy endeavored to conscientiously examine the performance of its own units. The paramount aim was to ensure that task forces were properly equipped and trained to defeat enemy forces, while at the same time avoiding excessive losses. In the final analysis, the Americans made good use of intelligence. The shortage of information, coupled with visible indications of the enemy's ability to inflict attrition, was viewed as indication that assessments concerning the relative capabilities of the opposing forces needed to lean toward wariness. The potential threat posed by the IJN's fleet was not discredited until combat losses had substantially reduced its strength, to a point where it was no longer capable of opposing the Allied advance toward the Home Islands. Most important, the intelligence gained through encounters with enemy forces was used to draw lessons on how the Pacific Fleet could fight more successfully.

4

The "Underdog in the Air War," Yet a Resourceful Opponent
INTELLIGENCE ON THE IJN'S AIR ARM 1943–45

U.S. assessments on the Imperial Japanese Navy Air Force (IJNAF) showed a considerably deeper understanding than was the case with the IJN's surface fleet. The achievement was due to two factors, the first of which was the abundance of opportunities that intelligence organizations had to secure raw data on the performance and characteristics of enemy aircraft. Secondly, in contrast to the IJN's fleet, its air arm remained active for the duration of the conflict. As the Pacific Fleet advanced toward the inner zone of Japan's empire, task forces regularly encountered aerial opposition, and witnessed the tactics that enemy air forces used when attacking naval targets. Operations against island positions also provided a means to gather information on how the Japanese used their naval air power to defend the skies above their conquered territories.

Nevertheless, the U.S. Navy faced considerable difficulties in developing an accurate knowledge, among the most important of which was that the available intelligence provided an array of contradictory evidence. As the war progressed, the IJN's air arm demonstrated that it did not possess the matériel to prevail in a protracted conflict. Assessments on the IJNAF's numerical strength put forward an undisputed conclusion that combat losses had considerably diminished the quantity of planes it could deploy. The performance of Japanese aircraft was also mediocre in terms of endurance and firepower. The relative capabilities of the U.S. Navy's air service, on the other hand, steadily rose, thanks to the introduction of a large number of technologically advanced planes. In addition, enemy pilots continued to show a declining level of fighting skill. By 1943, the majority of the IJN's top aviators had been either shot down or killed in accidents, and the air service failed to establish a training program to replace the lost pilots in a timely manner.

At the same time, the U.S. Navy and its air service paid due attention to indications that the Japanese still possessed a sizeable supply of aircraft, as well as aircrews with a high level of tactical aptitude. This was mainly because operational planning was based on the premise that the proper steps were needed to remain on guard against the damage that the enemy could cause, so as to ensure that the Pacific Fleet was able to prevail in the long run. Task force leaders and air commanders were aware that in order to defeat the IJNAF, they had to develop ingenious tactics that worked to overcome their opponent in the most efficient manner. Under the circumstances, evaluations of the IJN air arm were likely to highlight weaknesses that were open to exploitation. However, the Americans were also inclined to acknowledge that their opponent was able to execute damaging attacks on Allied vessels and aircraft. To complicate matters, the information did not always provide a full picture of enemy capabilities. The doctrines concerning the construction of planes and methods of their use were uncertain, and the possibility of improvements was not ruled out. The extent to which the Japanese had lost their aircraft and top-of-the-line pilots also could not be precisely calculated. During late 1944 and 1945, the appearance of kamikaze attacks reminded U.S. personnel that their opponent remained a significant threat. The naval establishment concluded that while the IJNAF did not pose the same danger as it did during the early stages of the conflict, it was a resourceful fighting force that had the capacity to inflict attrition on opponents who were not properly equipped.

Intelligence on the IJNAF's Numerical Strength

Among the most crucial indicators used to assess the IJNAF's ability to oppose Allied forces was the number of aircraft it had in operation. U.S. defense officials recognized that the destruction of Japanese air power was a crucial step toward achieving their objective of securing control over the Pacific Ocean and neutralizing the enemy's capacity to obstruct the advance toward the Home Islands. For this reason, concerns regarding the threat posed by the IJN's air arm were not dispelled unless credible data revealed that it no longer had the numerical strength to cause significant damage for Allied task forces. The main bodies responsible for handling quantitative information were the ONI and the Pacific Fleet. At the apex of the defense establishment, the JIC, along with its superiors in the JCS, provided overall assessments of Japanese air strengths and their effect on the strategic situation. Although naval intelligence was not always able to obtain a full collection of data, reliable pieces of evidence suggested that combat attrition and aircraft malfunctions had substantially diminished Japan's forces. Industries also did not have the productive capacity to replace losses. At the same time, the intelligence pointing to the IJNAF's growing numerical inferiority vis-à-vis its opponents provided limited grounds for optimism. In spite of their depleted capabilities, the Japanese maintained a sizeable air service that was capable of interfering with the U.S. Navy's operations. Moreover, as the Pacific Fleet began to operate in areas closer to the heart of Japan's empire, where the bulk of the enemy's planes were held in reserve, naval crews and airmen conceded that they were most likely to face greater levels of resistance.

Estimates of Japanese aircraft production were not based on accurate figures. Insofar as sources were concerned, signals intelligence, captured documents, and nameplates from downed planes pointed toward the number of machines that had been deployed. The data were patchy, and did not allow firm calculations. To provide a key example, in October 1943, the U.S. and British air intelligence staffs convened a conference at London. The existing documents revealed that the available sources provided "very little evidence."[1] Nameplates rarely referred to aircraft produced before early 1943. Moreover, intelligence on current strengths did not permit predictions of future developments. As late as 1945, data on manufacturing capabilities were lacking, to the point where precise estimates were almost impossible. At the Washington conference on the Japanese air force held in February, where representatives from naval intelligence were in attendance, the delegates could not agree whether the loss of raw material supplies from the southern regions, resulting from the destruction of the merchant fleet, was likely to result in declining output.[2] The ONI admitted that without a firsthand examination of plants and written records of industrial production, the statistics on Japan's aircraft construction was "necessarily very incomplete."[3]

Calculations of Japanese production were therefore largely based on data that had been secured prior to the conflict, coupled with speculation on the extent to which the aircraft industry was able to increase its efficiency in wartime. Indeed, as the Pacific War progressed, the Japanese faced mounting complexities in assembling an adequate number of planes. As early as 1941, manufacturers were short on key metals, including iron ore and aluminum.[4] In an attempt to facilitate the allocation of resources, the government created a munitions board in November 1943, which was assigned to administer matters such as the distribution of manpower and of raw materials. An intensive effort was also made to divert resources from the civilian sector so as to ensure that war industries received priority. The main beneficiaries of the move were aircraft firms, whose output peaked during 1944.[5] The U.S. Strategic Bombing Survey concluded that the achievement was "not inconsiderable . . . in view of the essential limitations within which the Japanese economy had to operate."[6] Yet, the results were far short of those accomplished by Japan's opponents, most notably the United States. By 1945, the prolonged submarine attacks on the merchant fleet worked to cut off the Home Islands from all supplies of raw materials, to the point where industrial activity came to a virtual standstill.[7] The bombing raids on Japan's cities also brought about a dramatic decline, down to 50 percent below the high point reached in 1944.[8]

Although U.S. naval intelligence did not have access to exact statistics, the available data did allow the Americans to deduce that the Japanese were burdened with a number of bottlenecks. Industrialization had begun late in comparison with the West, and although considerable progress had been made, factories were not as well organized as their U.S. counterparts.[9] Manufacturers also relied heavily on imports for special steels and machine tools, while trained labor was lacking. As a result, Japan's war industries suffered from "definite deficiencies" both in the quantity and quality of equipment they could produce.

The IJNAF's inability to provide sufficient aircraft for its frontline units was a key manifestation of its dwindling strength. Again, estimates were prone to a margin of error. Following the carrier strikes on Okinawa and Formosa in October 1944, the Pacific Fleet could only conclude that recent losses had reduced the IJNAF "to a shoestring not much longer than the one with which it started the war."[10] Nevertheless, the reduced scale of aerial attacks faced by

U.S. forces clearly showed that the enemy's supply of planes had diminished. As early as June 1943, the commander, Air Force Pacific Fleet (COMAIR-PAC), noted how the Japanese had been compelled to downsize their operations in the South Pacific and New Guinea.[11] Attacks by large squadrons took place less frequently, and in an apparent effort to avoid further losses, enemy forces tended to choose targets where fighter defenses were known to be minimal. Commenting on the decrease in enemy air activity, the JIC surmised that Japan had enough planes only for the purpose of protecting its conquered territories.[12] As long as the Allies continued to inflict attrition, there were few prospects of engaging in any offensive operation that required heavy air support. Although production was expected to continue increasing, operational and combat losses were bound to negate the results.[13] Under the circumstances, the Japanese could do little to alter the fact that the Allied air power ranged against them was "overwhelming and impossible to undermine."[14]

The prediction that waning strengths would result in correspondingly reduced opposition was proven correct during the U.S. Navy's operations against the key bastions of Japan's empire in 1944. Intelligence staffs, both in Washington and the Pacific, deduced that the IJNAF was no longer capable of carrying out sustained attacks against task forces, at least in the outlying territories. In the Gilberts-Marshalls area, the Japanese were reported to be "desperately short" of Betty bombers, which were needed for search and interdiction missions.[15] Following the Japanese losses during the Marianas campaign, the Joint Staff Planners asserted that enemy forces were much easier to overcome than during the early part of the year.[16] The majority of air units had been withdrawn to rear bases in the Philippines, with the remainder dispersed across the western Pacific. As a result, when attacking any island position, U.S. forces could expect air raids only during the initial phases.

Nevertheless, U.S. officials were careful not to become complacent, and paid due attention to the fact that the Japanese remained capable of amassing aircraft to carry out damaging attacks. This became especially true when the U.S. Navy began to operate in areas closer to the Home Islands, where the enemy kept the bulk of its reserves. Furthermore, intelligence staffs were inclined to be prudent when confronted with incomplete data on Japanese air strengths. During spring 1944, the JIC was tasked with calculating the opposition likely to be encountered in the Luzon-Formosa area, between the period two days before the landing, to twenty days afterwards.[17] Estimates ranged as high as 1,500 aircraft at the commencement, reinforced by another 1,405 within the interval. The Japanese were considered capable of putting up even more resistance in their mainland. The JIC claimed that in the event U.S. forces invaded the southern island of Kyushu, Japan could deploy up to four thousand combat aircraft and an equal number of training planes.[18] A large number of air bases were also within easy reach of the Allied task force, and up to five hundred sorties could be flown in any twenty-four-hour period. Even if enemy airfields were subjected to preemptive strikes, Japanese air strength was unlikely to be diminished by more than 20 percent by the moment of the invasion.

Defense planners also acknowledged the intelligence pointing to the IJNAF's continued possession of a large air force, and concluded that efforts to neutralize the enemy were bound to be laborious. For example, when planning the capture of the Palaus, the Joint Staff Planners agreed that the complete destruction of Japanese planes prior to the invasion was almost impossible, since previous experiences in the Pacific had proved that airfields remained serviceable unless they were bombarded constantly.[19] The damage inflicted by carrier-based raids had been limited, because task forces were not able to remain close to an island objective for any length of time, owing to logistical factors and the danger posed by counterattacks. In order to ensure that the IJNAF could not oppose the Pacific Fleet, U.S. forces needed to undertake a series of quick and overpowering strikes.[20] A slow and indecisive advance, on the other hand, was more likely to permit the Japanese to bring forth every weapon at their disposal. The U.S. defense establishment's evaluations concerning the IJN air arm's quantitative features thus reflected how the information regarding the enemy's weaknesses was not treated as a reason to discredit its fighting potential. On the contrary, intelligence organizations, along with naval commanders, remained wary about the losses that the IJNAF was able to inflict. In the absence of the unlikely scenario whereby Japan's supply of aircraft had been completely eliminated, the Pacific Fleet was more likely to feel compelled to maintain a close watch on its opponent.

Development of the U.S. Navy's Air Intelligence Capabilities

By mid-1944, the Pacific Fleet's ability to gauge the IJN's air arm was considerably enhanced, thanks to the establishment of an effective machinery to do

so at the theater level. As was the case when the U.S. Navy handled information on the IJN's surface fleet, the overriding concern that shaped intelligence
activities concerning the IJNAF was to determine its capacity to engage the
Allies in a drawn-out conflict. However, the available information again portrayed what was often an incomplete picture. Because intelligence organizations wished to avoid miscalculations that were likely to elicit criticisms from
their clients in the Navy and its air arm, assessments on future trends tended
to veer toward the watchful side, and paid heed to the fact that enemy forces
had demonstrated their capacity to put up a significant challenge. Ship commanders and aircrews acknowledged the possibility that the Japanese could
introduce modifications, and thereby complicate the situation confronting
U.S. forces.

In terms of organization, the efforts undertaken to bolster the U.S. Navy's
air intelligence network reflected the extent to which commanders were eager
to process the growing number of available sources in a methodical manner,
and promote a more informed image of the IJNAF. Although the South Pacific
Force continued to produce its weekly air battle notes, as the focus of operations shifted to the central Pacific, the Americans carried out a corresponding
expansion of their machinery. JICPOA, which worked under the auspices of
the commanders in chief, Pacific Fleet and Pacific Ocean Areas (CINCPAC-
CINCPOA), managed the collection and translation of data obtained from
captured sources, including POWs and enemy documents, until the U.S.
Navy established its centralized technical air intelligence center in 1944. The
office of the commander, Air Force Pacific Fleet (COMAIRPAC), also set up
its own operational intelligence section. For obvious reasons, COMAIRPAC
focused on aerial combat, with the Pacific Fleet examining enemy attacks
against shipping targets. The intelligence bodies working under the Navy
Department in Washington, including the ONI, continued to play an active
role, but were mainly responsible for circulating the information to personnel
due to embark on their assignments. As the number of organizations dealing
with air intelligence matters grew, fleet units were burdened with an overload
of information.[21] To complicate matters, there was no bureau tasked to coordinate intelligence activities. This was largely because the Navy had a greater
interest in creating bodies that could evaluate the IJNAF, in order to provide
personnel with a better idea of the elements they had to deal with. However,

the setup resulted in a situation where the theater-level organizations often worked independently of the ONI, with few mechanisms for oversight.

The available intelligence also did not provide details concerning the ideas that influenced the IJNAF's conduct of its operations. The Americans needed a better understanding of an enemy whose weapons designs and fighting techniques were largely shaped by cultural factors. Like the IJN's surface fleet, the air service followed a concept that called for concerted measures to compensate for Japan's inability to produce the same quantity of weaponry as its Allied opponents, by focusing on quality. The construction of aircraft, along with the training of pilots, was geared to enable the Japanese to overcome U.S. forces through tactical finesse. At the outbreak of war, the IJN air arm was superior to the competing maritime powers. Zero fighters ranked among the most advanced combat aircraft of their time. In terms of flying skill, the IJNAF developed a highly dedicated corps of pilots who were able to carry out the IJN's main missions, namely, to achieve air superiority, and inflict crippling blows on enemy surface vessels.

The main failing was that the Japanese did not build their air forces with a view to conducting an extended war effort. Aircraft production targets were modest when compared to the Western powers, while the design of bombers and fighters did not enable them to engage in intensified battles. In particular, planes were fitted with small amounts of armament or armor. The practice was natural, given Japan's shortage of raw materials and productive plants, which in turn prevented industries from assembling large quantities of aircraft. Yet the deficiency also stemmed from mistaken perceptions, which maintained that the Japanese air arm's performance could overcome any material advantages the Allies enjoyed. Japanese naval planners, along with their intelligence staffs, asserted that the Zero had the equivalent capability of up to five enemy fighter planes.[22] To make matters worse, the initial successes created a false sense of confidence, and the air service felt no need to enhance its capabilities.[23] In reality, the IJNAF could maintain its lead only while it faced weaker opponents, since it was unable to replace aircraft losses at the same rate as the Allies.

When the IJNAF realized that it had incurred an excessive level of attrition, and that the United States was catching up both in quality and quantity by early 1943, the situation was virtually irreversible. The Japanese had neither the resources nor the expertise to produce planes that could compete with their rivals. Newly introduced models of the Zero, while equipped with armor, were still thinly protected, which rendered them vulnerable to the heavy gunfire delivered by the Corsair and Hellcat. In contrast to their U.S. counterparts, Japanese air commanders did not identify the need to provide planes with better protection until a late stage. This was largely due to previous experiences in China, where the Japanese had incurred relatively few losses. Subsequently, the IJNAF developed a belief that it was invincible.[24] Military traditions also glorified less well-armed warriors overcoming more powerful opponents through skilful maneuvering. Aircrews adhered to the credo, and considered defensive armor to be unnecessary.[25] As a result, the navy air service did not press manufacturers to construct more durable machines. Although top officials in the IJNAF eventually acknowledged the Zero's inadequacies, they simultaneously faced the pressing need to continue putting out a large number of fighter aircraft, in order to compensate for losses. Industries therefore could not readily be requested to phase the Zero out of production, and overhaul their plants to make way for the construction of new fighter types.[26] Bombers were handicapped by similar faults. The Kate, which had served as the main carrier-based bomber in China, became obsolete during the early stages of the Pacific War owing to its lack of armor plate.[27] Likewise, the Frances was equipped with only one forward-firing and one rear-firing flexible gun, and relied heavily on speed to defend against enemy interceptors.[28]

In addition to poor equipment, the IJNAF suffered from a dwindling supply of manpower, and did not foresee the need to build a large reserve of aircrews. By 1944, the vast majority of skilled aviators had been lost in combat or plane crashes, and most units were manned by inexperienced personnel. For example, Air Group 652, which suffered heavy casualties at Rabaul, ended up providing only two months of training for its replacement pilots.[29] During the Marianas campaign, squadrons proved incapable of coordinating their tactics. Raids consisted mainly of small and widely separated formations, which U.S. task forces found easy to counter.

At the same time, while the Japanese were slow to innovate, they did manage to bring about incremental changes. The Emily flying boat was heavily armored, mainly because its range was beyond that of escorting fighters, and the plane thus required extra protection.[30] The Jill, which replaced the Kate as the main torpedo bomber, was also fitted with enhanced plating, and made its first appearance during the Marianas campaign.[31] The vulnerability of the Zeros was partially reduced by fitting them with protective glass, as well as automatic fire extinguishers in the fuel tanks. Japan also managed to enhance its aircraft technology by continuing to rely on foreign help. Between 1943 and 1945, in return for deliveries of raw materials to Germany from Southeast Asia, U-boats transported numerous samples of the latest weapons that the Nazis had to offer, including jet aircraft and flying bombs, along with licenses for Japanese companies to construct copies of the equipment.[32] The war machine benefited "immeasurably" from the exchange, particularly in the development of radar. Although the Japanese had a delayed start, and were not able to produce enough devices to equip all of their aircraft, a modest number were fitted. As a result, pilots were more able to carry out accurate attacks. In regard to fighting skill, even though the IJNAF had lost many of its top aviators, a large number continued to demonstrate competence. Aircrews were adroit at circumventing the obstacles posed by the U.S. Navy's enhanced antiaircraft and fighter defenses, by employing tactics that emphasized speed, surprise, and determination.

Under the circumstances, U.S. personnel had to evaluate an opponent with a multifarious assortment of traits. Yet while the available data described the material features of the air service, they did not explain the enemy's ideas concerning aerial combat. Because information on cultural factors was rare, the naval establishment did not expend a great effort in drawing conclusions. Japanese tactics were noted to demonstrate some distinct features, among the most discernible of which was aggressiveness. Horizontal bombing methods were described to exemplify national characteristics, including "courage, indifference to losses, and an adherence to preconceived plans."[33] However, assessments of the IJNAF tended to focus on features that could be clearly examined, such as the characteristics of its planes and the maneuvers its pilots carried out in battle. Even toward the closing stages of the conflict, the U.S. Navy establishment accepted the fact that it was not able to identify the trends that affected its enemy's ways of fighting. When the IJNAF demonstrated a conspicuous inability to introduce significant advancements in its aircraft technology, the weakness was not attributed to flawed doctrine but cited as a byproduct of Japan's resource shortages. Moreover, intelligence staffs and combat personnel tended to concentrate more on how the enemy's faults affected its combat performance, rather than surmise on the underlying causes. U.S. officials also declared that there were few reasons to dismiss the possibility of the Japanese altering their capabilities. The appearance of kamikaze attacks did compel the Americans to pay closer attention to the mentality that led their enemy to carry out suicidal moves. Nevertheless, attention continued to focus on the strengths and weaknesses of Japanese tactics, and their implications for the U.S. Navy's operations.

In spite of the limitations, intelligence efforts were augmented by the increasing range of sources that became available as the conflict progressed. On matters concerning the particulars of Japanese planes, technical intelligence was the main source. Included in this category were specimens of recovered enemy aircraft that had either crashed or been shot down, as well as captured documents and blueprints. Enemy pilots who were taken prisoner also provided information. The material revealed a wealth of data on the construction of enemy planes and the weapons they carried. POWs and captured papers also described the maneuvers that Japanese aircrews were trained to carry out. The available pool of intelligence was further enhanced by the U.S. Navy's practice of relying upon outside bodies. The USAAF, along with the air services of America's allies, notably Great Britain and Australia, were actively engaging the Japanese, and thus supplied useful material.

The first source of intelligence was POWs. Opportunities to capture enemy pilots were few and far between, for a number of reasons. In terms of geography, the campaigns in the Pacific took place over large stretches of ocean, which meant that downed aircrews frequently died from injuries or drowning before they could be recovered. Even when planes crashed over land areas, the mountainous jungles that prevailed in areas such as the Solomons made it hard to find surviving aviators. Last but not least, Japanese airmen were strongly imbued with the belief that surrendering to the enemy was tantamount to high treason, and thus tended to commit suicide before the Allies could capture them.

On occasions when enemy airmen were taken prisoner, interrogations revealed some interesting information. In a significant development, a collection of POW reports received during the latter half of 1943 confirmed the extent to which the IJNAF was compelled to produce its cohort of airmen in a rushed manner, and thus unable to provide extensive training. The instruction program had been streamlined to a point where aircrews learned only the most basic maneuvers. The time devoted was drastically reduced from the one thousand hours that had been common during the early stages of the war to a mere two hundred hours in some cases.[34] In another instance, a pilot who had formerly been assigned to the surface fleet was sent directly to intermediate flying school, without the benefit of pre-flight preparation.[35]

At the same time, the intelligence received from captured pilots had to be treated with reserve. Enemy pilots were often familiar with the equipment and tactics used by their individual units, but less knowledgeable on the overall situation prevailing within the IJNAF. Frontline personnel were not always updated on the decisions made by the high command, owing to the latter's practice of keeping the information secret, as well as the hindrances involved in communicating matters to units stationed in the outlying areas. The limitation was apparent when POWs described aircraft designs. In one instance, the Technical Air Intelligence Center noted how Japanese aircrews had suggested that their navy was equipping its fighters with 40-mm cannon, similar to those its army counterparts had been fitted with. However, the data were questionable, since the naval air arm was not known to be using weapons made for its rival service.[36]

Captured aircraft and enemy documents were a more reliable source of information on equipment. At the theater level, CINCPAC headquarters issued periodic bulletins on the designation systems that the Japanese used to name their aircraft, thus enabling U.S. aircrews to clear away the confusion arising from the overwhelmingly large number of plane types that enemy forces had deployed.[37] Intelligence officials from BuAer in Washington also disseminated reports on the test flights carried out on captured enemy aircraft. As early as November 1942, the experiments with the Zero fighter that had crash-landed in the Aleutian Islands revealed vital data.[38] The Zero was found to be "far inferior" to the F4U Corsair in terms of speed at level flight and in diving at all altitudes, while at medium heights, the Zero was slightly better at ascending.[39] Nevertheless, the Zero did not keep up with the Corsair in high-speed chases. Experiments carried out by the USAAF also indicated how the Japanese plane performed in relation to its U.S. counterparts.

The Zero fighter had superior maneuverability over the P-38 at speeds below three hundred miles per hour. Nevertheless, at altitudes above 25,000 feet, the P-38 could outmaneuver its opponent, owing to better climbing ability and speed.[40] Against the P-39, the Zero was inferior in all respects, while the P-51 Mustang was able to dive away from its opponent at any time.[41] The information revealed how, at the very best, the Zero was marginally better than its U.S. counterparts in certain maneuvers, while in other categories it had a decisive disadvantage vis-à-vis the newer models of American aircraft. By January 1943, the intelligence obtained through test flights was regularly used to brief U.S. pilots.

Although the apparatus provided good information, the U.S. Navy judged that a centralized organization was needed to process and disseminate technical data more efficiently. If the rival services, including the Army, along with the other Allied air forces operating in the Asia-Pacific theaters, continued to carry out their own activities, the necessary intelligence was unlikely to be properly shared. In addition, organizations faced the risk of duplicating each other's efforts, thereby causing a dissipation of limited resources. The Air Information Division, operating under the deputy CNO, was renamed the Air Technical Analysis Division (designated OP-35) in September 1943, and four months later, the division was incorporated as a branch of the ONI. Recognizing the need for a more coordinated effort, in mid-1944, OP-35 decreed that the Division of Naval Intelligence was the central body responsible for evaluating and disseminating technical material.[42] OP-35 was amalgamated with the Technical Air Intelligence Center (TAIC), based at the naval air station in the Washington, D.C., suburb of Anacostia. The center provided the necessary organization and facilities for handling the relevant information on the Japanese air forces, both naval and army. The War Department and USAAF, along with the British Royal Air Force, were to forward their findings to the TAIC. Commencing in August, the center issued a weekly summary that contained a detailed collection of diagrams and photographs describing the particulars of enemy aircraft. The reports were based on enemy documents, photographic reconnaissance, and most important, data obtained from inspections of crashed planes.

The information obtained from captured aircraft was particularly useful for finding answers to the pressing question concerning the extent to which the enemy had introduced new designs, but was less reliable for obtaining data on key aircraft components, the most important of which was radar. U.S. aviators did provide a steady flow of reports, which confirmed that the IJN air arm did not possess aircraft that equaled their Western counterparts. However, aircrews often witnessed Japanese planes that had an enhanced capacity to withstand gunfire. The development raised concerns that U.S. forces could encounter a tougher opponent.

The most visible flaw in enemy planes was their lack of armament and protection. The consequences were highlighted in the fact that Japanese losses in the South Pacific were over four times greater than the Allies'. Air combat intelligence could safely conclude that the IJNAF's qualitative and quantitative inferiority was the major weakness that saddled it with the unenviable status of "the underdog in the air war."[43] U.S. naval intelligence lost no time in recognizing that Japanese air capabilities were declining. In one mission over Truk, more than twenty Zekes were shot down, while VF-32 suffered minor damage to only one of its planes. The participating pilots attributed the success to the fact that the F6F-3 model of the Hellcat was superior in all phases of flight, with the possible exception of making turns at slow speeds.[44] During another encounter in the western Pacific, eight Hellcats from Fighting Squadron 22 intercepted and dispersed up to eighteen fighter-bombers, and destroyed another fourteen when enemy formations attempted to attack a carrier task force.[45]

At the same time, U.S. pilots observed that enemy planes showed higher durability, and the development indicated that the IJNAF had introduced modifications. An excerpt from a combat report stated that a number of Zeros exposed their bellies while breaking away, and tracer fire was seen to bounce off.[46] Another series of accounts stated that very few Zeros had been downed from directly astern, and suggested that back and head protection for the pilot was installed on some machines. However, the intelligence secured through observations did not clearly reveal aircraft designs and armament, and the details could not be ascertained when engaging the enemy at a distance. In July 1944, a technical summary noted how the available information did not permit a precise estimate on the development of new plane types.[47] A suggestion was made that the Japanese did not have the capacity to upgrade their plant facilities and facilitate the production of more modern designs. The inference was based on the fact that a large number of the aircraft captured in the

Pacific theaters were obsolete, and not on hard data concerning the machines actually being assembled. COMINCH could only state, "There is a possibility that some Zeros are equipped with armor protection, although no confirmation is available at this time from actual examination of crashed aircraft."[48] Documentary intelligence did confirm suspicions that the Japanese planned to introduce better airplanes. COMAIRPAC noted how, although Allied units had not sighted a new enemy fighter for several months, a captured document had described how the Japanese had "long been hard-pressed" to catch up with their opponents.[49] Yet without concrete evidence in the form of enemy equipment, the precise characteristics could not be determined.

As a growing number of enemy aircraft were recovered, inspections showed that they were in fact fitted with more powerful weapons and improved armor. The evidence was treated as a strong hint that the Americans faced the possibility of confronting an enhanced challenge. Specimens of the George and Jack navy interceptors mounted several 20-mm cannon, in addition to a number of larger-caliber machine guns.[50] A technical air intelligence summary issued in September 1944 warned, "A new modern air force is in the making that will be a serious threat . . . if the Japanese have sufficient time to realize their program."[51] The quality and design of aircraft were also described to be "excellent." In particular, torpedo bombers such as the Grace and Frances carried larger payloads, and their use on a large scale was deemed to pose a distinct obstacle to the U.S. Navy's operations.

Apprehensions concerning new Japanese machines were not dispelled until concrete data revealed that the IJNAF was unable to rival the technological advancement and performance of the U.S. Navy air arm. Although Japanese fighters were equipped with heavier ordnance, the rate of fire was well below the standard U.S. pattern.[52] Test flights of the new model of the Zero, the Zeke 52, showed that in spite of its maneuverability, it had a significantly lower speed than the F6F and F4U at virtually all altitudes.[53] Following a test of a captured George 11, conducted at Clark Field in the Philippines, the general conclusion was that the plane had an excellent rate of ascent and high speed, but it "did not impress the [test] pilot with the feeling of confidence that one normally gets in a good substantial plane."[54] Inspections of Japanese aircraft therefore provided foolproof confirmation that better construction could not significantly reverse their disadvantages.

While technical intelligence staffs had abundant opportunities to obtain details concerning Japanese aircraft, they were less successful in securing radar devices. Captured planes were often not equipped with the gadgets, and even when they were, Allied technical inspectors found it hard to recover samples. Unlike airframes and engines, search equipment usually did not withstand crash damage. Consequently, a crucial aspect of the IJN air arm, namely, the extent to which its pilots could locate aerial and shipping targets, remained unclear. The Japanese did not appear to have made substantial advances, and their efficiency was affected in two key areas. First, attacks could not be carried out with precision. During the preliminary bombing raids on the Marianas, the standard practice was to have aerial patrols find ships, and thereafter call the bombers into the scene.[55] The raids were rarely concentrated, and in no instance had squadrons shown that they knew the exact position of U.S. task forces. Second, the enemy's poor search capability resulted in an uneconomical use of air power. During a nighttime mission in the Rabaul area, Japanese fighters were reported to pursue their targets aimlessly and patrol certain areas of the sky, waiting for the attacking planes to arrive.[56]

Yet the extent to which the IJN had fitted its planes with search devices was open to speculation. A technical summary issued in February 1944 noted, "So far, no aircraft have revealed the presence of radar equipment."[57] At the same time, enemy maneuvers suggested that devices had been installed on some planes. During the Tarawa operation, bombers approached from distances that were beyond visual contact with the task group, thereby raising the possibility that they had either radar or homing instruments to locate the signals transmitted by U.S. vessels.[58] Commenting on the opposition encountered during the Truk operation, the commanding officer of the *Oakland* noted how enemy pilots were able to locate the task group on a dark night with ease.[59] While the exact reasons could not be ascertained, naval commanders were disposed to concede that a number of Japanese aircraft were equipped with radar, even though the majority were not.[60] As late as 1944, assessments were based on sporadic evidence. The available information did suggest that the technological gap with which the Japanese started the war had been partially closed. Yet in citing evidence for the claim, CINCPAC could only state that radar intercepts had picked up signals of a much higher frequency than previous ones.[61] COMAIRPAC deduced that, in terms of range, Japanese aerial searching was comparable to its Allied counterparts.[62] The statement was based on a combination of assumptions concerning how enemy technology had progressed, and the uncertainty remained largely unresolved for the duration of the conflict. The only definite fact was that the IJNAF had a comparatively late start, and its tactical use of the equipment was lagging. Nevertheless, the U.S. Navy was careful to concede that if their opponent continued with its improvements, U.S. task forces were likely to be subjected to greater levels of destruction.

Technical intelligence staffs also relied on photographs and enemy documents supplied by JICPOA. Oftentimes, the material offered a useful supplement to captured equipment. Blueprints permitted a clear analysis of the Emily, and provided more data than crashed specimens could offer. The plane was not only equipped with 20-mm guns, but also two quarter-inch steel plates behind the pilot and co-pilot, offering better protection for the crew.[63] A document translated by JICPOA supplied one of the first pieces of evidence that the Japanese navy planned to deploy a new type of interceptor, the Raiden, which could climb to almost 30,000 feet in less than fifteen minutes.[64] Photographic reconnaissance also revealed information on the introduction of the Tenzan (Jill) torpedo bomber.[65] Printed material and photographs thus foretold the types of aircraft U.S. forces were likely to encounter.

However, when written evidence revealed information on aircraft that the Allies had not yet engaged, the material provided only a vague hint on how the IJNAF's fighting capabilities could be affected. The problem was apparent when intelligence staffs attempted to predict trends in aero-engine designs. In spring 1944, JICPOA received intelligence suggesting that fighter planes, as well as the Betty and Emily bombers, were being equipped with a new type of power plant, the Kasei, which had a greater propulsion capacity than any of its predecessors.[66] However, the Kasei's performance was ascertained only when specimens were recovered.[67] Again, in November, the TAIC received diagrams that suggested that experiments with more powerful engines were being carried out. Nevertheless, it was "impossible" to foresee if and when they could be produced in mass quantities.[68] Intelligence officials admitted that the only certain conclusion was that changes had taken place, and similar developments needed to be monitored.

Captured documents also described the ideas that influenced the IJNAF's combat methods. The use of surprise and concentrated attacks continued to form the cornerstone of enemy doctrine. A manual translated by JICPOA stated that the main objective of an engagement involving the use of carrier-based aircraft was to deal a "death blow" at the outset, by launching a surprise raid with an "overwhelmingly superior force."[69] Thereafter, a succession of "relentless attacks" was to be carried out to prevent the enemy from regaining the initiative. The document also laid out operational procedures. Torpedo planes commenced the raid, while bombers were to fly in close formation so they could concentrate their machine-gun fire against fighters. Allowance was also made for the various types of opposition that the Japanese could encounter. Combat regulations laid out a variety of scenarios, from situations where antiaircraft and fighter opposition were substantial, to those where friendly forces had attained air supremacy.[70] In instances where enemy ships were able to deliver large amounts of flak, the idea was to minimize the time during which the planes were exposed.[71] To achieve this end, the dives were to be made at short intervals and varying angles, so as to deny the defending forces extra time to adjust their guns. The material highlighted how the Japanese had arranged a meticulous set of instructions for aircrews, and paid painstaking attention to detail.

Nevertheless, the information supplied by captured documents was not comprehensive, mainly because it did not specify whether the stated doctrines were accepted by the entire air service. Naval intelligence took into account how the IJNAF's training program had fallen into disarray. Given the large number of student recruits the Japanese were attempting to process, the main flight instruction schools did not provide all of the necessary preparation. Individual units thus had to set up their own procedures. Commenting on a set of draft battle rules for fighter units, the Pacific Fleet warned that there was little basis for determining whether the tactics applied to any other groups besides the 251st Air Group based at Truk.[72] A more troubling issue was the possibility that the theories committed to writing differed from actual practices. A report on enemy tactics, based on a collection of official documents, was prefaced with a proviso that significant time had lapsed since the material was secured and translated.[73] For this reason, the IJN air arm's concepts may have easily changed as a result of battle lessons learned in the intervening period. Units in a particular area were also not necessarily bound by a prescribed doctrine, and could alter their methods according to their own experiences. The intelligence was considered useful only insofar as it provided a background for the study of Japanese tactics.

Technical intelligence sources, including captured documents and equipment, therefore proved useful on matters such as the characteristics of Japanese aircraft. The material revealed how improvements in designs enabled the IJNAF to exert increased challenges for the U.S. Navy, but in the long run, enemy forces were unable to significantly remedy their substandard endurance and striking power. However, the available intelligence did not allow firm conclusions on other aspects, including the development of radar and aero-engines. The Americans exercised discretion in dealing with the uncertainty, and recognized that the Japanese had taken measures to increase their own fighting capabilities. The doctrines that influenced the IJN air arm's combat methods also remained ambiguous. The Japanese air service's tactical proficiency therefore could not be determined until U.S. forces conducted an extensive series of engagements with enemy forces.

Battle Lessons

U.S. combat personnel supplied the most reliable information on the IJNAF's tactical performance. In addition to the action reports prepared by Navy aviators and ship crews, the accounts provided by Marine air units were a useful source, especially after August 1944, when they were assigned to be based on escort carriers and to conduct strike operations against land targets.[74] Last but not least, USAAF units, operating under the Allied Air Forces, Southwest Pacific Area (AAFSWPA), supplied data on the maneuvers that the Japanese carried out. The available intelligence showed a mixed picture. On the liability side, Japan's supply of qualified pilots suffered a noticeable decline, owing to the casualties accumulated through combat losses and accidents. The situation negated any hope of the Japanese winning the air war. Nevertheless, the IJN air arm still possessed its share of trained crews who were able to carry out skillful maneuvers, and inflict harm on Allied task forces. To complicate the situation, the available intelligence precluded a complete knowledge of the trends governing the IJNAF's methods. Because the organizational ethos of the U.S. Navy and its air service called for concerted measures to understand the difficulties that enemy forces were able to put up, the Americans tended to assess the contradictory, and oftentimes fragmentary, information in a cautious manner. The ultimate aim was to develop effective tactics against the damage that the Japanese were able to cause. Intelligence officials and combat personnel were therefore similarly inclined to recognize that they faced a difficult opponent, and hesitated to conclude that its fighting skills had no prospects of getting better.

Among the most important observations made by U.S. pilots was that a growing proportion of IJN aviators they encountered were not the most competent type. Rear Admiral Osborne Hardison, commanding the South Pacific Fleet air division, noted that during the opening stages of the conflict, the Japanese could be described as the "hounds," and the Americans as the "rabbits."[75] However, the situation during 1943 had reversed, and U.S. aircrews had developed a tactical superiority to the point where, on every mission, they hoped enemy forces would appear and thereby expose more of their aircraft and pilots. Following the Marshall Islands operation, where the Japanese lost three times more aircraft than the U.S. task force, Nimitz wrote in his monthly operational summary that the encounter was "typical of what may be expected in the future."[76]

Yet many Japanese pilots continued to demonstrate their proficiency. The situation was summarized in an ONI bulletin issued in autumn 1943, based on action reports received since the start of the Guadalcanal campaign.[77] Following Midway, there was noticeable deterioration in overall pilot quality. The Japanese often made "glaring tactical mistakes," such as separating their units and thereby losing mutual support. Bomber and fighter crews alike ceased to display the aggressiveness that characterized their earlier techniques. The ONI correctly speculated that the development was due to the depletion of the IJN's talented aviators, coupled with the increasing scale of the air war in the Pacific, both of which required the Japanese to remedy their losses expeditiously and rely on inexperienced men. Yet while the shortage of aircrews was one of Japan's "gravest handicaps," the IJN still possessed its share of skilled personnel, and naval intelligence warned that the Allies had no justification to become overconfident. The only reassurance was that operations against the Japanese were unlikely to encounter the same level of opposition as during the early stages of the conflict. At the highest levels of the intelligence machinery, the JIC expressed a similar wariness. During the latter part of 1943 and early 1944, the Japanese had shown a "more striking ineptitude in the employment of their available air strength than at any previous time during the war."[78] Nevertheless, because a large part of the IJNAF had not engaged in extensive operations, it still possessed a pool of better trained pilots that could be placed in frontline units.[79] While the Japanese were bound to incur further manpower losses, even in early 1944 the shortage of crews had not been a "serious limiting factor." The IJNAF remained active, and continued to put up opposition, albeit on a diminished scale.

In regard to the particulars of fighter tactics, U.S. pilots noted how their opponents showed less determination. One fighter ace recalled how he noticed the dramatic rise in the kill ratios achieved by his squadron. Whereas during the early stages of the war, when the Japanese were "extremely tough," the proportion was only 5-to-1, at Palau and Hollandia it more than doubled.[80] Airmen who carried out air raids against Truk observed that on the few instances when Japanese fighters appeared, their attacks were not pressed home with anything more than a "half-hearted purpose."[81] As a result, the F6Fs were able to "clean the air of enemy opposition," leaving the dive-bombers and torpedo planes free to concentrate on shipping targets.

Yet on many occasions, aviators reported that their opponents were fully capable of putting up a challenge. Naval intelligence tended to pay heed to the IJNAF's continued demonstration of tactical talent, as evidenced by the dissemination of a large number of reports that highlighted this feature. The Japanese demonstrated their skill at taking advantage of their aircraft's maneuverability. On a mission over the Solomons area, Fighting Squadron 17 encountered a bomber formation covered by Zekes disposed all the way around it. When attacked, the fighters dispersed in several directions to intercept the approaching planes. Japanese pilots proved that they were by no means easy opponents, and were credited for handling their planes "beautifully."[82] Against heavy bomber aircraft such as the B-24, enemy crews carried out aerobatic maneuvers, including loops, slow rolls, and corkscrew dives.[83] During one operation over New Guinea, Zekes launched high frontal attacks, diving toward the B-24s at angles of 60 to 75 degrees, and from sectors where U.S. aircraft were unable to deliver their machine-gun fire. The interception was described as a "brilliant display" of Japanese tactics.[84] Pilots encountered over Rabaul were "more expert, determined, and combative" than those engaged in the Solomons.[85] Among the most notable moves was a concentrated attack on bombers, with the main targets being stragglers and planes flying out of formation. The Japanese also showed a "first-class" knowledge of American weaving tactics, and made their runs when the planes were furthest apart and not in a position to provide mutual support. Japanese gunnery showed greater accuracy, while the ability to conduct sharp turns and climbs had not declined.[86] Aerial opposition collapsed only at the end of nine weeks of bombing, and even then, only after the IJN's source of reinforcements at Truk had been subjected to a sustained assault.[87] U.S. aircrews perceived the lessons of combat experience as a stern warning against expecting weak resistance. Captain David McCampbell, commanding VF-15 on the carrier *Essex*, recalled how, as a precautionary measure, he assumed all enemy pilots to be of equal ability, since he could never tell when he would encounter a "topnotch airman."[88]

Toward the latter stages of the conflict, from mid-1944 to summer 1945, one of the most outstanding aspects was the increasing disparity in the flying skill of Japanese pilots. U.S. aircrews hesitated to dismiss the IJNAF's capacity to put up obstacles, since they did not have full details of its skill or the doctrines it followed, and the opposition witnessed varied from one U.S. squadron to another. Following the Battle of the Philippine Sea, most aviators concluded that the Japanese were no longer of full combat quality.[89] The most basic defensive measures, such as providing fighter cover for bombers, appeared to be neglected. Judys were mostly dispersed, making them "most vulnerable."[90] The Zekes and Hamps attempted to fight off the F6Fs only when attacked.[91] Even when enemy forces outnumbered their attackers by 2-to-1, their tactics were "erratic and disorganized," with pilots showing a reluctance to carry through with their pursuits.[92] Yet one squadron commander, based on the *Bunker Hill*, described his opponents as "the most skillful yet encountered" by his unit.[93] Hamp fighters made sharp nose-down turns into formations of Hellcats, thus requiring the latter to take frequent evasive measures.

Aircrews also noted how the Japanese failed to coordinate their maneuvers, and did not achieve sufficient teamwork. At Palau, while some planes attempted to intercept, once they were scattered, pilots seemed to have "no idea of joining up for mutual protection, and lost all apparent interest in offensive action, each apparently interested only in saving [himself]."[94] During the preliminary assaults on the Philippines, air squadrons flying over Clark

Field noted how the Japanese did not concentrate their fighter strength, with the planes carrying out individual attacks that were not very effective.[95] After making a failed attempt at interception, enemy pilots often preferred to escape rather than position themselves for another shot. The operational use of air forces revealed how the IJN suffered an acute shortage of crews. At Leyte, in an effort to concentrate their planes, the Japanese teamed up their ship-borne units with land-based units on Luzon prior to the operation.[96] As a result, U.S. planes attacking the carrier force met what was described as a "scanty" level of opposition.

At the same time, the IJNAF continued to fight effectively on many occasions, and the Americans remained alert to the dangers they had to cope with. In particular, the Japanese maintained their capacity to use camouflage and deception. Zeke pilots encountered during the air raids on Iwo Jima took evasive action by heading toward the direction of the sun and cloud cover to conceal their movements.[97] In the Philippines, enemy crews utilized their familiarity with the terrain to fly up ravines and valleys, thus enabling them to blend in with the landscape.[98]

The operations carried against the Japanese Home Islands during 1945 often encountered a level of opposition that raised concern. Following an attack on Kure naval base, Marine aviators from VMF-123 described their counterparts as "anything but scrub league."[99] Immediately after reaching the coast of Honshu, the Corsairs were pursued from the rear, with enemy planes surrounding the formation and attacking from all directions. The marksmanship and flying skill were "as fine as the squadron had ever seen." A Marine squadron that raided airfields in the Hiroshima area reported that a formation of thirty enemy aircraft made an overhead pass in a "very professional manner," with two-plane sections making coordinated attacks.[100] An air captain wrote in his official report, "Enemy pilots were aggressive," and showed the same skill as they had at Guadalcanal.[101] The incidents indicated that the Japanese were aiming to conserve their dwindling reserve of qualified aircrews for a last-ditch defense of the mainland. U.S. personnel therefore had to take adequate precautions. During an attack on Kyushu, pilots based on the *Hornet* did not attempt to pursue the Zekes that tried to escape, out of fear that by doing so the squadron would have ended up breaking its defensive position and exposing itself to dogfights in which the Japanese were likely to hold the advantage.[102] As far as U.S. Navy aviators were concerned, the only reassurance was that the average quality of their enemy's aircrews had substantially declined and, as a fighting force, the IJNAF could not compete with its Allied counterparts. Yet a further depletion of skilled pilots could not be achieved unless the Americans carried out sustained attacks.

Enemy raids against ship targets also remained a matter of significant concern during the campaigns in the Pacific theater. Again, because full details on the general trends that governed bombardment methods were not available, U.S. personnel refrained from disparaging their opponent. By 1943, intelligence officials in Washington accumulated enough information to formulate a knowledgeable assessment. Although enemy tactics demonstrated some weaknesses, they had the potential to cause considerable damage. The ONI air intelligence group prepared a statistical summary that showed that at most altitudes the Japanese achieved a significantly lower proportion of hits than those that U.S. air attacks had attained.[103] Yet the information was not deemed conclusive enough to arrive at a firm conclusion that the IJNAF's techniques were inferior.

Furthermore, Japanese pilots were expected to learn from their mistakes. For example, torpedo planes often made a slow and straight approach, and made themselves vulnerable to antiaircraft fire.[104] The failure to provide adequate fighter support caused further losses. Likewise, dive-bombing techniques, while effective, were not exceptional, since planes did not hit their targets when faced with fighter opposition. At the same time, prior combat experience was seen as a good reason to believe that enemy forces were adept at striking targets in the open sea. The Japanese had coordinated the deployment of their various types of bombers, and the sinking of the *Hornet* during the Guadalcanal campaign was cited as an excellent example of the efficiency that the IJNAF could achieve. Although rapid innovations were rare, since pilots were not taught to use individual initiative, over a longer period changes were frequent. The relative lack of success that aircrews had achieved in striking U.S. vessels during the early part of 1943 was most likely to convince them to devote a considerable effort to reform their anti-shipping tactics.

Equally impressive were Japanese attempts to alleviate the disadvantages they suffered through their lack of radar equipment. In the area of search and communications, maneuvers were carried out effectively. The Air Information

Division referred to the report of a U.S. carrier that engaged in the Solomons, which stated, "At all times the enemy seemed to have no difficulty in finding our forces. . . . Their reconnaissance, [along with] the communication of contact reports by submarines or patrol planes, must have been excellent."[105] During night attacks, when visibility was limited, the common practice was to guide the bombers by saturating the target area with parachute flares and float lights. Reconnaissance actions did not end with the air raid. Oftentimes, scouts were kept close to the target in order to keep contact. U.S. planes, after beating off a raid, failed to find all of the snoopers, thus leaving task forces open to further shadowing and a renewed attack. The operational plan for the attacks on Japanese shipping in the Shortland Islands area was based on the assumption that detection by enemy forces prior to the mission was "highly probable," owing to the efficient manner in which they had previously carried out their missions.[106]

The Japanese also resorted to radar countermeasures (RCM), in an attempt to lessen the search capabilities of U.S. vessels. During an operation in the vicinity of New Ireland and Rabaul in February 1944, a task force consisting of the destroyers *Charles Ausburne*, *Claxton*, and *Dyson* reported that enemy planes dropped reflecting devices known as "phantoms." Blips appeared on the screens and concealed the approaching aircraft for up to twelve minutes.[107] COMAIRPAC concluded that phantom was an "excellent radar deception device," since it was capable of producing reflections over a wide frequency band. If the Japanese used phantom extensively, the size and number of false echoes could render large portions of the indicator scopes useless.[108] Because actual targets could not be easily distinguished from phantoms, radar operators needed to undergo extra training to identify enemy aircraft. Ship crews also reported that the enemy was using metal strips, more commonly known as "window." When the Japanese were first observed using window during spring 1944, the initial impression was that it did not cause confusion.[109] Window was often dropped haphazardly, and personnel who were alert to the blips could easily recognize the bogies. However, during the Marianas campaign, the enemy achieved good results. At Saipan, window affected the *Wasp*'s air search radars on several occasions.[110] Japanese planes dropped their chaff while orbiting the task force, and left the infected area only to attack from a different direction. In light of the increased frequency and skill with which RCM were being employed, CINCPAC warned that the Japanese were "ingenious and resourceful," and they had to be expected to make every effort to improve their ways of alleviating whatever advantages the Pacific Fleet accrued from its superior radar equipment.[111] Naval commanders conceded that they did not have full details concerning the types of equipment that the Japanese were developing, and for this reason, the safer option was to anticipate improvements.

The threat posed by Japanese RCM was dismissed only after a series of encounters proved that it was incapable of creating significant interference. At Okinawa, the Japanese did not achieve anything close to a complete saturation of radar, and their efforts at deceptive tactics were described as "more of a nuisance."[112] Even in instances when window was used in large quantities, the Japanese dropped them without coordinating their maneuvers. Attacking planes did not attempt to mask their approach by circling the infected area, but continued to cross while leaving the trail of window behind them. Japanese pilots had failed to develop an effective doctrine for employing RCM, and assumed that the mere dropping of window would help them evade combat air patrols and antiaircraft fire.[113]

Japanese bombing techniques, on the other hand, raised apprehensions for the duration of the conflict. Observations of the IJNAF's performance during the operations carried out against island positions between late 1943 and mid-1944 reinforced the U.S. Navy's perception that enemy pilots had a high level of aptitude. The majority of attacks did not score hits, mainly because task forces enjoyed the advantages of fighter protection, coupled with improved antiaircraft defenses. Some commanders were prepared to conclude that the IJNAF could no longer sink many vessels. During the Marshalls campaign, the commanding officer of the cruiser *Portland* reported that even with bright moonlight, enemy planes did not launch a single coordinated attack on the task group.[114] However, most naval officers emphasized how enemy planes frequently missed their objectives by a dangerously narrow margin. Commenting on the Rabaul operation, the commander of the *Essex* noted that while the task force suffered minimal damage, enemy dive-bombers and torpedo planes did reach their attack positions, and dropped their ordnance at a close distance to the carrier decks.[115]

Due attention was also paid to the possibility that the Japanese could vary their methods, and thereby carry out more devastating raids. As was the case when U.S. crews evaluated enemy fighter tactics, they could not foretell whether skilled pilots were likely to be encountered. For this reason, assessments on the matter tended to urge vigilance. The commander of Task Force 50 concluded that if the enemy had fought in a more synchronized manner at Tarawa, and attacked simultaneously from several directions, a large number of vessels could have been hit.[116] Rear Admiral Arthur Radford, who commanded the Gilberts invasion force, warned that the Japanese were getting better at nighttime torpedo-bombing.[117] In future operations, task force leaders had to assume that the Japanese would profit from their own failures. The IJN air arm relied heavily on torpedo planes to defend island positions, and such attacks constituted the major threat to surface task forces.[118] The U.S. Navy therefore had to give an "immediate and searching analysis" to the problem, so that a workable set of countermeasures could be introduced.

The IJN air arm's poor performance in a particular operation was therefore not taken as a sign that the U.S. Navy was likely to face minimal dangers in future encounters. During the bombardment raids prior to the Marianas operation, the Japanese did not counterattack with torpedo planes under the cover of darkness, and daylight actions consisted mainly of uncoordinated raids. However, the commanding officer of the *Essex* warned, "It would be dangerous to accept as a precedent the lack of quality displayed."[119] On the contrary, the safest assumption was that the U.S. task force had caught the enemy off guard. Following their successful attempt at repelling Japanese attacks during the Philippine Sea encounter, pilots reported to combat air intelligence officers that enemy dive-bomber and torpedo plane crews were "loath to keep their defensive formations, and separated, thus losing all chances of scoring hits."[120] Yet ship-based personnel concluded that the Japanese were capable of doing better. The commanding officer of the battleship *Alabama* noted how the raids were made by separate formations flying in widely spaced waves. Had the same number of planes been concentrated, they could have saturated the air defenses of the U.S. vessels and caused much heavier losses.[121]

As the Pacific Fleet began to operate closer to the Home Islands, the Japanese were expected to put up significantly greater resistance to protect the heart of their empire. In July 1944, COMAIRPAC warned that while enemy forces were visibly inferior, the situation was unlikely to continue if they modified their techniques. Aircraft carriers remained vulnerable when the IJNAF attacked in an organized fashion, and for this reason overconfidence was not justified.[122] Due attention was also paid to the fact that the skills of Japanese aircrews varied widely from one unit to another. For example, in response to Admiral Mitscher's suggestion in September that the IJN had lost virtually its entire remaining pool of trained pilots following the strikes on the Formosa-Luzon area, Halsey maintained that he was not convinced that U.S. task forces were likely to encounter decreased opposition. Observations of enemy forces had shown that they consisted of a disparate mixture of various plane types, thereby indicating that the IJNAF was facing troubles in organizing proper air units.[123] However, there was little evidence to confirm that the Japanese were categorically incompetent.

The conviction that the IJN possessed its share of trained crews was also confirmed by action reports. IJNAF pilots exploited the weak spots in their opponent's defenses. At Leyte, a destroyer commander remarked how, owing to the American pilots' reluctance to conduct patrol missions under the cover of darkness, enemy forces often had air supremacy after sundown.[124] The Japanese used the opportunity to attack escort carriers from the moment fighter cover was reduced. Although intruders seldom caused damage, they "made the night hideous with red alerts and antiaircraft fire." Aviators also made good use of concealment. Torpedo aircraft attacking Task Group 38.4 during the preliminary bombardment missions on Luzon approached at low altitudes, and used the rain squall to hide their presence.[125] That the task force escaped damage was attributed to good fortune. In another mission against the Home Islands, one of the most effective Japanese tactics was to launch surprise attacks from areas affected by cloud cover and directly over the U.S. task force.[126] The move was often undertaken when carriers were launching their planes, and made good use of the fact that radar screens became saturated with friendly aircraft to the point where operators could not identify enemy forces.

The advent of kamikaze attacks during the closing stages of the Pacific War further highlighted the enemy's ability to create significant troubles for naval units that were not adequately protected. In judging the threat posed by kamikaze pilots, U.S. personnel tended to focus on the damage they inflicted, but also tried to understand the mindset that motivated the Japanese to undertake suicide raids. The key aim was to realistically gauge the threats that the Pacific Fleet faced, so that suitable countermeasures could be developed. The move initially did appear to entail a reckless expenditure of dwindling resources at a stage when Japan's defeat was only a matter of time. While kamikaze aircraft caused high casualties when they scored hits, they could not sink a large proportion of U.S. ships.[127] Commenting on the losses suffered by the destroyer pickets at Okinawa, Nimitz concluded, "We can produce destroyers faster than they [the Japanese] can build planes."[128] The *Baka* suicide rocket also proved ineffective, since the parent plane was vulnerable to both defending fighters and antiaircraft fire.[129]

Historical accounts have explained how the decision to resort to kamikaze tactics reflected a desperate effort on the part of the Japanese naval command to change the course of the conflict.[130] The Sho (victory) operations were to rely on suicide attacks to destroy U.S. task forces as they approached the Philippines; however, the ever-quickening tempo of the Allied offensive allowed little time for adequate preparations, either in terms of amassing aircraft or the training of aircrews.[131] The 201st Air Corps of the First Air Fleet was assigned to execute the operation to defend Leyte, and staff officers were told, "The situation is so grave that the fate of the empire depends on the outcome of the Sho operation." Japanese commanders judged that, given their shortage of aircraft, conventional methods were unlikely to achieve results, and suicide crash-dives offered the only viable solution.[132] Moreover, the initial sorties were often flown by experienced pilots, since novice airmen were considered incapable of striking their targets. The result was a further diminution of what little remained in Japan's pool of qualified aviators.[133] As the IJN's supply of aircraft and crews began to dwindle, it had to enlist the help of army aviators, as well as volunteers, neither of whom had the skill to hit naval vessels in the open sea. Yet while both branches of the Japanese military were committed to cooperate in fighting the Americans, navy pilots continued to be assigned to attack warships, while the army concentrated on convoys and troop carriers.[134] The latter were easier targets, owing to their relatively weak antiaircraft defenses, and pilots required less training. Toward the end of the Okinawa operation, Japanese forces were running so short of their reserves of fuel, aircraft, and pilots that Imperial General Headquarters in Tokyo ordered the majority of suicide planes to be withdrawn, and held in readiness to meet the expected invasion of the Home Islands.[135]

However, in terms of their ability to harm task forces in the short term, kamikaze attacks did provide a relatively economical weapon, since pilots could achieve a higher ratio of hits than in conventional raids. Tactics were also planned in detail, and pilots learned that certain methods worked better than others.[136] Approaches were made either at extremely high or low altitudes, in order to evade radar detection. Against carriers, the best points of aim were the deck elevators, since their destruction ensured that the vessel would be disabled from launching its aircraft.

U.S. naval commanders were apt to view suicide raids as an effective tactic, rather than belittle them as an irrational act. Nimitz observed how kamikaze planes provided the Japanese with a valuable weapon, because they could be intentionally guided against their targets until the moment of impact.[137] Likewise, Spruance recalled how, once committed to an attack, the planes were fast and maneuverable, so that a ship of any size had "little chance" of evading a hit.[138] In a postwar memoir, Halsey wrote that he was confident that U.S. forces could deal with suicide attacks, but admitted, "I would be a damn fool to pretend that individual kamikazes did not scare me for a moment."[139]

Likewise, task force leaders who participated in the Philippines campaign credited kamikaze pilots for achieving considerable results. Commenting on the Lingayen Gulf operation, the commander of Battleship Squadron 1 noted how most pilots conducted evasive maneuvers when faced by antiaircraft fire.[140] Stealth and surprise were also noticeable elements. Instead of flying directly toward the objective, planes often flew a course that appeared to be directed toward a nearby ship. Thereafter, at a short range from the apparent target, pilots suddenly changed course by banking steeply toward the selected vessels. Attacks were also carried out with a view to preventing ships from opening their batteries in a timely manner, by concealing planes in cloud cover, or exploiting the low visibility that prevailed during dawn and dusk.[141] Another common move was to use several planes against a single ship, in an effort to overwhelm the antiaircraft defenses. At Iwo Jima, a squadron of four planes approached from the same sector simultaneously, yet maintained enough separation to compel gun crews to disperse their flak.[142] The situation was further complicated because kamikaze pilots did not appear to follow a consistent tactic, and methods were adapted in accordance with the opposition encountered. Early action reports reported that while some planes headed for the ship's stern to avoid antiaircraft fire, others approached from the bow or other angles. Approaches were reported at altitudes ranging from fifty feet up to eight thousand feet, with aircraft engaging in violent evasive maneuvers and straightening out only when committed to their targets. Methods of diving varied from those carried out vertically to a low approach.

Of equal importance, when viewed in light of cost-benefit ratios, suicide raids entailed a minimal expenditure of resources, since a single plane could potentially sink or disable a large vessel such as an aircraft carrier or battleship.[143] Top-ranking admirals noted how more warships had been sunk by kamikaze attacks during the three months of the Philippines operations than had been lost or damaged in all of the previous naval battles, including Pearl Harbor.[144] Even when they did not sink ships, kamikaze planes could substantially damage the fighting capabilities of U.S. forces. The carrier *Ticonderoga* reported having lost half of its defensive capacity after its antiaircraft director and a large number of its guns had been hit.[145]

Finally, the training of kamikaze units was not a complicated task. Although documentary evidence on the attitudes that led enemy pilots to embark on suicide missions did not become available until after the war, U.S. personnel did note how cultural factors placed the Japanese in a favorable position to create a large pool of dedicated crews. As a matter of fact, a large portion of the personnel in the special attack forces (*tokkotai*) stoically accepted suicide, owing to deep-seated religious and patriotic convictions. Airmen were ordered to recite the parts of the Imperial Rescript to soldiers and sailors that emphasized loyalty and an unquestioning acceptance of orders from higher authorities.[146] The primary motivation was to die in what Japanese traditions viewed as the most glorious act of sacrifice. Nevertheless, most pilots claimed to be driven by more practical concerns, and the belief that one needed to sacrifice his life in order to safeguard the Japanese nation. The recruits consisted mainly of university students, who were not fully aware that they were signing up for suicide squadrons until after they reported to the training base. Writings left behind by volunteers reveal that an important reason to go forward, when informed of their mission, was a sense of admiration for those who did join the *tokkotai*, and a strong desire not to protect their own lives while they saw their comrades offering theirs.[147] A Pacific Fleet summary explained that while it appeared illogical for the enemy to whittle away its qualified pilots in suicide missions, the Imperial forces had been known for resorting to similar measures, such as the use of human torpedoes.[148] The most salient fact was that Japanese traditions demanded combat personnel to put on a constant show of valor. For this reason, pilots were more prepared to undertake moves that entailed self-sacrifice than their Western counterparts.

Because the Japanese appeared well placed to carry out kamikaze attacks on a larger scale, intelligence personnel judged that the Pacific Fleet needed to be fully informed on the dangers it faced. As early as November 1944, the head of the *Wasp*'s CIC team suggested that information on suicide tactics be vigorously disseminated in order to familiarize ship crews who had not yet encountered them.[149] Yet until the Okinawa campaign, the U.S. Navy was not prepared to encounter kamikaze attacks on a large scale. Most Americans could not comprehend the extent to which the Japanese were willing to forfeit human lives. Enemy forces were known to be committed to defending their key island bastions in every possible way. U.S. commanders were also apprehensive of what the Japanese could do to their task forces, since the operation was scheduled to take place within proximity of the Home Islands, where enemy forces had several airfields, as well as an estimated three thousand planes.[150] Nor was there any reason to downplay the possibility that enemy forces could perfect their methods. Nevertheless, most naval personnel were not aware of the intensity or length of time with which the suicide attacks were to continue.[151] Nor did they believe that enough recruits could be mustered to make the kamikaze corps an effective fighting force.[152] Experiences during the opening phases of the Okinawa operation also created misperceptions. During the preparatory raid on the Kerama archipelago, almost seven hundred enemy planes were shot down, with only a handful of U.S. destroyers and ammunition ships sunk. The statistics indicated that kamikazes were no longer as lethal as they had been in the Philippines, and intelligence estimates concluded that the Imperial air forces' strengths were reaching the end of their tether.[153]

Encounters at Okinawa showed the U.S. Navy that kamikaze attacks could be conducted in a coordinated manner, and on a magnitude that created significant destruction. The Japanese also conducted their raids with increased aggressiveness. Only a negligible number of sorties failed to locate the target area, and few planes were seen to have turned back after encountering CAPs or antiaircraft opposition. The rise in the number of ships damaged and sunk was attributed to the fact that kamikaze planes were employed in larger numbers than at Leyte and Lingayen.[154] To complicate the situation, suicide raids were far from "static," and were continually adjusted, with the tactics employed depending largely on the individual pilot.[155] While new methods could not be foreseen, a number of common characteristics could be discerned. Isolated ships that were weakly supported proved particularly vulnerable, and the attrition suffered by destroyers reached a serious magnitude.[156] Planes operating in small groups were reported to have been detected on various bearings. While some units turned away, others dropped to the water to attack from low altitudes.[157] This form of raid was most difficult to destroy with combat air patrols, since enemy planes were dispersed over a wide area.

The intensity with which the Japanese carried out kamikaze raids during the Okinawa campaign provided ominous indications of the catastrophes that U.S. forces could face during their invasion of the Home Islands. Although enemy air strengths were expected to be substantially depleted through preliminary raids, the JIC predicted that all available aircraft would be committed to the "full limit of Japanese capabilities, and without regard to the further conservation of strength."[158] During the early phase of the operation, enemy forces were expected to have the capacity to make a maximum effort, consisting of approximately two hundred to three hundred sorties daily. As long as Japan possessed reserve of aircraft, their employment in suicide missions was to be expected. Although the attacks were likely to diminish as the Japanese expended the remnants of their strength, the damage that the Allied task forces could incur remained open to conjecture, and a matter of grave concern.

Conclusion

As was the case when the U.S. Navy evaluated the IJN's surface fleet, intelligence efforts concerning the naval air arm were largely shaped by prevailing concepts on how the Japanese were to be dealt with. Strategic thinking placed a paramount importance on destroying enemy air power, so that task forces could be protected as they advanced across large expanses of ocean. Any evidence of the IJNAF's capacity to inflict damage was therefore likely to be closely examined. The available information permitted a more extensive assessment than was the case with the Imperial Japanese fleet. The ONI, along with the organizations operating at the theater level, drew upon a wide range of technical sources, including captured equipment and documents. The material was useful for determining the performance and design features of Japanese planes. Although the Japanese managed to introduce new aircraft designs with improved firepower, durability, and speed, reliable pieces of evidence confirmed that the IJNAF was unable to compete with its Allied counterparts in terms of quality. Technical information proved less helpful in supplying qualitative data, especially on matters such as the ideas that shaped the enemy's combat techniques. U.S. naval intelligence was careful to note that it did not have the knowledge to formulate a thorough evaluation, and warned that a vigilant watch had to be maintained on the IJN air arm's activities.

Firsthand observations of the IJNAF's performance in battle provided the most concrete information concerning the challenges it was able to pose for the Americans, as well as weaknesses that were open to exploitation. At the same time, U.S. intelligence staffs and combat personnel were apt to recognize the difficulties involved in obtaining data on the main trends of the enemy's doctrine, and exercised caution when assessing its capabilities. As the Pacific War progressed, Japanese pilots showed a visibly diminished level of flying skill, and did not fight with the aggressiveness and determination they did previously. The situation suggested that the Imperial Navy's air arm could not replace the manpower losses it had incurred. Nevertheless, on many occasions, most notably during the operations against the Gilbert and Marshall Islands, and the aerial assault on Rabaul, U.S. airmen and naval crews reported that they continued to encounter opponents who were able to put up tough resistance. Fighter pilots carried out attacks on air formations with a good amount of aerobatic skill, while bombing attacks on task forces often missed their targets only by a narrow margin. The available intelligence also did not permit firm conclusions as to whether further combat losses could bring about the complete elimination of Japan's supply of skilled pilots, or whether the IJNAF was likely to improve its tactical methods. The Pacific Fleet showed a reluctance to dismiss the dangers it faced, and assessments were based on the understanding that U.S. forces needed to prepare for a variety of scenarios. Although the defeats suffered by the Japanese during the Marianas campaign demonstrated how they had lost the capacity to forestall

the Allied advance, the U.S. naval establishment did not lapse into complacency. On the contrary, commanders became apprehensive that as the Pacific
Fleet began operating in areas within closer proximity to the Home Islands,
they were likely to encounter larger scales of opposition. The challenges posed
by kamikaze attacks during the Philippines campaign, and later at Okinawa,
highlighted the extent to which the IJNAF was still able to use its dwindling
resources to inflict attrition on its opponents.

U.S. intelligence organizations, along with personnel within the Pacific
Fleet, did use their available information in an effectual manner. Technical
intelligence sources on the performance and design features of enemy aircraft
were collated to put forward a comprehensive collection of data on virtually every plane the Japanese produced. On other matters, most notably the
IJNAF's doctrine, intelligence staffs accepted the fact that the available material did not permit firm conclusions. Firsthand observations of the Japanese
naval air service's combat performance, which showed a mixed picture of its
fighting capabilities, were analyzed in a calibrated manner. Moreover, the
lack of firm evidence concerning the number of skilled pilots and aircraft
that the Japanese possessed, and future trends of their tactical doctrine, was
treated as an indication that their capacity to put up a challenge could not
be entirely dismissed. Assessments of the IJNAF therefore reflected a widespread aspiration on the part of the American naval establishment to create a
balanced estimate of the situation it had to confront.

5

Knowledge of the Enemy Applied

THE EVOLUTION OF U.S. NAVAL AIR COMBAT DOCTRINE

For U.S. naval crews and aviators, the evidence pointing to the IJNAF's combat capabilities not only indicated that they needed to develop effective defenses against aerial attacks. More importantly, the changing nature of the opposition put up by the Japanese required the Pacific Fleet to undertake corresponding adjustments. For the purpose of devising ways to fight the IJN air arm, frontline personnel managed most stages of the intelligence process, including the collection and analysis of data, as well as implementing the material into a working set of combat procedures. Action reports frequently provided a detailed explanation of battle lessons and the tactics that worked to defeat the Japanese. The intelligence services were more involved in disseminating information. The ONI's air intelligence group propagated the lessons collated via COMAIRPAC and CINCPAC headquarters. The intelligence division of the office of the chief of naval operations also periodically issued summaries on subjects such as antiaircraft defense and fighter cover.

By late 1943, the Pacific Fleet was able to identify the various maneuvers that the Japanese air services habitually carried out against shipping targets and in aerial battles. In regard to the interrelation between intelligence and fighting techniques, the U.S. Navy had created a large part of its armaments and ways of their use either prior to or during the early stages of the Pacific War. American military thinking had called for defeating enemy forces by relying heavily on material and technological prowess. The key components of the Navy air arm's arsenal, including high performance fighters such as the Corsair and Hellcat, as well as radar-controlled fighter direction systems, signified this doctrine. The development of advanced equipment and methods of their use was motivated by a recognition of the need to fight an intensified campaign. For this reason, intelligence on the IJN air arm did not initially play a decisive role in shaping tactical doctrine and weapons. Rather, the information helped the U.S. Navy amend its ways of using its resources.

In attempting to improve their own performance, the Americans faced two key challenges, the first of which was to figure out how to defeat a resilient adversary that proved capable of introducing modifications in its aircraft and fighting techniques. The U.S. Navy's concepts concerning the conduct of warfare had a marked influence on the manner in which it applied its understanding of the IJNAF. Naval doctrine stipulated that the fleet needed to secure control of the airspace over the areas where it operated. Fighters and antiaircraft guns were to prevent enemy aircraft from menacing surface ships. Air forces also had to eliminate the opponent's interceptors, so that friendly units could carry out their operations without facing formidable opposition. The Americans thus had a clear vision of the objectives to be achieved at the battlefront level. Naval commanders also continued to insist that disproportionate casualties had to be averted by all possible means, and were therefore well placed to keep a vigilant watch on the elements they needed to confront in a prolonged and intensified campaign. Ship-based officers and aviators were constantly requested to reform their procedures so that they could cope with the threats that the IJN air arm was known to pose. The shortage of accurate intelligence on many aspects of Japanese fighting capabilities was also perceived as a sign that the Americans needed to prepare for a variety of scenarios. Tactics were developed while paying due attention to evidence indicating that in spite of the IJNAF's declining strengths and tactical skill, it continued to show a good level of efficiency, and the possibility of encountering strong resistance could not be ruled out. The Pacific Fleet therefore tended to avoid getting rid of its apprehensions concerning the Japanese air service until its own forces had proven their competence.

A second, and equally important, problem was that while U.S. personnel comprehended the measures needed to fight the IJNAF, their weapons did not offer a complete remedy. In regard to antiaircraft defenses, radar equipment was not designed to detect the low-altitude and high-speed attacks that the Japanese often carried out. As a result, battery crews were often unable to direct accurate fire against their targets. The U.S. Navy's capacity to employ its fighter defenses, on the other hand, made significant progress, thanks to the introduction of more modern planes, coupled with the development of tactics that worked to shoot down formations with greater success. Aircrews also learned how to conduct preemptive strikes against Japanese airfields and thereby destroy enemy aircraft before they could be brought into action. However, the Pacific Fleet's fighter control system frequently failed to vector the planes properly toward the attackers, owing to inadequate radar and communications equipment. The intelligence pointing to the challenges posed by the IJN air arm thus did not always give rise to an immediate upgrading of the U.S. Navy's capabilities. Technological changes frequently took several months to implement on a large scale. In other cases, the Americans did not have the resources to introduce new weapons. Instead, personnel were requested to deploy their weapons and manpower more skillfully. The efforts undertaken to combat kamikaze attacks during late 1944 and early 1945 illustrated a key example of this aspect.

Evolution of the U.S. Navy's Antiaircraft Defense Capabilities

Toward the middle stages of the conflict, the intelligence gained through combat experience enabled the Pacific Fleet to prescribe a set of actions that antiaircraft personnel could follow in order to deal with the IJNAF's most common maneuvers. Although the tactical skill of Japanese aircrews had shown a marked downturn, on many occasions U.S. vessels came dangerously close to being hit. Among the main elements that received attention was the manner in which the Japanese executed a variety of moves, including torpedo bombing, dive-bombing, and horizontal bombing raids, all of which required gunnery crews to use different countermeasures. Enemy forces also showed a preference for fighting at night and taking advantage of the limited visibility afforded by the darkness. The U.S. Navy's overall aim was to use its matériel in an economical manner, and bring down planes without unnecessarily expending its ammunition. Equally important was to reduce the damage that the IJN air arm could cause. Yet naval commanders conceded that the necessary procedures often could not be executed. The main problem was that in spite of significant advances, U.S. industries and technical facilities lacked the capacity to produce large quantities of the advanced equipment required to neutralize enemy bombers. In particular, fire-control radar did not consistently provide accurate bearings. In terms of fighting proficiency, a large proportion of personnel found themselves unprepared, owing to the shortage of opportunities to carry out exercises. The difficulties were circumvented through the improvised use of the U.S. Navy's available resources.

The Pacific Fleet's antiaircraft doctrine prescribed a number of tactics that were effective against the Japanese. PAC-10 (Current Tactical Orders and Doctrine, U.S. Pacific Fleet), issued in June 1943, laid out general rules.[1] Against dive-bombing and torpedo attacks, where planes closed in at low altitudes, the best method was to open fire as soon as the attackers reached the firing range of batteries and deliver the maximum volume of flak. Horizontal bombers, on the other hand, approached at high elevations, in which case only the longest-range batteries, such as the 5-inch gun, were likely to work.

Nevertheless, the Navy did not have the equipment and skilled manpower to fully transform its doctrine into practice. Antiaircraft weaponry consisted of three standard guns, including the 5-inch, 38-caliber dual-purpose battery, the Swedish 40-mm Bofors cannon, and the Swiss 20-mm Oerlikon. The armament had been built for the general purpose of dealing with air attacks, and virtually every vessel was fitted with a mixed complement of these devices. The 38-caliber, with a range of ten miles and a 30,000-foot ceiling, combined with a capacity to fire up to fifteen rounds per minute, provided the most reliable defense for fast carrier forces. To alleviate the problems arising from the swift maneuvers that Japanese pilots carried out, the Americans used a proximity, or variable-time fuse, shell, which was equipped with a radio transmitter at the head that could gauge the distance from the target before detonating.[2] Gunnery crews were able to fire at the approximate vicinity of enemy planes and still disable them. The 40-mm was the preferred weapon, since it could be used in mounts consisting of up to four guns, and each gun was capable of firing 160 two-pound projectiles per minute, although the maximum rate was never achieved because the batteries were loaded manually.[3] However, the 40-mm was not available in large numbers until the latter stages of the war. The majority of guns were of the 20-mm type. Its main advantage was the capacity to deliver short-range and high-frequency fire, but the projectiles were too small to take down aircraft. The defect was highlighted during the operations in the Gilberts-Marshalls area, and the commander of the *Independence* suggested that all carriers needed to be reequipped with the 40-mm gun, which had twice the range.[4] Task force commanders insisted that until their ships could be more properly defended, naval units needed to avoid placing themselves within striking distance of enemy shore-based planes, and be prepared to take evasive measures.[5]

A more serious deficiency arose from the lack of advanced radar equipment that could be used to control antiaircraft fire. One of the U.S. Navy's most significant wartime achievements was to develop methods of using radar not only to locate enemy planes, but also to provide gunnery crews with information on where to deliver their flak. From the early stages of the conflict, encounters with Japanese forces showed how they often did not approach in a straight path, but made frequent changes in course, altitude, and speed. The situation required a careful tracking of incoming aircraft. In instances where radar-directed fire was not used, battery crews often missed their targets, and simply wasted their shells. Blind fire also tended to expose the location of ships, without bringing any benefits.[6] Naval officers continued to develop their concepts of fire control during the Pacific campaign, and by 1944, each ship was instructed to operate a coordinated lookout system that covered all sectors.[7] In order to facilitate data distribution, a CIC was established to intercept enemy communications and forward the information to task force commanders.[8] The CIC was also responsible for providing fire-control stations with the data obtained through search devices, thereby enabling gunnery crews to launch their flak in a timely manner.[9] Last but not least, the CIC directed the task force's maneuvers so as to ensure that gun batteries were facing the correct direction.[10] The improvements signified how the U.S. Navy's thinking placed a high value on utilizing its knowledge of the threats posed by the IJNAF, and enabling personnel to deploy their resources in a way that was suitable for countering their opponent.

Yet in spite of a working doctrine, the existing instruments demonstrated shortcomings, and the Pacific Fleet's antiaircraft capabilities were consequently hampered. All carriers of the *Essex* class were fitted with radar to determine the composition and formation of incoming flights. Search devices had been developed largely with the help of the National Research Laboratories, and performed well.[11] The Mark 3 and Mark 4, installed during late 1941 and early 1942 and equipped with more precise range circuits, became a mainstay of the fleet throughout the war. The Mark 8, with its 30-square-foot antenna, transmitted a more powerful microwave beam, and became available in 1943.[12] Control systems for 5-inch guns consisted of a mechanical computer into which operators could feed information on the target's initial speed and trajectory, and thereafter the device estimated the flight path. Although the equipment helped to lessen the damage incurred by task forces, commanding officers acknowledged that the key challenge was to design and install a device that could track the low-level attacks that Japanese pilots routinely carried out.[13] The Mark 4, even with its horizontal sweep, could not detect planes that flew within ten degrees above the horizon.[14] The situation caused considerable complications for radar operators and antiaircraft crews. Vice Admiral Fitzhugh Lee, observing the activities of Essex's CIC unit, recalled spending "many unhappy hours" watching the blips appear and fade as enemy planes approached, knowing that battery personnel could not be supplied with the data needed to strike their targets.[15]

The situation was rendered more alarming because the IJNAF continued to possess its share of trained aviators, and task group leaders were conscious that they had to prepare for more troubling situations. The Pacific Fleet also faced the ever-present possibility that the enemy could reform its tactics and equipment. Efforts to defend against night attacks were particularly complicated. In engagements under the cover of darkness, the Japanese tended to approach at low altitudes so they could detect the silhouettes of ships more easily. At Vella Lavella in the Solomons, torpedo plane pilots were noted to have taken advantage of the limited visibility and attacked their targets with "relative impunity."[16] Following the Tarawa operation, destroyer commanders raised concerns that the Japanese were conducting torpedo raids with increased persistence, and top priority thus had to be given to installing equipment that could provide a full picture on the position of enemy planes.[17] The U.S. Navy also struggled to introduce a single device that could operate at all ranges. Fire-direction radar was found to be incapable of discerning targets more than ten thousand yards away.[18] The installation of SK radar, with its longer beam, remedied the flaw, but did not track targets at closer range. Following a raid on Palau, the commander of the Alabama warned that the deficiency could assume "dangerous proportions" if the Japanese managed to launch a large and coordinated wave of planes.[19] Although the IJNAF did not pose the same menace that it had during the early stages of the war, U.S. commanders were wary of becoming overconfident about their capacity to deal with aerial attacks.

In order to circumvent the shortcomings posed by radar and antiaircraft ordnance, task forces attempted to maximize their defensive power by sailing in formation and providing mutual support. Again, the idea of having ships coordinate their movements had already been developed prior to the war, and wartime experiences were used as a basis for improving the U.S. Navy's practices. Drawing upon the lessons from Coral Sea and Midway, where carriers sailed independently and ended up exposing themselves to piecemeal attack, commanders insisted that carriers needed to operate in groups.[20] PAC-10 emphasized that task forces needed to be concentrated in a single formation, and that splitting the carriers could only dissipate their cumulative strength. Naval commanders also treated the damage that the IJN air arm was able to inflict on U.S. vessels as a clear indication that protective screens needed to be positioned further away from the capital ships and aircraft carriers. At Tarawa, the *Oakland* was stationed at a distance of six miles from the center of the carrier group. The commander of Task Force 50 asserted that "excellent results" were achieved, and the encounter confirmed the benefits accrued by subjecting planes to flak at an early stage.[21] War instructions stipulated that the vanguard be placed 1,500 yards from the center of the task force.[22] The disposition was considered the most effective defense against torpedo-plane and horizontal bombing attacks, as well as nighttime raids.

More important, the Pacific Fleet was apt to modify its procedures in accordance with the frequent variations in Japanese techniques. In the aftermath of the Marianas campaign, where enemy forces launched a series of attacks from their airfields at Guam, the accepted conclusion was that future operations were most likely to encounter shore-based opposition.[23] The scenario was judged to be probable as U.S. forces began to operate within proximity of large island chains such as the Philippines and Formosa. Under the circumstances, battleships were expected to become vital. Proper measures were also taken against the different maneuvers that the Japanese carried out. When confronted by dive-bombers, ships sailing far away from carriers were unlikely to bring down the planes, owing to the sharp angles at which the latter approached. Heavy support ships therefore had to be properly distributed, with a sufficient number stationed closer to the center.[24] Following the increased opposition encountered during the carrier strikes against Luzon, commanders reiterated the contention that dispositions had to be laid out to provide protection against all forms of attacks. The formation had to be symmetrical all around, so as to ensure that there were no weak sectors. Ships also had to be sufficiently separated, in order to enable them to take radical maneuvers in case evasive action became necessary.[25] The ideal screen included a number of ships armed with heavy batteries concentrated at the center, with smaller ships stationed further out, to provide early warnings of attacks.

In regard to personnel, the U.S. Navy noted how efforts to enhance its own efficiency were obstructed by the lack of proper training. Prewar doctrine had addressed the tasks facing antiaircraft crews. Officers realized that specialized training was needed to hit airborne targets, since they moved at higher speeds than surface vessels.[26] A knowledge regarding the capabilities of the various items of matériel, including guns, directors, and ammunition, was described as "the foundation on which to build success." However, gun crews initially proved not fully capable of utilizing the more sophisticated technology at their disposal, the most important of which was radar. Naval commanders not only feared that the weakness could preclude the optimal use of resources; they also feared that the inefficient employment of radar could compromise the advantages that U.S. forces enjoyed, especially in the event the Japanese improved their own equipment. In May 1943, during a discussion with Spruance, Towers raised concerns that many officers did not have a complete knowledge of how search devices could help detect incoming planes and direct antiaircraft fire.[27] Training had to emphasize essential measures, including the tracking of targets, evaluating information provided by the CIC, and handling night attacks.[28] Procedures for firing at practice targets, also known as drones, specified that crews needed to become accustomed to the "weaving" maneuvers that enemy forces frequently carried out.[29] During torpedo or horizontal bombing runs, planes were to frequently change their trajectory.

Nevertheless, antiaircraft teams did not have many opportunities to practice. Ironically enough, naval units were committed to operations at sea for long periods but did not regularly face aerial attacks. One machine-gun control officer pointed out how ship crews were unable to familiarize themselves with the measures for combating Japanese planes.[30] For this reason, training centers had to be established at advance bases, so that personnel could rehearse whenever they were in port. Exercises had to emphasize the frequent use of automatic weapons, and the shooting of high-speed targets. A further problem was that naval personnel tended to become overconfident that friendly fighter aircraft could contain enemy forces before they approached the task forces. Proper instruction was made all the more urgent because, until redesigned radar became available, the only feasible solution was to have antiaircraft crews rely on their own skill. The use of human vision was important. During an operation against Truk, two Japanese dive-bombers penetrated the air patrol screen of Task Group 58.3 without being molested, and thereafter dropped their ordnance within close range of the *Lexington*.[31] The encounter was taken as a clear warning that battery personnel needed to be more observant.

Toward the closing stages of the war, antiaircraft crews did manage to achieve greater accuracy, thanks to combat experience and the subsequently improved use of equipment. During the Marianas engagement, teams on board the *Bunker Hill* found that dive-bombers were visible only for short periods, and consequently, the action depended entirely on individual initiative and "instinctive quick action."[32] The Mark 4 fire-direction radar did not receive optical assistance because of cloud cover, and ships avoided expending their flak by launching it only after the Japanese emerged in plain sight.

At the same time, the Pacific Fleet found itself having to prepare for the increased scale of air attacks the Japanese were able to bring. U.S. naval commanders maintained that every possible effort had to be devoted toward enhancing the efficiency of all ships, because in most areas of the western Pacific enemy forces had ample reserves of planes. The U.S. Navy's antiaircraft weaponry was deemed not entirely satisfactory, and for this reason ship crews still needed to improve their defenses by optimizing the available resources.

Radar remained unreliable for providing consistent bearings. One of the most serious defects arose from blind spots, and the weakness became pronounced when operations were carried out within proximity of land masses. The reflections created by shore lines and mountains restricted the area where radar could follow movements. In the Philippines, the Japanese took full advantage of the situation by approaching over land whenever the option was available. Antiaircraft batteries were not effective, owing to the resulting delay in detecting targets.[33] The encounters reinforced the conviction that enemy forces were capable of inflicting much greater attrition if they had more aircraft at their disposal. New methods of using search devices were needed. Although SM radar detected planes at low altitudes and at greater distances, it transmitted a narrow directional beam that could not keep a constant tracking. On other occasions, attacking planes appeared overhead without any warning and could not be monitored by SK and SC devices, since they showed long fade areas at high altitudes.[34] The fault was remedied by having radar operators use a trial and error process of sweeping the antenna through various bearings and elevation angles to home in on their targets.

Countermeasures were also sought by increasing the proficiency of antiaircraft personnel. By September 1944, Halsey expressed confidence that his crews had made good use of the "extensive opportunities" to carry out the training prescribed by CINCPAC headquarters.[35] Combat action reports confirmed how battery teams performed more effectively. During the Formosa operation, torpedo bombers were taken by intense and accurate gunfire from automatic weapons that were opened immediately after the planes were detected by visual means.[36] Serious damage was prevented by the "grim determination of the gunners." Personnel also devised methods of calibrating the location of aircraft by compiling data from various sources, including radar and rangefinders.[37] Thereafter, the information was quickly tabulated to provide a median calculation of the target's speed and flight path. The use of multiple fire directors, to provide a triangulated tracking of planes, also proved helpful.

Yet, while improvements were visible in a large number of units, a significant proportion of crews complained that they faced troubles. During the Philippines campaign, ships that were frequently called out on operational duty did not have enough time for exercises. Even when naval forces were in port, the bulk of the time was spent preparing for operations, refueling, and loading supplies. Task force commanders insisted that a more rigorous instruction program be implemented. The situation was complicated because the standard manuals did not provide sufficient scope for variation. The existing instructions were criticized for prescribing an inflexible set of moves that were not suitable for many types of attacks, including those carried out by torpedo planes.[38] Training maneuvers also needed to be specifically geared to recreate the moves that were characteristic of Japanese pilots, with arrangements made for bombing attacks during periods of sunrise and sunset, when the enemy made good use of the camouflage afforded by the combination of darkness and strong sunlight.[39] The successes that U.S. forces achieved in defeating Japanese attacks were therefore not seized by naval crews as evidence that their gunnery and the methods of its use were satisfactory. On the contrary, even toward the closing stages of the conflict, the most frequently cited feature was that antiaircraft defenses showed ample room for improvement. Even though the enemy's resources were rapidly dwindling, in many instances its forces did manage to sink and damage vessels. Subsequently, the casualties that the U.S. fleet was likely to face as it started to conduct frequent operations in the vicinity of the Home Islands, where the Japanese had considerably larger concentrations of planes, were a cause for worries. The Americans were thus disposed to draw a reserved level of reassurance from their experiences, which suggested that their fighting efficiency was on the rise.

Fighter Defense

The improvements achieved in the Pacific Fleet's aerial combat capabilities were most visible in the area of fighter tactics. U.S. pilots utilized their knowledge of the IJNAF's advantages and weaknesses to devise measures that worked to substantially diminish its supply of aircraft. Fighting methods were geared to exploit the lack of armor protection and firepower on board Japanese aircraft, while at the same time matching their capacity to conduct abrupt maneuvers. At the operational level, the declining strength of enemy forces offered an opportunity to conduct offensive operations on a larger scale. Aircrews also realized that the determination and aggressiveness that characterized Japanese attacks made them hard to intercept once the planes were within proximity of task forces. For this reason, the most effective means to counter the IJN air arm was to conduct preemptive strikes against its land bases. However, while the performance of American aircraft and pilots showed considerable progress, the U.S. Navy's methods of controlling the movements of its aircraft continued to reveal shortcomings. In particular, fighter direction was unsatisfactory on many occasions, largely because radar could not provide accurate bearings on incoming planes. Communication between aircrews and flight control personnel was also hindered by the shortage of radio devices that could handle large volumes of traffic. Consequently, fighter squadrons were unable to engage enemy forces in a timely manner. In the area of night fighting, the Pacific Fleet continued to be hindered by the lack of equipment and trained crews. As was the case when the Americans developed their antiaircraft defenses, the problems were overcome by deploying the existing assets more efficiently.

The U.S. Navy's development of its air arm demonstrated how its doctrine placed a prime importance on procuring a sizeable supply of matériel and manpower to execute a large-scale war effort. Although antiaircraft batteries proved useful for reducing the damage inflicted on surface forces, naval commanders maintained that air power constituted the first line of defense. Fighter planes were able to break up formations of enemy bombers, while at the same time compelling enemy pilots to make haphazard approaches toward ships, thereby diminishing the accuracy of the raids.[40] Most aircraft designs had not been built specifically to fight the Japanese. The overriding concern was to enable the Navy air arm to wage an intensified campaign, where planes had to be equipped with large amounts of firepower to destroy enemy forces. Equally important was to provide sufficient armor to friendly air units and to protect them against attrition. By the latter half of 1943, the Americans could express an unreserved confidence in their own capabilities, thanks to the availability of a greater quantity of modern machines. The newly produced F6F Hellcat, with its three .50-caliber machine guns fixed on each wing, fired over a thousand rounds per minute, and its destructive power was vastly superior to that of the Zero. American pilots unanimously agreed that the F4U Corsair was at least equal to the Zero in maneuverability, and possibly superior in conducting climbs at altitudes above 15,000 feet.[41] In a mission over Malaita, a squadron of Corsairs managed to shoot down three Bettys by carrying out a slight dive, using a minimal amount of engine power, and achieving enough speed to catch up with their opponents.[42] When the new model of the Wildcat, the FM-2, was introduced in summer 1944, most airmen agreed that at any speed above two hundred knots, it was able to ascend and dive faster than the Zero.[43]

In addition to high-performance equipment, one of the most crucial requirements facing carrier task forces was to have a sizeable cohort of qualified aircrews. Again, instead of being specifically tailored for operations against the Japanese, the pilot training program was initially geared to meet the general demands of a protracted conflict.[44] At the commencement of the Pacific War, the cadet system that had been set up during the mid-1930s was expanded so that it could produce a larger pool of airmen. Preflight centers and basic flying schools were established for preliminary instruction. Student pilots thereafter proceeded to the advanced flight schools at Pensacola, Florida, and Corpus Christi, Texas, where each cadet received a total of nearly five hundred hours of practice time before qualifying for combat duty. Aviation officers had to possess a thorough knowledge of air strategy and tactics, as well as the capabilities of the air arm in aiding naval operations. The main problem was that aviation constituted the U.S. Navy's fastest-growing component, especially after 1943, when the scale of operations in the Pacific rose dramatically. The demand for experienced officers subsequently rose, and oftentimes the manpower supply was not sufficient.[45] In order to remedy the situation, optimal use was made of those pilots who managed to graduate. Younger officers were sent to the front line at the earliest opportunity. Air discipline and the development of unit cohesion were considered crucial ingredients for success. Aviators had to learn to depend on certain squadron leaders, and to develop confidence in their ability to carry out maneuvers.[46] To place untried airmen at the head of formations, on the other hand, tended to cause "uncertainty and confusion in the minds of all." Leaders who were unfamiliar with their units also lacked the knowledge of what their subordinates could do.

In addition to the Navy, the Marine Corps provided a valuable portion of the aircrews that fought with the Pacific Fleet. In response to the increased tempo of operations during 1944, General Alexander Vandegrift, commandant of the Marine Corps, met with Nimitz, and a Marine aircraft carrier program was approved and specifically geared to provide amphibious forces with close air support.[47] Nevertheless, pilot instruction also focused largely on achieving air superiority in the area of operations, by eliminating fighter opposition.

As the balance of forces shifted toward the Allies, aviators endeavored to exploit the IJNAF's shortcomings by developing offensive tactics. Admiral Mitscher insisted that task group commanders not only needed to be experts in the handling of air squadrons, but also have the characteristics of aggres-siveness and courage.[48] Training was conducted with a view to placing planes in a position to initiate attacks. The development of maneuvers was aided by increased experience, and a subsequently enhanced knowledge of how to cope with enemy forces. The most important aim was to maximize the com-bined power of fighters. Planes needed to be supplied with a combination of armor-piercing, incendiary, and tracer bullets in order to take advantage of the relatively weak protective armor on board Japanese aircraft.[49] Pilots also utilized the strengths they accrued through superior firepower, speed, and armor protection. On one of the first missions carried out by a Hellcat squad-ron against Wake Island, pilots learned that the best way to engage the Japa-nese was to maintain a high velocity and pursue enemy planes in a dive, in order to close in on the Zeke before it could make a sharp turn.[50]

At the same time, action reports stressed the need to prepare for all types of opposition, and commanders continued to be wary of the challenges they had to contend with. In addition, uncertainties arose from the lack of intel-ligence on the precise extent of the IJNAF's losses of its aircraft and qualified pilots. Operations therefore had to be planned with the understanding that the IJN air arm was still capable of putting up resistance. The improvements that the Japanese were pursuing also remained open to speculation, and future trends in their tactics and airplane designs could not be predicted. Under the circumstances, adequate precautions were essential. As late as September 1944, Nimitz warned, "It would be unwise to deduce a too rigid theory for all future warfare," especially when U.S. forces engaged a more effective enemy air force.[51] Any trend toward parity was likely to result in greater casualties for the Americans.

Tactics were therefore devised to counter a Japanese airman that was known to retain a large, albeit diminishing, number of planes, along with air-crews that carried out skillful moves. Enemy pilots had to be denied any op-portunities for making use of the benefits that their aircraft possessed, such as speed and maneuverability. Newly arrived pilots were instructed that shoot-ing down Zeros was often a complicated task. Corsair and Hellcat pilots re-marked how the Zero was able to maneuver itself out of the "jaws of death" with relative ease.[52] When pursuing Zeros, the most effective approaches were from below and rear, where enemy pilots did not have good visibility.[53] Aviators learned that a bullet aimed at the wing roots, where fuel was stored, often sent Japanese planes up in flames, owing to their lack of self-sealing tanks.[54] U.S. forces also continued to face the need to take evasive action. On one of the first missions in the Solomons involving the use of Corsairs, Marine pilots were told that when chased by the Zero, a sharp turn to the left at high speed often worked to "lose" the enemy.[55]

Fighter doctrine emphasized teamwork, and stipulated that units coordinate their maneuvers in order to defend against interceptors. Because the fighter's primary role was to protect bombers, escort tactics received high emphasis. An analysis of air combat losses convincingly showed that the number of aircraft that returned safely from missions was directly proportional to the amount of cover provided.[56] In instances where bombers were not defended, their capacity to destroy ground and naval targets could not be fully exploited. During a number of raids conducted against Rendova and Bougainville, pilots noted how inadequate VF protection required bombers to spend a large part of their time evading interceptors.[57] One of the key recommendations was to increase the ratio of fighters to bombers within formations that operated in areas where Japanese planes were known to be capable of interfering with air strikes. The general idea was to give the bombers "the coverage they needed during all phases of the attack," and thereby enable them to "devote their whole energy to laying their bombs accurately on the proper target."[58] Because the Japanese were able to get in the air and hide in sectors where they could remain undetected, there was no way of determining whether enemy VF would be present until they appeared.[59] Hence, a portion of the U.S. fighter force had to cover bombardment groups continuously, while flying to and from the target area and during the attack itself.

In addition to protecting bombers, one of the essential requisites was that fighter units maintain formation. Any pilot that got separated was most likely to become a target for a determined chase, and the lesson was learned by virtually all squadrons. Pilots from VF-33 noted how Japanese pilots preferred to make a head-on approach, and thereafter position themselves behind their targets.[60] On the other hand, if sections stayed together, the Japanese could be denied any opportunities to target planes that did not enjoy mutual support. Caution also had to be exercised against decoy Zeros that attempted to lure planes into combat. In a mission over Rabaul, groups of U.S. fighters were placed in several stacks above the bombers. As the latter commenced their dives, the two lower levels of fighters followed to provide cover against approaching interceptors.[61] Meanwhile, the fighters flying at higher levels made a circular sweep to deal with Zeros that attempted to interfere. Airmen were also instructed that one of the best evasive maneuvers was to dive at terminal velocity, and make a sharp turn to the right, because when faced with such moves Zero pilots opted not to carry through with the pursuit.[62] Instead of assuming that the tactical and technological advantages enjoyed by U.S. forces enabled them to defeat the Japanese easily, aircrews acknowledged that they frequently faced a difficult opponent. The situation was considered to provide a stark indication that Navy pilots needed to properly make use of their strengths, while at the same time minimizing the casualties that enemy forces were able to cause.

Despite the substantial progress that the U.S. Navy's fleet air arm made in the area of fighter tactics, the development of its capabilities in nighttime operations remained problematic. Improvements were made urgent because the IJNAF had frequently resorted to attacks under the cover of darkness. Combat experience suggested that nighttime raids were becoming an integral component of the IJNAF's practices. Enemy pilots evidently realized that daylight attacks were becoming unfruitful, because the task forces were well protected by fighter cover and radar-controlled antiaircraft batteries. Operations in limited visibility, on the other hand, achieved greater success at a lower cost, because planes could lurk in the target area and make repeated runs. The damage suffered by U.S. task forces during previous campaigns in the Solomons was also not forgotten. Prior to the Gilbert Islands operation, Spruance and Rear Admiral Charles Alan Pownall (who commanded the Pacific Fast Carrier Forces) expressed apprehensions about the Japanese attacking at night, and suggested that aircraft be used primarily to defend the task force, rather than be committed to the bombardment of land targets.[63]

Among the most significant moves to enhance the Pacific Fleet's ability to deploy its planes in nighttime conditions concentrated on equipping fighters with search instruments, so that pilots could pinpoint their opponents. As early as 1942, even before the IJNAF's capabilities were fully known, the Navy had already started its own Project Affirm, at the naval air station in Quonset Point, Rhode Island, to train fighter pilots in the use of airborne radar sets. When Rear Admiral John S. McCain Sr., who commanded the naval air campaign in the Solomons, became chief of BuAer in October, he initiated an investigation of ways to deal with Japanese night fighters.[64] The first specialized squadron, VF(N)-75, was created in April 1943.[65] The Grumman aircraft manufacturing company was also commissioned to develop the heavily armed twin-engine XF-7F Tigercat, and the first production model flew in December. In addition, the land-based version of the F4U Corsair was reconfigured to be deployed on carriers, and used as a night fighter when the Americans began conducting operations in the Central Pacific. Commencing in October, VF(N)-75 carried out a number of operations against Munda in New Georgia. Following the Marcus Island operations during that same autumn, Rear Admiral Pownall recommended that a standardized night-fighter doctrine be adopted so that aircrews could understand the procedures for intercepting enemy planes.[66] Pownall supported the suggestion that Nimitz had put forward earlier, to the effect that a minimum of four dedicated fighters be placed on board each carrier. The fighter director school at Pearl Harbor also attempted to develop a standard set of instructions.

U.S. commanders insisted that task forces had to be supplied with advanced search devices, as well as qualified crews, but unfortunately, the Navy did not have the matériel and manpower to meet its targets. In regard to equipment, Spruance ordered the installation of the Mark 12 and Mark 22 radars, which had a much higher range.[67] American manufacturers also built airborne pulse-search instruments that were considerably lighter than their predecessors, and could detect aircraft at distances up to five miles. The devices were installed on selected planes within a number of air groups, including those of the *Essex*, *Hornet*, *Wasp*, and *Lexington*. However, U.S. industries needed to expend substantial time and effort before they could produce high-performance radar sets in mass quantities. In terms of manpower, carrier deck crews were primarily assigned for daytime operations, and often too exhausted at night to conduct a long series of launches and recoveries.[68] Night fighters were therefore used for duties that required the use of small squadrons, such as search and rescue, and guiding lost planes back to the carriers, but rarely for extensive combat operations.[69] Measures to enlarge the supply of pilots were also fraught with obstacles. Training was stepped up, with an emergency syllabus issued to each fast-carrier captain. Carriers were to be supplied with at least two specialized teams, consisting of Hellcats.[70] Naval officers also suggested that several fleet aircraft carriers (CVs) be assigned for night operations, with fighter crews carrying out regular practices in searching and intercepting.[71] However, the wartime demand for airmen meant that the training course for night flying lasted only twenty-nine weeks, which meant the necessary teams remained a scarce commodity.[72] Under the circumstances, tactical methods were likely to take considerable time before they could advance beyond the experimental stage.

While attention continued to be paid to defensive maneuvers, at the operational level, as the Americans began to secure a clear ascendancy in numbers, the Pacific Fleet's doctrine started to take on a more aggressive tone. Whereas during the early stages of the conflict U.S. forces concentrated primarily on protecting task forces against air attack, by late 1943 the situation in the Pacific theaters had evolved to a point where carriers and air groups were seeking opportunities to utilize their striking power. The introduction of the *Essex*–class carriers, with their increased aircraft complements, significantly bolstered the U.S. Navy's offensive capabilities. The construction of light carriers (CVLs) in large numbers also complemented the air power based on fleet carriers. Following the autumn 1943 Marcus Island operation, CVLs were assigned to cover task forces, while larger vessels sent their planes against land targets for bombing and strafing missions.[73]

With the balance of strength tilting in the U.S. Navy's favor, commanders became convinced that they could conduct preemptive strikes against enemy airfields more frequently. War instructions did stipulate that a CAP composed of fighters had to be stationed directly over the task group, since from that position the planes could easily be vectored to intercept attacking forces.[74] At the same time, the growing consensus was that enemy planes had to be engaged as far away as possible from friendly forces. During late 1943 and early 1944, when the U.S. Navy carried out a series of landing operations in the South Pacific, the IJNAF's bastion at Rabaul was subjected to constant raids, in an effort to prevent enemy aircraft from interdicting the amphibious forces. The operation highlighted the value of neutralizing Japanese airfields.[75] On many occasions, the probability of encountering a strong counterattack was welcomed, on the premise that it enabled U.S. forces to annihilate a large portion of the enemy's air force. Halsey recalled that the plan to attack the

Japanese airfield on Bougainville, and maintain a continuous patrol over the landing site, was based on a calculated risk.[76] The launching of long-range attacks against Iwo Jima in July 1944, in an effort to defend U.S. invasion forces in the Marianas, and the success achieved in shooting down the defending fighters gave rise to the conclusion that air groups needed to fully exploit the maximum combat radius of carrier-borne planes, and thereby pose an increasingly larger threat to Japanese positions.[77]

Aircrews endeavored to develop methods for carrying out preemptive raids. The preferred move was to strike while Japanese planes were still on the ground. Fighter sweeps were conducted at low altitudes, followed by bombers that laid incendiaries and fragmentation clusters on the target.[78] At Rabaul, a proportion of U.S. fighters was used to form a circle around the airfield and destroy enemy bombers, while the remainder made diving attacks against Zekes that attempted to intercept the formation.[79]

The Navy air arm was also aware that it needed to maintain an adequate tactical supremacy over the IJNAF. Air squadrons were instructed to adapt their procedures to deal with the opposition that the Japanese were able to put up. The persistent use that enemy forces made of their airfields in the Marianas necessitated more effective methods. The placing of delayed action fuses on runways, coupled with the maintenance of a CAP to prevent reinforcements being flown in, was considered viable solutions.[80] Experiences during the attacks on Saipan and the Bonin Islands showed that fighter sweeps conducted at different altitudes were not sound when facing an air force of equal numbers, since enemy planes flying higher than the attacking force could concentrate on each small element, and eliminate them piecemeal.[81] For this reason, a full strike, consisting of bombers and fighter escorts, had to fly in at high altitude, and remain concentrated until opposition was neutralized.

By the latter half of 1944, the devastation that the Americans managed to mete out on the Japanese provided encouragement to speed up the counteroffensive. The heavy aircraft losses that the enemy was estimated to have suffered during the bombardment of Luzon in September 1944, carried out in conjunction by the U.S. Navy, Marine Corps, and Fifth Air Force, convinced Halsey that the IJNAF could no longer offer a great deal of resistance, and the central Philippines was "a hollow shell" that formed a vulnerable point in Japan's empire.[82] The admiral decided to push forward the date of the Leyte invasion, and while the possibility that the Japanese might launch shuttle attacks against the Third Fleet was acknowledged, Halsey maintained that U.S. forces needed to undertake offensive operations in order to neutralize the remnants of enemy air power.[83]

Nevertheless, aircrews were reluctant to rest reassured that their operations would not encounter obstacles. This was largely because they recognized the complexities arising from ground-based antiaircraft opposition. The situation was expected to become more menacing in areas closer to the Home Islands, where defenses were of a "more permanent and effective nature" than in other parts of the Pacific.[84] During the Marianas campaign, enemy flak became the main cause of losses, and studies needed to be conducted on the most efficient ways to destroy Japanese positions.[85] Shore batteries were described as "intense and very accurate," requiring a large number of planes to be directed against the guns before they could target other objectives such as aircraft revetments and hangars.[86] In many cases, antiaircraft positions consisted of a number of batteries arranged in widely scattered groups, with each battery separately revetted.[87] The arrangement forced pilots to execute piecemeal attacks on a multitude of small targets. Low-level strafing attacks succeeded in driving enemy antiaircraft crews to seek cover in nearby shelters. However, as soon as the planes completed their runs, the crews often re-manned their positions.[88] Enemy gun crews also used the opportunity to improvise their tactics with each successive attack, thereby rendering the destruction of batteries progressively harder. Air attacks therefore had to be carried out repeatedly, rather than at intervals, so as to deny the Japanese any opportunity to reconstitute their defenses.

The Americans also bore in mind that as they began bombarding large islands that contained a significantly higher number of airfields and installations, attacks had to be more coordinated, with efficient use made of the available air power. In order to achieve the maximum results, an accurate knowledge of enemy defenses was an absolute necessity. By autumn 1944, Halsey was raising concerns that the facilities for processing photographic data in the forward areas were lacking, and information on targets in the Home Islands had not been gathered in any vigorous manner.[89] The success achieved during the attacks on Japanese airfields in the Philippines was not taken as a sign that U.S. forces had perfected their reconnaissance capabilities.

On the contrary, the operations showed numerous cases where squadrons did not have good intelligence. The volume of flak encountered around Manila Bay, and the incidents where novice leaders guided their formations to the vicinity of intense antiaircraft fire, gave rise to strong recommendations that strike leaders had to be chosen on the basis of their familiarity of the target area.[90] The commander of Air Group 22 noted that a thorough survey was crucial, particularly when details of the target area, including the number of planes on the ground and layout of antiaircraft defenses, were incomplete.[91] A secret tactical bulletin, issued by COMAIRPAC in April 1945, warned, "There is no substitute for a well planned attack which . . . makes use of the best combination of weapons, tactics, and confusion of the enemy's defense, within the numerical limitations of the force to be employed."[92] Yet as late as the Okinawa operation, U.S. aircrews had yet to find a satisfactory solution. Because task groups often alternated their targets, pilots did not always have the most updated information.[93] The absence of a centralized intelligence organization in the forward areas meant that data were not always disseminated systematically. To complicate matters, the supply of trained surveillance teams was inadequate. Personnel from the carrier *Intrepid* pointed out that most pilots had no instruction for six months prior to joining the unit, and had not practiced with the most advanced camera equipment.[94]

The situation became more complicated as U.S. operations were extended to the Japanese Home Islands, where enemy forces were able to rely on a large network of widely scattered air bases. Under the conditions, only a small number of Japanese aircraft were likely to be exposed to any single Allied raid, and the attackers were forced to expend a greater effort to hunt down their targets.[95] The Japanese also demonstrated considerable skill in dispersing and camouflaging their planes to hide them when an attack was imminent, or flying out of range when forewarned of strikes.[96] In many instances, aircraft were concealed in wooded areas and roadside locations, several miles away from the base. The planes spotted on runways were almost invariably decoys that had been placed to lure U.S. forces into areas where the Japanese could deliver flak.[97] Scouts needed to fly in prior to the attack and obtain thorough coverage. Aerial bombardments had to concentrate on the most important airfields and installations, in an effort to neutralize the IJNAF to a point where it was unable to carry out large-scale attacks. Nevertheless, task forces remained unable to eliminate all enemy planes. As late as August 1945, the Japanese had a total of four thousand combat-type planes, along with several thousand training aircraft.[98] U.S. pilots therefore needed to devote a greater effort to determine the locations where enemy forces were hiding their reserves, by making good use of photographic intelligence.

The efficacy of bombing operations was enhanced by assigning pilots to carry out reconnaissance missions on a regular basis. Crews were given more opportunities to operate their own cameras and assess the results of their own work, thereby enabling them to develop their skills at handling information.[99] Fields that were believed to have the greatest numbers of aircraft were surveyed as a matter of priority.[100] The photographs were then passed to aircrews, who studied the layout of the target. Thereafter, individual pilots were assigned with specific objectives to bomb. Air squadrons attacking the Kanoya airfield, which was known to have an extensive and well-protected concealment area, were instructed that every pilot had to know his assigned target "so well that he can find it unhesitatingly and hit it during the confusion of the attack."[101] As a result, air squadrons incurred much fewer casualties, while at the same time achieving a higher ratio of hits.

The evolution of aerial tactics, and the conduct of preemptive strikes against enemy bases, therefore showed how the U.S. Navy successfully exploited its intelligence on weaknesses that the IJNAF suffered as a result of its declining strength, as well as the inferior quality of its planes and pilots. Equally important, fighting methods continued to be formulated while taking into account the difficulties that the Japanese were able to pose. This achievement was due to the fact that the Pacific Fleet had the resources to convert its knowledge of the enemy into a set of effective procedures.

Efforts to develop a system for commanding and controlling aircraft, on the other hand, continued to face considerable difficulties. The U.S. Navy placed a high priority on improving its capacity to monitor the swift and evasive maneuvers that Japanese pilots frequently carried out, so that defending fighters could make accurate interceptions. Personnel were alert to the lessons learned from the early encounters, where inadequate fighter direction frequently resulted in the sinking of ships. The loss of the cruiser *Chicago* in January 1943 was blamed on the poor handling of protective air groups, which permitted enemy torpedo planes to attack without being molested.[102]

By mid-1944, the Americans had acquired the equipment and manpower to assemble a functioning apparatus. Naval doctrine also continued to emphasize that task forces needed to deploy their planes in a resourceful manner. The purpose of fighter direction was "to provide the best defense against air attack," by making the most efficient use of the available fighters, and preventing them from having to waste substantial time and fuel trying to locate enemy aircraft.[103] Although carriers received priority, all ships were eventually supplied with at least one FDO. SC and SK radars were used for aerial searches, while surface-level SG radar detected low-flying targets. Auxiliary vessels, including destroyers and cruisers, acted as pickets, sailing ahead of the carrier task force to provide early warnings.

The information obtained through search devices was also integrated with a system that could process the material and thereafter disseminate it to air units. Radar operators were subjected to an intensive nine-week course, during which time they were indoctrinated in the means to identify enemy raids, as well as to distinguish friendly and enemy aircraft through the use of identification-friend-or-foe (IFF) equipment.[104] Fighter direction teams occupied a special section of the radar plot room, where a chart table laid out the position of all known targets. The officer in tactical command of the carrier force guided the fighters, and instructed them to fly to a point where they could shoot down the enemy. The distribution of information was streamlined by incorporating the radar plot with the CIC. In February 1943, Admiral King outlined a plan to fit all ships larger than a cruiser with a CIC. Naval commanders asserted that personnel working in the CIC needed to be comprehensively trained to use the available radar facilities, as well as to analyze enemy signals so that aircraft could tracked.[105] By the end of the war, CICs were provided with large compartments with space for up to fifty inhabitants. The unit became the "location where knowledge of an action was concentrated," and replaced the bridge as the "nerve center."[106]

Nevertheless, the Pacific Fleet's fighter direction continued to reveal inadequacies. Aircrews faced particularly acute problems when they attempted to neutralize Japanese attacks at nighttime. The main problem was that the available radar devices did not always function well enough to permit large-scale interceptions. In order to develop an adequate system for vectoring planes, the Pacific Fleet had to procure better equipment. Commenting on the Tarawa operation, Admiral Radford concluded that the U.S. Navy did not "have an outfit that could touch them [the Japanese]" in aerial operations in conditions of darkness.[107] Hurried efforts were needed to assemble radar devices that could accurately determine the altitude of enemy aircraft, and detect them at greater distances. Most of the interceptions, while using a certain amount of radar-guided interceptors, had been effected largely by using searchlights and the moonlight, when the latter was available.[108] Further apprehensions arose from the uncertainty as to whether the IJNAF was holding back its best crews for a decisive engagement, and the flying skills of enemy pilots could not be determined until they were actually encountered. While the damage suffered by U.S. surface vessels had thus far been minimal, U.S. naval crews and pilots did not expect to see Japanese forces refraining from large-scale operations indefinitely. The Americans had to be prepared for attacks to be carried out more adeptly, in which case better fighter direction was an absolute necessity.[109] Complications were also bound to arise if the Japanese improved their ordnance. Skillful maneuvering and antiaircraft fire had neutralized the effects of most raids. Nevertheless, such moves were likely to become ineffective if the IJNAF introduced weapons such as the acoustically guided torpedo, in which case the bombers had to be shot down before they positioned themselves for an attack.[110] In addition, if a greater number of enemy planes were equipped with radar, their pilots could carry out more accurate raids with bigger formations.[111]

The lack of effective communications was also a hindrance. Within many carrier groups, messages were still transmitted through a single channel, which meant radio circuits often became overloaded. To remedy the situation, the Americans developed a four-channel ultra-high-frequency radio that permitted each ship to carry out several separate conversations, and at short range so as to prevent enemy forces from listening in.[112] However, the introduction of new equipment still did not offer a full solution. In many cases, especially when formations were returning from missions, there were too many aircraft to identify, and radar operators could not report the presence of those aircraft that failed to confirm their own frequency band. The situation offered the Japanese an ideal opportunity to mingle and avoid detection.[113] Task forces also had several ships assigned to detect incoming planes, without a clear delineation of sectors.[114] A disproportionate amount of time was spent interrogating individual pilots and confirming the identity of their aircraft, rather than singling out the attackers. The situation was further complicated because advance bases in the central Pacific area generally lacked the facilities necessary to instruct night-fighting crews and CIC teams on how to reform their procedures.[115]

The U.S. Navy's fighter direction capabilities were markedly enhanced by the latter half of 1944, largely due to a better knowledge of the necessary measures. Fighter crews were commended for providing a "valuable service" in intercepting formations heading for U.S. task forces.[116] Communication was also improved, with pilots trained to avoid making unnecessary transmissions. Additional channels were installed to ease the burden on radio circuits. Following the Japanese defeat at Saipan, Towers' staff stated that the operation had "conclusively" proved the defensive abilities of the Navy's fighter direction methods against "the pick of the [enemy] air force."[117] Admiral Mitscher noted that Task Force 58's success had proved that "the long and costly efforts in research, training, and the practical applications of radar have not been in vain." The *Hornet*'s action report described the coordination between fighter directors and pilots as "well-nigh perfect," with interceptions carried out "like clockwork."[118]

Nevertheless, the Pacific Fleet faced a host of complications when it began to operate in areas such as the Philippines and Formosa, where the fighting became considerably more intense. A communications system that enabled aircrews to operate in a more coordinated manner was deemed urgent. At Leyte, the number of planes using the same channels multiplied, and a larger number of important contact reports and instructions needed to be issued.[119] The provision of communications facilities had not kept pace, and carrier commanders feared that if the defects persisted, air squadrons would not be able to make proper interceptions, and more ships were bound to be hit. During the Formosa operation, the amount of information handled by the *Essex*'s CIC was described as "tremendous," but an improved apparatus could not be established until more efficient equipment became available.[120]

Nor did radar permit the control of large formations. Even when directing single planes, SM devices could not track planes at extremely high altitudes or extended distances.[121] Air commanders doubted that a determined attack of any size could be broken, mainly because a number of enemy aircraft frequently remained undetected. The installation of search devices with the capacity to detect low-flying attacks was "mandatory."[122] Radar devices also did not provide overhead cover. Adjacent task groups had to fill each other's blind spots, and report on the appearance of enemy planes within a specified range, so that fighters could be vectored.[123] Because the Japanese were fully aware of the limitations of the U.S. Navy's equipment, it was not safe to rely solely on radar, and lookouts had to remain alert.[124] Fighter direction teams had to use their own vision, and communicate directly with the CAP.

The U.S. Navy therefore conceded that its fighter defenses continued to require reforms, even at the closing stages of the Pacific War. On one hand, aircrews were confident that their planes had a greater level of endurance and firepower over their IJNAF counterparts, and these characteristics permitted them to defeat enemy forces in the vast majority of aerial battles. Nevertheless, the Japanese continued to demonstrate their skill at carrying out evasive maneuvers and surprise attacks, both of which required a careful tracking of incoming targets so that fighter planes could be vectored for interception. Unfortunately, the existing fighter direction equipment did not offer an entirely adequate countermeasure. Nor could radar devices and communication equipment always handle the increased opposition that U.S. forces had to encounter in areas closer to the heart of Japan's empire. For this reason, the defense of task forces depended on pilots neutralizing enemy opposition by using their aircraft more adroitly.

The Kamikaze Challenge

The appearance of suicide squadrons from late 1944 onwards caused substantial problems for U.S. antiaircraft crews and aviators, both among experienced as well as novice personnel. In dealing with kamikaze attacks, the Pacific Fleet abided by its practice of comprehensively examining the challenges that the IJNAF posed, and thereafter endeavoring to develop the correct countermeasures. The overriding principle of naval doctrine, namely, to enable task forces and air squadrons to neutralize the enemy by making optimal use of the available supply of advanced weapons, while at the same time preventing the attackers from inflicting losses, also remained unchanged. Many of the techniques that the U.S. Navy had learned during previous encounters in the Solomons and central Pacific proved applicable. The maintenance of a

CAP that covered all of the task force's flanks, while having ship-borne crews deliver large quantities of accurate flak against incoming planes, was a crucial move. The key task was to execute the tactics on a more thorough scale, and the development of adequate procedures became a matter of heightened concern when kamikaze pilots proved capable of damaging or destroying ships with just a single plane. Suicide raids also closed in with a speed and determination that had not been witnessed previously. Furthermore, U.S. naval commanders recognized that their crews continued to follow a number of ineffectual measures, such as the maneuvering of ships and disabling incoming planes, neither of which prevented the Japanese from scoring hits. Experiences during the Philippines campaign highlighted the extent to which the Navy needed to improve its capacity to counter suicide attacks. Although the lessons were applied at Okinawa, the existing fighter direction and antiaircraft control equipment continued to reveal shortcomings, and proved not fully capable of coping with the increased scales of attack that the Japanese executed. The Pacific Fleet therefore strove to enhance its capabilities by modifying the use of its aircraft and gunnery.

By the latter half of 1944, the U.S. Navy was aware that it needed to implement a number of practical steps to deal with the resistance that enemy forces were likely to put up in areas closer to Japan's Home Islands. The commander of Task Group 38 suggested that since the Japanese were able to conduct extensive bombing raids from their numerous island bases, the most urgent priority for fast carrier groups was to achieve air superiority in the main areas of operations.[125] Two-seater dive-bombers had to be removed in order to make space for fighters, since the former were of little use in shooting down aircraft.[126]

The early encounters with kamikaze attacks showed ominous indications of the substantial effort required to develop the Pacific Fleet's protection against the unique difficulties posed by such moves. In conventional raids, as long as 80 to 90 percent of enemy aircraft were destroyed, the results could be considered an "eminent success," since the remainder of the planes tended to abandon their missions. However, suicide attacks demanded a 100 percent kill ratio, since one strike could spell disaster.[127] Furthermore, under normal conditions, fighters and antiaircraft guns only had to cause sufficient structural damage until the attacking plane could no longer drop its ordnance accurately, but such actions did not stop the Japanese from deliberately crashing into vessels.[128]

In terms of equipment, aircrews and antiaircraft personnel acknowledged the need to be supplied with significantly larger amounts of firepower. Encounters in the Philippines proved that existing doctrines that called for the deployment of fighter formations amounting to half of the attacking force's size were obsolete with the advent of suicide bombers.[129] As a basic emergency measure, the fighter-bomber ratio on board carriers was raised to a proportion of over 2-to-1.[130] CAP teams took on a larger part of the burden, mainly because antiaircraft crews did not have the capacity to act in a timely manner. Once the enemy planes evaded the fighter defense, the time available for lookouts to spot their targets was a matter of minutes, or in some cases, a few seconds.[131] That window of opportunity did not permit ship crews to adjust their batteries. Suiciders also approached more quickly than conventional bombers, because they did not use brakes, and were often at terminal velocity when reaching their targets.[132] In such cases, flak tended to lag behind the planes. Yet the frequency with which kamikaze planes penetrated the CAP screen meant that antiaircraft batteries constituted an important safety net. For this reason, improvements in both areas were treated as a necessity.

Naval vessels had to be fitted with stronger guns. COMINCH conceded that the suicide attack represented "by far the most difficult antiaircraft problem yet faced."[133] Planes diving at speeds over 450 knots became, in effect, "low-velocity projectiles" with a momentum that often could not be deflected, even with a great volume of hits.[134] In addition, because the Japanese resorted to evasive measures such as weaves and climbs, battery crews were often unable to achieve accurate hits.[135] Many officers concluded that 20-mm and 40-mm devices were of little use, especially following the sinking of the destroyer *Abner Read*. Although machine guns delivered accurate and continuous fire, the quantity of flak was not enough to destroy aircraft.[136] Fire-support ships therefore had to be fitted with 5-inch batteries that could launch fused projectiles. The Mark 32, fired from .38- and .25-caliber guns, and directed by fire-control radar, was considered the only weapon with any promise of shooting down planes at a sufficient range. Personnel also needed to fire a large volume of 5-inch fire during the short space of time in which a suicide attack was within the target ship's range. Yet following the Battle of Lingayen Gulf, complaints were raised about the delays that had been placed on installing guns that could deal with low-level attacks, which enemy forces carried out on an increasingly frequent basis.[137] Refitting all ships was likely to be time-consuming, and personnel had to contend with the limitations by making good use of their available weapons.

Furthermore, providing larger quantities of firepower was seen as only one of the requisite measures. Equally important was to set up a system that enabled task forces to deploy their weapons more accurately. In regard to fighter defenses, the use of an overwhelming number of planes did reduce the number of attacks. A statistical analysis carried out by COMINCH head-quarters showed that larger CAP groups achieved a significantly higher ratio of interceptions.[138] Nevertheless, bigger fighter forces did not necessarily guarantee protection. The damage that kamikaze forces inflicted, as well as the frequency with which Allied ships came dangerously close to being hit, highlighted the need to develop a way to properly vector the squadrons.[139] Commenting on the Lingayen operation, the commander of Battleship Squad-ron 1 recalled how, during the approach phase, even when forty fighters were stationed above the ships, kamikaze raids were not stopped.[140] Air cover therefore did not hinge on the quantity of planes, but on technological factors such as the types of fighters used and, more important, effective radar. When carriers operated beyond the cover of shore-based aircraft, it was essential to maintain patrols in all directions from which the Japanese could approach.[141] SM and SP type radars were to keep a constant low-level search to facilitate the early detection of planes. CIC teams also had to maintain constant com-munication with the fighter direction center, in order to formulate a complete picture of the situation.[142]

However, progress continued to be hindered because the existing equip-ment did not always serve its intended purposes. Although a large number of action reports opined that the tactical use of air cover during the Philip-pines operations was satisfactory, there were many noted failures. The repeated instances where the Japanese attacked without being detected, and the in-creased number of fighters that were used by U.S. task forces, necessitated a better method of command and control. Kamikaze raids often appeared at varying bearings and altitudes, and fighters were not able to get into the correct position. Admiral Towers noted how enemy aircraft headed directly toward the task forces from distances of up to ninety miles, with scouts used to provide a full knowledge of the target's location.[143] While frequent interceptions were made, CVEs were not equipped with altitude-determining devices, and the lack of accurate information permitted many enemy planes to get through. The defending fighters could not be used in the most efficient manner.[144] Because radar could not always be relied upon, fighters had to be dispatched any time a blip on the screen was suspected to emanate from an enemy plane. Suicide bombings were also frequently carried out by small formations, thereby further complicating efforts to detect the attackers.[145] Task force commanders needed a substantial fighter force under their immediate control, so they could patrol at all elevations and sectors.[146]

The shortcomings posed by the available radar also affected antiaircraft defenses. When fire-control instruments were used, calculations often proved inaccurate because enemy pilots took evasive action.[147] Batteries thus had to be opened from the moment the attackers were initially detected. Furthermore, at elevations below fifty feet, neither SK nor SG equipment picked up targets further than eight to ten miles.[148] Given that up to two minutes were needed to evaluate a contact and alert the gun crews, by the time a proper estimate could be made, the bombers had often hit their targets.

In response to the faults demonstrated by their equipment, task forces learned to use what they had in a more ingenious manner. Following Leyte, naval commanders recommended that the coverage of task forces be extended by stationing auxiliary vessels at the perimeter of the formation, whose specific assignment was to monitor the enemy's movements.[149] Ships sailing in formation also needed to coordinate their tracking to prevent aircraft from evading detection.[150] The situation was complicated because the Japanese often trailed U.S. formations returning from a mission. In such instances, enemy planes could not be easily distinguished from friendly ones. U.S. pilots needed to reduce the signals of their transponders so they could make minimal radar contact when within range of friendly forces.[151] Returning strike planes were also required to make a full turn around designated picket destroyers, in order to properly distinguish themselves from kamikaze planes, in a process known as "delousing."[152]

Most important, naval crews were compelled to continue relying on their own tactical finesse. Commanders acknowledged how the training of antiaircraft personnel had to be reformed. Detecting suicide bombers required "intense diligence and speed on the part of the radar operators," with the latter trained to determine the size and altitude of the approaching formation.[153] Fire-control doctrine was premised on the understanding that until new equipment was developed, battery personnel needed to fall back on "last-resort" weapons, such as visual lookouts.[154] Antiaircraft personnel were to identify enemy planes without over-relying on the CIC.[155] Gun crews also needed to become acclimatized to kamikaze tactics. However, exercises too often took the form of tactics used by U.S. air groups, namely, a massed attack, rather than individual and small formation raids.[156] As a solution, "Exercise Moose Trap" was devised, where pilots executed a number of maneuvers, including flying in pairs and at varying heights, in an attempt to divide the antiaircraft fire. Pilots who flew the practice targets were also instructed to simulate the deceptive moves that the Japanese carried out, such as riding down the null spots of radar and making use of the sun and clouds to conduct surprise attacks.[157] The measures signified how the Pacific Fleet conceded that, in the absence of better equipment, it had few alternatives aside from improving the quality of its personnel and helping them develop the aptitude needed to deal with kamikaze attacks.

Fighter crews learned to cope with the imperfect system for detecting enemy planes by carrying out missions at a greater distance from the task forces. Defending aircraft were positioned so that incoming attackers could be shot down before reaching strike range.[158] Formations were set up at three different circles, approximately two thousand, five thousand, and ten thousand feet away from the task group.[159] CAPs also needed to be stationed at sufficiently high elevations to ensure that the fighters had altitude advantage when contact was made, and disposed so they were prepared to deal with raids coming from several directions and heights.[160]

Naval commanders also became convinced that preemptive attacks against enemy airfields offered the most viable way to circumvent the complexities involved in destroying enemy planes when they got close to U.S. vessels. Many officials, including Halsey, voiced reservations about relegating fighters to a defensive role, and favored a more aggressive use of their air power.[161] Yet the neutralization of Japanese air forces was rarely an easy task. Kamikaze missions could be flown from an array of fields in the Philippines, and enemy aircraft had to be subjected to persistent attacks if they were to be denied opportunities to jeopardize U.S. task forces.[162] Operations were also planned on the assumption that the Japanese were likely to put up heavy opposition. Air groups needed to be provided with replacement planes and crews so that the momentum could be maintained.[163] To complicate matters, the propor-tion of fighters on board carriers proved insufficient to immobilize enemy forces. During the Luzon operation, the existing number of VF did not simul-taneously permit constant patrols over land bases and adequate cover for task groups.[164] Nor did air groups have enough fighters to stay above the target long enough to destroy all of the aircraft that the Japanese had at their dis-posal.[165] At the same time, bomber complements could not be reduced, since they were needed to destroy runways, installations, and munitions depots, and thereby put enemy bases out of action.

Efforts to subject airfields to constant bombardment also entailed a sub-stantial expenditure of resources. The idea of conducting a "blanket" CAP was criticized because fighters often spent their time flying around the target without engaging enemy planes, thereby wasting fuel, while at the same time causing pilot fatigue.[166] Yet naval commanders continued to face the overrid-ing need to carry out preemptive attacks. The solution was to conduct shuttle runs, and Vice Admiral McCain instituted a tactic designed to use the avail-able aircraft more economically. The "Three Strike" system, whereby one fighter patrol stayed over an enemy airfield, while a second one prepared to take off, with the third one flying en route to the objective, ensured that Japa-nese bases were kept under constant pressure, and their planes subsequently grounded.[167] In the meantime, back in the task group area, a CAP consist-ing of two dozen Hellcats was disposed, with another four pairs of fighters, known as "Jack patrols," whose job was to intercept suiciders who managed to evade radar detection positioned at low level. The doctrine was eventually adopted by the Third Fleet, and proved effective. By carefully scheduling launch and recovery times throughout the day, air groups could cover targets with only a ten-minute gap between strikes. As a result, enemy forces were prevented from "achieving the presumably considerable organization neces-sary" for sending out a strong raid, and carrier units were subjected to very few major attacks.[168]

The U.S. Navy's ability to deal with kamikaze attacks showed significant improvements by the time of the Okinawa operation, in the sense that enemy forces were often neutralized at the earliest available opportunity. Even before the invasion was launched, task force commanders anticipated an intensification in Japanese resistance, and attempted to bombard all enemy airfields and planes within striking distance of the operations area. Halsey ordered carrier groups to launch assaults against bases as far afield as Kyushu. In total, carrier-based planes alone dropped up to thirteen tons of bombs, and fired over two hundred rockets on the airfields within range of Okinawa.[169] The USAAF also played an important role. In January 1945, the Fifth Air Force commenced a series of raids with its B-24 and B-25 medium bombers against airdromes in Formosa, where a large proportion of the Japanese army air service's suicide squadrons were based. On virtually every mission, planes were reported to have been destroyed on the ground, and by the end of April, estimates suggested that the Japanese had lost more than four-fifths of their air strengths on the island.[170] In March 1945, the representatives of CINCPOA headquarters, the Army Air Forces Pacific Ocean Areas, and General Curtis LeMay's XXI Bomber Command drew up a plan to use B-29 Superfortresses in support of the Okinawa operation. Attacks against air installations in Kyushu were to commence ten days prior to the scheduled invasion, with Nimitz having the power to select the targets.[171] LeMay did not agree with the plan, on the grounds that it diverted his heavy bombers away from their primary mission of attacking Japanese cities and industrial centers. Nevertheless, under pressure from his superiors, including General Henry "Hap" Arnold, the Army Air Forces chief of staff, LeMay informed Nimitz that the Navy could use the XXI Bomber Command "whenever the B-29s could have a decisive effect." In effect, CINCPOA headquarters had virtual control of the bombing effort in the weeks leading up to the landing. The weight of the bombardment significantly diminished the number of suicide raids that the Japanese could launch, with most of their planes immobilized and ground personnel prevented from repairing any of the damaged facilities.[172]

However, the destruction of Japanese air power was still judged to be time-consuming and laborious. COMAIRPAC noted how carrier forces struggled to simultaneously protect friendly vessels and dispatch their aircraft on missions against land targets.[173] Nor did preemptive strikes achieve a complete kill ratio, and when kamikaze squadrons managed to launch an attack, destroying them remained a difficult job. The Division of Naval Intelligence concluded at the end of the Okinawa campaign that even though CAPs had shot down many enemy planes, between 40 to 60 percent of suicide sorties managed to reach the vicinity of their target area.[174] Furthermore, while the work performed by the CAPs was appreciated by all surface-vessel crews, in areas where enemy air action was most apparent, there appeared to be either too few or no friendly aircraft, since a large proportion of them were preoccupied in bombing enemy airfields.

The success that the Pacific Fleet achieved in its preemptive strikes was therefore perceived as a limited confidence builder. U.S. personnel remained aware that they needed to keep casualties at an acceptable level, and the larger number of ships sunk during the Okinawa campaign raised concerns. Naval commanders and air squadron leaders also continued to complain about the inadequate performance of fighter direction teams, who faced what was described as their "most strenuous test."[175] Although personnel were well trained and experienced, search devices could not follow the evasive maneuvers that Japanese pilots carried out. U.S. carrier forces supporting the aerial attacks on bases in Kyushu were subjected to surprise attacks carried out from high altitudes and areas where cloud cover tended to conceal the attackers' presence. Because the fade areas of the SK and SG radars did not permit accurate tracking, fighter direction teams could not vector the planes.[176] Nor did the available equipment pick up formations consisting of anything less than a handful of aircraft. The Japanese appeared to know how to exploit the shortcoming, by spreading themselves in small groups for widely scattered raids. Kamikaze pilots also trailed U.S. formations, counting on the latter's transponders to conceal their presence.[177] Another common move was to tune in to the same radio frequency bearings as U.S. forces, thereby making it almost impossible to distinguish between the aircraft that appeared on the screen.[178] The number of blips was far greater than what could be handled by radar operators and plotters.

Task forces also continued to face troubles in fighting off kamikaze attacks at nighttime. The Japanese frequently used hecklers to intercept planes that were returning to the carriers at dawn.[179] Because the number of squadrons dedicated specifically to night operations was still only a handful, suicide planes were able to operate freely over U.S. vessels under the cover of darkness, and the appropriate CAP techniques had to be developed, as a matter of urgency.[180] The most viable alternative was to capture island bases and establish radar stations, thereby supplementing the coverage that destroyer pickets provided.[181] Yet the delays involved in securing Japanese-held islands meant that large numbers of ships had to be held in the vicinity to offer air support for the landing forces. When undertaking such missions, task forces became lucrative targets. The only feasible remedy was to establish sufficient carrier-based air strength to ensure that enemy forces were kept sufficiently grounded.

Until new search devices became available to refit all ships, U.S. methods of fighter defense were developed while accepting the fact that a certain number of enemy planes were bound to evade the CAPs, particularly when the Japanese coordinated their movements. To provide more early warnings, a radar screening line composed of up to three destroyer divisions, manned by experienced CIC personnel, was established on the flanks where planes were most likely to appear. Admiral Richmond Turner, commanding the amphibious landing force, devised a plan where pickets were disposed around Okinawa at distances of fifteen to one hundred miles from shore.[182] While radar operators were able to pinpoint the enemy, fighter direction could be improved only if interceptions were initiated at greater ranges. To accomplish this end, destroyers needed to be equipped with a more powerful, SP-type radar.

The introduction of new equipment that could accurately distinguish enemy and friendly aircraft was also essential. A number of naval units managed to acquire more efficient systems, and subsequently made good use of their fighter aircraft. The carrier *Randolph* installed the AN/APX-2 airborne interrogator in its Mark 37 directors, which produced a code response on the scope.[183] The *Wake Island* had its planes equipped with transmitters emitting a standard frequency, and thanks to extensive pre-flight testing, not a single friendly plane was intercepted.[184]

Nevertheless, the majority of vessels were not equipped to identify enemy planes until they were within striking range. Task groups thus needed to rely on a "thorough knowledge" of the tactics that the Japanese used most frequently.[185] Equally important was to use the available aircraft and pilots in a way that prevented enemy forces from carrying out successful attacks. Rear Admiral Gerald Bogan, commanding Carrier Division 4, noted how sending fighters toward the general direction of the incoming raid was ineffective, and each group had to be assigned a precise sector.[186] The standard practice of stationing fighters to cover all of the formation's flanks, which had been learned in previous campaigns, needed to be implemented on an enlarged scale. CAP divisions were positioned at various altitudes, with a view to saturating the area with friendly aircraft.[187] To provide full protection, three divisions had to fly a continuous orbit around the task force, with an additional group stationed directly overhead, to look out for approaching formations.[188] Fighters were also kept at prearranged stations, thus providing an optimum number of interceptors available at each position. To defend against low-level attacks, one division of CAPs was kept at three thousand feet over the formation, under the control of fighter direction officers who used their own vision to detect enemy planes.

Individual fighter tactics were also adjusted. The commanding officer of the *Enterprise* noted how, given the enemy's ability to evade the screen, the most advantageous way to shoot down planes was to engage them in high-speed chases.[189] Again, the method was identical to the one used from the early stages of the conflict, with the only difference being that the move needed to be carried out much more skillfully. The momentum of the interception was to be maximized by placing patrols at higher altitudes, from where fighters could commence dives and thereby gain velocity. The improvements that the U.S. Navy achieved in employing its fighter defenses therefore demonstrated how tactical methods were developed while paying due attention to the challenges posed by kamikaze attacks. More important, however, task force commanders and aircrews accepted the fact that the existing control systems did not provide a complete solution, owing to the shortcomings of radar and communications technology. Enhanced protection needed to be sought by utilizing the flying skills of U.S. pilots and deploying aircraft in sufficient quantity to prevent the Japanese from menacing the Pacific Fleet.

The limitations of the U.S. Navy's antiaircraft defenses were also further exposed during the Okinawa campaign. Fire-control devices remained unable to track planes that carried out rapid maneuvers. The SP radar was considered an "excellent piece of equipment," but when task forces were attacked by planes flying independently, at high altitudes and speeds, the results were "definitely negative."[190] While fire was directed at distant targets with relative ease, when formations split up prior to the final approach, radar did not afford the close range necessary for accurate bearings. Enemy pilots also altered their tactics, in a manner that diminished the effectiveness of the available instruments. On many occasions, small groups and single planes made high-level approaches to exploit the lack of overhead cover. To counter such moves, the installation of zenith radars was urgent. Although the APS-6 was installed on most carriers, it was not designed to distinguish between friendly and enemy planes.[191] The SCR-720, which had been used on board P-61 fighters, provided overhead cover, but was in short supply.[192]

The decreased effectiveness of suicide attacks against U.S. carriers and battleships during the closing stages of the Okinawa campaign was largely attributed to the skillful use of the matériel at hand. Target acquisition was improved, thanks to a closer liaison between the CIC and gunnery crews. Destroyer pickets also provided antiaircraft crews with advance warnings by making radar contacts as well as visual checks. Picket stations extended the coverage by up to sixty miles from the area of operations. Rear Admiral Allan Smith, commanding Task Force 54, reported that the cordon of destroyer radar pickets around Okinawa gave timely information on approaching enemy planes, and this was "the most important factor in the security of the entire operation."[193] Destroyers were credited for accomplishing their purpose in "an effective manner" and sharply reducing the number of surprise attacks.

At the same time, many task forces leaders expressed the belief that antiaircraft teams were not properly equipped. Officers feared that their defenses would not work against an air force that possessed an ability equal to their own.[194] If the Japanese started to carry out more coordinated and intensified attacks, U.S. vessels were likely to face much greater levels of destruction. Picket vessels also became the target of kamikaze raids, since they were stationed at the far reaches of the formation, where ships were not well protected. Destroyer crews noted how suicide pilots had discovered that while it was preferable to hit heavy ships, kamikaze raids could also sink a light vessel with the same expenditure of material.[195] A statistical analysis of Allied shipping losses during the Okinawa campaign showed that destroyer losses were extreme, especially since they made up only 10 percent of the force but 30 percent of the total number of ships hit.[196] Yet as the Pacific Fleet began operating within proximity of the Home Islands, destroyers were expected to play a crucial role in providing an antiaircraft screen. Picket vessels needed to be equipped with adequate defenses, and supported by other surface craft insofar as possible.[197] Captain Frederick Moosbrugger, commanding the amphibious force screen, noted that during the initial stages, most destroyers lacked the proper fire-control radars and heavy automatic weapons.[198] Commanding officers of the *Fletcher* class, which constituted the most numerous of the destroyer types, commented that additional guns were needed.[199] Torpedo tubes, which were of little use on radar picket stations, could be replaced with a combination of 40-mm and 20-mm batteries.

However, overhauling destroyers was a laborious task that required them to be withdrawn from action for lengthy periods. For this reason, improved protection had to be sought through tactical reforms. Task forces promulgated a formation whereby ships sailed in a single circle, with destroyers and heavier ships placed in alternate stations. The arrangement allowed maximum fire to be brought against all approaches.[200] The U.S. Navy's operations research group concluded that the best defensive method for destroyers was to face their beam toward the kamikazes attempting a high dive.[201] By doing so, antiaircraft crews could bring to bear their maximum firepower. Against low-level attacks, turning the ship to present the bow or stern to the approaching plane minimized the area where the attacker could crash. Fighter aircraft also played an important role, and CAPs needed to be stationed as far as possible from the picket station so they could shoot down incoming kamikazes.

The impediments to procuring new equipment also compelled commanders to seek better ways of using the available batteries. Anticipating the need to deal with significantly larger opposition during the invasion of the Home Islands, the Navy commissioned a special investigation. In June 1945, Admiral King established a defense section at Casco Bay, Maine, the purpose of which was "to expedite readiness to defeat Japanese suicide attacks."[202] The center was headed by Vice Admiral Willis Lee, commander of Task Force 58. Men, ships, and planes were requisitioned to test new maneuvers, and the section produced an "Anti-Aircraft Action Summary" in late July. The more advanced fire-control equipment, such as the Mark 51 and 57, provided an effective range solution, thus enabling the projectiles to be directed accurately against targets. However, these devices were in short supply, and as late as July, BuOrd conceded that considerable time was needed to refit a number of battleships, including the *Arkansas*, *Texas*, and *New York*.[203] The Mark

37 radar, the most commonly used control instrument, could not achieve an accurate bearing against fast-moving aircraft. Although BuOrd made every effort to improve the gun director, a more efficient piece was needed to control fire against targets at all ranges.[204]

At the battlefront level, crews established procedures for shooting down targets at extended ranges. As aircraft closed in to 4,500 yards, the information was passed to the machine-gun control officer, who immediately ordered battery crews to commence firing.[205] A spotting system, based on observations of the differences between the actual elevation and the calculated height, was used to direct the fire at the general area where enemy planes were located. The method worked to subject incoming aircraft to a large volume of flak. However, because Japanese tactics called for evasive maneuvers until they were within short range of the ships, a large proportion of aircraft were not shot down until they were within striking distance.[206] Training thus needed to be stepped up, with naval crews given adequate opportunities to practice against fast-moving targets that simulated the moves carried out by kamikaze pilots.[207] Drones approached at long ranges, and used radical maneuvers to masthead height before veering off at the last moment.[208] Personnel were subjected to dummy surprise attacks, in an effort to teach them to act rapidly while under pressure.[209] CIC teams learned to detect targets at ranges up to eighty miles, while radar tracking of CAP sectors enabled radar operators to calibrate the altitudes of incoming planes.[210]

The improvements introduced in the aftermath of the Okinawa campaign were not put to test, since Japan's forces surrendered before the Allies launched their planned invasion of the Home Islands. Yet the development of antiaircraft defenses against kamikaze attacks provides a further example of how the U.S. Navy properly used its knowledge of its opponent to devise the moves necessary to protect friendly forces from excessive damage. The determination with which enemy pilots carried out suicide dives meant that gun crews needed to deliver large amounts of accurate fire. The existing radar devices did not always permit the timely opening of batteries, nor did the equipment provide a reliable calculation on the speed and location of enemy planes. For this reason, ship crews had to use their available weaponry more effectively. In order to achieve this end, they relied more on human skill, rather than technological resources.

Conclusion

The main reason why the U.S. Navy extensively drew upon the information gained through combat experience was that its strategic culture heavily emphasized efforts to base its fighting methods on a sound comprehension of enemy strengths and weaknesses. At the onset of the war, a large part of the Pacific Fleet's weaponry and concepts regarding its use had not been developed specifically to fight the IJN, owing to the lack of intelligence. Nevertheless, the Americans were aided by the fact that their antiaircraft equipment and fighter defenses, along with the doctrines governing their use, had been geared for operations against opponents that were able to conduct large-scale aerial attacks. Under the circumstances, naval officers and air commanders were well placed to develop suitable practices for engaging the IJNAF. By the middle stages of the conflict, observations of the Japanese air service's performance revealed that its aircraft and the flying skills of its pilots were becoming increasingly inferior in relation to its enemies. U.S. aviators seized the opportunity to exploit the shortcomings by making good use of their growing supply of technologically advanced planes and talented aviators. The aim was to shoot down Japanese aircraft whenever possible. At the same time, enemy forces continued to retain their share of good crews, and proved capable of introducing minor changes in their aircraft designs. Both factors enabled the IJNAF to harm opponents that were not properly equipped and trained. Furthermore, because the U.S. Navy did not have many opportunities to obtain information on the enemy's ideas concerning aerial combat, the possibility of refinements could not be ruled out. The Americans acknowledged the need to mitigate the damage that the Japanese were able to cause. Fighter planes had to provide close protection for bombers, while at the same time flying in tight formations to prevent enemy forces from carrying out successful interceptions. Equally important was to protect task forces from air attack.

Toward the closing stages of the conflict, U.S. aviators and naval commanders developed procedures to destroy Japanese aircraft before they could be brought into action, by attacking enemy airfields. Yet, while the move worked to reduce opposition, the situation became more difficult as the U.S. fleet's operations were extended to the western Pacific and Japan's Home Islands, where enemy forces had a larger reserve of planes and antiaircraft defenses at their disposal. Preemptive strikes were carried out on an enhanced scale, to ensure that the IJNAF was subjected to a consistent diminution of its strengths. The successes achieved in perfecting the U.S. Navy's methods for neutralizing enemy aircraft were largely due to the availability of resources to transform knowledge of the enemy into effective countermeasures.

The situation was not as favorable in other aspects of the Pacific Fleet's air defenses, most notably antiaircraft gunnery and fighter control. In spite of their knowledge of the proper measures, the Americans conceded that their weapons technologies did not permit the establishment of a fully reliable protective system. Consequently, naval personnel and aircrews were requested to reform their ways of using the available equipment and manpower. The development of antiaircraft methods highlighted this aspect. Because Japanese pilots conducted various types of maneuvers, including torpedo, dive-bombing, and horizontal bombing attacks, all of which were conducted at various altitudes, U.S. antiaircraft gun crews needed to adjust their fire in accordance with the situation they faced. In order to enable battery personnel to direct their flak at the correct points, radar operators had to determine the location of enemy aircraft and provide an accurate calculation of their flight path. However, when the Japanese carried out low-altitude attacks, their movements could not be tracked. Antiaircraft crews therefore had to use their own vision, instead of relying on technological remedies. The appearance of kamikaze attacks in late 1944 further revealed how radar could not always provide precise bearings. Suicide pilots resorted to deceptive measures by frequently changing their trajectory. The U.S. Navy's use of destroyer pickets, stationed at further distances away from the task force, partially remedied the situation, since it expanded the radar coverage and supplied earlier warnings of incoming raids. Nevertheless, a large number of planes managed to avoid detection, and antiaircraft crews needed to perfect their methods of locating targets by relying on human skill and maneuvering their guns to bring down fast-moving planes.

Improvements in the area of fighter direction were also introduced through the optimal deployment of resources. The Japanese frequently carried out air attacks at nighttime, which necessitated the development of fighters that were fitted with radar, to help pilots detect enemy aircraft in conditions of limited visibility. The U.S. Navy also needed to designate certain carriers to engage solely in night operations, in order to ensure that it had a sufficient complement of aircraft assigned for such duties. Yet the Americans faced problems in procuring enough devices to equip all of their fighters. Nor were they able to train a sufficient cohort of deck crews and pilots to form a dedicated carrier group, until at a late stage in the conflict. The Pacific Fleet's capabilities showed a significant improvement by the time of the Marianas campaign in June 1944, thanks to the better use of radar and communications. Nevertheless, as operations were extended to the western Pacific, where the Japanese were able to put up greater opposition, U.S. forces needed to deploy a correspondingly increased number of fighters. The available devices often proved incapable of monitoring the situation in intensified aerial battles. Kamikaze attacks posed particular problems, since they were carried out by formations composed of no more than a handful of planes, which were too small to be detected by radar. Japanese pilots also frequently changed their trajectory, making it difficult to vector the interceptors to the correct location. The problem was circumvented by reducing the dependence on fighter direction, and having a large number of planes cover all of the task force's flanks, with the pilots relying on their own vision to locate incoming attacks.

In the end, the Pacific Fleet's use of its knowledge of the IJNAF's capabilities fulfilled its own requirements. The difficulties in effecting technological and tactical improvements stemmed from resource shortages rather than a poor understanding of the enemy. The situation was remedied by carefully investigating the ways in which existing assets could be used more effectively. On many occasions, the Navy did manage to neutralize its opponent, and alleviated the casualties incurred by its task forces and air units. The successes can be attributed to the U.S. Navy's organizational culture. Officials developed a clear concept of the objectives they wished to attain, and were inclined to remain alert to the potential obstacles. Equally important, personnel were consistently encouraged to formulate a workable set of procedures for engaging their enemies. While the availability of intelligence was a contributing factor, the manner in which the Americans placed a high value on the proper application of that intelligence played a distinct role in laying the grounds for their achievements.

Conclusion

The Effectiveness of U.S. Naval Intelligence during the Pacific War
CAUSES AND CONSEQUENCES

The U.S. Navy's intelligence activities against the IJN highlight a number of key patterns that emerge when armed forces attempt to assess their opponents. First, a defense establishment's reaction to the challenges posed by its rivals is largely conditioned by the concepts that its officers hold on how operations should be conducted. Similarly, the military leadership's wartime objectives have a decisive influence on how it uses the available information in order to develop the means to overcome its enemy. The Navy's intelligence capabilities were a by-product of the thinking that had pervaded American officials during the period prior to the Pacific War, and were geared to determine the IJN's capacity to oppose the Allies in a prolonged confrontation. Strategic culture during the interwar years dictated that in any confrontation against a major power, U.S. forces were to fully exploit the large quantities of advanced armaments that their parent nation's industries were able to produce. Once hostilities began, war plans also called for bringing about the complete destruction of the Axis powers' military forces, and defeating them in a total conflict. The naval establishment's intelligence efforts thus reflected the ambitious strategies that it had drawn up. Instead of intelligence shaping ideas on how the Japanese were to be defeated, personnel used the material secured through wartime experiences to apply their tactical doctrines and weapons technologies in a way that worked to neutralize the particular challenges their enemy put up.

Second, even when military organizations try to understand their opponents, they cannot always collect the necessary data. The situation becomes even more complicated when intelligence bodies are assigned to assess foreign actors who hold alien mindsets and cultural characteristics, as was the case with the IJN. Even when personnel manage to collect information, they are not able to tell whether the material indicates enemy strengths, or whether it represents weaknesses that hamper its performance. Chapter One illustrated how, prior to the outbreak of hostilities, the U.S. Navy faced formidable difficulties in calculating the Imperial fleet's efficiency, because the Japanese authorities severely restricted the extent to which foreign observers could monitor their rearmament program. As a result, the Navy's preparations for war were based on an incomplete knowledge of its future enemy. Chapters Three and Four also revealed how the Americans continued to face problems arising from limited intelligence after they began to fight the IJN, although encounters with enemy forces facilitated the gathering of a wider pool of information. The principles and ideas that governed the construction of Japanese weapons and their methods of deployment remained not fully known until the end of the conflict. In particular, the U.S. Navy could not arrive at definite conclusions as to whether the Imperial forces were likely to improve their capabilities in future operations, nor could they predict the moves their opponent was likely to carry out. Combat personnel did not have access to a complete picture of the situation they needed to deal with, and countermeasures were subsequently devised through a process of experimentation.

Third, and not least, the previous chapters have demonstrated how, in wartime, defense organizations are confronted with obstacles that hamper them from improving their performance, despite their possession of good intelligence on the dangers that enemy forces can exert. The situation partly stems from the fact that during the previous period of peace, weapons technologies were developed without a clear knowledge of future foes. By the time hostilities break out, commanders find that innovations require a long time to mature before they can affect the conduct of operations. A more serious hindrance is that armed forces do not have the equipment required to execute new tactics. Yet the rapid pace of the campaign calls for quick action, and for this reason, military institutions need to do the best they can with the available matériel. In order to cope effectively with the IJN and its air arm, the Pacific Fleet needed to procure more modern radar and communications equipment. Unfortunately, U.S. industries and technical facilities were not able to assemble large quantities of the necessary hardware in a timely manner. For this reason, intelligence on the Japanese did not lead to the introduction of improved weapons. A more accurate argument is that commanders used their knowledge of the enemy in order to devise new ways of utilizing their available armaments.

The U.S. Navy needed to fight the IJN over an extended period, and in actual combat conditions, before it could comprehend enemy forces and the means to defeat them. The collection of accurate data on foreign fleets was made especially important during the interwar period and the Pacific War, when rapid advances in technology gave rise to advanced weapons systems such as maritime aviation and the submarine, along with new ideas on how to carry out naval operations. In many respects, the Americans were well placed to identify the challenges they had to confront. From the geopolitical viewpoint, the Asia-Pacific region was considered a vital area for U.S. economic and commercial interests, and its protection became a top national security concern. The Navy also had a long-standing tradition of keeping a lookout on potential adversaries, and as early as the 1880s the ONI had been established to systematically handle information on foreign fleets. Assessments of rival forces played an important role in shaping policy, and officers based their war plans on a sober calculation of strategic realities. From the time when War Plan Orange was conceived in 1907, the neutralization of Japanese naval power was acknowledged as an arduous undertaking. The American fleet was to carry out a protracted campaign, while at the same time avoiding setbacks that could hinder its ability to prevail in the long run. Developing an accurate evaluation of the IJN's ability to oppose the Pacific Fleet was therefore treated as an urgent task. Subsequently, the ONI was assigned to collect information on Japan's forces, and assess the material in a calibrated manner. Under the circumstances, naval intelligence was bound to have a positive impact on helping the Navy improve its fighting capabilities.

The IJN, by contrast, made a minimal effort to gauge the obstacles it had to contend with, because Japanese military culture placed a low value on intelligence activities. A combination of historical factors, ranging from an extended period of isolation from the outside world to a centuries-old belief in self-superiority, combined to lay the foundations for a view that suggested knowledge of the enemy was a feature that made little or no difference.[1] IJN officials preferred to base their calculations on the belief that the Imperial fleet's technological resources and tactical prowess guaranteed victory against the numerically superior U.S. fleet. The neglect of proper intelligence also reflected the high command's strategic concept of a limited war, where Japan's forces were expected to achieve a quick victory and thereafter wait for the United States and its allies to offer peace. Intelligence efforts thus focused on matters of short-term interest such as the current state of enemy forces. The U.S. Strategic Bombing Survey did note how, prior to the conflict, the government had developed a "vast organization throughout the world for collecting intelligence by relying on its overseas diplomatic and military representatives, together with a large network of spies.[2] The success that human agents achieved in ascertaining the layout of Allied bases and the position of enemy ships was a key factor that enabled the Japanese navy and its air arm to inflict crippling losses on their opponents during the opening months of the Pacific War. However, Japan's leaders did not methodically investigate wider issues such as the U.S. fleet's potential to fight a protracted war, where superiority in weapons production and deployment played a critical role in determining the outcome.[3] Consequently, naval authorities made serious errors in estimating America's recuperative powers following the Pearl Harbor attack. Wishful thinking thus led the IJN to overlook the need to gauge its Allied opponents, and the misperception was a key factor that gave rise to its decision to commence a war effort for which it was poorly equipped to prevail in the long run.

The disregard for intelligence activities had a number of adverse effects on the IJN's capacity to handle information. While the Japanese proved competent at collecting data, their intelligence machinery was seriously handicapped by their failure to establish organizations that could systematically analyze the material and thereafter disseminate it throughout the various levels of the command.[4] Assessments were most often produced by operational planners, and the role of intelligence departments was simply to provide information to their superiors on demand. Within the IJN, the main organs were the Third (Intelligence) Division and the Fourth (Communications)

Division, neither of which played a significant role in advising commanders on the formulation of strategy and policy. One officer in the Third Division recalled how his section exercised "very little influence" on other bureaus in the naval general staff, and lamented that IJN authorities tended to treat the work produced by his peers in a "perfunctory" manner. Naval intelligence also had to operate with an undermanned staff, and thus struggled to perform its assigned functions.[5] For example, a lone officer was tasked to compile material on Allied air forces, including technical, statistical, and order-of-battle data. Any intelligence on important issues, such as U.S. industrial production, was brushed aside. In March 1941, the IJN's attaché in Washington, who had managed to foster close ties with Rear Admiral Richmond Turner, the director of naval war plans, warned Tokyo that caution needed to be exercised before embarking on a war against America.[6] The warning apparently went unheeded.

During the period leading up to December 1941, the Americans did make a number of mistaken judgments of the Japanese. This was mainly due to the shortage of accurate information. Racial prejudices did have a visible effect on the U.S. Navy's perceptions, but they were not the most important contributing factor. The U.S. Navy did abide by an accepted view that suggested Japan was a backward nation, both in terms of economic advancement and technological expertise. Furthermore, officers tended to believe that their own weapons and combat methods were superior. Because the Navy's doctrine called for the use of overwhelming force to defeat its opponents, its evaluations of rival forces focused on material strength. The Imperial fleet could not deploy the same quantity of ships and aircraft as its U.S. counterpart, and was hence not deemed a serious challenge. Under this mindset, the naval establishment was most likely to reject evidence suggesting that the Japanese had constructed an effective fighting force.

Nevertheless, the fact of the matter was that neither the ONI nor its superiors within the Navy Department had the means to formulate an accurate picture. The Japanese were exceptionally successful at concealing their rearmament program and war plans from foreign observers, which made intelligence collection a most difficult task. As a result, the available information illustrated how the Imperial fleet faced a host of problems that hindered its efficiency, including a lack of experience in carrying out a large-scale conflict involving the use of modern armaments. To complicate matters, the Americans did not have a reliable benchmark for gauging the IJN. The last occasion when Japan had been involved in a major campaign was during the turn of the twentieth century, when it fought weaker enemies such as China and Tsarist Russia. Its capacity to engage a more powerful opponent remained open to question.

The tendency to belittle the Japanese also has to be viewed alongside the fact that significant sections of the Navy leadership did acknowledge how the IJN could cause considerable difficulties. In particular, the General Board, along with officers at the Naval War College, paid close attention to how the Japanese had assembled a large fleet consisting of modern vessels, including aircraft carriers, battleships, and submarines, that were fully capable of impeding the U.S. Navy's advance across the Pacific Ocean. Yet the shortage of intelligence on the IJN's operational plans meant that officials could only speculate on what their opponent was likely to do in the event of hostilities. Conventional doctrine stated that a fleet with inferior strength could not afford to risk high losses during the opening stages, since such scenarios invariably diminished one's prospects of winning. The Americans concluded that the IJN would remain cognizant of its own inadequacies, and thereby avoid moves that entailed a large-scale confrontation against the U.S. Navy, at least until the latter's strength had been significantly diminished. Assessments concerning the potential scope of enemy operations were thus based on an underlying preconception that dictated that Japanese commanders would follow the same guarded line of thinking as those accepted by their Western counterparts. An assault against the Pacific Fleet's main base at Pearl Harbor was therefore deemed improbable. Leading authorities within the Navy Department did not comprehend the extent to which the deterioration in U.S.-Japanese relations between 1940 and 1941 was more likely to encourage IJN leaders to conduct a preemptive strike rather than convince them to remain on the defensive.

The U.S. Navy was not alone in miscalculating its rivals, and its problems were similar to those that the majority of the world's leading armed services suffered during the interwar period. For example, British assessments of Japan were frequently tainted by racial views suggesting that it was "an ancient yet still virile culture" that had managed to adopt some traces of Western sophistication in terms of economic and military development.[7] As a result, policymakers did not grasp the extent to which the Japanese could menace Western interests in the Far East. Attempts to gauge Nazi Germany were also fraught with obstacles, even without the ethnic divide that tended to cloud opinions of Japan. Although U.S. intelligence collected substantial information on the German army, it was less able to scrutinize the Luftwaffe, owing to secrecy as well as the lack of inside sources.[8] British moves to evaluate Germany were similarly hindered by the rapid pace of the latter's rearmament program. Assessments were often based on conjecture, with "untested preconceptions" concerning the conduct of warfare being "interwoven with hard facts."[9] Among the most significant misperceptions was that because the United States and Britain were constructing their air forces with the aim of carrying out strategic bombing missions, the Germans were most likely to be doing likewise, when in reality the Luftwaffe's main purpose was to provide tactical support for the army. Yet, in the absence of a direct encounter between friendly forces and their foreign counterparts, the relative qualities of the opposing sides could not be determined with a great deal of accuracy. The U.S. Navy's prewar intelligence concerning the IJN was no exception to the prevalent dilemma.

The lack of information on the Japanese fleet also hindered efforts to devise effective countermeasures. In most areas, including surface operations and the use of the air arm, the procedures developed by U.S. naval leaders reflected their overarching doctrine regarding maritime warfare, which emphasized that when facing enemies that were able to deploy a substantial number of ships and aircraft, fleet units needed to deploy correspondingly superior matériel. The strategic culture prevailing within the naval establishment was also conducive to innovation.[10] War planning was carried out with a view to fighting a specific opponent, and achieving a defined objective, namely, to emasculate the IJN's capacity to fight. Staff exercises were conducted to determine the Blue fleet's ability to cope with the various obstacles that the Orange navy could put up. However, without accurate intelligence on the IJN, the U.S. Navy's weapons and tactical procedures could not be adjusted in accordance with the threats exerted by its adversary. In particular, encounters with the Japanese during the opening stages of the conflict showed how the Americans needed to substantially improve their performance in night operations, as well as supply their air arm with greater numbers of modern aircraft and trained pilots, before they could fight the Imperial forces on equal terms.

Following the outbreak of the Pacific War, strategic priorities continued to affect the manner by which the Americans assessed the Japanese. From the onset, the defense establishment's objective was to dismantle the Axis powers' hold on their conquered territories. The U.S. Navy therefore used intelligence to enable its forces to defeat the IJN in a large-scale campaign. However, in the aftermath of the debacles the Pacific Fleet suffered during the opening phases of the conflict, including the loss of a large portion of its vessels anchored at Pearl Harbor, the naval establishment was more concerned with its short-term objective, namely, to curb further enemy advances. Japan's forces proved beyond doubt their capacity to achieve a dominant position in the western Pacific, and to oppose Allied attempts to reestablish their hold on the area. The overriding priority was to understand the threats that the Japanese exerted, so that the Navy could develop the appropriate means to counter them. The ONI, along with the intelligence organizations working at the theater level, was also supplied with increased resources so it could carry out its functions more efficiently. More important, U.S. personnel adopted a more cautious method of evaluating their enemy, and opinions of Japanese martial qualities undertook a dramatic swing by focusing on their strengths. The phenomenon did give rise to an unfortunate development, in that the Imperial Navy's prowess was exaggerated. However, neither the intelligence services nor the Pacific Fleet was culpable for creating the "superior enemy" image. The opinion was natural, in light of the trauma that pervaded the naval establishment after the Japanese achieved their unexpected spate of triumphs. A more realistic assessment could emerge only after the IJN was faced with defeats. Only then could the Americans gain concrete indications of the extent to which their enemy's shortcomings affected its performance.

The Pacific Fleet's ability to apply the lessons of defeat and thereafter formulate better ways of engaging the IJN was also significantly restricted. This was mainly because until mid-1943, U.S. forces did not have the strength to launch large-scale offensives against Japan, since their resources were largely committed to fighting Germany. The losses incurred at Pearl Harbor also meant that the Navy possessed a numerical inferiority in virtually all categories of vessels, and faced problems even when it tried to hold out against the scale of attack that the Imperial fleet was able to put up. The immediate aim was to remain on the defensive, while at the same time preparing to carry out minor attacks against the periphery of Japan's empire. The IJN's setbacks at Coral Sea and Midway resulted in the loss of a large number of its carriers and accompanying aircraft, and gave U.S. naval leaders a sense of confidence that they could step up the tempo of the campaign in the Pacific. However, assessments of the Imperial fleet warned against lapsing into over-optimism, and noted how it still had substantial resources with which to impede Allied operations.

The tactical skill and technological capabilities of enemy forces also remained largely unknown, and the Americans conducted their campaign in the Solomons during autumn 1942 without knowing the challenges they had to deal with. Combat experience revealed how the IJN and its air arm remained difficult opponents. In surface operations, the Japanese fleet proved adept at conducting nighttime operations, and exploiting the limited visibility afforded by the cover of darkness to launch surprise attacks. Enemy torpedoes caused a level of destruction that bewildered American ship crews. The IJNAF also continued to demonstrate its capacity to wreak havoc on task forces, even though it had lost a large number of its trained pilots through attrition. By early 1943, when the Solomons campaign had reached its conclusion, the Pacific Fleet learned the initial lessons on ways to confront an adversary whose capabilities had been unknown. Although the success at preventing the Japanese from establishing a foothold at Guadalcanal provided a reassurance that they could be defeated, the accepted conclusion was that the U.S. Navy was not fully capable of engaging the Imperial fleet and its air arm in a more intensified campaign. Commanding officers realized that greater quantities of the most modern equipment, along with substantially improved tactics, were needed to defeat the Japanese without incurring excessive casualties. In surface operations, the pressing concern was to develop procedures for night fighting, which was an area that fleet officers had overlooked prior to the conflict. While the use of radar helped task force leaders detect enemy ships and deliver accurate fire on them, technological resources did not offer foolproof protection. Search devices did not function well in areas where land masses and rough seas concealed the presence of vessels, and in such circumstances, the Japanese were adept at concealing their presence. U.S. commanders also needed to establish a system for disseminating information on the location of enemy units to all ship crews, so that they could take timely action. Owing to the shortcomings of radar, the Pacific Fleet was compelled to develop better tactics by learning how to conduct surprise moves, as well as taking evasive action when faced by enemy attacks.

In aerial combat operations, the U.S. Navy had a realistic idea of the measures it had to take in order to fight the Japanese, but did not have the necessary resources. Encounters with the IJNAF showed that the swift maneuvers it carried out could be countered only when task forces made good use of a combination of antiaircraft fire and fighter defenses. Even before the war began, and the IJN air arm's capabilities became apparent, the Americans had already set out to develop the capacity to neutralize opponents who were able to deliver large-scale attacks, as evidenced by their plans to construct high performance fighters such as the Corsair and Hellcat. Of equal importance, the Navy had established a system for using radar to detect enemy planes and vector fighter formations against their precise location. The main problem facing U.S. forces during the opening phases of the conflict was that advanced weaponry had yet to be produced and deployed in mass quantities. The available radar devices also proved inadequate for determining the altitude of incoming aircraft, and fighter direction could not perform its intended task. Consequently, the Navy air service needed to manage with its available technological capabilities. For example, the Wildcat, which constituted the majority of the Pacific Fleet's carrier-based fighters, had greater firepower than the Zero, but was inferior in terms of maneuverability and often vulnerable when confronted with high-speed chases. Aircrews solved the problem by learning to fly in formation so that they could provide mutual protection. The shortcomings of radar were dealt with by indoctrinating personnel with the uses and limits of the equipment. At the same time, the development of the most efficient measures still hinged on the Americans undergoing further encounters, and thereby obtaining a more comprehensive picture of how the Japanese fought.

As the pace of operations against Japan gained momentum after mid-1943, following the deployment of larger forces to the Pacific theater, U.S. intelligence efforts against the IJN started to reflect the long-term objectives of defense officials, namely, to wrest control of Japan's conquests from the empire and to prepare positions for an eventual assault on the Home Islands. The Navy's strategic aim, of defeating the Japanese in a large-scale war effort, had three important effects on how it gauged the Imperial forces. First, intelligence activities were geared to help American crews understand the full range of factors that shaped their opponent's capabilities. While numerical strength and operational plans constituted crucial matters, equally important was to determine the IJN's combat methods and the state of its weapons. Second, the Pacific Fleet endeavored not only to know the current fighting potential of the Imperial fleet and its air arm. A substantial effort was also made to figure out how their tactics and technology could evolve, so that the Americans could be better prepared to encounter enhanced opposition in future operations. Third, and of equal importance, U.S. commanders wished to avoid losses that could erode their capacity to prevail. For this reason, they tended to view any indication that the Japanese were able to inflict delay and attrition on Allied forces with considerable apprehension.

However, in attempting to comprehend the Japanese, the naval establishment faced a formidable obstacle, namely, that it did not have the means to secure all of the necessary intelligence on an adversary whose practices and mindset were esoteric to most American observers. In particular, the U.S. Navy achieved limited success in obtaining information on the ideas and doctrines that shaped the enemy's ways of carrying out its operations, mainly because the IJN managed to keep the relevant information secret until the closing stages of the conflict.

The difficulties were largely alleviated because officials dealt with the uncertainties surrounding the Imperial fleet in a cautious manner. The overriding principle was to avoid miscalculations that could expose U.S. forces to unnecessary losses. The Navy tasked the ONI and the organizations working at the theater level to process a wide range of sources, including captured documents and equipment, POWs, and last but not least, action reports prepared by combat personnel who had engaged the Japanese. Dedicated bodies were set up to collect and analyze the various types of information, and thereafter disseminate the material within the naval establishment in an expeditious manner. Naval officers and aircrews also undertook a large part of the tasks related to handling intelligence, by producing accounts of the challenges that they encountered in their operations. The material was distributed either by the intelligence services or the respective naval and air commands. As a result, the Pacific Fleet was able to develop a better idea of the elements it had to contend with.

The U.S. Navy circumvented the problems arising from the shortage of intelligence concerning Japanese fighting techniques by basing its conclusions on a calibrated analysis of the information that was available. Assessments were prepared by examining aspects that could be observed, such as the equipment that the Japanese deployed and the moves they carried out. Intelligence staffs, along with combat personnel, realized that the Americans were engaging an opponent whose values and thought patterns were unique, and discerned a number of ways in which cultural factors influenced the IJN's ways of conducting its operations. The Japanese were noted to lack the ability to use individual initiative, which meant that naval officers were often slow to adjust their procedures. However, because information on the characteristics that influenced the capabilities of Japan's armed forces was difficult to obtain, the naval establishment did not expend a large effort inferring on the matter. For example, the problems that the Imperial Navy and its air arm faced in developing modern equipment, such as radar and advanced aircraft types, largely stemmed from the fact that Japanese authorities held an unquestioning belief that their martial qualities were superior to the Allies, and that improvements were therefore unnecessary. At the same time, because U.S. intelligence did not fully understand the IJN's attitudes, the shortcoming was most often attributed to Japan's shortage of economic and technical resources, which prevented industries from producing large quantities of high-performance weapons.

Racial perceptions therefore did not lay the grounds for negative judgments. Instead, the U.S. Navy concentrated on the features that rendered the Japanese a testing adversary. The Imperial forces did show visible signs that they were not able to produce weapons that could match those of their Allied counterparts. Simultaneously, they demonstrated a number of important qualities, including a capacity to develop a modest number of sophisticated machines and deploy them in an effective manner. For example, the IJN's surface fleet was handicapped because it did not have adequate radar devices to locate enemy ships, and as a result, naval crews could not direct their fire accurately.

Japanese units were also vulnerable to surprise attacks. Nevertheless, the Imperial fleet's torpedoes sank U.S. vessels on many occasions. Another noted characteristic was aggressiveness. The IJNAF proved adept at destroying American aircraft and warships until the closing stages of the conflict, even though it had lost a large portion of its skilled pilots, and faced problems in putting out aircraft with better endurance and firepower. After autumn 1944, the damage that kamikaze units wrought on task forces demonstrated how the Japanese were able to use their limited resources in an adroit manner. U.S. intelligence organizations, along with naval officers and air commanders, concluded that although the IJN was inferior to the U.S. Navy in terms of the quality of equipment and methods of use, it was still a resourceful opponent that was able to inflict considerable levels of delay and attrition on its opponents.

The Americans were also aware that they were not always able to identify the trends that governed the development of Japanese technology and fighting techniques, and for this reason, they tended to avoid making unfounded assumptions. This aspect was particularly visible when officers attempted to determine whether the Imperial Navy and its air arm were likely to enhance their performance. The only certain conclusion was that the enemy had proven its competence at developing weapons and tactics suited for impeding the progress of U.S. forces. Japan's forces were thus deemed to possess the capacity to introduce improvements. A show of ineptitude in one operation was not taken as an indication that the Imperial fleet and its air arm were categorically incapable of putting up a challenge. Nor did the IJN's lack of progress in innovating its weapons rule out the prospect of its forces becoming better equipped. The cautious method of threat assessment reflected the Navy's strategic thinking, which dictated that the Japanese needed to be defeated in a total war, where the main objective was to bring about the complete destruction of the enemy's fighting capabilities. U.S. forces were tasked with carrying out a prolonged series of campaigns and deploying their forces in the most cost-effective manner. To achieve this objective, the Americans had to gain adequate intelligence on the obstacles that the Japanese were able to put up. In the final analysis, the Pacific Fleet's success at formulating a realistic view of the IJN owed itself primarily to the culture that prevailed within its parent defense establishment. Knowledge of the enemy's capacity to conduct an intensified and extended war effort was considered crucial in order to develop the means to overcome the Japanese in the long run, and intelligence activities were geared toward this end.

Strategic culture also influenced the Pacific Fleet's ways of using intelligence to reform its ways of fighting the Japanese. While information on the IJN played a direct role in shaping the U.S. Navy's perceptions, the impact on the development of combat capabilities was less straightforward. This was largely because the Americans had already developed a large part of their weapons and tactics prior to December 1941, when their knowledge of the Imperial Navy was limited. Procedures were based on the U.S. Navy's concepts regarding the conduct of maritime warfare, which stipulated that when engaging a strong opponent, battle fleets were to use large quantities of modern equipment in an effort to neutralize the latter's forces. The Pacific Fleet's arsenal was created with similar objectives in mind. For this reason, intelligence did not have a decisive effect on how U.S. forces engaged their opponent, at least during the opening stages of the conflict. The information obtained in wartime was more useful for the purpose of modifying the Navy's existing practices.

From 1943 onwards, when the Navy was able to deploy a growing portion of its strength for operations against Japan, the main factor that facilitated the development of combat methods was that U.S. personnel understood that they were engaging a strong opponent, and success depended on the skillful use of their vast supply of modern armaments. The key task was to apply the available knowledge of the IJN in order to enhance the capabilities of both surface forces and air units. U.S. Navy officials maintained that their forces needed to engage in a prolonged campaign in order to defeat the Japanese. Equally important was to avoid excessive losses that could diminish the fleet's capacity to secure a long-term victory. To achieve these ends, the rank and file were encouraged to formulate their fighting methods while bearing in mind the enemy's weaknesses that were open to exploitation, as well as the dangers it exerted. In many areas, good intelligence significantly aided the operations of U.S. task forces and air units. The IJN surface fleet's capacity to launch damaging torpedo attacks was alleviated by using radar to detect Japanese vessels and direct gunfire on them. The move also took advantage of the enemy's inadequate means to locate its attackers in a timely manner. Aerial tactics were developed with a view to making good use of the relatively low amounts of armor protection and firepower that Japanese planes carried. Toward the closing stages of the conflict, when the IJNAF's numerical strength vis-à-vis the Allies underwent a significant decline, U.S. air commanders devised ways to carry out preemptive strikes against Japanese airfields, in an attempt to destroy their machines before they could be brought into action. At the same time, aircrews bore in mind that the IJN air arm remained capable of putting up difficult resistance. Enemy pilots proved adept at carrying out maneuvers that worked to intercept attacking planes and sink U.S. ships on many occasions. U.S. officers tended to avoid discarding their apprehensions regarding the Japanese until friendly forces developed suitable defensive tactics.

Nevertheless, in spite of the Pacific Fleet's conscientious effort to transform its knowledge of the IJN into an effective practice, two key problems were prevalent. First, on many aspects, the available intelligence on enemy forces was incomplete, and this factor hampered the development of tactics. The encounters with the Japanese aircraft carrier and battleship fleet illustrated this dilemma. The Imperial Navy's main units remained inactive following its defeat at the Solomons in early 1943, and did not reappear until June 1944, during the Marianas campaign. Officers therefore did not have a reliable means to assess how their opponent's capabilities had evolved in the intervening period. Subsequently, the U.S. Navy remained unsure as to whether its own procedures and equipment were sufficient to counter Japan's forces. As late as the Battle of Leyte Gulf, commanders found themselves identifying deficiencies in their capacity to interdict Japanese vessels, and seeking ways to improve their performance.

The second key impediment was that even when U.S. officers understood the moves they needed to execute, the required weapons were not available. The development of antiaircraft defenses and fighter direction systems hinged on task forces being equipped with radar sets that could monitor enemy planes, so that flak and defending aircraft could be deployed efficiently. However, American industries and technical facilities were not able to provide search devices that could track the evasive maneuvers that Japanese air formations frequently carried out. The problem became particularly acute when U.S. task forces faced kamikaze attacks during the closing stages of the conflict. Because technological resources did not provide a complete remedy, countermeasures had to be provided by using the Pacific Fleet's available resources more ingenuously. Antiaircraft crews learned to rely on their own vision to detect incoming planes. Fighter units also had to maintain a constant patrol around the areas where surface vessels operated, and to station a sufficient number of aircraft so that they could intercept any enemy formation that attempted to attack. Again, the naval establishment had a clear idea of its objective, namely, to achieve air superiority in the areas in which it operated, so that task forces could be protected from aerial attacks. This vision, coupled with the continued desire to defeat enemy forces in the most economical manner, was the key impetus that led American personnel to closely examine the challenges posed by the Japanese naval air service, and develop the means necessary to cope with them.

Intelligence played a pivotal role in paving the way for the U.S. Navy's triumph over the IJN. While the possession of numerically superior forces with technologically advanced armaments was a key prerequisite, the proper deployment of resources was often of equal importance. The availability of good information facilitated the Pacific Fleet's effort to gauge the Japanese and thereafter develop the appropriate ways to combat them. However, intelligence needed to be used effectively if it was to have any value. After all, one of the most critical phases in the intelligence process lies in convincing the leadership to make use of the information supplied to them.[11] Much depended on whether decision-makers were open-minded enough to accept criticism and take in accurate, albeit unpleasant, information. The extent to which officials are receptive to ideas put forward by intelligence organizations often depends upon the service culture prevailing within a particular organization. Military organizations also need to establish a suitable means of measuring their own performance against their opponents'.[12] This is best achieved by determining the defense establishment's ultimate goals. Officials must thereafter not only ascertain whether their resources are adequate to fulfill the prescribed objectives, they also face the task of carefully studying the actions they need to follow at the strategic, operational, and tactical levels.

The U.S. Navy's experience during the Pacific War therefore illustrates how organizations that follow a realistic military culture, and have a clear idea of their aims along with the means to achieve them, are more likely to create an objective evaluation of their environment. American task force leaders, along with commanders of their accompanying air units, understood that defeating the Japanese entailed carrying out a large-scale war effort, and the Navy's intelligence efforts were geared toward determining the IJN's capacity to do likewise. U.S. officials applied their knowledge of the Imperial forces in order to facilitate the Pacific Fleet's efforts to achieve its strategic objective of destroying enemy forces and securing control over Japan's home waters. The U.S. Navy's use of intelligence was therefore primarily shaped by its thinking during the Pacific War, which dictated that overcoming the Japanese fleet required a full and efficient deployment of the available resources. While effective intelligence was a key factor that enabled the Americans to reform their existing practices, more importantly, the success must be primarily attributed to the fact that the defense establishment held a good understanding of the type of conflict being fought, and conscientiously endeavored to determine the proper means to confront its opponent.

Notes

Introduction

1. Sun Tzu, *The Art of War*, trans. and with a historical introduction by Ralph Sawyer (Boulder, CO: Westview, 1994), 184.

2. Christopher Andrew and David Dilks, eds., introductory essay in *The Missing Dimension: Governments and Intelligence Communities in the Twentieth Century* (Chicago: Illinois University Press, 1985), 1–2.

3. H. Random, "Intelligence as a Science," in *Studies in Intelligence* (Spring 1958), cited in Michael Warner, "Wanted: a Definition of 'Intelligence,'" *Studies in Intelligence* 46, no. 3 (2002): 15–22.

4. For a description of the intelligence cycle, see Michael Herman, *Intelligence Power in Peace and War* (Cambridge, England: Cambridge University Press / London: Royal Institute of International Affairs, 1996), 36–40.

5. Loch Johnson, "Bricks and Mortar for a Theory of Intelligence," *Comparative Strategy* 22 (2003): 2.

6. John Ferris, "Intelligence," in *The Origins of World War Two: The Debate Continues*, ed. Robert Boyce and Joseph Maiolo (Basingstoke, England: Palgrave/Macmillan, 2003), 308.

7. Len Scott and Peter Jackson, "The Study of Intelligence in Theory and Practice," *Intelligence and National Security* 19, no. 2 (2004): 143, 151.

8. Christopher Andrew, "Intelligence, International Relations, and 'Under-theorization,'" *Intelligence and National Security* 19, no. 2 (2004): 174.

9. Samuel Morison, *Coral Sea, Midway, and Submarine Actions, May 1942 to August 1942*, History of United States Naval Operations in World War II, vol. 4 (Boston: Little, Brown and Co., 1988); *The Struggle for Guadalcanal, August 1942 to February 1943*, History of United States Naval Operations in World War II, vol. 5 (Boston: Little, Brown and Co., 1989); *Breaking the Bismarks Barrier, 22 July 1942 to 1 May 1944*, History of United States Naval Operations in World War II, vol. 6 (Boston: Little, Brown and Co., 1988); *Aleutians, Gilberts, and Marshalls, June 1942 to April 1944*, History of United States Naval Operations in World War II, vol. 7 (Edison, NJ: Castle Books, 2001); *New Guinea and the Marianas, March 1944 to August 1944*, History of United States Naval Operations in World War II, vol. 8 (Edison, NJ: Castle Books, 2001); *Leyte, June 1944 to January 1945*, History of United States Naval Operations in World War II, vol. 9 (Boston: Little, Brown and Co., 1988); *The Liberation of the Philippines: Luzon, Mindanao, the Visayas, 1944–45*, History of United States Naval Operations in World War II, vol. 13 (Urbana and Chicago: University of Illinois Press, 2002); *Victory in the Pacific, 1945*, History of United States Naval Operations in World War II, vol. 14 (Edison, NJ: Castle Books, 2001).

10. Examples include: James Belote and William Belote, *Titans of the Seas: The Development and Operations of Japanese and American Carrier Task Forces during World War II* (New York: Harper & Row, 1975); Clark Reynolds, *The Fast Carriers: The Forging of an Air Navy* (New York: McGraw Hill, 1968). For more recent works, see: Eric Bergerud, *Fire in the Sky: The Air War in the South Pacific* (Boulder, CO: Westview, 1999); John Lundstrom, *The First Team and the Guadalcanal Campaign: Naval Fighter Combat from August to November 1942* (Annapolis, MD: Naval Institute Press, 1994).

11. Examples include: David Dickson, *The Battle of the Philippine Sea* (London: Ian Allan, 1975); David MacIntyre, *Leyte Gulf: Armada in the Pacific* (London: MacDonald & Co., 1969); William Y'Blood, *Red Sun Setting: The Battle of the Philippine Sea* (Annapolis, MD: Naval Institute Press, 1981). Recent works are: Richard Frank, *Guadalcanal: The Definitive Account of the Landmark Battle* (New York: Penguin, 1990); Vincent O'Hara, *The U.S. Navy against the Axis: Surface Combat, 1941–45* (Annapolis, MD: Naval Institute Press, 2007); Barrett Tillman, *Clash of the Carriers: The True story of the Marianas Turkey Shoot of World War II* (New York: NAL Caliber, 2005).

12. John Ellis, *Brute Force: Allied Strategy and Tactics in the Second World War* (London: Andre Deutsch, 1990), 495, 538. Similar arguments can be found in Paul Kennedy, *The Rise and Fall of the Great Powers: Economic Change and Military Conflict from 1500 to 2000* (London: HarperCollins, 1988), 456, 458–9; Allan Millett and Williamson Murray, *A War to be Won: Fighting the Second World War* (Cambridge, MA: Harvard University Press / Belknap Press, 2000), 204, 337–8, 351–2, 527–45; Gerhard Weinberg, *A World at Arms: A Global History of World War II* (Cambridge, England: Cambridge University Press, 1994), 338.

13. Ronald Spector, *Eagle against the Sun: The American War with Japan* (New York: Viking, 1985), 560.

14. Richard Overy, *Why the Allies Won* (New York: Norton, 1995), 2, 5–6, 192, 318, 345.

15. Michael Handel, introductory essay in *Intelligence and Military Operations* (London: Frank Cass, 1990), 65–6.

16. Alan Bath, *Tracking the Axis Enemy: The Triumph of Anglo-American Naval Intelligence* (Lawrence: Kansas University Press, 1998); John Prados, *Combined Fleet Decoded: The Secret History of American Intelligence and the Japanese Navy in World War II* (Annapolis, MD: Naval Institute Press, 1995); John Winton, *ULTRA in the Pacific: How Breaking Japanese Codes and Cyphers Affected Naval Operations against Japan, 1941–1945* (London: Leo Cooper, 1993).

17. Michael Handel, *War, Strategy, and Intelligence* (London: Frank Cass, 1989), 239.

18. Ellis Zacharias, *Secret Missions: The Story of an Intelligence Officer* (New York: G. Putnam's & Sons, 1946), 88.

19. Herman, *Intelligence Power*, 100–112.

20. Carl von Clausewitz, *On War*, indexed edition, edited and translated by Michael Howard and Peter Paret (Princeton, NJ: Princeton University Press, 1984), 117.

21. Handel, *Intelligence and Military Operations*, 14.

22. Stéphane Lefebvre, "A Look at Intelligence Analysis," *International Journal of Intelligence and Counterintelligence* 17, no. 2 (2004): 240.

23. Peter Jackson, "Historical Reflections on the Uses and Limits of Intelligence," in *Intelligence and Statecraft: The Use and Limits of Intelligence in International Society*, ed. Peter Jackson and Jennifer Siegel (Westport, CT: Greenwood, 2005), 51.

24. Martin van Creveld, *Command in War* (Cambridge, MA: Harvard University Press, 1985), 256–6.

25. Colin Gray, *Strategy for Chaos: Revolutions in Military Affairs and the Evidence of History* (London: Frank Cass, 2002), 118.

26. Cynthia Grabo, *Anticipating Surprise: Analysis for Strategic Warning* (Lanham, MD: University Press of America, 2004), 20.

27. Herman, *Intelligence Power*, 140.

28. Andrew and Dilks, *The Missing Dimension*, 13.

29. Williamson Murray, "Innovation: Past and Future," in *Military Innovation in the Interwar Period*, ed. Allan Millett and Williamson Murray (Cambridge, England: Cambridge University Press, 1996), 301–4. Also see Williamson Murray and MacGregor Knox, "Thinking about Revolutions in Warfare," and "The Future Behind Us," in *The Dynamics of Military Revolution, 1300–2050* (Cambridge, England: Cambridge University Press, 2001), 14, 185; Handel, *War, Strategy, and Intelligence*, 21–4.

30. Alfred Mahan, *The Influence of Sea Power on History, 1660–1783* (London: Constable & Co., 1987), 3–11.

31. Julian Corbett, *Some Principles of Maritime Strategy* (London: Longmans, 1911; Annapolis, MD: Naval Institute Press, 1988), 107. Citations refer to the Naval Institute Press edition.

32. Barry Watts and Williamson Murray, "Military Innovation in Peacetime," in Millett and Murray, *Military Innovation*, 406.

33. Ernest May, "Capabilities and Proclivities," in *Knowing One's Enemies: Intelligence Assessment before the Two World Wars* (Princeton, NJ: Princeton University Press, 1984), 509, 520–1.

34. Murray, "Innovation: Past and Future"; Allan Millett, "Patterns of Military Innovation in the Interwar Period," in Millett and Murray, *Military Innovation*, 349–59.

35. See Watts and Murray, "Military Innovation in Peacetime," 312–3; Ken Booth, *Strategy and Ethnocentrism* (New York: Holmes & Meier, 1979), 14; Colin Gray, *Modern Strategy* (Oxford: Oxford University Press, 1999), 138; Alastair Johnston, "Thinking about Strategic Culture," *International Security* 19, no. 4 (1995): 46–8; A. Macmillan et al., "Strategic Culture," in *Strategic Cultures in the Asia-Pacific Region*, ed. Ken Booth and Russell Trood (Basingstoke, England: Macmillan, 1999), 8.

36. Williamson Murray, "Does Military Culture Matter?: The Future of American Military Culture," *Orbis* 43 (1999): 33.

37. Allan Millett et al., "The Effectiveness of Military Organizations," *International Security* 11, no.1 (1986): 37–71.

38. On the interwar period, country-specific studies include: Antony Best, *British Intelligence and the Japanese Challenge in Asia, 1914–1941* (London: Macmillan, 2002); Thomas Mahnken, *Uncovering Ways of War: U.S. Intelligence and Foreign Military Innovation, 1918–1941* (Ithaca, NY: Cornell University Press, 2002); Wesley Wark, *The Ultimate Enemy: British Intelligence and Nazi Germany, 1933–1939* (London: I. B. Tauris, 1985).

39. Geoffrey Smith, "An Uncertain Passage: The Bureaus Run the Navy, 1842–1861," 82–3, 95–102; Lance Buhl, "Maintaining 'an American Navy,' 1865–1889," 149–50, 153–5, 160–5; Ronald Spector, "The Triumph of Professional Ideology: The U.S. Navy in the 1890s," 177–84; Richard Turk, "Defending the New Empire, 1900–1914," 186–202—all in *In Peace and War: Interpretations of American Naval History, 1775–1984*, ed. Kenneth Hagan, 2nd ed. (London: Greenwood,

1984); Kenneth Hagan, *This People's Navy: The Making of American Sea Power* (New York: Free Press, 1991), Chapters 4, 6–7; Michael Vlahos, *The Blue Sword: The Naval War College and the American Mission, 1919–1941* (Newport, RI: Naval War College Press, 1980), 3–14.

40. Edward Miller, *War Plan Orange: The U.S. Strategy to Defeat Japan, 1897–1945* (Annapolis, MD: Naval Institute Press, 1991), 19–114; Michael Vlahos, "The Naval War College and the Origins of War Planning against Japan," *Naval War College Review* 33 (July–August 1980): 31–5. "Orange" was the color code that U.S. defense planners designated for Japan's forces.

41. Eliot Cohen, "The Strategy of Innocence?: The United States, 1920–1945," in *The Making of Strategy: Rulers, States, and War*, ed. Williamson Murray et al. (Cambridge, England: Cambridge University Press, 1994), 429–38, 441–61; R. Weigley, *The American Way of War: A History of United States Military Strategy and Policy* (Bloomington, IN: Indiana University Press, 1973), 245–6.

42. Norman Friedman, *The U.S. Maritime Strategy* (London: Jane's 1988), 213, 235.

43. Wyman Packard, *A Century of U.S. Naval Intelligence* (Washington, DC: Office of Naval Intelligence/Naval Historical Center, 1996), 16.

44. Naoko Sajima, "Japan: Strategic Culture at the Crossroads," in *Strategic Cultures*, ed. Booth and Trood, 76.

45. John Chapman, "Japanese Intelligence, 1918–1945: A Suitable Case for Treatment," in *Intelligence and International Relations, 1900–1945*, ed. Christopher Andrew and Jeremy Noakes (Exeter, England: Exeter University Press, 1987), 168–69.

46. See William Beasley, "Modernization and Imperialism," chap. 3 in *Japanese Imperialism, 1894–1945* (Oxford: Oxford University Press, 1987); Ruth Benedict, "The Meiji Reform," chap. 4 in *The Chrysanthemum and the Sword: Patterns in Japanese Culture* (Cambridge, MA: Riverside, 1946); Carol Gluck, "Ideology and Imperial Japan," "The Late Meiji Period," "The Language of Ideology," and "Ideology in Modern Japan," chaps. 1–2, 8, and Epilogue in *Japan's Modern Myths: Ideology in the Late Meiji Period* (Princeton, NJ: Princeton University Press, 1985); Chushichi Tsuzuki, *The Pursuit of Power in Modern Japan, 1825–1995* (Oxford: Oxford University Press, 2000), 113–5.

47. Forrest Morgan, *Compellence and the Strategic Culture of Imperial Japan: Implications for Coercive Diplomacy in the Twenty-first Century* (Westport, CT: Praeger, 2003), 64–5, 174.

48. Nobutake Kondo, "Some Opinions Concerning the War," in *The Pacific War Papers: Japanese Documents of World War II*, ed. Donald Goldstein and Katherine Dillon (Washington, DC: Potomac Books, 2004), 306–8.

49. David Kahn, "The United States Views Germany and Japan in 1941," in May, *Knowing One's Enemies*, 476–501; Mahnken, "Japan: Assessing a Rising Regional Power," chap. 3 in *Uncovering Ways of War*.

50. Stephen Rosen, *Winning the Next War: Innovation and the Modern Military* (Ithaca, NY: Cornell University Press, 1991), 51–2, 57–8, 61–4.

51. Edward Luttwak, *Strategy: The Logic of War and Peace* (Cambridge, MA: Harvard University Press / Belknap Press, 1987), 20.

52. John Dower, *War without Mercy: Race and Power in the Pacific War* (New York: Pantheon, 1986).

53. Rosen, *Winning the Next War*, 27–30, 34–6.
54. Ibid., 253.

Chapter 1: Gauging an Untested Opponent
U.S. PERCEPTIONS OF THE IMPERIAL JAPANESE NAVY, 1918–41

1. Richard Betts, "Analysis, War, and Decision: Why Intelligence Failures are Inevitable," *World Politics* 31, no. 1 (October 1978): 61. Also see Loch Johnson, "Preface to a Theory of Strategic Intelligence," *International Journal of Intelligence and Counterintelligence* 16, no. 4 (2003): 653.

2. Richards Heuer, "The Limits of Intelligence Analysis," *Orbis* 49, no.1 (Winter 2005): 84–7.

3. See ibid., 78–83; Richards Heuer, *The Psychology of Intelligence Analysis* (Washington, DC: Center for the Study of Intelligence, 1999), 4–16, 21–9; Robert Jervis, *Perception and Misperception in International Politics* (Princeton, NJ: Princeton University Press, 1976), 117, 143–57; Herman, *Intelligence Power*, 239.

4. William Dunn, "Intelligence and Decision-making," in *Intelligence: Policy and Process*, ed. Alfred Maurer et al. (Boulder, CO: Westview, 1985), 226.

5. See Booth, *Strategy and Ethnocentrism*, 15, 45, 65, 103–5.

6. In addition to the works cited in Note 49 of Introduction, see Douglas Ford, "U.S. Naval Intelligence and the Imperial Japanese Fleet during the Washington Treaty Era, c.1922–1936," *Mariner's Mirror* 93, no. 3 (2007): 281–306.

7. Richard Betts, *Surprise Attack: Lessons for Defense Planning* (Washington, DC: Brookings Institution, 1982), 120–2; Handel, *War, Strategy, and Intelligence*, 242, 250; Herman, *Intelligence Power*, 228; Mark Lowenthal, "The Burdensome Concept of Failure," in *Intelligence*, ed. Maurer et al., 44, 49.

8. Mark Lowenthal, *Leadership and Indecision: American War Planning and Policy Process, 1937–1942* (New York: Garland, 1988), vol. 1, 427, vol. 2, 594.

9. See Willard Matthias, *America's Strategic Blunders: Intelligence Analysis and National Security Policy from 1936 to 1991* (University Park, PA: Pennsylvania State University Press, 2001), 12–3.

10. Calvin Christman, "Franklin D. Roosevelt and the Craft of Strategic Assessment," in *Calculations, Net Assessment, and the Coming of World War II*, ed. Williamson Murray and Allan Millett (New York: Free Press, 1992), 235–6.

11. Kahn, "The United States Views Germany and Japan in 1941," 476.

12. James Morley, *The Fateful Choice: Japan's Advance into Southeast Asia, 1939–41*, translated version of official history series, *Taiheiyo Senso e no Michi: Kaisen Gaikoshi* [Japan's Road to the Pacific War] (New York: Columbia University Press, 1980), 235–7.

13. James Morley, *The Final Confrontation: Japan's Negotiations with the United States, 1941*, translated version of official history series *Taiheiyo Senso e no Michi: Kaisen Gaikoshi* (New York: Columbia University Press, 1994), 163–7; Nobutaka Ike, ed., *Japan's Decision for War: Records of the 1941 Policy Conferences* (Stanford, CA: Stanford University Press, 1967), 112–29.

14. Ike, *Japan's Decision for War*, 131–2, 135–8, 160.

15. Thaddeus Tuleja, *Statesmen and Admirals: Quest for a Far Eastern Naval Policy* (New York: W.W. Norton, 1963), 19.

16. "Japan: Estimate of Political-Military Situation," in ONI Monthly Intelligence Bulletin (ONIMIB), no. 8 (15 August 1923), ONI, Security Classified Publications, Box 13, RG 38, National Archives and Records Administration, Washington, D.C. (NARA 1).

17. Louis Morton, *Strategy and Command: The First Two Years*, United States Army in World War II: The War in the Pacific (Washington, DC: Office of the Chief of Military History, 1962–1989), 27.

18. Philip Rosen, "The Treaty Navy, 1919–1937," in Hagan, *In Peace and War*, 231.

19. Vlahos, *Blue Sword*, 72–3, 82–5, 117–29. Also see "The Influence of Families, Clans, and the Military Class of the Japanese Government," lecture at Naval War College, delivered by Commander F. F. Rogers (USN), May 1926, Records of the Chief of Naval Operations (CNO), Intelligence Division, Box 466, Folder C-9-e, RG 38, NARA 1.

20. Mahnken, *Uncovering Ways of War*, 19.

21. "The Office of Naval Intelligence: Its Purpose and Its Work," in ONIMIB 11, no. 9 (March 1929), ONI, Security Classified Publications, Box 16, RG 38, NARA 1.

22. Packard, *A Century of U.S. Naval Intelligence*, 17.

23. Jeffery Dorwart, *Conflict of Duty: The U.S. Navy's Intelligence Dilemma, 1919–1945* (Annapolis, MD: Naval Institute Press, 1983), 4–8.

24. "Information to be sought regarding Japanese capital ships," Bureau of Construction and Repair to DNI, 19 March 1925, and "Request for Ordnance Information: Japan," BuOrd to DNI, 18 February 1928, Box 319, Folder S/QN/EF37, and "Firing of Torpedoes from Submarines," Director of Fleet Training to DNI, 28 August 1933, Box 123, Folder A5–2/QN/EF37, Director of Naval Intelligence (DNI), General Correspondence, RG 38, NARA 1.

25. "Information desired re: Aviation Activities and Development in Japan," Chief of BuAer to DNI, 14 February 1925, DNI, General Correspondence, Box 66, Folder A3-1/QN/EF37, RG 38, NARA 1.

26. Dorwart, *Conflict of Duty*, 26.

27. Mahnken, *Uncovering Ways of War*, 25, 46–7.

28. "Notes on the Airplane Carrier *Akagi*," in ONIMIB 8, no. 9 (March 1926), and "Japan: Naval Notes—Airplane Carrier *Kaga*," in ONIMIB 8, no. 10 (April 1926), ONI, Security Classified Publications, Box 14, RG 38, NARA 1.

29. See "Big Japanese Naval Budget to Include the Proposed 8:8 Building Program Expenses" (from *Nichi Nichi*), provided by Naval Attaché (Tokyo) to DNI, 9 October 1919, Office of Naval Records and Library, 1911–1927, Box 703, Folder 4, RG 45, NARA 1.

30. Data on Japanese Naval Vessels, Naval Attaché (Tokyo) to DNI, 8 October 1921, ONI Confidential Files, Box 81, Folder 21088–192, RG 38, NARA 1.

31. Japanese Ambassador (Washington) to Secretary of State, 12 February 1932, and Secretary of State to Secretary of Navy, 21 January 1935, DNI, General Correspondence, Box 327, Folder CA/QN/EF37, RG 38, NARA 1.

32. Dorwart, *Conflict of Duty*, 45.

33. Regulations for the enforcement of the Military Resources Secrets Law, 11 July 1939, Secret Naval Attaché Reports, 1936–43, Box 3, Vol. 2, Serial No. 155, RG

38, National Archives and Records Administration, College Park, MD (NARA 2). All documents henceforward, unless otherwise stated, were consulted at NARA 2.

34. Naval policy and trends from the Diet proceedings, 17 February 1938, Secret Naval Attaché Reports, 1936–43, Box 3, Vol. 1, Serial No. 43, RG 38.

35. Capital ship construction, 16 January 1939, Vol. 2, Serial No. 8, Box 3, and Naval Construction at Kawasaki dockyard, Kobe, 16 March 1939, Box 20, ONI, Foreign Intelligence Branch, Naval Attaché Reports from Tokyo, RG 38.

36. Japanese capital ship building program, 11 October 1939, Secret Naval Attaché Reports, 1936–43, Box 3, Vol. 2, Serial No. 231, RG 38.

37. Zacharias, *Secret Missions*, 56.

38. "Japan—General Characteristics: Industry and Ability of Japanese," Naval Attaché (Tokyo) to DNI, 20 February 1935, Records of the CNO, Intelligence Division, Box 1330A, Folder U-1-b, RG 38, NARA 1.

39. "Summary of Information Bearing on Japanese Preparation for War," in ONIMIB, no. 9-1921 (September 1921), in ONI Security Classified Publications, Box 12, RG 38, NARA 1.

40. "Japan: Efficiency in Gunnery," in ONIMIB, no. 12-20, December 1920, in ONI Security Classified Publications, Box 12, RG 38, NARA 1.

41. Anthony Watts and Brian Gordon, *The Imperial Japanese Navy* (New York: Doubleday, 1971), 40–1, 52–8.

42. Hansgeorg Jentschura et al., *Warships of the Imperial Japanese Navy, 1869–1945*, trans. A. Preston and J. Brown (Annapolis, MD: Naval Institute Press, 1992), 35; M. J. Whitley, *Battleships of World War II: An International Encyclopedia* (London: Arms & Armour, 1998), 200–202.

43. See Masataka Chihaya, "Some Stories Concerning the Construction of the *Yamato*–class Battleships," in Goldstein, and Dillon, eds., *Pacific War Papers*, 94–7.

44. Janusz Skulski, *The Battleship Yamato: Anatomy of the Ship* (London: Conway, 1988), 15–17; Whitley, *Battleships*, 210–1.

45. Mark Peattie, *Sunburst: The Rise of Japanese Naval Air Power, 1909–1941* (Annapolis, MD: Naval Institute Press, 2001), 17–20. Also see John Ferris, "A British 'Unofficial' Aviation Mission and Japanese Naval Developments, 1919–1929," *Journal of Strategic Studies* 5 (September 1982): 416–39.

46. Jiro Horikoshi, *Eagles of Mitsubishi: The Story of the Zero Fighter*, trans. Shojiro Shindo and Harold Wantiez (London: Orbis, 1981), 15.

47. Akira Yoshimura, *Zero Fighter*, trans. Retsu Kaiho and Michael Gregson (Westport, CT: Praeger, 1996), 39–49. For a firsthand account, see Horikoshi, *Eagles of Mitsubishi*, 3–8, 32–64.

48. "Gun Elevations of Japanese Vessels," Memorandum for DNI, 17 November 1924, and "Gun Elevations on board Japanese Capital Ships," Acting Naval Attaché (Tokyo) to DNI, 13 January 1925, in DNI, General Correspondence, Box 319, Folder S/QN/EF37, RG 38, NARA 1.

49. "Maximum ranges of Main Battery Guns of Japanese Capital Ships," DNI to President of Naval War College, 12 June 1924, in DNI, General Correspondence, Box 319, Folder S/QN/EF37, RG 38, NARA 1.

50. Characteristics and armament of Type 97 fighter, 17 September 1940, Report No. 152, Box 21, in ONI, Foreign Intelligence Branch, Naval Attaché Reports from Tokyo, RG 38.

51. Aviation Notes, 13 December 1939, Report No. 265, Box 20, in ONI, Foreign Intelligence Branch, Naval Attaché Reports from Tokyo, RG 38.

52. The aircraft industry in Japan, 3 August 1939, Serial No. 172, in Secret Naval Attaché Reports, 1936–43, Vol. 2, Box 3, RG 38.

53. Annual naval aviation digest, 30 June 1938 to 30 June 1939, Serial No. 178 in Secret Naval Attaché Reports, 1936–43, Vol. 2, Box 3, RG 38.

54. "Situation in the Pacific: Studies Prepared under Direction of Admiral Yarnell (Commander-in-Chief Asiatic Fleet)," 26 November 1938, Navy General Board, Subject File, Box 151, Folder 429, RG 80, NARA 1.

55. David Evans and Mark Peattie, *Kaigun: The Strategy, Tactics, and Technology of the Imperial Japanese Navy, 1887–1941* (Annapolis, MD: Naval Institute Press, 1997), 187–8, 194–201, 205–12, 238–9.

56. Minoru Genda, "Tactical Planning in the Imperial Japanese Navy," *Naval War College Review* 22 (October 1969): 45–7.

57. Jisaburo Ozawa, "Development of the Japanese Navy's Operational Concept against America," in *Pacific War Papers*, ed. Goldstein and Dillon, 73.

58. Hiroyuki Agawa, *The Reluctant Admiral: Yamamoto and the Imperial Navy*, trans. John Bester (Tokyo: Kodansha, 1979), 220–9.

59. Annual Report of Naval Activities, operating year 1936, dated 28 January 1937, Secret Naval Attaché Reports, 1936–43, Box 3, Vol. 1, RG 38; Air show at Haneda Airport, 3 October 1939, Report No. 222, ONI, Foreign Intelligence Branch, Naval Attaché Reports from Tokyo, Box 20, RG 38.

60. Night Training and Operations, 18 October 1934, Naval Attaché (Tokyo), Report No. 261, ONI Monograph Files, Box 77, RG 38.

61. Operating schedule of Combined Fleet, 13 May 1941, Secret Naval Attaché Reports, 1936–43, Vol. 3, Serial No. 75, Box 4, RG 38.

62. Ronald Lewin, *The Other ULTRA: Codes, Cyphers, and the Defeat of Japan* (London: Hutchinson, 1982), 28.

63. Mahnken, *Uncovering Ways of War*, 58.

64. See Mahnken, *Uncovering Ways of War*, 25, 46–7, 58, 74–5; Malcolm Muir, "Rearming in a Vacuum: U.S. Navy Intelligence and the Japanese Capital Ship Threat, 1936–1945," *Journal of Military History* 54, no. 4 (1990): 477.

65. Various reports on Japanese Grand Fleet maneuvers, June–August 1933, dated 7 March 1934, Commander-in-Chief, Asiatic Fleet, SRH-223, Papers of Edwin T. Layton, Box 21, Manuscripts Collection, Naval War College, Newport, RI (NWC).

66. Captain Thomas Dyer, interview by Paul Stilwell, 29 August 1983, pages 135–6, Oral History Collection, NWC.

67. See Richard Aldrich, "Conspiracy or Confusion?: Churchill, Roosevelt, and Pearl Harbor," chap. 5 in *Intelligence and the War Against Japan: Britain, America, and the Politics of Secret Service* (Cambridge, England: Cambridge University Press, 2000); Christopher Andrew, *For the President's Eyes Only: Secret Intelligence and*

the American Presidency from Washington to Bush (London: HarperCollins, 1995), 108–20; John Costello, *The Pacific War, 1941–1945* (New York: Rawson-Wade, 1982), 670–714; Ladislas Farago, *The Broken Seal: The Story of "Operation Magic" and the Pearl Harbor Disaster* (New York: Random House, 1967); David Kahn, *The Codebreakers* (London: Weidenfeld & Nicolson, 1973), 12–3, 44–5; Prados, *Combined Fleet Decoded*; Gordon Prange, *At Dawn We Slept: The Untold Story of Pearl Harbor* (London: Michael Joseph, 1981); Roberta Wohlstetter, *Pearl Harbor: Warning and Decision* (Stanford, CA: Stanford University Press, 1962). For a firsthand account, see Oral History of Captain Joseph J. Rochefort, 113–18, Oral History Collection, NWC.

68. An alternative explanation, to the effect that the Pearl Harbor attack force (Kido Butai) did transmit radio communications, and the ONI was in fact reading JN-25, can be found in Timothy Wilford, *Pearl Harbor Redefined: U.S. Navy Radio Intelligence in 1941* (Lanham, MD: University Press of America, 2001). However, virtually all reliable sources indicate that the Kido Butai refrained from communicating via radio. For a recent analysis of the issue, see Ken Kotani, "Pearl Harbor: Japanese Planning and Command Structure," in *The Pacific War Companion: From Pearl Harbor to Hiroshima*, ed. Daniel Marston (New York: Osprey, 2007), 31–45.

69. Prados, *Combined Fleet Decoded*, 163.

70. "Observation on Japan and the Japanese with particular reference to the Japanese Navy," Commander F. J. Horne (USN) to Secretary of the Navy, 7 May 1919, Records of the CNO, Intelligence Division, Box 1330A, Folder U-1-b, RG 38, NARA 1.

71. Notes on naval subjects, 27 June 1941, Box 4, Vol. 3, Serial No. 72, in Secret Naval Attaché Reports, 1936–43, RG 38.

72. Yokosuka naval air station, 17 March 1937, Box 3, Vol. 1, Serial No. 62, in Secret Naval Attaché Reports, 1936–43, Vol. 2, Box 3, RG 38.

73. Report on Japanese assault landing operations in the Shanghai area, by First Lieutenant Victor H. Krulak, Assistant R-2, 4th Marines, 1937, ONI Monograph Files, Box 77, RG 38.

74. Sino-Japanese Conflict, 30 May 1938, by Commander-in-Chief, U.S. Asiatic Fleet, DNI, General Correspondence, Folder A8-2 FS, Box 196; Aerial Activities in Sino-Japanese Conflict, 15 and 29 August 1938, Commander, U.S. Asiatic Fleet, South China Patrol, Folder A8-2, Box 194, RG 38, NARA 1.

75. Aviation statistical summary, 1 July 1938, Secret Naval Attaché Reports, 1936–43, Box 3, Serial No. 207, Vol. 2, RG 38.

76. Peattie, *Sunburst*, 109–21.

77. Ikuhiko Hata and Yasuho Izawa, *Japanese Naval Aces and Fighter Units in World War II*, trans. Don Gorham (Annapolis, MD: Naval Institute Press, 1989), 90.

78. Weekly intelligence summary for week ending 10 October 1937, by Commanding Officer, USS *Oahu* to Commander-in-Chief, U.S. Asiatic Fleet, DNI, General Correspondence, Box 194, Folder A8-2, RG 38, NARA 1.

79. Resumé of present China incident, 17 July 1938, ONI, Far Eastern Branch, Intelligence Reports from Headquarters 4th Marines, Shanghai, China, Box 3, RG 38, NARA 1.

80. "Japanese Navy's Participation in the Great War," prepared by ONI for Secretary of State, 23 September 1921, ONI Confidential Files, Box 81, Folder 21088-192, RG 38, NARA 1.

81. "Training and Instruction of Personnel," in ONIMIB 10, no. 5 (November 1927), ONI, Security Classified Publications, Box 16, RG 38, NARA 1.

82. "Conclusions and Inferences re: Orange," by W. D. Puleston (DNI), 13 September 1934, DNI Official Correspondence, Box 2, RG 38, NARA 1.

83. For a parallel account of British intelligence, see Arthur Marder, *Old Friends, New Enemies: The Royal Navy and the Imperial Japanese Navy, 1936–45*, vol. 1, *Strategic Illusions, 1936–41* (Oxford: Oxford University Press, 1981), 342–6; Wesley Wark, "In Search of a Suitable Japan: British Naval Intelligence in the Pacific before the Second World War," *Intelligence and National Security* 1, no. 2 (1986): 189–212.

84. "Japanese Racial Characteristics: A Study of Their Effects on the Conduct of a Modern War," in ONIMIB, no. 7-1922 (July 1922), ONI, Security Classified Publications, Box 13, RG 38, NARA 1.

85. Mahnken, *Uncovering Ways of War*, 58–9, 65, 70.

86. "Japanese Grand Maneuvers, 1930," in ONIMIB 13, nos. 6 and 7 (December 1930 and January 1931), Box 18, in ONI, Security Classified Publications, RG 38, NARA 1.

87. "Japanese Gunnery Training," September 1931, File 907-5800, Box 82, in ONI, Security Classified Publications, RG 38, NARA 1, and "Japan: Naval Gunnery School at Yokosuka," in ONIMIB 10, no. 11 (May 1928), Box 16 in ONI, Security Classified Publications, RG 38, NARA 1.

88. "Night Battle Practice," December 1932, in Box 82, Folder 907-5800, in ONI Monograph Files, RG 38.

89. "Japanese Navy Operations and Target Practice," January 1941, Box 82, Folder 907-5800, in ONI Monograph Files, RG 38.

90. "Special Grand Naval Review," 11 November 1936, Box 77, Folder 907-3000, in ONI Monograph Files, RG 38.

91. See Evans and Peattie, *Kaigun*, 252.

92. Carl Boyd, "Japanese Military Effectiveness: The Interwar Period," in *Military Effectiveness*, ed. Allan Millett and Williamson Murray, vol. 2, *The Interwar Period* (Boston: Allen & Unwin, 1988), 160.

93. Mahnken, *Uncovering Ways of War*, 70–1.

94. "Heavy Cruiser Types for Future Construction," 23 March 1940, Memorandum by Captain C. M. Cooke (WPD, Office of Naval Operations) for Chairman of General Board, Navy General Board, Subject File, Box 78, Folder 420-6, RG 80, NARA 1.

95. Operations Problem I (Tactical), Blue Staff Solution, 8 August 1938, and Orange Staff Solution, August 1939, by Senior Class 1939, Student Problems and Solutions, Box 9, RG 12, NWC.

96. "Aviation, Japan," in ONIMIB, no. 1-1920 (January 1920), Box 12, in ONI Classified Publications, RG 38, NARA 1.

97. "Japan: Aeronautical," in ONIMIB 10, no. 2 (August 1927), Box 16, in ONI

Classified Publications, RG 38, NARA 1, and "Japanese Naval Air Maneuvers, 1929," in ONIMIB 12, no. 11 (May 1930), Box 17, in ONI Classified Publications, RG 38, NARA 1.

98. "Japanese Aviation: Personnel, Training and Operations," in ONIMIB 16, no. 1 (July 1935), Box 18, in ONI Classified Publications, RG 38, NARA 1.

99. "Aviation Notes: Japan," in ONIMIB 12, no. 1 (July 1929), Box 12, in ONI Classified Publications, RG 38, NARA 1.

100. "Japan: Naval Aviation," in ONIMIB 8, no. 4 (October 1925), Box 14, in ONI Classified Publications, RG 38, NARA 1.

101. "Summary of Japanese Aviation," data taken from ONI publication "Monograph–Japanese," ca. 1932, DNI, General Correspondence, Box 192, Folder A8-2/EF37, RG 38, NARA 1.

102. "Aviation Notes: Japan," in ONIMIB 14, nos.5–8 (November 1931–February 1932), ONI, Security Classified Publications, Box 18, RG 38, NARA 1.

103. "Conclusions and Inferences re: Orange," by W. D. Puleston (DNI), 13 September 1934, DNI Official Correspondence, Box 2, RG 38, NARA 1.

104. John Thach, "Butch O'Hare and the Thach Weave," in *Carrier Warfare in the Pacific: An Oral History Collection*, ed. E. T. Wooldridge (Washington, DC: Smithsonian Institution, 1993), 10–2; Jim Rearden, *Cracking the Zero Mystery: How the U.S. Learned to Beat Japan's Vaunted WWII Fighter Plane* (Harrisburg, PA: Stackpole, 1990), 17.

105. William Halsey and J. Bryan, *Admiral Halsey's Story* (New York: McGraw Hill, 1947), 70–1.

106. Masatake Okumiya and Jiro Horikoshi, with Martin Caidin, *Zero!: The Story of the Japanese Navy Air Force, 1937–1945* (London: Cassell, 1956), 38–9.

107. Thomas Hone et al., *Battle Line: The United States Navy, 1919–1939* (Annapolis, MD: Naval Institute Press, 2006), 69–71.

108. Hone et al., *Battle Line*, 77–80. Also see FTP 138, Tentative Battleship Tactical Instructions, 1933, and FTP 143, War Instructions, 1934, in Box 107 and Box 108, respectively, Fleet Tactical Publications, U.S. Navy, Operational Archives, World War II Command File, United States Naval Historical Center, Washington, D.C. (NHC).

109. Thomas Hone et al., *American and British Aircraft Carrier Development, 1919–1941* (Annapolis, MD: Naval Institute Press, 1999), 46–7. Also see Richard Turk, "Edward Walter Eberle," in *The Chiefs of Naval Operations*, ed. Robert Love (Annapolis, MD: Naval Institute Press, 1980), 41–2.

110. Geoffrey Till, "Adopting the Aircraft Carrier: The British, American, and Japanese Case Studies," in *Military Innovation*, ed. Millett and Murray, 203; John Kuehn, *Agents of Innovation: The General Board and the Design of the Fleet that Defeated the Japanese Navy* (Annapolis, MD: Naval Institute Press, 2008), 89–91.

111. Study of uses of aircraft carriers in connection with determination of a carrier policy, prepared by BuAer for General Board, 1 August 1931, Navy General Board, Subject File, Box 80, Folder 420-7, RG 80, NARA 1. Also see Hone et al., *Carrier Development*, 51–5; Wayne Hughes, *Fleet Tactics: Theory and Practice* (Annapolis, MD: Naval Institute Press, 1986), 87–8.

112. Archibald Turnbull and Clifford Lord, *History of United States Naval Aviation* (New Haven, CT: Yale University Press, 1949), 161.

113. Norman Friedman, *U.S. Aircraft Carriers: An Illustrated Design History* (Annapolis, MD: Naval Institute Press, 1983), 38–9, 120–1.

114. Ronald Spector, *Professors of War: The Naval War College and the Development of the Naval Profession* (Newport, RI: Naval War College Press, 1977), 145–8.

115. Friedman, *U.S. Aircraft Carriers*, 34–5.

116. FTP 143, War Instructions, 1934, Fleet Tactical Publications, U.S. Navy, Box 108, Operational Archives, World War II Command File, NHC.

117. William McBride, "Challenging a Strategic Paradigm: Aviation and the U.S. Navy Special Policy Board of 1924," *Journal of Strategic Studies* 14, no. 1 (1991): 76–81.

118. Fleet Organization and Command, 1 October 1934, by Commander-in-Chief, U.S. Fleet, Papers of Ernest J. King, MF 396, Reel 1, Microfilm Collection, NWC.

119. Friedman, *U.S. Aircraft Carriers*, 13.

120. Malcolm Muir, "The United States Navy in World War II: An Assessment," in *Re-evaluating Major Naval Combatants of World War II*, ed. James Sadkovich (Westport, CT: Greenwood, 1990), 4.

121. Foreword for 1945 edition of the *Annual*, Papers of Ernest J. King, Box 30, Library of Congress, Washington, D.C. (LOC).

122. George Baer, *One Hundred Years of Sea Power: The US Navy, 1890–1990* (Stanford, CA: Stanford University Press, 1994), 85.

123. Miller, *War Plan Orange*, 19–114. Also see Louis Morton, "War Plan Orange: Evolution of a Strategy," *World Politics* 11, no. 2 (January 1959): 227, 230–1.

124. Strategic Survey of the Pacific, prepared by General Board, for Secretary of the Navy, 26 April 1923, Navy General Board, Subject File, Box 130, Folder 425, RG 80, NARA 1.

125. Hagan, *This People's Navy*, 267.

126. "Budget 1926: Estimate of the Situation and Base Development Program," prepared by Director of War Plans Division, for CNO, 17 March 1924, Folder 425, Box 130, in Navy General Board, Subject File, RG 80, NARA 1.

127. Aircraft Carriers, prepared by Chief of BuAer, for Secretary of Navy, 6 January 1927, Folder 420-7, Box 80, in Navy General Board, Subject File, RG 80, NARA 1.

128. Lawrence Douglas, "Robert Edward Coontz," in *The Chiefs of Naval Operations*, ed. Love, 30.

129. "Explanation of the needs of the Navy–Topic C: Steps actually taken which could influence our course," prepared for Secretary of Navy, 3 November 1924, Folder 420-2, Box 61, and Five-year Building Program, prepared for Secretary of Navy, 27 September 1927, Folder 420-2, Box 62, in Navy General Board, Subject File, RG 80, NARA 1.

130. "Blue" was the color code designated for the U.S. Fleet.

131. Building Program: Fiscal Year 1937, prepared for Secretary of Navy, 24 May 1935, Box 62, Folder 420-2, in Navy General Board, Subject File, RG 80, NARA 1.

132. Building Program for Fiscal Year 1941, prepared for Secretary of Navy, 26 April 1939, Box 63, Folder 420-2, in Navy General Board, Subject File, RG 80, NARA 1.

133. CNO, Memorandum for the General Board on battleship building program, 20 March 1939, Box 63, File 420-2, in Navy General Board, Subject File, RG 80, NARA 1.

134. Expedition of Shipbuilding Program and Emergency Defense Preparations in General, prepared for Secretary of Navy, 14 May 1940, Box 63, Folder 420-2, in Navy General Board, Subject File, RG 80, NARA 1.

135. "Are We Ready?," Part III, prepared for Secretary of the Navy, 14 June 1941, Box 134, Folder 425, in Navy General Board, Subject File, RG 80, NARA 1.

136. Problem II-1937-SR: Blue Staff Solution, 4 January 1937, Publications by the Department of Operations, Box 80, RG 4, NWC.

137. Ibid. Also see Operations Problem V (Strategic), Blue Staff Solution, February 1939, by Senior Class 1939, Student Problems and Solutions, Box 9, RG 12, NWC.

138. Analysis of Tactical Problem I-1936-SR, September 1935, Publications by the Department of Intelligence, Box 74, RG 4, NWC.

139. Hedley Willmott, *Empires in the Balance: Japanese and Allied Pacific Strategies to April 1942* (Annapolis, MD: Naval Institute Press, 1982), 439, 451–6, 458–60; Evans and Peattie, *Kaigun*, 488–92. The most recent analysis is James Wood, *Japanese Military Strategy in the Pacific War: Was Defeat Inevitable?* (Lanham, MD: Rowman & Littlewood, 2007), 26–8.

140. See Problem II-1931-SR, Blue Solution, and Problem V-1932-SR, Revision of Problem IV-1931-SR, Blue Solution, March 1932, and Problem II-1936-SR, Blue Solution, December 1935, in Publications by the Department of Operations, Box 54, Box 59, Box 75, respectively, RG4; Problem IV-1936-SR, Estimate of the Situation by C-in-C Blue Fleet, April 1936, Student Problems and Solutions, Box 7, RG 12, NWC.

141. Operations Problem V (Strategic), Blue Staff Solution, February 1939, by Senior Class 1939, in Student Problems and Solutions, Box 9, RG 12, NWC.

142. Blue Statement of Problem, January 1939, in Student Problems and Solutions, Box 9, RG 12, NWC.

143. Estimate of Special Situation, Orange, 28 September 1938, Office of the CNO, War Plans Division, 1918–41, Strategic Plans Division Records, Miscellaneous Subject File, Box 64, RG 38.

144. William Puleston, *The Armed Forces of the Pacific: A Comparison of the Military and Naval Power of the United States and Japan* (New Haven, CT: Yale University Press, 1941), 121–2, 168–9.

145. Basic Studies for Landing Operations in a Blue-Orange War, 23 June 1939, Office of the CNO, War Plans Division, 1918–41, Strategic Plans, Box 28, WPL-35, RG 38.

146. Maurice Matloff and Edwin Snell, *Strategic Planning for Coalition Warfare*, United States Army in World War II: The War Department (Washington, DC: Office of the Chief of Military History, 1950–1955), 13–4.

147. Lester Brune, *The Origins of American National Security Policy: Sea Power, Air Power and Foreign Policy, 1900–1941* (Manhattan, KS: MA/AH Publishing, 1981), 116.

148. Morton, *Strategy and Command*, 81–2; Jonathan Utley, *Going to War with Japan, 1937–1941* (Knoxville: Tennessee University Press, 1985), 113–4.

149. Joint Army and Navy Basic War Plan, Rainbow 5, May 1941, Appendix I: Office of the CNO, War Plans Division, 1918–41, Strategic Plans, Box 34, WPL-46, RG 38.

150. Ibid.

151. Samuel Morison, *The Rising Sun in the Pacific, 1931–April 1942*, History of United States Naval Operations in World War II, vol. 3 (Urbana and Chicago: Illinois University Press, 2001), 129–31.

Chapter 2: Dismantling the "Lesser Foe" and "Superior Enemy" Images
DECEMBER 1941 TO EARLY 1943

1. Dorwart, *Conflict of Duty*, 189–90.

2. Thomas Buell, *Master of Sea Power: A Biography of Admiral Ernest J. King* (Boston: Little, Brown and Co., 1980), 176.

3. Packard, *A Century of U.S. Naval Intelligence*, 147.

4. Bath, *Tracking the Axis Enemy*, 176.

5. See Charter for the Joint Intelligence Committee, n.d., ca. February/March 1942, Records of the JCS, Central Decimal File, 1942–45, Box 201, RG 218.

6. Wilfred Holmes, *Double-edged Secrets: U.S. Naval Intelligence Operations in the Pacific during World War II* (Annapolis, MD: Naval Institute Press, 1979), 11.

7. Record of Costello and Pineau interview of Layton, May 1983, Papers of Edwin T. Layton, Box 30, Manuscript Collection, NWC.

8. Packard, *A Century of U.S. Naval Intelligence*, 171.

9. "Action in the Macassar Strait," in ONI Weekly, no. 11 (8 April 1942), ONI Security Classified Publications, Box 5, RG 38.

10. Appreciation of the Pacific situation as at 15 January 1942, Papers of Chester Nimitz, Series 1, Box 9, World War II Command Series, NHC.

11. Steven Ross, *American War Plans, 1941–1945* (London: Frank Cass, 1997), 24.

12. U.S. Pacific Fleet, Estimate of the Situation, 24 December 1941, Papers of Chester Nimitz, Series 1, Box 9, World War II Command Series, NHC.

13. Grace Hayes, *The History of the Joint Chiefs of Staff in World War II: The War against Japan* (Annapolis, MD: Naval Institute Press, 1982), 108–20; Robert Love, "Ernest Joseph King," in *The Chiefs of Naval Operations*, ed. Love, 148–9.

14. Costello, *The Pacific War*, 187–90, 239.

15. Ernest King and Walter Whitehill, *Fleet Admiral King: A Naval Record* (London: Eyre & Spottiswoode, 1953), 164.

16. Costello, *The Pacific War*, 241.

17. Elmer Potter, *Nimitz* (Annapolis, MD: Naval Institute Press, 1976), 49.

18. "Notes on Mitsubishi Navy Type 96 twin-engine bomber," in Pacific Fleet Intelligence Bulletin (PFIB), no. 7-42, in Box 7, Folder A8, JICPOA (hereafter, BLUE 644), Naval Forces Operating in the Pacific, RG 313 (hereafter, RG 313).

19. "Japanese bombing of U.S. naval vessels in the ABDA area, 4–5 February 1942," by Op-16-F-2, Box 5, Folder A8/(12), Serial 34-42, BLUE 644, RG 313.

20. Estimate of the situation, 22 April 1942, Papers of Chester Nimitz, Series 1, Box 9, World War II Command Series, NHC.

21. Japanese ship-borne aircraft and aircraft types, 22 April 1942, by Op-16-F-2, Confidential Reports of Naval Attachés, 1940–1946, Box 1217, Folder O-12-c, 12484-D, Serial 44-42, RG 38.

22. Appreciation of the Pacific situation as at 15 January 1942, Papers of Chester Nimitz, Series 1, Box 9, World War II Command Series, NHC.

23. Attacks on the *Prince of Wales*, *Repulse*, and on Pearl Harbor, 17 December 1941, and Japanese high-level bombing attacks in the ABDA area, 15 March 1942, by Op-16-F-2, Serial 83-41 and Serial 35-42, respectively, Box 5, Folder A8/(19), BLUE 644, RG 313.

24. Japanese ship-borne aircraft and aircraft types, 22 April 1942, by Op-16-F-2, Confidential Reports of Naval Attachés, 1940–1946, Box 1217, Folder O-12-c, 12484-D, Serial 44-42, RG 38.

25. "Raiding the Island Bases," in ONI Weekly, Confidential Issue, no.11 (10 June 1942), ONI Security Classified Publications, Box 1, RG 38.

26. Composition and employment of Japanese task forces in southward advance, 10 April 1942, by CINCPAC, Commander, Aircraft South Pacific Force (hereafter, BLUE 242), Box 14, RG 313. For a secondary account, see Walter Karig, *Battle Report: Pearl Harbor to Coral Sea* (New York: Farrar & Rinehart, 1944), 169.

27. ONI Combat Narratives, Java Sea Campaign, dated 13 March 1943, http://www.ibiblio.org/hyperwar/USN/USN–CN–Java/index.html (accessed 17 February 2009).

28. Ernest King, *The U.S. Navy at War: First Report to the Secretary of the Navy* (Washington, DC: Headquarters of the Commander-in-Chief, U.S. Fleet, 1944), 46.

29. See John Lundstrom, *The First Team: Naval Air Combat from Pearl Harbor to Midway* (Annapolis, MD: Naval Institute Press, 1984), 182; Dan Vandervat, *The Pacific Campaign* (London: Hodder & Stoughton, 1991), 224.

30. "Japanese air tactics," in PFIB, no.1-42, 12 January 1942, BLUE 644, Box 7, Folder A8, RG 313.

31. Richard Bueschel, *Mitsubishi A6M1/2 Zero-sen in Imperial Japanese Naval Air Service* (Oxford: Osprey, 1970), 14–5.

32. "Tactical lessons learned from aircraft in combat," prepared by Lieutenant General George H. Brett, for Chief of USAAF, in PFIB, no. 8-42 (26 March 1942), Box 7, Folder A8, in BLUE 644, RG 313.

33. "Japanese fighter tactics and activities," in Commander, Allied Naval Forces, SWPA, Intelligence Information Bulletin, no. 2/1942 (27 May 1942), Box 5, A8/(19), in BLUE 644, RG 313.

34. "Japanese air tactics," in ONI Weekly, no. 17 (20 May 1942), ONI Security Classified Publications, Box 5, RG 38.

35. "Personal observations from an Army flight officer participating in Java action," in PFIB, no. 5-42, in Box 7, Folder A8, BLUE 644, RG 313.

36. "Information received from USAAC officers returning from the Netherlands East Indies, Philippines, and Australia area," in PFIB, no. 5-42, in Box 7, Folder A8, BLUE 644, RG 313.

37. "Aerial combat experience in the Far East," in ONI Weekly, no. 5 (25 February 1942), ONI Security Classified Publications, Box 5, RG 38.

38. "Japanese fighter tactics and activities," in Commander, Allied Naval Forces, SWPA, Intelligence Information Bulletin, no. 2/1942 (27 May 1942), Box 5, A8/(19), in BLUE 644, RG 313.

39. "Intelligence information, Japanese aircraft: performances, fields of fire and methods of attack," 8 December 1941, BLUE 644, Box 5, Folder A8/(17), RG 313.

40. "Air combat intelligence officers," 1 May 1942, written by Chief of BuAer to COMINCH, BLUE 644, Box 10, Folder A8–2/a, RG 313. Also see Packard, *A Century of U.S. Naval Intelligence*, 171–2.

41. "Destroyers, Battle Force, War Bulletins," in COMINCH, Information Bulletin, no. 11, in ONI Security Classified Publications, World War II, Box 1, RG 38.

42. "The Twenty-millimeter machine gun, June 1942," in Machine Gun Bulletin, no. 2, in ONI Security Classified Publications, World War II, Box 1, RG 38.

43. "Japanese aviation operations and tactics," in PFIB, no. 7-42, BLUE 644, Box 7, Folder A8, RG 313.

44. Clark Reynolds, *Admiral John H. Towers: The Struggle for Naval Air Supremacy* (Annapolis, MD: Naval Institute Press, 1991), 371.

45. "Estimated strength of the Japanese navy," in ONI Weekly, Confidential Issue, no. 23 (1 July 1942), in Box 1, ONI Security Classified Publications, RG 38.

46. "Japanese iron and steel production," in ONI Weekly, no. 48 (23 December 1942), in Box 5, ONI Security Classified Publications, RG 38.

47. "The Economic Capacity of Japan as a Belligerent" (article based on material furnished by the Board of Economic Warfare), in ONI Weekly, Confidential Issue, no. 25 (15 July 1942), in Box 1, ONI Security Classified Publications, RG 38.

48. Summary of Japanese warships built, 3 August 1942, by Op-16-F-2, BLUE 644, Box 5, Folder A8/(11), Serial #76-42, RG 313.

49. Hayes, *Joint Chiefs*, 177–86.

50. Jack Coombe, *Derailing the Tokyo Express: The Naval Battles for the Solomon Islands that Sealed Japan's Fate* (Harrisburg, PA: Stackpole, 1991), 117.

51. Future operations in the Solomons Sea area, 8 December 1942, Papers of Chester Nimitz, Series 1, Box 11, World War II Command Series, NHC.

52. "Axis torpedoes," in ONI Weekly, no. 36 (30 September 1942), in ONI Security Classified Publications, Box 5, RG 38.

53. "The Fifth Battle of the Solomons," in ONI Weekly, no. 46 (9 December 1942), in ONI Security Classified Publications, Box 5, RG 38.

54. "Naval Task Forces, March 1943," in ONI Monographs, Box 77, Folder 907-175, RG 38.

55. "Japanese destroyer tactics, March 1943," in ONI Monographs, Box 77, Folder 907-175, RG 38.

56. Solomons Islands Campaign, Part II: The Battle of Savo Island, 9 August 1942, and Part III, The Battle of the Eastern Solomons, 23–25 August 1942, ONI Security Classified Publications, Combat Narratives, 1942–44, Box 5, RG 38. All ONI combat narratives referred to in the notes, while issued several months after the actual engagement, were based on reports originally written by participating officers.

57. Bruce Loxton and Chris Coulthard-Clark, *The Shame of Savo: Anatomy of a Naval Disaster* (Annapolis, MD: Naval Institute Press, 1994), 263.

58. Action Report, Commanding Officer, USS *President Jackson*, dated 9 August 1942, ADM 199/1328, United Kingdom National Archives, London (UKNA).

59. Frederick Bell, *Condition Red: Destroyer Action in the South Pacific* (New York: Longmans, 1943), 29.

60. Richard Bates, *The Battle of Savo Island, August 9, 1942: Strategic and Tactical Analysis* (Newport, RI: Naval War College, 1950), 356.

61. Louis Brown, *Technical and Military Imperatives: A Radar History of World War II* (Philadelphia: Institute of Physics, 1999), 248.

62. Denis Warner et al., *Disaster in the Pacific: New Light on the Battle of Savo Island* (Annapolis, MD: Naval Institute Press, 1992), 215–6.

63. Frank, *Guadalcanal*, 122. Also see Bernard Edwards, *Salvo: Classic Naval Gun Actions* (London: Arms & Armour, 1999), 142–3.

64. George Dyer, *The Amphibians Came to Conquer: The Story of Admiral Richmond Kelly Turner* (Washington, DC: Naval Historical Center, 1969), 361.

65. Morison, *The Struggle for Guadalcanal*, 61–2.

66. Solomons Islands Campaign, Part IV, Battle of Cape Esperance, 11 October 1942, and Part V, Battle of Santa Cruz Islands, 26 October 1942, ONI Security Classified Publications, Combat Narratives, 1942–44, Box 5, RG 38.

67. Charles Cook, *The Battle of Cape Esperance: Encounter at Guadalcanal* (Annapolis, MD: Naval Institute Press, 1968), 149–50; Frank, *Guadalcanal*, 311.

68. Solomons Islands Campaign, Part VI, Battle of Guadalcanal, 11–15 November 1942, ONI Security Classified Publications, Combat Narratives, 1942–44, Box 5, RG 38.

69. Action report, Night of 14–15 November 1942, Commanding Officer, USS *Washington*, in Commander Battleships and Cruisers, Pacific Fleet (hereafter, BLUE 360), Box 2, RG 313.

70. Commander, Task Force 64, Report of night action, 14–15 November 1942, dated 18 February 1943, in BLUE 360, Box 2, RG 313. Also see Coombe, *Derailing the Tokyo Express*, 127–8.

71. Hughes, *Fleet Tactics*, 118–9.

72. James Grace, *The Naval Battle of Guadalcanal: Night Action, 13 November 1942* (Annapolis, MD: Naval Institute Press, 1999), 49–50.

73. Solomon Islands Campaign, Torpedoing of *Saratoga*, *Wasp*, and *North Carolina*, dated 31 October 1942, Reprint of CINCPAC Reports of actions and campaigns, February 1942 to February 1943 (hereafter, CINCPAC Reports), ADM 199/1493, UKNA.

74. Russell Crenshaw, *South Pacific Destroyer: The Battles for the Solomons from Savo Island to Vela Gulf* (Annapolis, MD: Naval Institute Press, 1998), 20.

75. Solomon Islands Campaign, Part VII, Battle of Tassafaronga, 30 November 1942 ONI Security Classified Publications, Combat Narratives, 1942–44, Box 5, RG 38.

76. Night action of 30 November to 1 December, dated 4 December 1942, Commanding Officer, USS *New Orleans*, World War II Action Reports, Box 23, Folder CA32/A16-3, RG 38.

77. Russell Crenshaw, *The Battle of Tassafaronga* (Baltimore, MD: Nautical & Aviation Publishing Company of America, 1995), 87–8, 105.

78. Commander, Task Force 64, Report of night action, 14–15 November 1942, dated 18 February 1943, BLUE 360, Box 2, RG 313.

79. Future operations in the Solomons Sea area, 8 December 1942, Papers of Chester Nimitz, Series 1, Box 11, World War II Command Series, NHC.

80. Solomon Islands Campaign, Battle of the Solomons, 11–15 November 1942, dated 18 February 1943, by CINCPAC, BLUE 360, Box 2, RG 313.

81. Kenneth Poolman, *The Winning Edge: Naval Technology in Action, 1939–1945* (Annapolis, MD: Naval Institute Press, 1997), 168–9.

82. Crenshaw, *Tassafaronga*, 101–3.

83. Future operations in the Solomons Sea area, 8 December 1942, Papers of Chester Nimitz, Series 1, Box 11, World War II Command Series, NHC.

84. Atsushi Oi, "Why Japan's Anti-submarine Warfare Failed," in *The Japanese Navy in World War II: In the Words of Former Japanese Naval Officers*, ed. David Evans, 2nd ed. (Annapolis, MD: Naval Institute Press, 1986), 387.

85. Boyd, "Japanese Military," 149; M. Chihaya, "An Intimate Look at the Japanese Navy," in *The Pearl Harbor Papers: Inside the Japanese Plans*, ed. Donald Goldstein and Katherine Dillon (Dulles, VA: Brassey's, 1993), 323; Toshiyuki Yokoi, "Thoughts on Japan's Naval Defeat," in *The Japanese Navy in World War II*, ed. Evans, 511.

86. Mark Parillo, *The Japanese Merchant Marine in World War II* (Annapolis, MD: Naval Institute Press, 1993), 7–12, 14–7.

87. Enemy Anti-submarine measures, 22 November 1942 to 15 January 1943, by USS *Halibut*, in Box 81, File 907-5550, ONI Monographs, RG 38.

88. Report on Enemy Anti-submarine Measures, war patrol in Japanese coastal waters, 24 March 1943, by USS *Flying Fish*, in Box 82, File 907-5900, ONI Monographs, RG 38.

89. Report on Enemy Anti-submarine Measures, 18 May 1942, by USS *Grayback*, in Box 82, File 907-5900, ONI Monographs, RG 38.

90. J. E. Talbott, "Weapons Development, War Planning, and Policy: The U.S. Navy and the Submarine, 1917–1941," *Naval War College Review* 37 (May–June 1984): 56–8, 64–8. Also see Gary Weir, "The Search for an American Submarine Strategy and Design, 1916–1936," *Naval War College Review* 44 (Winter 1991): 41–4.

91. Morison, *Coral Sea*, 230–1.

92. Ibid., 221.

93. Ibid., 256–7.

94. Clay Blair, *Silent Victory: The U.S. Submarine War against Japan* (New York: J. B. Lippincott, 1975), 374–7.

95. Ibid., 280.

96. Narrative of Japanese anti-shipping attacks, 1941–43, prepared by Op-35, August 1943, ONI, Air Intelligence Group (Op-16-V), Serials and Publications, Box 12, RG 38.

97. Relation of action reports and combat intelligence to tactical orders and procedure, 11 December 1942, by Commander, Air Force Pacific Fleet, Naval Operating Forces in the Pacific, Commander, Second Carrier Task Force (hereafter, BLUE 627), Box 20, Folder A8, RG 313.

98. Rearden, *Cracking the Zero Mystery*, 30–1. Also see Lundstrom, *Guadalcanal Campaign*, 532–6.

99. Commander L. J. Dow, USN, interview, VF-3, USS *Lexington*, at BuAer, 17 June 1942, ADM 199/461, UKNA.

100. Stanley Johnston, *The Grim Reapers* (London: Jarrolds, 1943), 26–7.

101. Interview of Lieutenant Commander E. J. O'Neill, USN, VF-8 pilot, USS *Hornet*, at BuAer, 18 June 1942, ONI, Air Intelligence Group (Op-16-V), Box 5, RG 38.

102. Comparison of American and Japanese fighter aircraft, 9 August 1942, CINC-PAC to Carriers, Pacific Fleet, BLUE 644, Box 5, Folder A8/(17), RG 313; Lundstrom, *The First Team*, 442.

103. Analysis of Air Operations, Solomons Campaign, January 1943, by Commander Air Force, Pacific Fleet to CINCPAC, Papers of Henry Hap Arnold, Microfilm Reel no. 107, LOC.

104. "Estimate: An offensive for the capture and occupation of Tulagi and vicinity," 6 July 1942, Papers of Chester Nimitz, Series 1, Box 10, World War II Command Series, NHC.

105. Walter Karig, *Battle Report: Pacific War, Middle Phase* (New York: Rinehart, 1947), 40.

106. Bergerud, *Fire in the Sky*; Lundstrom, *The First Team*, 441.

107. "Fighters at Guadalcanal" (personal account of operations given by a major of the USMC, given at BuAer), in Air Ministry Weekly Intelligence Summary (hereafter, AMWIS), no. 175, 9 January 1943, AIR 22/77, UKNA.

108. Performance of P-400 and F4F-4 in Guadalcanal area, 28 September 1942, BLUE 242, Box 15, RG 313.

109. Okumiya and Horikoshi, *Zero!*, 33.

110. Dallas Isom, *Midway Inquest: Why the Japanese Lost the Battle of Midway* (Bloomington, IN: Indiana University Press, 2007), 164–6.

111. Henry Sakaida, *Imperial Japanese Navy Aces, 1937–1945* (Oxford: Osprey, 1999), 22.

112. Peattie, *Sunburst*, 181–4.

113. Jonathan Parshall and Anthony Tully, *Shattered Sword: The Untold Story of the Battle of Midway* (Washington, DC: Potomac, 2005), 404–6.

114. Report of Fighter Direction during attack on Enterprise, 24 August 1942, in Information Bulletin, no. 21, by Aviation Intelligence Branch, BuAer, Technical Aviation Intelligence, Commander Battleships and Cruisers, Pacific Fleet (hereafter, BLUE 361), Box 11, Folder A8, RG 313.

115. Naval air combat intelligence, 22 September 1942, by Aircraft South Pacific Force, BLUE 644, Box 17, Folder A16–3/VV, RG 313.

116. Japanese monograph ONI-49, and Japanese naval building program, by Op-16-FE, Serial 54-43, Confidential Reports of Naval Attachés, 1940–1946, Box 196, Folder O-12-c, 7206-S, RG 38.

117. Lundstrom, *Guadalcanal Campaign*, 138, 141.

118. Narrative of Japanese anti-shipping attacks, 1941–43, Comment by Commanding Officer, USS *Hornet*, on Battle of Santa Cruz, 26 October 1942, in ONI, Air Intelligence Group (Op-16-V), Serials and Publications, Box 12, RG 38.

119. Comment by Commander Cruiser Task Force, on Santa Cruz, in ONI, Air Intelligence Group (Op-16-V), Serials and Publications, Box 12, RG 38.

120. CINCPAC, Gunnery Bulletin No. 2-42, ADM 199/461, UKNA.

121. Japanese aircraft tactics and night torpedo attacks, 16 March 1943, by COMSOPAC, BLUE 242, Box 14, RG 313.

122. Solomon Islands campaign, Battle of Tassafaronga, 30 November 1942, CINCPAC Reports.

123. Solomon Islands campaign, 11–15 November, dated 18 February 1943, by CINCPAC, World War II Action Reports, Box 20, Folder Pac-90-mb/A16-3/SOL, RG 38.

124. Interview of Lieutenant L. J. Dow, USN, Communications Officer on Admiral Halsey's staff, at BuAer, 29 September 1942, ADM 199/461, UKNA.

125. Solomon Islands campaign, from 6 January through Vila bombardment of 23–24 January 1943, CINCPAC Reports.

126. Lundstrom, *Guadalcanal Campaign*, 62–3.

127. "Interception of enemy fighters over the Russell islands, April 1, 1943," 15 April 1943, in Air Battle Notes from the South Pacific, no. 14, ONI, Air Intelligence Group (Op-16-V), Serials and Publications, Box 8, RG 38.

128. Action of August 24, dated 5 September 1942, by Commanding Officer, USS *Enterprise*, World War II Action Reports, Box 14, Folder CV6/A16–3/(10–My), RG 38.

129. Bergerud, *Fire in the Sky*, 331–5.

130. Battle of Midway Island, 4–6 June, dated 8 June 1942, by Commanding Officer, USS *Enterprise*, World War II Action Reports, Box 20, Folder CV6/A16–3, RG 38.

131. Report on Air Operations against the Japanese in the Guadalcanal area, 11 September to 16 October 1942, by Commander, Aircraft South Pacific Force, for CINCPAC, Papers of Henry Hap Arnold, Microfilm Reel no. 107, LOC.

132. Reynolds, *Admiral John H. Towers*, 401.

133. Ronald Spector, *At War at Sea: Sailors and Naval Combat in the Twentieth Century* (New York: Viking, 2001), 203.

134. Air Force Pacific Fleet, Air Operations Memorandum 1-42, 25 November 1942, BuAer, Confidential Correspondence, 1922–44, Box 201, RG 72.

135. Thomas Miller, *The Cactus Air Force* (New York: Harper & Row, 1969), 72.

136. Interview of Commander L. C. Stevens, U.S. Navy, upon return from visit to Pacific Fleet, in Technical Aviation Intelligence, Information Bulletin no. 21, by Aviation Intelligence Branch, BuAer, BLUE 361, Box 11, Folder A8, RG 313.

137. Spector, *At War*, 217–8.

138. Fighting Squadron Ten, Report of action, 10–17 November 1942, ADM 199/1323, UKNA.

139. John Lindley, *Carrier Victory: The Air War in the Pacific* (New York: Elsevier-Dutton, 1978), 90–1. For an account of how John Thach conceived the tactic before the outbreak of the Pacific War, see Thach, "Butch O'Hare," 11–2; Rearden, *Cracking the Zero Mystery*, 17–19.

140. Preliminary report of action, 26 October, dated 30 October 1942, Commander, Task Force Seventeen, World War II Action Reports, Box 21, Folder A16-3(11t), RG 38.

141. FTP 134, Gunnery Instructions, 1933, Fleet Tactical Publications, U.S. Navy, Box 107, Operational Archives, World War II Command File, NHC.

142. Secret and personal letter, dated 17 November 1942, by CINCPAC, Papers of Chester Nimitz, Series 13, Personal Correspondence with COMSOPAC, NHC.

143. Report of action, 24 August 1942, by Commander, Cruisers, Task Force 16, ADM 199/1303, UKNA.

144. Action of 24 August 1942, by Commanding Officer, USS *North Carolina*, World War II Action Reports, Box 14, Folder BB55/A16-3, RG 38.

145. Report of gunnery performance during anti-aircraft engagement on 24 August 1942, Commanding Officer, USS *Atlanta*, BLUE 361, Box 12, RG 313.

146. Battle of Midway, 3–6 July, ONI Security Classified Publications, Combat Narratives, 1942–44, Box 5, RG 38.

147. Bergerud, *Fire in the Sky*, 295–9.

148. Reynolds, *Fast Carriers*, 57–8.

149. Recent operations, dated 10 September 1942, by Commander, Task Force 16, BLUE 361, Box 12, RG 313. Also see Lundstrom, *Guadalcanal Campaign*, 163–4.

150. Interview of G. D. Murray (USN), at BuAer, 25 November 1942, ONI, Air Intelligence Group (Op-16-V), Box 2, RG 38.

151. The Battle of the Coral Sea, dated 8 January 1943, ONI Security Classified Publications, Combat Narratives, 1942–44, Box 5, RG 38.

152. See Preliminary Report on Naval Detection Methods, by E. G. Bowen (British Technical Mission), 1 October 1940, AVIA 10/1, UKNA.

153. Henry Guerlac, *Radar in World War II*, History of Modern Physics, 1800–1950, vol. 8 (Philadelphia: American Institute of Physics, 1987), 925–7. For a description of the Royal Navy's development of fighter direction during the early phases of the war, see Derek Howse, *Radar at Sea: The Royal Navy in World War II* (Basingstoke, England: Macmillan, 1993), 55–7, 64–5. I am also grateful to Eric Grove, who was kind enough to lend me a copy of his paper "The Aircraft Carrier Fighter Control Revolution: How the Aircraft Carrier became an Effective Anti-air Warfare System" (presented at King Hall Naval History Conference, Canberra, Australia, July 2007), which provides a concise overview of the subject.

154. Guerlac, *Radar in World War II*, 929–31.

155. Grove, "Fighter Control Revolution," 9.

156. Brown, *Military Imperatives*, 237–8, 368–70.

157. Peter Mersky, *The Grim Reapers: Fighting Squadron Ten in World War II* (Mesa, AZ: Champlin Fighter Museum, 1986), 28–9.

158. Eric Hammel, *Carrier Strike: The Battle of the Santa Cruz Islands, October 1942* (St. Paul, MN: Zenith, 2004), 200.

159. Action of *Hornet* Air Group in carrier action north of Santa Cruz Islands, on 26 October, dated 8 November 1942, by Commander Task Force 61, World War II Action Reports, Box 21, Folder A16-3, RG 38. For a secondary account of the problem, see Eric Hammel, *Carrier Clash: The Invasion of Guadalcanal and the Battle of the Eastern Solomons, August 1942* (St. Paul, MN: Zenith, 2004), 231–2.

160. Reports of Action by various Fighting Squadron 10 Pilots, BLUE 242, Box 18, RG 313.

161. Solomon Islands campaign, Makin Island diversion, dated 20 October 1942, CINCPAC Reports.

162. Morison, *Coral Sea*, 162.

163. Action of August 24, including air attack , dated 5 September 1942, by Commanding Officer, USS *Enterprise*, World War II Action Reports, Box 14, Folder CV6/A16-3/(10-My), RG 38.

164. Operations of carrier task forces, 5 January 1943, Commander, Task Force 65, BLUE 242, Box 7, Folder A4-3, RG 313.

165. Report by Nimitz, on Solomon Islands Campaign, 23–25 August, 1942, Papers of Henry Hap Arnold, Microfilm Reel no. 107, LOC.

166. Wesley Craven and James Cate, *The Army Air Forces in World War II*, vol. 4, *The Pacific: Guadalcanal to Saipan, August 1942 to July 1944* (Washington, DC: Office of Air Force History, 1983), 68.

167. Memorandum for Commander Kernodle, 25 September 1942, BLUE 242, Box 15, RG 313.

Chapter 3: The Elusive Enemy
U.S. NAVAL INTELLIGENCE AND THE IMPERIAL JAPANESE
NAVY'S FLEET, 1943–45

1. Hayes, *Joint Chiefs*, 299–301.

2. Costello, *The Pacific War*, 417.

3. Hayes, *Joint Chiefs*, 427–8; Ross, *War Plans*, 69.

4. King and Whitehill, *Fleet Admiral King*, 235.

5. Gunnery doctrine and standard fire-control procedures, CPTB 1-43, August 1943, by Cruisers Pacific Fleet, BLUE 361, Box 18, Folder A5-1, RG 313.

6. FTP 143(A), War Instructions, 1944, Fleet Tactical Publications, U.S. Navy, Box 108, Operational Archives, World War II Command File, NHC.

7. Secret and personal letter from Halsey to Nimitz, 28 September 1944, Papers of William F. Halsey, Box 15, LOC.

8. Morison, *Leyte*, 336.

9. Ibid., 187.

10. Packard, *A Century of U.S. Naval Intelligence*, 229–31.

11. Commander, Task Group 38.1, Action Report, 1 July to 15 August 1945, ADM 199/1542, UKNA.

12. F-22 to Op-16-FE, 27 July 1943, ONI Monographs, Box 90, Folder 912-200, RG 38.

13. Prados, *Combined Fleet Decoded*, 415.

14. ONI 222-Y, "The Japanese Navy: Official U.S. Navy Reference Manual," June 1945, ONI Monographs, Box 89, RG 38.

15. A. D. Baker, Introductory Section to ONI 225-J, *Japanese Naval Vessels of World War II: As Seen by U.S. Naval Intelligence* (Annapolis, MD: Naval Institute Press, 1987).

16. Paul Dull, *A Battle History of the Imperial Japanese Navy, 1941–45* (Annapolis, MD: Naval Institute Press, 1978), 299–300, 310; Evans and Peattie, *Kaigun*, 494, 515.

17. Chihaya, "Intimate Look," 319.

18. Evans and Peattie, *Kaigun*, 507–8.

19. Dull, *Battle History*, 60.

20. Akira Yoshimura, *Battleship Musashi: The Making and Sinking of the World's Biggest Battleship*, trans. V. Murphy (Tokyo: Kodansha, 1991), 150–1.

21. "The Japanese sailor" (from a report prepared by the Office of War Information), in ONI Weekly, Confidential Issue 4, no. 1 (3 January 1945), ONI Security Classified Publications, Box 4, RG 38.

22. Gunnery and Fire Control, March 1943, ONI Monographs, Box 82, Folder 907-5800, RG 38.

23. Radio-radar countermeasures in the Pacific, 25 February 1944, by CINCPAC, BLUE 360, Box 22, RG 313.

24. Estimate of the enemy situation, Pacific-Far East, Enclosure: report by Combined Intelligence Committee, 5 August 1944, CCS 643, Records of the JCS, Central Decimal File, 1942–45, Box 313, RG 218.

25. "Japanese naval guns," in ONI Weekly, Confidential Issue 3, no. 35 (30 August 1944), ONI Security Classified Publications, Box 3, RG 38,

26. Dower, *War without Mercy*, 85.

27. Morison, *Marianas*, 10–1.

28. Prados, *Combined Fleet Decoded*, 496.

29. CINCPAC-CINCPOA Preliminary POW Interrogation Report no. 74, in ONI Monographs, Box 93, Folder 912-800, RG 38.

30. Seventh Fleet Intelligence Center, New Japanese *Matsu*–class destroyers, 16 October 1944, in ONI Monographs, Box 93, Folder 912-800, RG 38.

31. JICPOA preliminary interrogation report no. 22, 20 February 1944, ONI Monographs, Box 90, Folder 912-200, RG 38.

32. "Japanese XCV-BB *Hyuga*," in U.S. Pacific Fleet and Pacific Ocean Areas, Weekly Intelligence (hereafter, PFWI) 1, no. 14 (13 October 1944), War Department, "P" File, Box 543, RG 165 (hereafter, RG 165).

33. "Japanese carriers sighted at Truk," in ONI Weekly 3, no. 17 (26 April 1944), ONI Publications, Box 7, RG 38.

34. "The *Agano* light cruiser class," in ONI Weekly 3, no. 17 (26 April 1944), ONI Publications, Box 7, RG 38.

35. "A new Japanese naval gun," in ONI Weekly 2, no. 34 (25 August 1943), ONI Publications, Box 6, RG 38.

36. Dorwart, *Conflict of Duty*, 220.

37. "The Navy's Japanese language school," in ONI Weekly 3, no. 8 (23 February 1944), ONI Publications, Box 7, RG 38.

38. Dorwart, *Conflict of Duty*, 177–8.

39. Prados, *Combined Fleet Decoded*, 351–2.

40. "Know Your Enemy!: Japanese striking force tactics," Addendum to CINCPAC-CINCPOA Weekly Intelligence 1, no. 10 (15 September 1944), ONI Monographs, Box 77, Folder 907-175, RG 38.

41. "Japanese carrier operations," Extracts from officer's professional notebook, Ref. JICPOA Item no. 2605-D, 12 June 1944, by Commander, Third Fleet, BLUE 360, Box 15, Folder A8, RG 313.

42. "Know Your Enemy!: Japanese radio communications and radio intelligence,"

in CINCPAC Bulletin 5-45, Papers of Edwin T. Layton, Box 21, Manuscript Collection, NWC.

43. "Japanese radar fire control against surface craft," in PFWI 1, no.16 (27 October 1944), Box 543, RG 165.

44. Study of foreign torpedoes, Project Re6a-201, Interim Report no. 1, by U.S. Naval torpedo station (Newport, RI), 10 May 1944, and Examination of Japanese 24-inch torpedo warhead, Foreign Ordnance Report no. 3-296, 27 March 1944, by BuOrd, in ONI Monographs, Box 86, Folder 910-3800, RG 38.

45. "Know Your Enemy!: Japanese torpedoes," May 1944, by Naval Combat Intelligence, South Pacific Force, in ONI Monographs, Box 86, Folder 910-3800, RG 38.

46. Hajime Fukaya, "Japan's Wartime Carrier Construction," United States Naval Institute *Proceedings* 81 (September 1955), 1031–7; Jentschura et al., *Warships*, 56.

47. "The Japanese shipping position," in ONI Weekly, Confidential Issue 2, no. 30 (28 July 1943), ONI Security Classified Publications, Box 2, RG 38.

48. "The Japanese shipping position," in ONI Weekly 2, no. 35 (1 September 1943), in Box 6, ONI Publications, RG 38.

49. "The Japanese shipping position," in ONI Weekly 3, no. 23 (7 June 1944), in Box 7, ONI Publications, RG 38.

50. Blair, *Silent Victory*, 584.

51. Japanese war economy, JIC 180/2, 8 April 1944, Records of the JCS, Geographic File, 1942–45, Box 112, RG 218.

52. Notes and estimates on Japanese aircraft carriers, n.d., ca. May 1943, by Intelligence Division South Pacific Force, BLUE 644, Box 4, RG 313.

53. "Notes on Japanese aircraft carriers," in ONI Weekly, Confidential Issue 2, no. 32 (11 August 1943), ONI Security Classified Publications, Box 2, RG 38.

54. Bath, *Tracking the Axis Enemy*, 176.

55. Aldrich, *Intelligence*, 238–40, 242–3.

56. Prados, *Combined Fleet Decoded*, 476.

57. Japanese reactions to certain operations, JIC 115, 19 June 1943, Records of the JCS, Geographic File, 1942–45, Box 129, RG 218.

58. Special edition of *U.S. at War*, "Activities of the United States Fleet in the Second Year of the War," September 1943, Papers of Ernest J. King, Box 30, LOC.

59. Re-organization for future naval war, 13 October 1943, by Special Planning Section, Navy Department, Papers of Ernest J. King, Reel 2, Reference no. 396, Microfilm Collection, NWC.

60. Thomas Buell, *The Quiet Warrior: A Biography of Admiral Raymond A. Spruance* (Boston: Little, Brown and Co., 1974), 183.

61. Ibid., 263–8; Emmet Forrestel, *Admiral Raymond A. Spruance: A Study in Command* (Washington, DC: Naval Historical Center, 1966), 137–8; Tillman, *Clash of the Carriers*, 100; Hedley Willmott, "The Battle of the Philippine Sea," in *Great American Naval Battles*, ed. Jack Sweetman (Annapolis, MD: Naval Institute Press, 1998), 331–2; Y'Blood, *Red Sun Setting*, 212–3.

62. Dickson, *Philippine Sea*, 32.

63. Walter Karig, *Battle Report: The End of an Empire* (New York: Rinehart & Co., 1948), 232–3; Clark Reynolds, *On the Warpath in the Pacific: Admiral Jocko Clark*

and the Fast Carriers (Annapolis, MD: Naval Institute Press, 2005), 354–5, 364–5; Theodore Taylor, *The Magnificent Mitscher* (New York: W. W. Norton, 1954), 215, 220–2; Y'Blood, *Red Sun Setting*, 215–7.

64. Tomiji Koyanagi, "The Battle of Leyte Gulf," in *Japanese Navy*, ed. Evans, 357–60. Also see Shigeru Fukudome, "The Air Battle off Taiwan, in *Japanese Navy*, ed. Evans, 335–6, 338–41.

65. D. C. Robertson, *Operations Analysis: The Battle for Leyte Gulf* (Newport, RI: Naval War College, 1993), 13–4. Also see Daniel Barbey, *MacArthur's Amphibious Navy: Seventh Amphibious Force Operations, 1943–1945* (Annapolis, MD: Naval Institute Press, 1969), 236.

66. Winton, *ULTRA in the Pacific*, 183.

67. Comer Vann Woodward, *The Battle for Leyte Gulf* (New York: Macmillan, 1947), 56.

68. See Thomas Cutler, *The Battle of Leyte Gulf, 23–26 October 1944* (New York: HarperCollins, 1994), 162–5, 215; Stanley Falk, *Decision at Leyte* (New York: W. W. Norton, 1966), 152–3; William, Halsey, "The Battle for Leyte Gulf," United States Naval Institute *Proceedings* 78 (May 1952), 494–5; MacIntyre, *Leyte Gulf*, 70–1, 76–7; James Merrill, *A Sailor's Admiral: A Biography of William F. Halsey* (New York: Thomas Y. Crowell, 1976), 153; Carl Solberg, *Decision and Dissent: With Halsey at Leyte Gulf* (Annapolis, MD: Naval Institute Press, 1995), 116–8; Hedley Willmott, *The Battle of Leyte Gulf: The Last Fleet Action* (Bloomington: Indiana University Press, 2005), 120–5, 194; Morison, *Leyte*, 193–4.

69. Estimate of the enemy situation, Pacific-Far East, CCS 643/2, Enclosure: report by Combined Intelligence Committee, 22 January 1945, Records of the JCS, Central Decimal File, 1942–45, Box 313, RG 218.

70. "Technical intelligence notes," in ONI Weekly, Confidential Issue 4, no. 23 (6 June 1945), ONI Security Classified Publications, Box 4, RG 38.

71. Morison, *The Liberation of the Philippines*, 157–8.

72. Ibid., 177.

73. Solomon Islands Campaign, Part X, Operations in the New Georgia Area, 21 June to 5 August 1943, ONI Publications, Combat Narratives, 1942–44, Box 5, RG 38.

74. Final report on battle action—*Selfridge*, *O'Bannon*, and *Chevalier* with enemy forces off Sauka Point, Vella Lavella, night of 6–7 October, dated 26 October 1943, by Commander, Destroyer Squadron Five, World War II Action Reports, Box 33, Folder FC4-4/A16-3, RG 38.

75. Action Report, Battle of Empress Augusta Bay, night surface action, 2 November 1943, in ONI Monographs, Box 82, Folder 907-5800, RG 38.

76. Action Report of Night Surface Engagement off Cape St. George, night of 24–25 November 1943, by Commanding Officer, USS *Charles Ausburne*, in ONI Monographs, Box 82, Folder 907-5800, RG 38.

77. Radio-radar countermeasures in the Pacific, 25 February 1944, by CINCPAC, BLUE 360, Box 22, RG 313.

78. Japanese reaction to recent operations in the Pacific, JIS 47/2, by Joint Intelligence Staff, 2 May 1944, Records of the JCS, Geographic File, 1942–45, Box 113, RG 218.

79. Appreciation and plan for the defeat of Japan, 31 July 1943, by Combined Intelligence Section, Records of the JCS, Geographic File, 1942–45, Box 127, RG 218.

80. "Japanese surface ship torpedoes and tactics," by Advanced Intelligence Center, Commander, Southwest Pacific Force, Enclosure: Battle of Kula Gulf, 5–6 July 1943, reports by Commander Task Group, and Commanding Officer, USS *Helena*, 12 February 1944, ONI Monographs, Box 86, Folder, 910-3800, RG 38.

81. Ibid., Enclosure, Report by Commanding Officer, USS *St. Louis*.

82. "Know Your Enemy!: Japanese torpedoes," May 1944, by Naval Combat Intelligence, South Pacific Force, ONI Monographs, Box 86, Folder 910-3800, RG 38.

83. Howard Sauer, *The Last Big-Gun Naval Battle: The Battle of Surigao Strait* (El Cerrito, CA: Glencannon, 1999), 116.

84. Leyte operation, 12–29 October 1944, by Commander, Carrier Division 22, BLUE 360, Box 21, RG 313.

85. Robert Cox, *The Battle off Samar: Taffy III and Leyte Gulf* (Groton, CT: Ivy Alba, 2003), 65.

86. Reprint of reports on operations in the Pacific Ocean Areas,, by CINCPAC, Enclosure: Operations in the Pacific Ocean Areas, October 1944, ADM 199/1493, UKNA.

87. Leyte operation, 12–29 October 1944, by Commander, Carrier Division 22, BLUE 360, Box 21, RG 313.

88. COMINCH, Secret Information Bulletin no. 22, Battle Experience, Leyte Gulf, 23–27 October 1944, dated 1 March 1945, http://www.ibiblio.org/hyperwar/USN/rep/Leyte/BatExp (accessed12 February 2009), (hereafter, Battle Experience, Leyte Gulf), Enclosures: Comments on Ammunition, by Commanding Officer, USS *Denver*; Gunnery Officer, USS *Maryland*; Commander Battleship Division 3; Commander Task Group 77.2; "The probable Japanese concept," dated 28 October 1944, Enclosure A to COMCARDIV 26 Serial 00014, Papers of William E. Riley, Box 2, LOC.

89. Cox, *The Battle off Samar*, 71, 161–3.

90. Commander Task Group 77.4 (Commander, Cruiser Division 4), Action Reports, Battle of Surigao Strait, 25 October 1944, http://www.ibiblio.org/hyperwar/USN/rep/Leyte/CTG–77.4 (accessed 12 February 2009), Enclosure: USS *Claxton* (DD 571).

91. Mark Stille, *Imperial Japanese Navy Aircraft Carriers, 1921–45* (Oxford: Osprey, 2005), 9–21.

92. "Anti-aircraft tactics of Japanese task groups," October 1944, in Flak Information Bulletin no. 3, ONI, Air Intelligence Group (Op-16-V), Serials and Publications, Box 12, RG 38.

93. Action against the Japanese Fleet, 18 to 22 June 1944, Appendix 1: Enemy fleet disposition, composition and maneuvers, by Commander, Carrier Division 3, World War II Action Reports, Box 220, Folder FB2-3/A16-3(11-wpc), RG 38. Also see "Defensive tactics of Japanese task forces subjected to air attack," October 1944, ONI, Air Intelligence Group (Op-16-V), Serials and Publications, Box 12, RG 38.

94. "Carrier action notes: Cruising disposition of the Japanese fleet," 9 July 1944,

in COMAIRPAC Air Operations Memorandum No.38, ONI, Air Intelligence Group (Op-16–V), Box 6, RG 38.

95. "The Japanese navy today" (reprinted from ONI Weekly, n.d., ca. spring 1944), in Admiralty Weekly Intelligence Report (ADMWIR), no. 240, 13 October 1944, ADM 223/164, UKNA.

96. Naval Combat Intelligence, Weekly Report, 12–18 December 1943, by COMSOPAC, BLUE 360, Box 16, RG 313.

97. Radio-radar countermeasures in the Pacific, 25 February 1944, by CINCPAC, BLUE 361, Box 19, RG 313.

98. Battle Experience, Leyte Gulf, Enclosure: Commanding Officer, USS *Enterprise*, Comments on Enemy Anti–aircraft.

99. "Japanese AA weapons: 25-mm, Model 96, automatic cannon," in Flak Information Bulletin, no. 3 (October 1944), ONI, Air Intelligence Group (Op-16-V), Serials and Publications, Box 12, RG 38.

100. "The Role of Communication Intelligence in Submarine Warfare in the Pacific, January 1943 to October 1943: Intelligence furnished to submarine commanders, Pacific Fleet," in *Listening to the Enemy: Key Documents on the Role of Communications Intelligence in the War with Japan*, ed. Ronald Spector (Wilmington, DE: Scholarly Resources, 1988), 130–1, and "Comint Contributions, Submarine Warfare in WWII, 17 June 1947: Vice Admiral Lockwood on value of communications intelligence against the Japanese," in *Listening to the Enemy*, ed. Spector, 134.

101. Report on Enemy Anti-submarine Measures, USS *Steelhead*, war patrol, 30 June to 16 August 1943, in ONI Monographs, Box 82, File 907-5900, RG 38.

102. Report on Enemy Anti-submarine Measures, USS *Pike*, war patrol, 31 March to 7 May 1943, in ONI Monographs, Box 82, File 907-5900, RG 38.

103. Countermeasures and Deception: CINCPAC Summary of Information, Issue no. 3, Enclosure: Action report, USS *Tinosa*, 5th war patrol, 10 January to 4 March 1944, BLUE 360, Box 23, Folder A22, RG 313.

104. Blair, *Silent Victory*, 351–2.

105. Report on Enemy Anti-submarine Measures, USS *Tuna*, submarine war patrol report, ONI Monographs, Box 82, Folder 907-5900, RG 38.

106. Countermeasures and Deception: CINCPAC Summary of Information, Issue no. 5, n.d., ca. May 1944, BLUE 360, Box 23, Folder A22, RG 313.

107. New Japanese use of radar deception in anti-submarine warfare, 13 June 1945, by CINCPAC, BLUE 627, Box 26, Folder S67-1, RG 313.

108. "Japanese anti-submarine warfare operations," in Seventh Fleet Intelligence Center, Bulletin no. 10-45, 30 March 1945, ONI Monographs, Box 82, Folder 907-5900, RG 38.

109. Operation Plan 5-43, Commander, Cruiser Division 9, BLUE 242, Box 4, RG 313.

110. Morison, *Breaking the Bismarks Barrier*, 195.

111. Reprint of early reports of operations in the Pacific Ocean Areas (February to August 1943), by CINCPAC, Enclosure: Operations in the Pacific Ocean Areas, dated July 1943, ADM 199/1493, UKNA. Also see Crenshaw, *South Pacific Destroyer*, 134.

112. Hughes, *Fleet Tactics*, 119–20.

113. Ibid., 125.

114. Final report on battle action—*Selfridge*, *O'Bannon*, and *Chevalier* with enemy forces off Sauka Point, Vella Lavella, night of 6–7 October, dated 26 October 1943, by Commander, Destroyer Squadron 5, World War II Action Reports, Box 33, Folder FC4-4/A16-3, RG 38.

115. Morison, *Breaking the Bismarcks Barrier*, 309–10.

116. Ibid., 312–3.

117. FTP 143(A), War Instructions, 1944, Fleet Tactical Publications, U.S. Navy, Box 108, Operational Archives, World War II Command File, NHC.

118. Brown, *Technical and Military Imperatives*, 370.

119. Reprint of early reports of operations in the Pacific Ocean Areas (February to August 1943), by CINCPAC, Enclosure: Operations in the Pacific Ocean Areas, July 1943, ADM 199/1493, UKNA.

120. Torpedo installations in new design cruisers, 12 December 1943, by Commander, Fifth Amphibious Force, U.S. Pacific Fleet, Fifth Fleet (hereafter, RED 136), Box 4, Folder S75, RG 313.

121. Morison, *Marianas*, 244–5; Dickson, *Philippine Sea*, 87.

122. Evans and Peattie, *Kaigun*, 496–7.

123. Carl Boyd and Akihiko Yoshida, *The Japanese Submarine Force and World War II* (Annapolis, MD: Naval Institute Press, 1995), 34–5, 50–1, 124–5, 189–90.

124. Digest of Minutes of Conference on anti-submarine warfare, held at Headquarters of the CINCUS, 25 July 1942, Enclosure F: Anti–submarine training in Destroyers, Pacific Fleet, by Commander G. L. Sims, Bureau of Aeronautics, Confidential Correspondence, 1922–44, Box 206, RG 72.

125. Submarines, March 1943, ONI Monographs, Box 77, Folder 907-175, RG 38.

126. Boyd and Yoshida, *Submarine Force*, 52.

127. See FTP 143, War Instructions, 1934, Fleet Tactical Publications, U.S. Navy, Box 108, Operational Archives, World War II Command File, NHC.

128. "Anti-submarine screens," in Pacific Fleet Tactical Bulletin 3TB-43, 23 November 1943, by CINCPAC, BLUE 361, Box 23, RG 313.

129. Cruising formation for carrier task groups, 23 October 1944, by Commander, Third Fleet, in BLUE 627, Box 82, RG 313.

130. Recommendations for anti-submarine measures, n.d., ca. late 1944, in BLUE 627, Box 82, RG 313.

131. Memoranda for Files, 26 May 1944, Papers of John H. Towers, Box 1, LOC.

132. "Allied tactics: night bombing attacks on surface ships by carrier-based TBFs," 5 February 1944, in COMAIRPAC Air Operations Memorandum, no. 21, ONI, Air Intelligence Group (Op-16-V), Box 6, RG 38.

133. Anti-aircraft actions of 12, 15, and 19 June, dated 26 June 1944, by Commanding Officer, USS *South Dakota*, World War II Action Reports, Box 1439, Folder BB57/A16-2, RG 38.

134. Anti-aircraft actions of 12, 15, and 19 June, dated 26 June 1944, by Commander, Battleship Division 9, World War II Action Reports, Box 1439, Folder BB57/A16-2, RG 38.

135. "COMBATDIV-9 comments on air power," in COMAIRPAC Air Operations Memorandum no. 63, 12 January 1945, ONI, Air Intelligence Group (Op-16-V), Box 6, RG 38.

136. Battle Experience, Leyte Gulf, Enclosure: CTG 38.3 Comments on Effectiveness of Bombs against Enemy Heavy Ships.

137. Future planning for CVG aircraft complements, 21 April 1945, by Air Force Pacific Fleet, BLUE 627, Box 25, Folder F1, RG 313.

138. Excerpts from aircraft action reports and battle narratives, Torpedo attacks by U.S. naval aircraft in the Pacific, September to November 1944, by Air Intelligence Group, Enclosures: Task Group 38.2 (USS *Intrepid*, *Cabot*, *Langley*, and *San Jacinto*), BLUE 627, Box 82, RG 313.

139. Ibid., Enclosure: Task Group 38.3.

140. Report on effectiveness of aerial torpedoes, 6 December 1944, by Commander, Task Force 38, BLUE 627, Box 84, RG 313.

141. "Allied tactics, Torpedo attack on maneuvering ships," in COMAIRPAC Air Operations Memorandum, no. 21, 5 February 1944, ONI, Air Intelligence Group (Op-16-V), Box 6, RG 38.

142. First Supplement to Torpedo Attacks by U.S. Naval Aircraft in the Pacific, dated October 1944, by Air Intelligence Group, Office of the CNO, Enclosure: Commander J. M. Peters, Air Group 1, USS *Yorktown* AIR 40/1539, UKNA.

143. Operations against Ryukyu islands, Formosa and Philippines, 2–27 October, dated 28 October 1944, Commanding Officer, USS *Hornet*, World War II Action Reports, Box 1041, Folder CV12/A16-3, RG 38.

144. Gerald Wheeler, "Thomas C. Kinkaid: MacArthur's Master of Naval Warfare," in *We Shall Return!: MacArthur's Commanders and the Defeat of Japan, 1942–1945*, ed. William Leary (Lexington: Kentucky University Press, 1988), 139.

145. Battle Experience, Leyte Gulf, Enclosure: CTG 77.2, Comments on Gunnery.

146. Battle of the Philippines, 24–25 October 1944, by Commander, Task Group 38.3, ADM 199/1494, UKNA.

147. Battle Experience, Leyte Gulf, Enclosure: Commanding Officer, USS *Hutchins*, Comments on Gunnery.

148. Commander, Task Group 79.11 (COMDESRON 54), Report of Night Action in Surigao Strait, Philippine Islands, 24–25 October 1944, http://www.ibiblio.org/hyperwar/USN/rep/Leyte/CTG–79.11–Surigao (accessed 12 February 2009).

149. Vann Woodward, *Leyte Gulf*, 82.

150. Report of participation in naval battle of Surigao Strait, 25 October 1944, by Commanding Officer, USS *California*, in Box 19, BLUE 360, RG 313.

151. Commander, Seventh Fleet, Report of operation for the capture of Leyte Islands, including action report of engagements in Surigao Strait, dated 31 January 1945, in Box 84, BLUE 360, RG 313.

152. Action Report, Battle of Surigao Strait, on 25 October 1944, by Commander, Task Group 77.2, ADM 199/1495, UKNA.

153. War Instructions, 1943; Bureau of Aeronautics, Confidential Correspondence, 1922–44, Box 204, RG 72. Also see FTP 143(A), War Instructions, 1944, Fleet Tactical Publications, U.S. Navy, Box 108, and USF 10A, U.S. Fleet, Current

Tactical Orders and Doctrine, 1944, Box 271, Operational Archives, World War II Command File, NHC.

154. Gunnery Doctrine and Instructions, 26 November 1944, Battleships U.S. Pacific Fleet, Battleship Squadron 1 (hereafter, BATRON 1), Box 2, Folder 594, Folder A16-3, RG 313.

155. Action Report, 20–25 October, in the Philippine area, by Commanding Officer, USS *Gambier Bay*, ADM 199/1495, UKNA.

156. "Damage control in gunnery actions," in Pacific Fleet Confidential Bulletin OCL-45, 1 January 1945, BLUE 627, Box 15, Folder A12-11(9), RG 313.

157. Buell, *Quiet Warrior*, 354–5; Forrestel, *Spruance*, 204.

158. Action report, Bombardment and occupation of Okinawa: gunfire and covering force, dated 5 May 1945, by Commander Battleship Squadron One, ADM 199/85, UKNA.

Chapter 4: The "Underdog in the Air War," Yet a Resourceful Opponent
INTELLIGENCE ON THE IJN'S AIR ARM, 1943–45

1. Report of London Conference on Japanese Air Force, 18–30 October 1943, AIR 40/346, UKNA.

2. Report of the Japanese Air Order of Battle Conference, 5–23 February 1945, U.S. War Department, AIR 40/2201, UKNA.

3. "The Japanese Aircraft Industry," based on publications issued by the Army, Navy, Foreign Economic Administrations, and Office of Strategic Services, up to May 1945, ONI Monographs, Box 122, Folder 1000, RG 38.

4. René Françillon, *Japanese Aircraft of the Pacific War* (New York: Funk & Wagnalls, 1970), 5–15.

5. Akira Hara, "Japan: Guns before Rice," in *The Economics of World War II*, ed. Mark Harrison (Cambridge, England: Cambridge University Press, 1998), 247–9; Alan Milward, *War, Economy, and Society, 1939–1945* (London: Penguin, 1977), 83–6.

6. Alvin Coox, "The Effectiveness of the Japanese Military Establishment in the Second World War," in *Military Effectiveness*, ed. Allan Millett and Williamson Murray, vol. 3, *The Second World War* (Boston: Allen & Unwin, 1988), 21–2.

7. Jerome Cohen, *Japan's Economy in War and Reconstruction*, Japanese Economic History 1930–1960, vol. 2, ed. Janet Hunter (London: Routledge, 2000), 58, 113–4.

8. United States Strategic Bombing Survey, *Summary Report, Pacific War* (Washington, DC: Government Printing Office, 1946), 16–8.

9. "Deficiencies in Japanese Industry" (based on a survey by the U.S. Board of Economic Warfare), in AMWIS, no. 215 (16 October 1943), AIR 22/79, UKNA.

10. "Story of Japanese shore-based naval air force combat strength," in PFWI 1, no. 21 (1 December 1944), Box 543, RG 165.

11. Analysis of air operations in the Solomons, New Guinea, and Netherlands East Indies campaigns, June 1943, by COMAIRPAC, ADM 199/918, UKNA.

12. Estimate of Enemy Situation, 1944, prepared by JIC, 9 November 1943, Records of the JCS, Central Decimal File, 1942–45, Box 312, RG 218.

13. Appreciation and Plan for Defeat of Japan, 31 July 1943, by Combined Intelligence Section, in Box 127, Records of the JCS, Geographic File, 1942–45, RG 218.
14. Enemy Strength and Dispositions in the Western Pacific, 14 July 1944, JIC 188/3, in Box 167, Records of the JCS, Geographic File, 1942–45, RG 218.
15. "Thumbnail biographies of Japanese aircraft—Betty," in PFWI 1, no. 10 (15 September 1944), Box 542, RG 165.
16. Minutes of 165th Meeting, 28 August 1944, Joint Staff Planners, Records of the JCS, Central Decimal File, 1942–45, Box 216, RG 218.
17. Prados, *Combined Fleet Decoded*, 599.
18. Ross, *War Plans*, 158–9.
19. Minutes of Meeting, 8 March 1944, Joint Staff Planners, in Box 215, Records of the JCS, Central Decimal File, 1942–45, RG 218.
20. Estimate of Enemy Situation, Pacific-Far East, prepared by Combined Intelligence Committee, 5 August 1944, in Box 313, Records of the JCS, Central Decimal File, 1942–45, RG 218.
21. Action Report, 1 July to 15 August 1945, by Commander, Task Group 38.1, ADM 199/1542, UKNA.
22. Robert Mikesh, *Zero: Combat and Development History of Japan's Legendary Mitsubishi A6M Zero fighter* (Osceola, WI: Motorbooks, 1994), 42. Also see Michael Barnhart, "Japanese Intelligence before the Second World War: Best-case analysis," in *Knowing One's Enemies*, ed. May, 454.
23. Gerhard Krebs, "The Japanese Air Forces," in *The Conduct of the Air War in the Second World War: An International Comparison*, ed. Horst Borg (Oxford: Berg, 1992), 230.
24. Mikesh, *Zero*, 103–6.
25. Horikoshi, *Eagles*, 144.
26. Okumiya and Horikoshi, *Zero!*, 134. Also see Robert Mikesh, *Broken Wings of the Samurai: The Destruction of the Japanese Air Force* (Shrewsbury, England: Airlife, 1993), 22.
27. Robert Mikesh, *Japanese Aircraft: Code Names and Designations* (Atglen, PA: Schiffer, 1993), 87.
28. Ibid., 53.
29. Hata and Izawa, *Naval Aces*, 80.
30. Mikesh, *Japanese Aircraft*, 51, 145.
31. Ibid., 78.
32. Mark Felton, *Yanagi: The Secret Underwater Trade between Germany and Japan, 1942–1945* (Barnsley, England: Pen & Sword, 2005), 184–5.
33. "Japanese bombing tactics" (Appreciation prepared by BuAer), in AMWIS, no. 181 (24 July 1943), AIR 22/77, UKNA.
34. "The Japanese naval air training program," Serial 2-44, 5 January 1944, by Op-16-FE, Confidential Reports of Naval Attachés, 1940–1946, Box 123, Folder A-1-w, 17542-A, RG 38.
35. "Japanese naval air training," 13 October 1944, in PFWI 1, no. 14, Box 543, RG 165.
36. "Miscellaneous Japanese aircraft developments," in Technical Air Intelligence (TAI) Summary, no. 22, May 1944, ONI, Air Intelligence Group (Op-16-V), Serials and Publications, Box 10, RG 38.

37. See: "Japanese official aircraft designations," in CINCPAC-CINCPOA Bulletin, no. 35-44, 24 March 1944, Box 483, RG 165.

38. Rearden, *Cracking the Zero Mystery*, 30–31. Also see Lundstrom, *Guadalcanal Campaign*, 532–6.

39. "Performance and characteristics trials of Japanese fighter," 4 November 1942, in Technical Aviation Intelligence Brief, no. 3, by Aviation Intelligence Branch, BuAer, AIR 23/5275, UKNA. Also see Rearden, *Zero Mystery*, 115–22; Barrett Tillman, *Corsair: The F4U in World War II and Korea* (Annapolis, MD: Naval Institute Press, 1979), 19–20.

40. "Performance trials of United States Army fighters versus the Japanese Zero," in Air Information Summary, no. 1 (28 January 1943), by Air Information Branch, BuAer, ADM 199/1289, UKNA.

41. "Combat Notes on the Zero fighter" (based upon material assembled by the Intelligence Service, USAAF), in ONI Weekly, no. 5, 3 February 1943, ONI Publications, Box 6, RG 38.

42. "Technical air intelligence: organization and functions," 1 August 1944, in TAI Summary, no. 1, ONI, Air Intelligence Group (Op-16-V), Serials and Publications, Box 8, RG 38.

43. "Japanese air weaknesses in the South Pacific" (Air Combat Intelligence, South Pacific Force), 20 February 1944, in Air Command Southeast Asia Weekly Intelligence Summary, no. 14, AIR 23/7720, UKNA.

44. "The more there are, the faster they fall," in COMAIRPAC Air Operations Memorandum, no. 32, 29 May 1944, in Box 6, ONI, Air Intelligence Group (Op-16-V), RG 38.

45. "VF-22 destroys 14 in single CAP," in COMAIRPAC Air Operations Memorandum, no. 68, 23 February 1945, in Box 7, ONI, Air Intelligence Group (Op-16-V), RG 38.

46. "Miscellaneous Japanese aircraft developments," in TAI Summary, no. 22 (May 1944), in ONI, Air Intelligence Group (Op-16-V), Serials and Publications, Box 10, RG 38.

47. "New Japanese aircraft developments," in TAI Summary, no. 26 (July 1944), in ONI, Air Intelligence Group (Op-16-V), Serials and Publications, Box 10, RG 38.

48. "Japanese aviation," in COMINCH Information Bulletin, no. 16, ONI Security Classified Publications, World War II, Box 2, RG 38.

49. "Enemy planes and equipment: Japanese fighter plane developments," in COMAIRPAC Air Operations Memorandum, no. 37 (3 July 1944), ONI, Air Intelligence Group (Op-16-V), Box 6, RG 38.

50. "Japanese aircraft armament," in PFWI 1, no. 38 (2 April 1945), Box 544, RG 165.

51. "New Japanese fighters and torpedo bombers," in TAI Summary, no. 5 (September 1944), ONI, Air Intelligence Group (Op-16-V), Serials and Publications, Box 10, RG 38.

52. "Trends in Japanese fighter design and production," in PFWI 1, no. 12 (29 September 1944), Box 542, RG 165.

53. "Combat evaluation of Zeke 52 with F4U-1D, F6F-5, and FM-2," in TAIC Report, no. 17 (November 1944), and "Performance of new Japanese aircraft,"

in TAI Summary, no. 11 (October 1944), in ONI, Air Intelligence Group (Op-16-V), Serials and Publications, Box 10, RG 38.

54. "George 11," TAI Summary, no. 33 (July 1945), in ONI, Air Intelligence Group (Op-16-V), Serials and Publications, Box 10, RG 38.

55. Report of the carrier air strike on the Saipan-Tinian area, 22 February, dated 3 March 1944, by Commander, Task Group 58.3, World War II Action Reports, Box 225, RG 38.

56. Interview of Commander R. A. Winston, USN, Commander, Fighting Squadron 31, and Air Group 21 USS *Cabot*, 17 July 1944, ONI, Air Intelligence Group (Op-16-V), Box 4, RG 38.

57. "Japanese aircraft radar," in TAI Summary, no. 16 (February 1944), ONI, Air Intelligence Group (Op-16-V), Serials and Publications, Box 10, RG 38.

58. Diary entry, 11 November 1943, Papers of John J. Ballentine, Box 1, LOC.

59. Action report, USS *Oakland*, 21–22 February 1944, in Countermeasures and Deception: CINCPAC Summary of Information, Issue no. 3, in BLUE 360, Box 23, Folder A22, RG 313.

60. Action report, CARDIV 3, 16–17 February 1944, in BLUE 360, Box 23, Folder A22, RG 313.

61. Japanese radar, ship-borne and airborne, in CINPCAC Summary of Information, Issue no. 4, 24 April 1944, in BLUE 360, Box 23, Folder A22, RG 313.

62. "How good is Japanese radar?" in COMAIRPAC Air Operations Memorandum, no. 77 (20 April 1945), ONI, Air Intelligence Group (Op-16-V), Box 7, RG 38.

63. "Miscellaneous Japanese aircraft developments," in TAI Summary, no. 27 (July 1944), in ONI, Air Intelligence Group (Op-16-V), Serials and Publications, Box 12, RG 38.

64. "New trends in Japanese aircraft," in COMAIRPAC Air Operations Memorandum, no. 38 (9 July 1944), in ONI, Air Intelligence Group (Op-16-V), Serials and Publications, Box 12, RG 38.

65. "First photos of new Japanese torpedo plane," and "Technical intelligence provides further information on new torpedo plane," in COMAIRPAC Air Operations Memorandum, no. 22 (15 February 1944), in ONI, Air Intelligence Group (Op-16-V), Serials and Publications, Box 12, RG 38.

66. "Enemy planes and equipment: Japanese fighters with more powerful engines slated to appear," in COMAIRPAC Air Operations Memorandum, no. 31 (18 May 1944), in ONI, Air Intelligence Group (Op-16-V), Serials and Publications, Box 12, RG 38.

67. "Miscellaneous Japanese aircraft developments," and "Estimates of Jill engines," in TAI Summary, no. 27 (July 1944), and no. 21 (May 1944), respectively, in ONI, Air Intelligence Group (Op-16-V), Serials and Publications, Box 10, RG 38.

68. "Evolution of Japanese airplane engines," in TAI Summary, no. 16 (November 1944), in ONI, Air Intelligence Group (Op-16-V), Serials and Publications, Box 10, RG 38.

69. "Japanese air combat doctrine," in COMAIRPAC Air Operations Memorandum, no. 39 (16 July 1944), ONI, Air Intelligence Group (Op-16-V), Box 6, RG 38.

70. "Japanese aerial tactics," in CINCPAC-CINCPOA Bulletin, no. 87-45, Special Translation no. 57 (3 April 1945), Box 500, RG 165.

71. "Enemy standard bombing tactics," in COMAIRPAC Air Operations Memorandum, no. 36 (25 June 1944), ONI, Air Intelligence Group (Op-16-V), Box 6, RG 38.

72. "Japanese night fighter tactics" (originally translated as CINCPAC-CINCPOA Item no. 10,133), in PFWI 1, no. 10 (15 September 1944), in Box 542, RG 165.

73. "Know Your Enemy!: Japanese aerial tactics against ship targets", 20 October 1944, in PFWI 1, no. 15, in Box 543, RG 165.

74. See Robert Sherrod, *History of Marine Corps Aviation in World War II* (Washington, DC: Combat Forces Press, 1952), 327–9.

75. Interview of Rear Admiral O. R. Hardison, Commander, Fleet Air, South Pacific, in the Air Technical Analysis Division, 14 January 1944, ONI, Air Intelligence Group (Op-16-V), Box 3, RG 38.

76. Taylor, *Mitscher*, 179–80.

77. "Japanese naval pilots" (from article in ONI Weekly), in ADMWIR, no. 195 (3 December 1943), ADM 223/160, UKNA.

78. Enemy Strength and Dispositions in the Western Pacific, JIC 188/3, 14 July 1944, in Box 167, Records of the JCS, Geographic File, 1942–45, RG 218.

79. Japanese aircraft and shipping situation, JIC 169, 29 February 1944, in Box 113, Records of the JCS, Geographic File, 1942–45, RG 218.

80. Wendy Wendorf, "Blood over Kwajalein," in *Aces against Japan*, vol. 2, ed. Eric Hammel (Pacifica, CA: Pacifica Press, 1996), 183.

81. "Enemy tactics, Enemy fighter opposition at Truk," in COMAIRPAC Air Operations Memorandum, no. 21 (5 February 1944), in ONI, Air Intelligence Group (Op-16-V), Box 6, RG 38.

82. "Japanese fighter tactics in the Solomons," in COMAIRPAC Air Operations Memorandum, no. 22 (15 February 1944), in ONI, Air Intelligence Group (Op-16-V), Box 6, RG 38.

83. "B-24 attack," in COMAIRPAC Air Operations Memorandum, no. 2 (March 1944) in ONI, Air Intelligence Group (Op-16-V), Box 6, RG 38.

84. "Enemy VF display new tactics against B-24 formation" (extract from Allied Air Forces, Southwest Pacific intelligence summary), in COMAIRPAC, Air Operations Memorandum, no. 36 (25 June 1944), in ONI, Air Intelligence Group (Op-16-V), Box 6, RG 38.

85. "Improved Japanese pilots over Rabaul," in COMAIRPAC Air Operations Memorandum No.22, 15 February 1944, in ONI, Air Intelligence Group (Op-16-V), Box 6, RG 38.

86. "Enemy tactics, Japanese fighter tactics over Rabaul," in COMAIRPAC Air Operations Memorandum No.21, 5 February 1944, in ONI, Air Intelligence Group (Op-16-V), Box 6, RG 38.

87. "The air neutralization of Rabaul," compiled from information contained in reports of Naval Air Combat Intelligence Section, Commander South Pacific Force, August 1944, Air Intelligence, OpNav-16-V, Office of the CNO, Division of Naval Intelligence, Air Operations Research Group, Box 81, Operational Archives, World War II Command File, NHC.

88. David McCampbell, "Doctrine for a Fighter Pilot," in *Carrier Warfare*, ed. Wooldridge, 196–7.

89. Dickson, *Philippine Sea*, 179.

90. COMAIRPAC Air Operations Memorandum, no. 40 (23 July 1944), ONI, Air Intelligence Group (Op-16-V), Box 6, RG 38.

91. When they originally spotted it over the Solomons in late 1942, Allied observers believed that the Hamp, which was in fact a clipped-wing version of the Zero, was a new design. When the Americans learned that the fighter was a modified Zero, the designation "Hamp" was dropped in favor of "Zeke 32." See Mikesh, *Japanese Aircraft*, 63.

92. Second Supplement to Japanese aircraft combat performance, Excerpts from aircraft action reports and battle narratives, June to September 1944, Air Intelligence, OpNav-16-V, Office of the CNO, Division of Naval Intelligence, Air Operations Research Group, Box 81, Operational Archives, World War II Command File, NHC.

93. Tillman, *Clash*, 148–9.

94. "Fighting Squadron Five analyzes Japanese tactics at Palau," in COMAIRPAC Air Operations Memorandum, no. 29 (20 April 1944), ONI, Air Intelligence Group (Op-16-V), Box 6, RG 38.

95. Second Supplement to Japanese aircraft combat performance, Excerpts from aircraft action reports and battle narratives, June to September 1944, Air Intelligence, OpNav-16-V, Office of the CNO, Division of Naval Intelligence, Air Operations Research Group, Box 81, Operational Archives, World War II Command File, NHC.

96. "The Philippine Fleet Action, October 23–26" (derived from PFWI), in ONI Weekly 3, no. 47 (22 November 1944), ONI Publications, Box 7, RG 38.

97. "Carrier action notes: Twelve make a baker's dozen," in COMAIRPAC Air Operations Memorandum, no. 43, 15 August, in ONI, Air Intelligence Group (Op-16-V), Box 6, RG 38.

98. "More aggressive Japanese fighters," in COMAIRPAC Air Operations Memorandum, no. 57 (1 December 1944), in ONI, Air Intelligence Group (Op-16-V), Box 6, RG 38.

99. "April 16 on board the *Hornet*," in COMAIRPAC Air Operations Memorandum, no. 82 (25 May 1945), ONI, Air Intelligence Group (Op-16-V), Box 7, RG 38.

100. John Condon, *Corsairs and Flattops: Marine Carrier Air Warfare, 1944–1945* (Annapolis, MD: Naval Institute Press, 1998), 54–5.

101. Joe Lynch, "The Last Dogfight," in *Aces against Japan*, vol. 1, ed. Eric Hammel (Pacifica, CA: Presidio, 1992), 297.

102. Bob Coats, "Slipping the Leash," in *Aces*, vol. 2, ed. Hammel, 246.

103. Statistical Studies of Data contained in Anti-Aircraft Action Summaries, with suggestions for revision of the Form for Reporting by Surface Ships, 29 January 1944, ONI, Air Intelligence Group (Op-16-V), Serials and Publications, Box 12, RG 38.

104. "Tactics employed by Japanese naval forces in attacks on merchant and naval shipping," August 1943, by Air Information Division, Office of the CNO, Confidential Reports of Naval Attachés, 1940–1946, Box 170, Folder A-1-z, 20171, RG 38.

105. Ibid.

106. Operation plan 5-43, 15 June 1943, by Commander, Task Group 36.2, BLUE 242, Box 13, RG 313.

107. Countermeasures and Deception: Summary of Information, Issue no. 3, by CINCPAC, Enclosure: Action report, USS *Dyson*, 3 February 1944, in BLUE 360, Box 23, Folder A22, RG 313.

108. Countermeasures: Intercept and D/F on enemy radar, by Air Force Pacific Fleet, n.d., ca. summer 1944, in BLUE 360, Box 23, Folder A22, RG 313.

109. Countermeasures and Deception: CINCPAC Summary of Information, Issue no. 4 (24 April 1944), Enclosure: Enemy Radar Deception, in BLUE 360, Box 23, Folder A22, RG 313.

110. Countermeasures and Deception: CINCPAC Summary of Information, Issue no. 7 (31 July 1944) in BLUE 360, Box 23, Folder A22, RG 313.

111. Countermeasures and deception: CINCPAC Summary of Information, Issue no. 8 (28 August 1944), BLUE 627, Box 85, Folder S67, RG 313.

112. Action Report, Okinawa support and associated operations for period 5 April through 31 May 1945, by Commanding Officer, USS *Randolph* (CV-15), ADM 199/87, UKNA.

113. Action Report, Bombardment and fire support of landings on Okinawa Island, 21 March to 24 April 1945, by Commanding Officer, USS *West Virginia*, ADM 199/105, UKNA.

114. Japanese aerial torpedo attacks against U.S. task forces (including radar countermeasures used by the enemy), July 1944, by Office of the CNO, Division of Naval Intelligence, Air Operations Research Group, Air Intelligence, OpNav-16-V, Operational Archives, World War II Command File, Box 80, NHC.

115. Operations in Rabaul area, 11 November, dated 22 November 1943, by Commanding Officer, USS *Essex*, World War II Action Reports, Box 974, RG 38.

116. Report of enemy air attacks during night of 4–5 December 1943, dated 3 January 1944, by Commander, Task Force 50, BLUE 360, Box 18, RG 313.

117. Morison, *Gilberts*, 143.

118. Galvanic operation, 18–25 November, dated 8 December 1943, by Commanding Officer, USS *Essex*, in Box 974, World War II Action Reports, RG 38.

119. Attack on Saipan-Tinian, 22 February, dated 10 March 1944, by Commanding Officer, USS *Essex*, in Box 975, Folder CV9/A16-3, World War II Action Reports, RG 38.

120. Morison, *Marianas*, 283–4.

121. Action report of engagements with enemy planes off Saipan, 19 June 1944, by Commanding Officer, USS *Alabama*, BLUE 360, Box 27, RG 313.

122. Reynolds, *Fast Carriers*, 220, 252.

123. Secret and personal letter from Halsey to Nimitz, 28 September 1944, Papers of William F. Halsey, Box 15, LOC.

124. Morison, *Leyte*, 350.

125. Operations from 24 September to 20 October 1944, Commanding Officer, USS *Biloxi*, World War II Action Reports, Box 162, Folder CL80/A16-3, RG 38.

126. "Enemy tactics: comments by CV skipper," in COMAIRPAC Air Operations

Memorandum, no. 78 (27 April 1945), ONI, Air Intelligence Group (Op-16-V), Box 7, RG 38.

127. Action report, Bombardment and occupation of Okinawa: Gunfire and covering force, dated 5 May 1945, by Commander Battleship Squadron 1, ADM 199/85, UKNA.

128. Morison, *Victory*, 256.

129. Observed suicide attacks by Japanese aircraft against Allied ships, 23 May 1945, ONI, Air Intelligence Group (Op-16-V), Serials and Publications, Box 13, RG 38.

130. Albert Axell and Hideaki Kase, *Kamikaze: Japan's Suicide Gods* (London: Pearson, 2002); Rikihei Inoguchi et al., *The Divine Wind: Japan's Kamikaze Force in World War II* (Annapolis, MD: Naval Institute Press, 1958); Rikihei Inoguchi and Tadashi Nakajima, "The Kamikaze Attack Corps," in *Japanese Navy*, ed. Evans, 415–39; Raymond Lamont-Brown, *Kamikaze: Japan's Suicide Samurai* (London: Arms & Armour, 1997).

131. Inoguchi and Nakajima, "The Kamikaze Attack Corps," 418–22.

132. Inoguchi et al., *Divine Wind*, 6–7, 18–9; Lamont-Brown, *Kamikaze*, 53.

133. Axell and Kase, *Kamikaze*, 35–7.

134. Robin Rielly, *Kamikazes, Corsairs, and Picket Ships: Okinawa, 1945* (Philadelphia: Casemate, 2008), 82.

135. Denis Warner et al., *The Sacred Warriors: Japan's Suicide Legions* (New York: Von Nostrand Reinhold, 1982), 268.

136. Inoguchi et al., *Divine Wind*, 56–8, 81–4.

137. Reprint of early reports of operations in the Pacific Ocean Areas (February to August 1943), by CINCPAC, Enclosure, Operations in the Pacific Ocean Areas, November 1944, ADM 199/1493, UKNA.

138. Letter from Spruance to Elmer Potter, 6 May 1960, Papers of Raymond A. Spruance, NHC.

139. Halsey and Bryan, *Halsey's Story*, 182.

140. Action Report, Bombardment and fire support of Lingayen Gulf, by Commander, Battleship Squadron 1, 3–18 January 1945, ADM 199/1499, UKNA.

141. Reprint of early reports of operations in the Pacific Ocean Areas, by CINCPAC, Enclosure: Operations in the Pacific Ocean Areas, November 1944, ADM 199/1493, UKNA.

142. Action report for 21 February, dated 26 February 1945, by Commanding Officer, USS *Saratoga*, World War II Action Reports, Box 1409, Folder CV3/A16–3/ (10–es), RG 38.

143. Reprint of early reports of operations in the Pacific Ocean Areas (February to August 1943), by CINCPAC, Enclosure: Operations in the Pacific Ocean Areas, May 1945, ADM 199/1493, UKNA.

144. Lamont-Brown, *Kamikaze*, 82.

145. Report of battle damage, dated 27 January 1945, by Commanding Officer, USS *Ticonderoga*, ADM 199/1508, UKNA.

146. Yasuo Kuwahara and Gordon Allred, *Kamikaze* (New York: Ballantine, 1957), 46–7, 144–5.

147. Emiko Ohnuki-Tierney, *Kamikaze, Cherry Blossoms, and Nationalisms: The Mili-*

tarization of Aesthetics in Japanese History (Chicago: Chicago University Press, 2002), 169.

148. "Notes on suicide planes," 15 January 1945, in PFWI 1, no. 27, Box 543, RG 165.

149. Notes on kamikaze tactics, 16 November 1944, by CIC and ACI of USS *Wasp*, BLUE 627, Box 83, RG 313.

150. King, *U.S. Navy at War*, 176; Morison, *Victory*, 89.

151. Stephen Jurika, "The Franklin: Tragedy and Triumph," in *Carrier Warfare*, ed. Wooldridge, 252–3.

152. Halsey and Bryan, *Halsey's Story*, 229.

153. Morison, *Victory*, 197, 216.

154. Statistical analysis of Japanese suicide effort against Allied shipping during the Okinawa campaign, 23 July 1945, by Air Intelligence Group, Analysis Section, BLUE 627, Box 82, RG 313.

155. Observed suicide attacks by Japanese aircraft against Allied ships, 23 May 1945, ONI, Air Intelligence Group (Op-16-V), Serials and Publications, Box 13, RG 38.

156. Action report, Bombardment and occupation of Okinawa: Gunfire and covering force, dated 5 May 1945, by Commander, Battleship Squadron 1, ADM 199/85, UKNA.

157. "Report on Japanese tactics by CTG 58.1," in COMAIRPAC Air Operations Memorandum, no. 85, July 1945, ONI, Air Intelligence Group (Op-16-V), Box 7, RG 38.

158. "Japanese Reaction to Assault on Kanto Plain of Honshu," 13 August 1945, JIC 218/11, Records of the JCS, Geographic File, 1942–45, Box 90, RG 218.

Chapter 5: Knowledge of the Enemy Applied
THE EVOLUTION OF U.S. NAVAL AIR COMBAT DOCTRINE

1. Current Tactical Orders and Doctrine, PAC-10, June 1943, by Pacific Fleet, Box 231A, Operational Archives, World War II Command File, NHC.

2. Reynolds, *Fast Carriers*, 55–6.

3. Mark Stille, *U.S. Navy Aircraft Carriers* (Oxford: Osprey, 2007), 11.

4. Galvanic operation, dated 4 December 1943, by Commanding Officer, USS *Independence*, in Box 1056, World War II Action Reports, RG 38.

5. Operations in Kwajalein area, 4 December 1943, dated 4 January 1944, by Commander Task Force 50, in Box 974, World War II Action Reports, RG 38.

6. Japanese aerial torpedo attacks against U.S. task forces, including radar countermeasures used by the enemy, July 1944, by Air Operations Research Group, Office of the CNO, Enclosure: Commanding Officer, USS *Saratoga*, Operations against Sabang, 19 April 1944, Air Intelligence, OpNav-16-V, Division of Naval Intelligence, in Box 80, Operational Archives, World War II Command File, NHC.

7. FTP 143(A), War Instructions, 1944, Fleet Tactical Publications, U.S. Navy, in Box 108, Operational Archives, World War II Command File, NHC.

8. Oral History of Captain Edwin T. Layton, interviewed by E. Kitchen, 30 May 1970, Oral History Collection, NWC.

9. Basic gunnery doctrine and instructions for ships, 17 April 1944, by COMAIRPAC, BLUE 627, Box 23, Folder A16-3, RG 313.

10. Procedures for Destroyer Gunnery and Torpedo Practices, March 1944, by Commander, Destroyers Pacific Fleet, Bureau of Ordnance, Confidential Correspondence, 1944, Box 22, RG 74 (hereafter, RG 74).

11. Guerlac, *Radar in World War II*, 915–6.

12. N. J. M. Campbell, *Naval Weapons of World War II* (London: Conway, 2002), 108–10.

13. Operations against Saipan and Tinian Islands, 21–22 February, dated 23 February 1944, by Commanding Officer, USS *Yorktown*, World War II Action Reports, Box 1537, RG 38.

14. Reynolds, *Fast Carriers*, 54.

15. Fitzhugh Lee, "First Cruise of the *Essex*," in *Carrier Warfare*, ed. Wooldridge, 111.

16. Action report covering operations 14–16 August 1943 during landings on and occupation of Vella Lavella island, dated 26 September 1943, by Commander, Task Force 31, in Box 2, BLUE 242, RG 313.

17. Anti-aircraft action by Destroyer Squadron 23 during the period 30 November to 6 December 1943, Commander, Task Force 39, in Box 4, BLUE 242, RG 313.

18. Ordnance material performance during action, 1–2 November 1943, by Commanding Officer, USS *Montpelier*, BLUE 361, Box 18, Folder A5-1, RG 313.

19. Action report of engagements with enemy planes off Palau, by Commanding Officer, USS *Alabama*, 29–30 March 1944, BLUE 360, Box 18, RG 313.

20. Reynolds, *Fast Carriers*, 72; Lindley, *Carrier Victory*, 101–2.

21. Report of enemy air attacks during night of 4–5 December 1943, dated 3 January 1944, by Commander, Task Force 50, BLUE 360, Box 17, RG 313.

22. War Instructions, 1943, Bureau of Aeronautics, Confidential Correspondence, 1922–44, Box 204, RG 72. Also see FTP 143(A), War Instructions, 1944, Fleet Tactical Publications, U.S. Navy, Operational Archives, World War II Command File, Box 108, NHC.

23. Anti-aircraft actions of 12, 15 and 19 June 1944, by Battleship Division 9, BLUE 360, Box 27, RG 313.

24. Comment on carrier task group dispositions, 1 August 1944, by Commander, Cruiser Division 13, in BLUE 627, Box 81, RG 313.

25. Carrier air strikes on Luzon, 14–16 December, dated 18 February 1945, by Commander, Task Group 58.3, in BLUE 627, Box 81, RG 313.

26. See FTP 134, Gunnery Instructions, 1933, Fleet Tactical Publications, U.S. Navy, Operational Archives, World War II Command File, Box 107, NHC.

27. Memorandum for Admiral Nimitz on fleet radar, 9 May 1943, Papers of John H. Towers, Box 3, LOC.

28. Tentative Training Exercises, 19 October 1943, and Training Exercises, 29 November 1943, Commander, Cruiser Division 1, BLUE 361, Box 18, Folder A5-1, RG 313.

29. Pacific Fleet Confidential Notice 9CN-44, Procedure for Drone Firing, 13 March 1944, Box 22, RG 74.

30. General comment on practice, 9 June 1943, by Major C. V. Larsen, USS *Honolulu*, BLUE 361, Box 18, Folder A5-1, RG 313.

31. Operations against Truk, Satawan, and Ponape, 29 April to 1 May, dated 3 June 1944, by Commander, Task Force 58, BLUE 360, Box 18, RG 313.

32. Action report for the period 6–27 June, dated 13 July 1944, by Commanding Officer, USS *Bunker Hill*, World War II Action Reports, Box 876, Folder CV17/A16–3, RG 38.

33. Action Report, Bombardment and fire support of Lingayen Gulf, 3–18 January 1945, by Commander, Battleship Squadron 1, ADM 199/1499, UKNA.

34. Action Report, period 13–17 December 1944, Operations in support of Mindoro assault and occupation, by Commander, Cruiser Division 12, ADM 199/1496, UKNA.

35. Secret and personal letter from Halsey to Nimitz, 9 September 1944, Papers of William F. Halsey, Box 15, LOC.

36. Battle report, dated 22 October 1944, by Executive Officer, USS *San Jacinto*, World War II Action Reports, Box 162, Folder CVL30/A16-3, RG 38.

37. Calibration of rangefinders on Anti-aircraft targets, 26 October 1944, by Commanding Officer, USS *Alaska*, BATRON 1, Box 6, Folder 594, S71, RG 313.

38. Operations of the Western Pacific Task Forces and the Third Fleet, dated 25 January 1945, by Commander, Third Fleet, World War II Action Reports, Box 41, Folder A16-3/(16), RG 38. Also see: Anti-aircraft training for task forces at sea in advanced areas, 5 November 1944, by Commander, Destroyers Pacific Fleet, BLUE 627, Box 30, Folder P11-1, RG 313.

39. Action report for period 30 December 1944 to 26 January 1945, dated 31 January 1945, by Commanding Officer, USS *South Dakota*, World War II Action Reports, Box 1440, Folder BB57/16-3, RG 38.

40. COMINCH Information Bulletin, no. 25, Anti-aircraft Action Summary, August 1944, ONI Security Classified Publications, World War II, Box 1, RG 38.

41. Interception of enemy fighters over the Russell Islands, 1 April 1943, by Intelligence Section, Air Command Solomon Islands, BLUE 242, Box 9, Folder A8, RG 313.

42. Interview of First Lieutenant Kenneth Walsh, USMC, VMF-124, in the Air Technical Analysis Division, DCNO (Air), 26 October 1943, in Box 3, ONI, Air Intelligence Group (Op-16-V), RG 38.

43. "Carrier action notes: Air combat reports on FM–2," 23 August 1944, in COMAIRPAC Air Operations Memorandum, no. 44, in Box 6, ONI, Air Intelligence Group (Op-16-V), RG 38.

44. Belote and Belote, *Titans of the Seas*, 212.

45. Admiral Yarnell's Report on Naval Aviation, prepared for Secretary of the Navy, 29 January 1944, Papers of Harry E. Yarnell, Box 11, NHC. Also see: Memorandum for Admiral King, by R. S. Edwards, 17 July 1943, Reference no. 396, Papers of Ernest J. King, Reel 3, Microfilm Collection, NWC.

46. "Tactics and operations: Air Group 15 commanding officer's comments," in COMAIRPAC Air Operations Memorandum, no. 42 (8 August 1944), ONI, Air Intelligence Group (Op-16-V), Box 6, RG 38.

47. Condon, *Corsairs*, 88–90.

48. Arleigh Burke, "Spruance, Mitscher, and Task Force 58," in *Carrier Warfare*, ed. Wooldridge, 158.

49. The combat strategy and tactics of Major Gregory Boyington, USMCR, 19 Janu-

ary 1944, Headquarters, Marine Aircraft, South Pacific Fleet, Intelligence Section, ONI, Air Intelligence Group (Op-16-V), Serials and Publications, Box 8, RG 38.

50. Barrett Tillman, *Hellcat: The F6F in World War II* (Annapolis, MD: Naval Institute Press, 1979), 35.

51. Operations in the Pacific Ocean Areas during the month of September 1944, by CINCPAC, BLUE 627, Box 81, RG 313.

52. Bruce Porter, "First Kill," in *Aces*, vol. 2, ed. Hammel, 146.

53. Fighter tactics: excerpts from aircraft action reports and battle narratives, January to April 1944, by Air Intelligence Group, BLUE 627, Box 80, Folder A9, RG 313.

54. McCampbell, "Doctrine," 196.

55. Tillman, *Corsair*, 19.

56. Analysis of air combat losses and fighter superiority in the South Pacific Area, 10 January 1944, Air Operations Analysis Report no. 3, ONI, Air Intelligence Group (Op-16-V), Serials and Publications, Box 12, RG 38.

57. Interview of Captain S. C. Ring, USN (Operations Officer for Commander, Air-Sol), in Air Information Division, 14 September 1943, in Box 2, ONI, Air Intelligence Group (Op-16-V), RG 38.

58. "Coordination of air group strikes," 29 May 1944, in COMAIRPAC Air Operations Memorandum, no. 32, in Box 6, ONI, Air Intelligence Group (Op-16-V), RG 38.

59. Fighter tactics: excerpts from aircraft action reports and battle narratives, January to April 1944, by Air Intelligence Group, BLUE 627, Box 80, Folder A9, RG 313.

60. "Tactical lessons learned in the South Pacific," 29 May 1944, in COMAIRPAC Air Operations Memorandum, no. 32, in Box 6, ONI, Air Intelligence Group (Op-16-V), RG 38.

61. Interview of Lieutenant Commander T. Blackburn, USN, Commanding Officer VF-17, in the Office of the CNO, 7 April 1944, in Box 3, ONI, Air Intelligence Group (Op-16-V), RG 38. Also see COMAIRPAC Air Operations Memorandum, no. 24 (18 March 1944), RED 136, Box 12, RG 313. For a secondary account, see Morison, *Bismarcks Barrier*, 401.

62. Wendorf, "Blood over Kwajalein," in *Aces*, vol. 2, ed. Hammel, 179.

63. Morison, *Gilberts*, 89, 95–6.

64. Reynolds, *Fast Carriers*, 59.

65. James Gray, "Development of Naval Night Fighters in World War II," United States Naval Institute *Proceedings* 74 (July 1948): 848; Guerlac, *Radar in World War II*, 936.

66. Morison, *Gilberts*, 86.

67. Reynolds, *Fast Carriers*, 170.

68. "Advantages of and necessity for night carrier operations," 23 March 1944, by Pacific Fleet Radar Center, Radar Operators' School, BLUE 627, Box 85, Folder S67-1, RG 313; "Japanese night air attacks," dated 21 March 1944, by Commander, Central Pacific Force, World War II Action Reports, Box 216, RG 38.

69. James Trousdale, "The Birth of the Navy's Night Fighters," United States Naval Institute *Proceedings* 78 (June 1952): 623.

70. Reynolds, *Fast Carriers*, 131.

71. "Tactics and operations: carrier-based night operations," in COMAIRPAC Air Operations Memorandum, no. 39 (16 July 1944), ONI, Air Intelligence Group (Op-16-V), Box 6, RG 38.

72. Tillman, *Hellcat*, 170–3.

73. Ashley Halsey, "The CVL's Success Story," United States Naval Institute *Proceedings* 72 (April 1946): 529.

74. War Instructions, 1943, BuAer, Confidential Correspondence, 1922–44, Box 204, RG 72.

75. Reynolds, *Fast Carriers*, 101.

76. Operations in the South Pacific Area, 20 April 1942 to 15 June 1944, Papers of William F. Halsey, Box 37, LOC.

77. "280-mile fighter sweep of Iwojima," in COMAIRPAC Air Operations Memorandum, no. 38 (9 July 1944), in ONI, Air Intelligence Group (Op-16-V), Box 6, RG 38.

78. "Tactics and operations: Neutralization of enemy airfields," in COMAIRPAC Air Operations Memorandum, no. 26 (9 April 1944), in ONI, Air Intelligence Group (Op-16-V), Box 6, RG 38.

79. "Allied tactics: New fighter sweep tactics," in COMAIRPAC Air Operations Memorandum, no. 21 (5 February 1944), in ONI, Air Intelligence Group (Op-16-V), Box 6, RG 38.

80. "177 Japanese planes in 13 days: *Hornet* score," in COMAIRPAC Air Operations Memorandum, no. 42 (8 August 1944), in ONI, Air Intelligence Group (Op-16-V), Box 6, RG 38; Operations against the Marianas, 11–30 June, dated 1 July 1944, by Commanding Officer, USS *Princeton*, World War II Action Reports, Box 226, RG 38.

81. "Tactics and operations: Comments of Commander, Air Group 1," in COMAIRPAC Air Operations Memorandum, no. 38 (9 July 1944), ONI, Air Intelligence Group (Op-16-V), Box 6, RG 38.

82. Halsey and Bryan, *Halsey's Story*, 199.

83. Merrill, *Sailor's Admiral*, 134.

84. Anti-aircraft information for air combat information officers, May 1944, ONI, Air Intelligence Group (Op-16-V), Serials and Publications, Box 8, RG 38.

85. "Carrier action notes: First reports from Marianas operation," in COMAIRPAC Air Operations Memorandum, no. 35 (16 June 1944), in ONI, Air Intelligence Group (Op-16-V), Box 6, RG 38.

86. "Commander Air Group 28 comments on AA fire," in COMAIRPAC Air Operations Memorandum, no. 52 (26 October 1944), in ONI, Air Intelligence Group (Op-16-V), Box 6, RG 38.

87. Destruction of anti-aircraft batteries, 26 August 1944, by Commander, Carrier Air Group 14, BLUE 627, Box 82, RG 313.

88. "Tactics and operations: Commander Air Group 13 Comments," in COMAIRPAC Air Operations Memorandum, no. 48 (October 1944), ONI, Air Intelligence Group (Op-16-V), Box 6, RG 38.

89. Report on seizure of southern Palau Islands and Ulithi, and concurrent operations in support of the seizure of Morotai, dated 14 November 1944, Papers of William F. Halsey, Box 37, LOC.

90. "Tactics and operations: Comments of CVLG-22," in COMAIRPAC Air Operations Memorandum, no. 60 (9 December 1944), in ONI, Air Intelligence Group (Op-16-V), Box 6, RG 38.

91. "Comments of Commander Air Group 22," in COMAIRPAC Air Operations Memorandum, no. 51 (12 October 1944), in ONI, Air Intelligence Group (Op-16-V), Box 6, RG 38.

92. "Attack on Anti–aircraft positions," in COMAIRPAC Secret Air Tactical Bulletin, no. 1 SATB-45 (22 April 1945), BLUE 627, Box 82, RG 313.

93. Action Report, 14 March to 14 May 1945, by Commander, Task Group 58.4, ADM 199/87, UKNA.

94. Brief of action report, USS *Intrepid*, for period 18 March through 16 April 1945, by COMAIRPAC, ADM 199/91, UKNA.

95. Methods of neutralizing Japanese air strength, August 1945, ONI, Air Intelligence Group (Op-16-V), Serials and Publications, Box 14, RG 38.

96. Report of operations, 24 May to 13 June, dated 14 June 1945, by Commanding Officer, USS *Shangri-la*, in Box 39, BLUE 627, RG 313.

97. Report on locating and destroying aircraft on the ground, 22 August 1945, by Commanding Officer, USS *Shangri-la*, in Box 82, BLUE 627, RG 313.

98. "Knocking out more Japanese aircraft," 5 August 1945, by Commander, Task Group 38.1, in Box 20, Folder A8, BLUE 627, RG 313.

99. Action Report, 14 March to 14 May 1945, by Commander, Task Group 58.4, ADM 199/87, UKNA.

100. "Knocking out more Japanese aircraft," 5 August 1945, by Commander, Carrier Division 3, ADM 199/1542, UKNA.

101. Strike against Kanoya airfield, 5 June 1945, by Commander, Task Force 38, BLUE 627, Box 82, RG 313.

102. Interview with Elmer Potter, 10 August 1972, Papers of Edwin T. Layton, Box 30, Manuscript Collection, NWC.

103. Fighter Direction Doctrine, n.d., ca. early 1944, BLUE 360, Box 4, RG 313.

104. John Monsarrat, *Angel on the Yardarm: Memoir of a Naval Officer in World War II* (Newport, RI: Naval War College Press, 1979), 37, 56–7.

105. Air attack on TF 52, evening of 25 November 1943, by Commander, Fifth Amphibious Force, Papers of Richmond K. Turner, Box 4, NHC.

106. Brown, *Technical and Military Imperatives*, 369.

107. Morison, *Gilberts*, 143.

108. Interview of Rear Admiral O. R. Hardison, Commander, Fleet Air, South Pacific, in the Air Technical Analysis Division, 14 January 1944, ONI, Air Intelligence Group (Op-16-V), Box 3, RG 38.

109. Comments and recommendations on operations in Western Carolines, and analysis of enemy air attacks during nights of 29 to 31 March, dated 5 April 1944, by Commanding Officer, USS *Minneapolis*, BLUE 360, Box 17, RG 313; Operations against Saipan and Tinian Islands, 21–22 February, dated 23 February 1944, by

Commanding Officer, USS *Yorktown*, World War II Action Reports, Box 1537, RG 38. Also see: Interview of Major T. R. Hicks, USMCR, Senior Controller, VMF(N)-531, 3 May 1944, ONI, Air Intelligence Group (Op-16-V), Box 3, RG 38.

110. "Tactics and operations: the employment of night fighters from carriers," in COMAIRPAC Air Operations Memorandum, no. 25 (1 April 1944), ONI, Air Intelligence Group (Op-16-V), Box 6, RG 38.

111. Report of the carrier air strike on the Saipan-Tinian area, 22 February, dated 3 March 1944, by Commander, Task Group 58.3, World War II Action Reports, Box 225, RG 38.

112. Reynolds, *Fast Carriers*, 55; Lindley, *Carrier Victory*, 108.

113. Attacks on Truk Islands on 29–30 April, dated 7 May 1944, Commanding Officer, USS *Lexington*, in Box 1147, World War II Action Reports, RG 38.

114. Operations against Saipan and Tinian Islands, 21–22 February, dated 8 April 1944, by Commander, Task Force 58, in Box 1537, World War II Action Reports, RG 38.

115. Air engagement against the Japanese fleet, dated 18 July 1944, by Commander Carrier Division Four, in Box 227, Folder FB2-4/A16-3(2), World War II Action Reports, RG 38.

116. "Carrier action notes: night fighter operations," in COMAIRPAC Air Operations Memorandum, no. 42 (8 August 1944), ONI, Air Intelligence Group (Op-16-V), Box 6, RG 38.

117. Reynolds, *Fast Carriers*, 211, 221.

118. Morison, *Marianas*, 262.

119. Battle Experience, Leyte Gulf, Enclosure: CTG 38.1, and Commanding Officers, USS *Essex* and USS *Sangamon*, Comments on Fighter Direction and Radar.

120. Battle of Formosa, 12–14 October, dated 21 November 1944, by Commanding Officer, USS *Essex*, World War II Action Reports, Box 975, Folder CV9/A16-3, RG 38.

121. Brief of action report, Task Group 38.2, covering support of Lingayen landings, 30 December to 26 January 1945, by COMAIRPAC, BLUE 627, Box 81, RG 313.

122. Action Report of USS *Savo Island* for operations in support of Mindoro Attack Group, 10–19 December 1944, by Commander, Seventh Fleet, ADM 199/1497, UKNA.

123. Luzon strikes on 5–6 November, dated 11 November 1944, by Commanding Officer, USS *Santa Fe*, World War II Action Reports, Box 154, Folder CL60/C-A16-3, RG 38.

124. Battle Experience, Leyte Gulf, Enclosure: USS *Fanshaw Bay*, Comments on Radar and Fighter Direction.

125. Operations against Palau, Mindanao, Luzon, Celebes, and Morotai during period from 29 August through 28 September, dated 29 October 1944, by Commander, Task Group 38, World War II Action Reports, Box 144, Folder C2CTF/A16-3, RG 38.

126. Operations against Palau, Mindanao, Visayas, Luzon, Celebes, and Morotai during period 29 August to 28 September, dated 7 October 1944, by Commander, Task Group 38.1, BLUE 627, Box 38, RG 313.

127. Morison, *Liberation*, 58.

128. Japanese suicide attacks on carriers, 22 January 1945, by COMAIRPAC, BLUE 627, Box 83, RG 313.

129. Action Report, Luzon Operation. 29 December 1944 to 12 January 1945, Commanding Officer, USS *Kadashan Bay*, ADM 199/1054, UKNA.

130. Morison, *Victory*, 21.

131. "Defense against Japanese aerial suicide attacks on U.S. naval vessels, excerpts from aircraft action reports and battle narratives," October 1944, by Office of the CNO, Division of Naval Intelligence, Air Operations Research Group, Enclosure: Commanding Officer, USS *McCord*, Air Intelligence, OpNav-16-V, Box 81, Operational Archives, World War II Command File, NHC.

132. Operations in support of landings at Lingayen, culminating in loss of the ship, 1–4 January 1945, by Commanding Officer, USS *Omaney Bay*, ADM 199/1501, UKNA.

133. CINCUS Anti-aircraft Action Summary: Suicide Attacks, April 1945, Pacific Fleet, Box 258A, Operational Archives, World War II Command File, NHC.

134. Action Report, Luzon Attack Force, Lingayen Gulf, Musketeer-Mike One operation, dated 9 January 1945, by Commander, Seventh Fleet, ADM 199/1508, UKNA.

135. Action report by Commander, Third Amphibious Force, on Lingayen Gulf operation, 7 March 1945, Excerpt from Battle Damage Section, by COMAIRPAC, BLUE 627, Box 82, RG 313.

136. "Defense against Japanese aerial suicide attacks on U.S. naval vessels, excerpts from aircraft action reports and battle narratives," October 1944, by Office of the CNO, Division of Naval Intelligence, Air Operations Research Group, Enclosure: Commanding Officer, USS *Abner Read*, Air Intelligence, OpNav-16-V, Box 81, Operational Archives, World War II Command File, NHC.

137. Action Report, Bombardment and fire support of Lingayen Gulf, 6–18 January 1945, by Commander, Battleship Division 3, ADM 199/1499, UKNA.

138. CINCUS Anti-suicide Action Summary, August 1945, Pacific Fleet, Box 258A, Operational Archives, World War II Command File, NHC.

139. Japanese suicide attacks on carriers, 22 January 1945, by COMAIRPAC, BLUE 627, Box 83, RG 313.

140. Action Report, Bombardment and fire support of Lingayen Gulf, 3–18 January 1945, Commander, Battleship Squadron 1, ADM 199/1499, UKNA.

141. Battle of the Philippines, 24–25 October, dated 2 December 1944, by Commander, Task Group 38.3, World War II Action Reports, Box 153, Folder FB2-1/A16-3/Rug, RG 38.

142. "Comments on defense against suicides," in COMAIRPAC Air Operations Memorandum, no. 75 (6 April 1945), ONI, Air Intelligence Group (Op-16-V), Box 7, RG 38.

143. Memoranda for Files, 18 December 1944, Papers of John H. Towers, Box 1, LOC.

144. Action Report, USS *Bismarck Sea*, Musketeer-Mike One operation, 1–23 January 1945, ADM 199/1501, UKNA.

145. Leyte operation, 12–29 October 1944, by Commander, Carrier Division 22, BLUE 360, Box 21, RG 313; Action Report, Lingayen Gulf operations, Commanding Officer, USS *Makin Island*, ADM 199/1502, UKNA.

146. Anti-submarine and combat air patrols by U.S. Navy aircraft in the Pacific, June 1944 to January 1945, by Air Intelligence Group, Enclosure: Action Report by Commanding Officer, Task Force 79, BLUE 627, Box 82, RG 313.

147. CINCUS Anti-aircraft Action Summary: suicide attacks, April 1945, Pacific Fleet, Box 258A, in Operational Archives, World War II Command File, NHC.

148. "Defense against Japanese aerial suicide attacks on U.S. naval vessels, excerpts from aircraft action reports and battle narratives," October 1944, by Office of the CNO, Division of Naval Intelligence, Air Operations Research Group, Enclosure: Gunnery Officer, USS *Canberra*, Air Intelligence, OpNav-16-V, Box 81, in Operational Archives, World War II Command File, NHC.

149. Requirements for fighter direction and radar picket destroyers with SP radar, 5 February 1945, by Commander, Amphibious Forces Pacific Fleet, BLUE 627, Box 85, Folder S67, RG 313. Also see Monsarrat, *Angel on the Yardarm*, 119–20.

150. Proposal of flak coordination plan, 25 January 1945, by Commanding Officer, USS *Essex*, BLUE 627, Box 22, Folder A16-3, RG 313.

151. Battle of the Philippines, 24–25 October, dated 21 November 1944, by Commanding Officer, USS *Essex*, World War II Action Reports, Box 975, Folder CV9/A16-3, RG 38.

152. Morison, *Liberation*, 54–5.

153. "Defense against Japanese aerial suicide attacks on U.S. naval vessels, excerpts from aircraft action reports and battle narratives," October 1944, by Office of the CNO, Division of Naval Intelligence, Air Operations Research Group, Enclosure: Commanding Officer, USS *Essex*, Air Intelligence, OpNav-16-V, Box 81, Operational Archives, World War II Command File, NHC.

154. Action Report, Luzon Attack Force, Lingayen Gulf, Musketeer-Mike One operation, dated 9 January 1945, by Commander, Seventh Fleet, ADM 199/1508, UKNA.

155. Action report, dated 7 November 1944, by Commanding Officer, USS *Wasp*, Box 1503, CV18/A9-3/A12-1, World War II Action Reports, RG 38.

156. CINCUS Anti-aircraft Action Summary: suicide attacks, April 1945, Pacific Fleet, Box 258A, Operational Archives, World War II Command File, NHC.

157. John Thach, "The Big Blue Blanket," in *Carrier Warfare*, ed. Wooldridge, 265–6.

158. "Carrier action notes: Japanese death divers present difficult problem," 1 December 1944, in COMAIRPAC Air Operations Memorandum, no. 57, ONI, Air Intelligence Group (Op-16-V), Box 6, RG 38.

159. CINCUS Anti-aircraft Action Summary: Suicide Attacks, April 1945, Pacific Fleet, Box 258A, and "The Role of the Combat Air Patrol in Suicide Plane Attacks," 31 March 1945, by Office of the CNO, Division of Naval Intelligence, Air Operations Research Group, Air Intelligence, OpNav-16-V, Box 80, Operational Archives, World War II Command File, NHC.

160. "Defense against Japanese aerial suicide attacks on U.S. naval vessels, excerpts from aircraft action reports and battle narratives," October 1944, by Office of the CNO, Division of Naval Intelligence, Air Operations Research Group, Enclosure: Commanding Officer, USS *Wichita*, Air Intelligence, OpNav-16-V, Box 81, Operational Archives, World War II Command File, NHC. Also see: Sui-

cide plane attacks, 5 February 1945, by Commander, Amphibious Forces, Pacific Fleet, BLUE 627, Box 81, RG 313.

161. Replacement of SB2C by VF, 19 November 1944 by Commander, Third Fleet, BLUE 627, Box 84, Folder F1, RG 313.

162. Operations in support of the occupation by U.S. forces of the central and northern Philippines, 30 October 1944 to 26 January 1945, by Commander, Second Carrier Task Force Pacific, ADM 199/1503, UKNA.

163. Secret and personal letter from Halsey to Nimitz, 9 November 1944, Papers of William F. Halsey, Box 15, LOC.

164. Action off Luzon, 25 November 1944, by Commander, Task Group 38.3, ADM 199/1505, UKNA.

165. Brief of action report CTG-38.3, covering Luzon sweeps of 14–16 December 1944, dated 18 February 1945, by COMAIRPAC, BLUE 627, Box 81, RG 313.

166. Action Report: Operations in support of Luzon landings, 30 December 1944 through 26 January 1945, by Commander Task Group 38.3, ADM 199/1507, UKNA.

167. Reynolds, *Fast Carriers*, 290; Tillman, *Hellcat*, 153–4.

168. "The role of CAP in suicide plane attacks," 28 March 1945, ONI, Air Intelligence Group (Op-16-V), Serials and Publications, Box 14, RG 38.

169. "Night operations: CVG-90 in support of Okinawa operations," in COMAIR-PAC Air Operations Memorandum, no. 80 (25 May 1945), ONI, Air Intelligence Group (Op-16-V), Box 7, RG 38.

170. George Kenney, *General Kenney Reports: A Personal History of the Pacific War* (New York: Duell, Sloan, and Pearce, 1949), 526; Also see Bernhard Mortensen, "Cutting the Enemy's Lifeline," in *The Army Air Forces in World War II*, ed. Wesley Craven and James Cate, vol. 5, *The Pacific: Matterhorn to Nagasaki, June 1944 to August 1945* (Washington, DC: Office of Air Force History, 1983), 473–9; Thomas Griffith, *MacArthur's Airman: General George C. Kenney and the War in the Southwest Pacific* (Lawrence: Kansas University Press, 1998), 224–5; Brigadier General J. V. Crabb, *Fifth Air Force's Air War against Japan, September 1942 to August 1945* (February 1946), located at Air University Library, Maxwell Air Force Base, Montgomery, AL, 26–7, http://www.au.af.mil/au/aul/bibs/japan/jpnwwii.pdf.

171. James Cate and James Olson, "Urban Area Attacks," in *Matterhorn to Nagasaki*, ed. Craven and Cate, 629–34.

172. "Night operations: CVG-90 in support of Okinawa operations," in COMAIR-PAC Air Operations Memorandum, no. 80 (25 May 1945), ONI, Air Intelligence Group (Op-16-V), Box 7, RG 38.

173. Brief of action report, USS *Intrepid*, for period 18 March through 16 April 1945, by COMAIRPAC, ADM 199/91, UKNA.

174. Rielly, *Kamikazes, Corsairs, and Picket Ships*, 337.

175. Brief of action report, CTF 58, for period 14 March to 28 May, dated 17 July 1945, by COMAIRPAC, BLUE 627, Box 82, RG 313.

176. "*Hornet* reports on fighter direction," in COMAIRPAC Air Operations Memorandum, no. 83 (1 June 1945), ONI, Air Intelligence Group (Op-16-V), Box 7, RG 38.

177. Report of operations of Task Force 58 in support of landings at Okinawa, 14 March through 28 May, by Commander, Fifth Fleet, ADM 199/89, UKNA.

178. Operations in support of amphibious landings on Okinawa, Phase II, 5 to 13 April, dated 16 April 1945, by Commanding Officer, USS *Enterprise*, World War II Action Reports, Box 971, Folder CV6/A16-3(11-pe), RG 38.

179. "Carrier action notes: COMCARDIV 4 comments on fighter direction," in COMAIRPAC Air Operations Memorandum, no. 86 (22 June 1945), ONI, Air Intelligence Group (Op-16-V), Box 7, RG 38.

180. Action Report, Phases I and II of the Okinawa campaign, and Operations of Task Group 54.1, Task Unit 54.1.3 from 21 March to 30 April 1945, by Commander, Amphibious Group 11 and Commander, Cruiser Division 13, ADM 199/94, UKNA.

181. Report of participation in operations against Okinawa, from 21 March to 24 April 1945, by Commander, Cruiser Division 6, ADM 199/107, UKNA. Also see Forrestel, *Spruance*, 204.

182. Morison, *Victory*, 178–9.

183. AA Training, 7 July 1945, by Commander, Battleship Squadron 2, BATRON 1, Box 1, Folder 594, Folder A5-1, RG 313.

184. Tactical uses of radar, in Pacific Fleet Radar Center, Bulletin of Information, no. 4-45 (7 July 1945), BLUE 627, Box 26, Folder S67-1, RG 313.

185. Report of operations of Task Group 58.1 (Fast Carrier Group 1) in support of landings at Okinawa, 14 March to 30 April 1945, by COMAIRPAC and Commander, Carrier Division 5, ADM 199/94, UKNA.

186. "Carrier action notes: COMCARDIV 4 comments on fighter direction," in COMAIRPAC Air Operations Memorandum, no. 86 (22 June 1945), ONI, Air Intelligence Group (Op-16-V), Box 7, RG 38.

187. For a secondary account, see Gerald Astor, *Operation Iceberg: The Invasion and Conquest of Okinawa in World War II* (New York: Dell, 1995), 204–5.

188. Action Report, 2 July through 15 August 1945, by Commanding Officer, USS *Lexington*, ADM 199/1544, UKNA.

189. "*Enterprise* reports on fighter direction findings," in COMAIRPAC Air Operations Memorandum, no. 77 (20 April 1945), ONI, Air Intelligence Group (Op-16-V), Box 7, RG 38.

190. Report of capture of Okinawa Gunto, 24 May to 24 June 1945, by Commander, Task Unit 52.1.1, BLUE 627, Box 114, RG 313.

191. Gunnery Doctrine and Instructions, 26 November 1944, by Battleships U.S. Pacific Fleet, BATRON 1, Box 2, Folder 594, RG 313.

192. Tactical uses of radar, in Pacific Fleet Radar Center, Bulletin of Information, no. 4-45 (7 July 1945), BLUE 627, Box 26, Folder S67-1, RG 313.

193. Rielly, *Kamikazes, Corsairs, and Picket Ships*, 335.

194. Action Report on capture of Okinawa, Phases I and II, dated 1 June 1945, by Commanding Officer, USS *St Louis* (CL49), ADM 199/86, UKNA.

195. Rielly, *Kamikazes, Corsairs, and Picket Ships*, 4.

196. Ibid., 342–3.

197. Battle Experience: Radar pickets and methods of combating suicide attacks off

Okinawa, March–May 1945, in Secret Information Bulletin, no. 24, U.S. Fleet, Box 262, Operational Archives, World War II Command File, NHC.

198. Rielly, *Kamikazes, Corsairs, and Picket Ships*, 19–23.

199. Ibid., 31–2, 41–2.

200. Action Report, Operations of Task Group 54.1, Task Unit 54.1.3 and Cruiser Division 13 in Phases I and II of the Okinawa campaign from 21 March to 30 April 1945, by Commander, Amphibious Group 11 and Commander, Cruiser Division 13, ADM 199/94, UKNA.

201. Rielly, *Kamikazes, Corsairs, and Picket Ships*, 38–9.

202. Reynolds, *Fast Carriers*, 350.

203. USS *New York* and USS *Texas*: Installation of gunfire control systems Mark 57 and Mark 63, dated 9 July 1945, by BuOrd, BATRON 1, Box 6, Folder 594, File S71, and Condition and reliability of Mark 50 directors, 4 July 1945, by Commander, Service Force Pacific Fleet, RG 313.

204. Directors for control of 5-inch, .38-caliber battery, 9 July 1945, by Bureau of Ordnance, BLUE 627, Box 83, RG 313.

205. Operations in support of the campaign for the capture of Okinawa Gunto, 14 March to 27 May 1945, by Commanding Officer, USS *Astoria* (CL90), ADM 199/85, UKNA.

206. Report of operations of Task Force 58 in support of landings at Okinawa, 14 March through 28 May, including actions against Kyushu, Nansei Shoto, Japanese fleet at Kure, the *Yamato*, and operations in direct support of landings at Okinawa, by Commander, Fifth Fleet, ADM 199/89, UKNA.

207. Action report: Bombardment and occupation of Okinawa: Gunfire and covering force, dated 5 May 1945, by Commander, Battleship Squadron 1, ADM 199/85, UKNA.

208. Anti-aircraft training: dry-run tracking, 9 July 1945, by Commanding Officer, USS *Mississippi*, BATRON 1, Box 9, Folder 593, RG 313.

209. Training exercises for period 28 May to 10 June 1945, by Commanding Officer, USS *Quincy*, Box 30, Folder P11-1, and training for period 28 May to 10 June, dated 13 August 1945, by Commander, Battleship Squadron 8, Box 22, Folder A16-3, BLUE 627, RG 313.

210. Training for June 1945, dated 25 July 1945, by Commanding Officer, USS *Monterey*, Part V: CIC Officer's report, Box 17, Folder A5-1, BLUE 627, RG 313.

Conclusion: The Effectiveness of U.S. Naval Intelligence during the Pacific War: Causes and Consequences

1. See Douglas Ford, "Strategic Culture, Intelligence Assessment, and the Conduct of the Pacific War, 1941–1945: The British-Indian and Imperial Japanese armies in comparison," *War in History* 14, no. 1 (2007): 95. The IJN and its air service were marginally less blissful than the Imperial Army, in that they understood how adequate technology was essential when fighting the Allies. However, Japanese navy officials, like their army counterparts, were not inclined to undertake a measured evaluation concerning the prospects of overcoming their Western rivals. See Evans and Peattie, *Kaigun*, 415–6.

2. United States Strategic Bombing Survey (USSBS), *Japanese Military and Naval Intelligence Division* (Washington, DC: Government Printing Office, 1946), 1, consulted at U.S. Army Military History Institute, Carlisle, PA.

3. Ibid., 20–1.

4. Ken Kotani, *Japanese Intelligence in World War II*, trans. Chiharu Kotani (Oxford: Osprey, 2009), 107–8, 159.

5. USSBS, *Japanese Intelligence*, 18–20.

6. Sadao Asada, "The Japanese Navy and the United States," in *Pearl Harbor as History*, ed. Dorothy Borg and Shumpei Okamoto (New York: Columbia University Press, 1973), 257.

7. Best, *British Intelligence*, 195.

8. Mahnken, *Uncovering Ways of War*, 115–30.

9. Wark, *Ultimate Enemy*, 27.

10. For a description of the prerequisites for successful innovation, see Murray, "Innovation," 326–7; Murray and Knox, "The Future behind Us," 193.

11. Handel, *War, Strategy*, 252–3.

12. Rosen, *Winning the Next War*, 34–5.

Bibliography

Primary Sources
UNPUBLISHED DOCUMENTS
United States National Archives and Records Administration, Washington, D.C. (NARA 1)
    RG 38, Records of the Chief of Naval Operations
    Director of Naval Intelligence, General Correspondence
    Director of Naval Intelligence, Official Correspondence
    Director's Subject File
    Office of Naval Intelligence, ONI, Confidential Correspondence, 1913–24
    ONI, Far Eastern Branch, Far Eastern Theater Section
    ONI, Intelligence Division, Naval Attaché Reports
    RG 45, Office of Naval Records and Library
    Naval Intelligence, 1911–27
  RG 80, Records of the Secretary of the Navy
    Navy General Board, Subject File, 1900–47
    Office of the Secretary of the Navy, Formerly Confidential Correspondence

United States National Archives and Records Administration,
College Park, Maryland (NARA 2)
    RG 38, Records of the Chief of Naval Operations
    ONI, Air Intelligence Group (OP-16-V)
    ONI, Confidential Reports of Naval Attachés, 1940–46
    ONI, Foreign Branch, Naval Attaché Reports from Tokyo
    ONI, Monograph Files, Japan, 1939–46
    ONI, Planning Branch
    ONI, Secret Naval Attaché Reports, 1936–43
    ONI, Security Classified Publications, 1882–1954
    War Plans Division, 1918–41
    World War II Action Reports

RG 72, Records of the Bureau of Aeronautics
   Confidential Correspondence, 1922–44
   Secret Correspondence, 1937–47
RG 74, Records of the Bureau of Ordnance
   Confidential Correspondence, 1944
RG 165, Records of the War Department
   Security Classified Publications, "P" File
RG 218, Records of the Joint Chiefs of Staff
   Central Decimal File, 1942–45
   Geographic File, 1942–45
RG 313, Records of Naval Forces Operating in the Pacific
   Battleship Squadron One (BATRON 1)
   Commander, Air Force South Pacific (BLUE 242)
   Commander, Battleships and Cruisers Pacific Fleet (BLUE 360) and (BLUE 361)
   Commander, Second Carrier Task Force (BLUE 627)
   Fifth Fleet (RED 136)
   Joint Intelligence Center, Pacific Ocean Area (BLUE 644)

Naval Historical Center, Washington, D.C. (NHC)
   Operational Archives
   World War II Command Files

United States Naval War College, Newport, Rhode Island (NWC)
   RG 4, Publications
   RG 12, Student Problems and Solutions

United Kingdom National Archives, London, England (UKNA)
   ADM 199, War History Cases and Papers
   ADM 223, Naval Intelligence Files
   AIR 22, Air Ministry: Periodical Summaries and Bulletins
   AIR 23, Royal Air Force Regional Commands
   AIR 40, Air Ministry: Air Intelligence Files
   AVIA 10, Ministry of Aircraft Production: Records of the British Technical
       Mission to North America (Tizard Mission)

Private Papers
Library of Congress, Washington D.C. (LOC)
   General Henry "Hap" Arnold
   Rear Admiral John J. Ballentine
   Fleet Admiral William F. Halsey
   Fleet Admiral Ernest J. King
   Brigadier General William E. Riley, U.S. Marine Corps
   Admiral John H. Towers

Naval Historical Center (NHC)
   Fleet Admiral Ernest J. King
   Admiral Marc A. Mitscher

Fleet Admiral Chester Nimitz
Admiral Raymond A. Spruance
Admiral Richmond K. Turner
Rear Admiral Harry E. Yarnell

United States Naval War College (NWC)
Captain Thomas Dyer, Oral History Collection
Fleet Admiral Ernest J. King, Microfilm Collection
Captain Edwin T. Layton
Captain Joseph J. Rochefort, Oral History Collection

PUBLISHED SOURCES—OFFICIAL HISTORIES, EDITED DOCUMENTS, AND MEMOIRS

Barbey, Daniel. *MacArthur's Amphibious Navy: Seventh Amphibious Force Operations, 1943–1945*. Annapolis, MD: Naval Institute Press, 1969.

Bates, Richard. *The Battle of Savo Island, August 9, 1942: Strategic and Tactical Analysis*. Newport, RI: Naval War College, 1950.

Bell, Frederick. *Condition Red: Destroyer Action in the South Pacific*. New York: Longmans, 1943.

Burke, Arleigh. "Spruance, Mitscher, and Task Force 58." In *Carrier Warfare in the Pacific,* edited by E. T. Wooldridge. Washington, DC: Smithsonian Institution, 1993.

Chihaya, Masataka. "An Intimate Look at the Japanese Navy." In *The Pearl Harbor Papers: Inside the Japanese Plans*, edited by Donald Goldstein and Katherine Dillon. Dulles, VA: Brassey's, 1993.

————. "Some Stories Concerning the Construction of the *Yamato*–class Battleships." In *The Pacific War Papers: Japanese Documents of World War II*, edited by Donald Goldstein and Katherine Dillon. Washington, DC: Potomac Books, 2004.

Clancey, Patrick. "Hyperwar: U.S. Navy in World War II." Hyperwar: World War II on the World Wide Web. http://www.ibiblio.org/hyperwar/USN/ (accessed February 2009).

Cook, Charles. *The Battle of Cape Esperance: Encounter at Guadalcanal.* Annapolis, MD: Naval Institute Press, 1992.

Cox, Robert. *The Battle off Samar: Taffy III and Leyte Gulf.* Groton, CT: Ivy Alba, 2003.

Crabb, Brigadier General J. V. *Fifth Air Force's Air War against Japan, September 1942 to August 1945*. February 1946. (Located at Air University Library, Maxwell Air Force Base, Montgomery, AL.) http://www.au.af.mil/au/aul/bibs/japan/jpnwwii.pdf.

Craven, Wesley, and James Cate. *The Army Air Forces in World War II*. Vol. 4, *The Pacific: Guadalcanal to Saipan, August 1942 to July 1944*, and vol. 5, *The Pacific: Matterhorn to Nagasaki, June 1944 to August 1945*. Washington, DC: Office of Air Force History, 1983.

Crenshaw, Russell. *The Battle of Tassafaronga*. Baltimore, MD: Nautical & Aviation Publishing Company of America, 1995.

————. *South Pacific Destroyer: The Battle for the Solomons from Savo Island to Vela Gulf.* Annapolis, MD: Naval Institute Press, 1998.

Fukaya, Hajime. "Japan's Wartime Carrier Construction." United States Naval Institute *Proceedings* 81 (September 1955).

Genda, Minoru. "Tactical Planning in the Imperial Japanese Navy." *Naval War College Review* 22 (October 1969).

Gray, James. "Development of Naval Night Fighters in World War II." United States Naval Institute *Proceedings* 74 (July 1948).

Halsey, Ashley. "The CVL's Success Story." United States Naval Institute *Proceedings* 72 (April 1946).

Halsey, William. "The Battle for Leyte Gulf." United States Naval Institute *Proceedings* 78 (May 1952).

Halsey, William, and J. Bryan. *Admiral Halsey's Story.* New York: McGraw Hill, 1947.

Holmes, Wilfred. *Double-Edged Secrets: U.S. Naval Intelligence Operations in the Pacific during World War II.* Annapolis, MD: Naval Institute Press, 1979.

Horikoshi, Jiro. *Eagles of Mitsubishi: The Story of the Zero Fighter.* Translated by S. Shindo and H. Wantiez. London: Orbis, 1981.

Ike, Nobutaka, ed. *Japan's Decision for War: Records of the 1941 Policy Conferences.* Stanford, CA: Stanford University Press, 1967.

Inoguchi, Rikihei, Tadashi Najajima, and Roger Pineau. *The Divine Wind: Japan's Kamikaze Force in World War II.* Annapolis, MD: Naval Institute Press, 1958.

Inoguchi, Rikihei, and Tadashi Nakajima. "The Kamikaze Attack Corps." In *The Japanese Navy in World War II: In the Words of Former Japanese Naval Officers,* edited by David Evans. 2nd ed. Annapolis, MD: Naval Institute Press, 1986.

Jurika, Stephen. "The *Franklin*: Tragedy and Triumph." In *Carrier Warfare in the Pacific,* edited by E. T. Wooldridge. Washington, DC: Smithsonian Institution, 1993.

Karig, Walter. *Battle Report: The End of an Empire.* New York: Rinehart & Co., 1948.

————. *Battle Report: Pacific War, Middle Phase.* New York: Rinehart & Co., 1947.

————. *Battle Report: Pearl Harbor to Coral Sea.* New York: Farrar & Rinehart, 1944.

Kenney, George. *General Kenney Reports: A Personal History of the Pacific War.* New York: Duell, Sloan, and Pearce, 1949.

King, Ernest. *U.S. Navy at War, 1941–1945.* Washington, DC: Headquarters of the Commander-in-Chief, U.S. Fleet, 1946.

King, Ernest, and Walter Whitehill. *Fleet Admiral King: A Naval Record.* London: Eyre & Spottiswoode, 1953.

Kondo, Nobutake. "Some Opinions Concerning the War." In *The Pacific War Papers: Japanese Documents of World War II,* edited by Donald Goldstein and Katherine Dillon. Washington, DC: Potomac Books, 2004.

Koyanagi, Tomiji. "The Battle of Leyte Gulf." In *The Japanese Navy in World War II,* edited by David Evans. 2nd ed. Annapolis, MD: Naval Institute Press, 1986.

Kuwahara, Yasuo, and Gordon Allred. *Kamikaze*. New York: Ballantine, 1957.

Lee, Fitzhugh. "First Cruise of the *Essex*." In *Carrier Warfare in the Pacific*, edited by E. T. Wooldridge. Washington, DC: Smithsonian Institution, 1993.

Lynch, Joe. "The Last Dogfight." In *Aces against Japan*. Vol. 1, edited by Eric Hammel. Pacifica, CA: Presidio, 1992.

Matloff, Maurice, and Edwin Snell. *Strategic Planning for Coalition Warfare*. United States Army in World War II: The War Department. Washington, DC: Office of the Chief of Military History, 1950–1955.

McCampbell, David. "Doctrine for a Fighter Pilot." In *Carrier Warfare in the Pacific*, edited by E. T. Wooldridge. Washington, DC: Smithsonian Institution, 1993.

Monsarrat, John. *Angel on the Yardarm: Memoir of a Naval Officer in World War II*. Newport, RI: Naval War College Press, 1979.

Morley, James. *The Fateful Choice: Japan's Advance into Southeast Asia, 1939–41*, and *The Final Confrontation: Japan's Negotiations with the United States, 1941*. Translated versions of official history series *Taiheiyo Senso e no Michi: Kaisen Gaikoshi* [Japan's Road to the Pacific War]. New York: Columbia University Press, 1980–94.

Morton, Louis. *Strategy and Command: The First Two Years*. United States Army in World War II: The War in the Pacific. Washington, DC: Office of the Chief of Military History, 1962–1989.

Office of Naval Intelligence. ONI 225-J, *Japanese Naval Vessels of World War II: As Seen by U.S. Naval Intelligence*. Annapolis, MD: Naval Institute Press, 1987.

Oi, Atsushi. "Why Japan's Anti-submarine Warfare Failed." In *The Japanese Navy in World War II*, edited by David Evans. 2nd ed. Annapolis, MD: Naval Institute Press, 1986.

Okumiya, Masatake, and Jiro Horikoshi, with Martin Caidin. *Zero!: The Story of the Japanese Navy Air Force, 1937–1945*. London: Cassell, 1956.

Ozawa, Jisaburo. "Development of the Japanese Navy's Operational Concept against America." In *The Pacific War Papers: Japanese Documents of World War II*, edited by Donald Goldstein and Katherine Dillon. Washington, DC: Potomac Books, 2004.

Porter, Bruce. "First Kill." In *Aces against Japan*. Vol. 2, edited by Eric Hammel. Pacifica, CA: Pacifica Press, 1996.

Puleston, William. *The Armed Forces of the Pacific: A Comparison of the Military and Naval Power of the United States and Japan*. New Haven, CT: Yale University Press, 1941.

Robertson, D. C. *Operations Analysis: The Battle for Leyte Gulf*. Newport, RI: Naval War College, 1993.

Spector, Ronald, ed. *Listening to the Enemy: Key Documents on the Role of Communications Intelligence in the War with Japan*. Wilmington, DE: Scholarly Resources, 1988.

Thach, John. "Butch O'Hare and the Thach Weave" and "The Big Blue Blanket." In *Carrier Warfare in the Pacific*, edited by E. T. Wooldridge. Washington, DC: Smithsonian Institution, 1993.

Trousdale, James. "The Birth of the Navy's Night Fighters." United States Naval Institute *Proceedings* 78 (June 1952).

United States Strategic Bombing Survey. *Japanese Military and Naval Intelligence Division*. Washington, DC: Government Printing Office, 1946.

———. *Summary Report, Pacific War*. Washington, DC: Government Printing Office, 1946.

Wendorf, Wendy. "Blood over Kwajalein." In *Aces against Japan*. Vol. 2, edited by Eric Hammel. Pacifica, CA: Pacifica Press, 1996.

Yokoi, Toshiyuki. "Thoughts on Japan's Naval Defeat." In *The Japanese Navy in World War II*, edited by David Evans. 2nd ed. Annapolis, MD: Naval Institute Press, 1986.

Zacharias, Ellis. *Secret Missions: The Story of an Intelligence Officer*. New York: G. P. Putnam's Sons, 1946.

Secondary Sources

Agawa, Hiroyuki. *The Reluctant Admiral: Yamamoto and the Imperial Navy*. Tokyo: Kodansha, 1979.

Aldrich, Richard. *Intelligence and the War against Japan: Britain, America, and the Politics of Secret Service*. Cambridge, England: Cambridge University Press, 2000.

Andrew, Christopher. *For the President's Eyes Only: Secret Intelligence and the American Presidency from Washington to Bush*. London: HarperCollins, 1995.

———. "Intelligence, International Relations, and 'Under-theorisation.'" *Intelligence and National Security* 19, no. 2 (2004).

Andrew, Christopher, and David Dilks. "Introduction." In *The Missing Dimension: Governments and Intelligence Communities in the Twentieth Century*, edited by Christopher Andrew and David Dilks. Chicago: Illinois University Press, 1985.

Asada, Sadao. "The Japanese Navy and the United States." In *Pearl Harbor as History*, edited by Dorothy Borg and Shumpei Okamoto. New York: Columbia University Press, 1973.

Astor, Gerald. *Operation Iceberg: The Invasion and Conquest of Okinawa in World War II*. New York: Dell, 1995.

Axell, Albert, and Hideaki Kase. *Kamikaze: Japan's Suicide Gods*. London: Pearson, 2002.

Baer, George. *One Hundred Years of Sea Power: The U.S. Navy, 1890–1990*. Stanford, CA: Stanford University Press, 1994.

Barnhart, Michael. "Japanese Intelligence before the Second World War: Best-case Analysis." In *Knowing One's Enemies: Intelligence Assessment before the Two World Wars*, edited by Ernest May. Princeton, NJ: Princeton University Press, 1984.

Bath, Alan. *Tracking the Axis Enemy: The Triumph of Anglo-American Naval Intelligence*. Lawrence: Kansas University Press, 1998.

Beasley, William. *Japanese Imperialism, 1894–1945*. Oxford: Oxford University Press, 1987.

Belote, James, and William Belote. *Titans of the Seas: The Development and Operations of Japanese and American Carrier Task Forces during World War II*. New York: Harper & Row, 1975.

Benedict, Ruth. *The Chrysanthemum and the Sword: Patterns in Japanese Culture*. Cambridge, MA: Riverside, 1946.

Bergerud, Eric. *Fire in the Sky: The Air War in the South Pacific*. Boulder, CO: Westview, 1999.

Best, Antony. *British Intelligence and the Japanese Challenge in Asia, 1914–1941*. London: Macmillan, 2002.

Betts, Richard. "Analysis, War, and Decision: Why Intelligence Failures are Inevitable." *World Politics* 31, no. 1 (1978–79).

———. *Surprise Attack: Lessons for Defense Planning*. Washington, DC: Brookings Institution, 1982.

Blair, Clay. *Silent Victory: The U.S. Submarine War against Japan*. New York: J. B. Lippincott, 1975.

Booth, Ken. *Strategy and Ethnocentrism*. New York: Holmes & Meier, 1979.

Boyd, Carl. "Japanese Military Effectiveness: The Interwar Period." In *The Interwar Period*, vol. 2 of *Military Effectiveness*, edited by Allan Millett and Williamson Murray. Boston: Allen & Unwin, 1988.

Boyd, Carl, and Akihiko Yoshida. *The Japanese Submarine Force and World War II*. Annapolis, MD: Naval Institute Press, 1995.

Brown, Louis. *Technical and Military Imperatives: A Radar History of World War II*. Philadelphia: Institute of Physics, 1999.

Brune, Lester. *The Origins of American National Security Policy: Sea Power, Air Power, and Foreign Policy, 1900–1941*. Manhattan, KS: MA/AH Publishing, 1981.

———. *Master of Sea Power: A Biography of Admiral Ernest J. King*. Boston: Little, Brown and Co., 1980.

Buell, Thomas. *The Quiet Warrior: A Biography of Raymond A. Spruance*. Boston: Little, Brown and Co., 1974.

Bueschel, Richard. *Mitsubishi A6M1/2 Zero-sen in Imperial Japanese Naval Air Service*. Oxford: Osprey, 1970.

Buhl, Lance. "Maintaining 'an American Navy,' 1865–1889." In *In Peace and War: Interpretations of American Naval History, 1775–1984*, edited by Kenneth Hagan. 2nd ed. London: Greenwood, 1984.

Campbell, N. J. M. *Naval Weapons of World War II*. London: Conway, 2002.

Chapman, John. "Japanese Intelligence, 1918–1945: A Suitable Case for Treatment." In *Intelligence and International Relations, 1900–1945*, edited by Christopher Andrew and Jeremy Noakes. Exeter, England: Exeter University Press, 1987.

Christman, Calvin. "Franklin D. Roosevelt and the Craft of Strategic Assessment." In *Calculations, Net Assessment, and the Coming of World War II*, edited by Williamson Murray and Allan Millett. New York: Free Press, 1992.

Cohen, Eliot. "The Strategy of Innocence?: The United States, 1920–1945." In *The Making of Strategy: Rulers, States, and War*, edited by Williamson Murray, MacGregor Knox, and Alvin Bernstein. Cambridge, England: Cambridge University Press, 1994.

Cohen, Jerome. *Japan's Economy in War and Reconstruction*. Japanese Economic History, 1930–1960, edited by Janet Hunter, vol. 2. London: Routledge, 2000.

Condon, John. *Corsairs and Flattops: Marine Carrier Air Warfare, 1944–1945*. Annapolis, MD: Naval Institute Press, 1998.

Coombe, Jack. *Derailing the Tokyo Express: The Naval Battles for the Solomon Islands that Sealed Japan's Fate*. Harrisburg, PA: Stackpole, 1991.

Coox, Alvin. "The Effectiveness of the Japanese Military Establishment in the Second World War." In *The Second World War*, vol. 3 of *Military Effectiveness*, edited by Allan Millett and Williamson Murray. Boston: Allen & Unwin, 1988.

Corbett, Julian. *Some Principles of Maritime Strategy*. Annapolis, MD: Naval Institute Press, 1988. Originally published in 1911 by Longmans, London.

Costello, John. *The Pacific War, 1941–1945*. New York: Rawson-Wade, 1982.

Cutler, Thomas. *The Battle of Leyte Gulf, 23–26 October 1944*. New York: HarperCollins, 1994.

Dickson, David. *The Battle of the Philippine Sea*. London: Ian Allan, 1975.

Dorwart, Jeffery. *Conflict of Duty: The U.S. Navy's Intelligence Dilemma, 1919–1945*. Annapolis, MD: Naval Institute Press, 1983.

Douglas, Lawrence. "Robert Edward Coontz." In *The Chiefs of Naval Operations*, edited by Robert Love. Annapolis, MD: Naval Institute Press, 1980.

Dower, John. *War without Mercy: Race and Power in the Pacific War*. New York: Pantheon, 1986.

Dull, Paul. *A Battle History of the Imperial Japanese Navy*. Annapolis, MD: Naval Institute Press, 1978.

Dunn, William. "Intelligence and Decision-making." In *Intelligence: Policy, and Process*, edited by Alfred Maurer, Marion Tunstall, and James Keagle. Boulder, CO: Westview, 1985.

Dyer, George. *The Amphibians Came to Conquer: The Story of Admiral Richmond Kelly Turner*. Washington, DC: Naval Historical Center, 1969.

Edwards, Bernard. *Salvo: Classic Naval Gun Actions*. London: Arms & Armour, 1999.

Ellis, John. *Brute Force: Allied Strategy and Tactics in the Second World War*. London: André Deutsch, 1990.

Evans, David, and Mark Peattie. *Kaigun: The Strategy, Tactics, and Technology of the Imperial Japanese Navy, 1887–1941*. Annapolis, MD: Naval Institute Press, 1997.

Falk, Stanley. *Decision at Leyte*. New York: W. W. Norton, 1966.

Farago, Ladislas. *The Broken Seal: The Story of "Operation Magic" and the Pearl Harbor Disaster*. New York: Random House, 1967.

Felton, Mark. *Yanagi: The Secret Underwater Trade between Germany and Japan, 1942–1945*. Barnsley, England: Pen & Sword, 2005.

Ferris, John. "A British 'Unofficial' Aviation Mission and Japanese Naval Developments, 1919–1929." *Journal of Strategic Studies* 5 (September 1982).

———. "Intelligence." In *The Origins of World War Two: The Debate Continues*, edited by Robert Boyce and Joseph Maiolo. Basingstoke, England: Palgrave / Macmillan, 2003.

Ford, Douglas. *Britain's Secret War against Japan, 1937–1945*. Abingdon, England: Routledge / Taylor & Francis, 2006.

———. "Realistic Caution and Ambivalent Optimism: U.S. Intelligence Assessments and War Preparations against Japan, 1918–1941." *Diplomacy and Statecraft* 21 (2010).

————. "Strategic Culture, Intelligence Assessment, and the Conduct of the Pacific War, 1941–1945: The British-Indian and Imperial Japanese Armies in Comparison." *War in History* 14, no. 1 (2007).

————. "U.S. Naval Intelligence and the Imperial Japanese Fleet during the Washington Treaty Era, c.1922–1936." *Mariner's Mirror* 93, no. 3 (2007).

Forrestel, Emmet. *Admiral Raymond A. Spruance: A Study in Command*. Washington, DC: Naval Historical Center, 1966.

Françillon, René. *Japanese Aircraft of the Pacific War*. New York: Funk & Wagnalls, 1979.

Frank, Richard. *Guadalcanal: The Definitive Account of the Landmark Battle*. New York: Penguin, 1990.

Friedman, Norman. *U.S. Aircraft Carriers*. Annapolis, MD: Naval Institute Press, 1983.

————. *The U.S. Maritime Strategy*. London: Jane's, 1988.

Gluck, Carol. *Japan's Modern Myths: Ideology in the Late Meiji Period*. Princeton, NJ: Princeton University Press, 1985.

Grabo, Cynthia. *Anticipating Surprise: Analysis for Strategic Warning*. Lanham, MD: University Press of America, 2004.

Grace, James. *The Naval Battle of Guadalcanal: Night Action, 13 November 1942*. Annapolis, MD: Naval Institute Press, 1999.

Gray, Colin. *Modern Strategy*. Oxford: Oxford University Press, 1999.

————. *Strategy for Chaos: Revolutions in Military Affairs and the Evidence of History*. London: Frank Cass, 2002.

Griffith, Thomas. *MacArthur's Airman: General George C. Kenney and the War in the Southwest Pacific*. Lawrence: Kansas University Press, 1998.

Grove, Eric. "The Aircraft Carrier Fighter Control Revolution: How the Aircraft Carrier became an Effective Anti-air Warfare System." Paper presented at King Hall Naval History Conference, Canberra, Australia, July 2007.

Guerlac, Henry. *Radar in World War II*. History of Modern Physics, 1800–1950, vol. 8. Philadelphia: American Institute of Physics, 1987.

Hagan, Kenneth. *This People's Navy: The Making of American Sea Power*. New York: Free Press, 1991.

Hammel, Eric. *Carrier Clash: The Invasion of Guadalcanal and the Battle of the Eastern Solomons, August 1942*. St. Paul, MN: Zenith, 2004.

————. *Carrier Strike: The Battle of the Santa Cruz Islands, October 1942*. St. Paul, MN: Zenith, 2004.

Handel, Michael. Introductory essay. In *Intelligence and Military Operations*, edited by Michael Handel. London: Frank Cass, 1990.

————. *War, Strategy, and Intelligence*. London: Frank Cass, 1989.

Hara, Akira. "Japan: Guns before Rice." In *The Economics of World War II*, edited by Mark Harrison. Cambridge, England: Cambridge University Press, 1998.

Hata, Ikuhiko, and Yasuho Izawa. *Japanese Naval Aces and Fighter Units in World War II*. Translated by Don Gorham. Annapolis, MD: Naval Institute Press, 1989.

Hayes, Grace. *The History of the Joint Chiefs of Staff in World War II: The War against Japan*. Annapolis, MD: Naval Institute Press, 1982.

Herman, Michael. *Intelligence Power in Peace and War*. Cambridge, England: Cambridge University Press / London: Royal Institute of International Affairs, 1996.

Heuer, Richards. *The Psychology of Intelligence Analysis*. Washington, DC: Center for the Study of Intelligence, 1999.

———. "The Limits of Intelligence Analysis." *Orbis* 49, no. 1 (Winter 2005).

Hone, Thomas, Trent Hone, and Mark Mandeles. *American and British Aircraft Carrier Development, 1919–1941*. Annapolis, MD: Naval Institute Press, 1999.

———. *Battle Line: The United States Navy, 1919–1939*. Annapolis, MD: Naval Institute Press, 2006.

Howse, Derek. *Radar at Sea: The Royal Navy in World War II*. Basingstoke, England: Macmillan, 1993.

Hughes, Wayne. *Fleet Tactics: Theory and Practice*. Annapolis, MD: Naval Institute Press, 1986.

Isom, Dallas. *Midway Inquest: Why the Japanese Lost the Battle of Midway*. Bloomington: Indiana University Press, 2007.

Jackson, Peter. "Historical Reflections on the Uses and Limits of Intelligence." In *Intelligence and Statecraft: The Use and Limits of Intelligence in International Society*, edited by Peter Jackson and Jennifer Siegel. Westport, CT: Greenwood, 2005.

Jentschura, Hansgeorg, Dieter Jung, and Peter Mickel. *Warships of the Imperial Japanese Navy, 1869–1945*. Translated by A. Preston and J. Brown. Annapolis, MD: Naval Institute Press, 1992.

Jervis, Robert. *Perception and Misperception in International Politics*. Princeton, NJ: Princeton University Press, 1976.

Johnson, Loch. "Bricks and Mortar for a Theory of Intelligence." *Comparative Strategy* 22 (2003).

———. "Preface to a Theory of Strategic Intelligence." *International Journal of Intelligence and Counterintelligence* 16, no. 4 (2003).

Johnston, Alastair. "Thinking about Strategic Culture." *International Security* 19, no. 4 (1995).

Johnston, Stanley. *The Grim Reapers*. London: Jarrolds, 1943.

Kahn, David. *The Codebreakers*. London: Weidenfeld & Nicolson, 1973.

———. "The United States Views Germany and Japan in 1941." In *Knowing One's Enemies: Intelligence Assessment before the Two World Wars*, edited by Ernest May. Princeton, NJ: Princeton University Press, 1984.

Kennedy, Paul. *The Rise and Fall of the Great Powers: Economic Change and Military Conflict from 1500 to 2000*. London: HarperCollins, 1988.

Kotani, Ken. *Japanese Intelligence in World War II*. Translated by C. Kotani. Oxford: Osprey, 2009.

———. "Pearl Harbor: Japanese Planning and Command Structure." In *The Pacific War Companion: From Pearl Harbor to Hiroshima*, edited by Daniel Marston. New York: Osprey, 2007.

Krebs, Gerhard. "The Japanese Air Forces." In *The Conduct of the Air War in the Second World War: An International Comparison*, edited by Horst Borg. Oxford: Berg, 1992.

Kuehn, John. *Agents of Innovation: The General Board and the Design of the Fleet that Defeated the Japanese Navy.* Annapolis, MD: Naval Institute Press, 2008.

Lamont-Brown, Raymond. *Kamikaze: Japan's Suicide Samurai.* London: Arms & Armour, 1997.

Lefebvre, Stéphane. "A Look at Intelligence Analysis." *International Journal of Intelligence and Counterintelligence* 17, no. 2 (2004).

Lewin, Ronald. *The Other ULTRA: Codes, Cyphers, and the Defeat of Japan.* London: Hutchinson, 1982.

Lindley, John. *Carrier Victory: The Air War in the Pacific.* New York: Elsevier-Dutton, 1978.

Love, Robert. "Ernest Joseph King." In *The Chiefs of Naval Operations*, edited by Robert Love. Annapolis, MD: Naval Institute Press, 1980.

Lowenthal, Mark. "The Burdensome Concept of Failure. In *Intelligence: Policy and Process*, edited by Alfred Maurer, Marion Tunstall, and James Keagle. Boulder, CO: Westview, 1985.

———. *Leadership and Indecision: American War Planning and Policy Process, 1937–1942.* 2 vols. New York: Garland, 1988.

Loxton, Bruce, and Chris Coulthard-Clark. *The Shame of Savo: Anatomy of a Naval Disaster.* Annapolis, MD: Naval Institute Press, 1994.

Lundstrom, John. *The First Team and the Guadalcanal Campaign: Naval Fighter Combat from August to November 1942.* Annapolis, MD: Naval Institute Press, 1994.

———. *The First Team: Naval Air Combat from Pearl Harbor to Midway.* Annapolis, MD: Naval Institute Press, 1984.

Luttwak, Edward. *Strategy: The Logic of War and Peace.* Cambridge, MA: Harvard University Press / Belknap Press, 1987.

MacIntyre, David. *Leyte Gulf: Armada in the Pacific.* London: MacDonald & Co., 1969.

Macmillan, A., Ken Booth, and Russell Trood. "Strategic Culture." In *Strategic Cultures in the Asia-Pacific Region*, edited by Ken Booth and Russell Trood. Basingstoke, England: Macmillan, 1999.

Mahan, Alfred. *The Influence of Sea Power on History, 1660–1783.* London: Constable & Co., 1987.

Mahnken, Thomas. *Uncovering Ways of War: U.S. Intelligence and Foreign Military Innovation, 1918–1941.* Ithaca, NY: Cornell University Press, 2002.

Marder, Arthur. *Strategic Illusions, 1936–41.* Vol. 1 of *Old Friends, New Enemies: The Royal Navy and the Imperial Japanese Navy, 1936–45.* Oxford: Oxford University Press, 1981.

Matthias, Willard. *America's Strategic Blunders: Intelligence Analysis and National Security Policy from 1936 to 1991.* University Park, PA: Pennsylvania State University Press, 2001.

May, Ernest. "Capabilities and Proclivities." In *Knowing One's Enemies: Intelligence Assessment before the Two World Wars*, edited by Ernest May. Princeton, NJ: Princeton University Press, 1984.

McBride, William. "Challenging a Strategic Paradigm: Aviation and the U.S. Navy Special Policy Board of 1924." *Journal of Strategic Studies* 14, no. 1 (1991).

Merrill, James. *A Sailor's Admiral: A Biography of William F. Halsey.* New York: Thomas Y. Crowell, 1976.

Mersky, Peter. *The Grim Reapers: Fighting Squadron Ten in World War II*. Mesa, AZ: Champlin Fighter Museum, 1986.

Mikesh, Robert. *Broken Wings of the Samurai: The Destruction of the Japanese Air Force*. Shrewsbury, England: Airlife, 1993.

———. *Japanese Aircraft: Code Names and Designations*. Atglen, PA: Schiffer, 1993.

———. *Zero: Combat and Development History of Japan's Legendary Mitsubishi A6M Zero Fighter*. Osceola, WI: Motorbooks, 1994.

Miller, Edward. *War Plan Orange: The U.S. Strategy to Defeat Japan, 1897–1945*. Annapolis, MD: Naval Institute Press, 1991.

Miller, Thomas. *The Cactus Air Force*. New York: Harper & Row, 1969.

Millett, Allan. "Patterns of Military Innovation in the Interwar Period." In *Military Innovation in the Interwar Period*, edited by Allan Millett and Williamson Murray. Cambridge, England: Cambridge University Press, 1996.

Millett, Allan, and Williamson Murray. *A War to be Won: Fighting the Second World War*. Cambridge, MA: Harvard University Press / Belknap Press, 2000.

Millett, Allan, Williamson Murray, and Kenneth Watman. "The Effectiveness of Military Organizations." *International Security* 11, no. 1 (1986).

Milward, Alan. *War, Economy, and Society, 1939–1945*. London: Penguin, 1977.

Morgan, Forrest. *Compellence and the Strategic Culture of Imperial Japan: Implications for Coercive Diplomacy in the Twenty-first Century*. Westport, CT: Praeger, 2003.

Morison, Samuel. *The Rising Sun in the Pacific, 1931–April 1942*. History of United States Naval Operations in World War II, vol. 3. Urbana and Chicago: University of Illinois Press, 2001.

———. *Coral Sea, Midway, and Submarine Actions, May 1942 to August 1942*. History of United States Naval Operations in World War II, vol. 4. Boston: Little, Brown and Co., 1988.

———. *The Struggle for Guadalcanal, August 1942 to February 1943*. History of United States Naval Operations in World War II, vol. 5. Boston: Little, Brown and Co., 1989.

———. *Breaking the Bismarks Barrier, 22 July 1942 to 1 May 1944*. History of United States Naval Operations in World War II, vol. 6. Boston: Little, Brown and Co., 1988.

———. *Aleutians, Gilberts and Marshalls, June 1942 to April 1944*. History of United States Naval Operations in World War II, vol. 7. Edison, NJ: Castle Books, 2001.

———. *New Guinea and the Marianas, March 1944 to August 1944*. History of United States Naval Operations in World War II, vol. 8. Edison, NJ: Castle Books, 2001.

———. *Leyte, June 1944 to January 1945*. History of United States Naval Operations in World War II, vol. 9. Boston: Little, Brown and Co., 1988.

———. *The Liberation of the Philippines: Luzon, Mindanao, the Visayas, 1944–45*. History of United States Naval Operations in World War II, vol. 13. Urbana and Chicago: University of Illinois Press, 2002.

———. *Victory in the Pacific, 1945*. History of United States Naval Operations in World War II, vol. 14. Edison, NJ: Castle Books, 2001.

Morton, Louis. "War Plan Orange: Evolution of a Strategy." *World Politics* 11, no. 2 (January 1959).

Muir, Malcolm. "Rearming in a Vacuum: U.S. Navy Intelligence and the Japanese Capital Ship Threat, 1936–1945." *Journal of Military History* 54, no. 4 (1990).

———. "The United States Navy in World War II: An Assessment." In *Reevaluating Major Naval Combatants of World War II*, edited by James Sadkovich. Westport, CT: Greenwood, 1990.

Murray, Williamson. "Does Military Culture Matter?: The Future of American Military Culture." *Orbis* 43 (1999).

———. "Innovation: Past and Future." In *Military Innovation in the Interwar Period*, edited by Alan Millett and Williamson Murray. Cambridge, England: Cambridge University Press, 1996.

Murray, Williamson, and MacGregor Knox, "Thinking about Revolutions in Warfare," and "The Future Behind Us." In *The Dynamics of Military Revolution, 1300–2050*, edited by Williamson Murray and MacGregor Knox. Cambridge, England: Cambridge University Press, 2001.

O'Hara, Vincent. *The U.S. Navy against the Axis: Surface Combat, 1941–45*. Annapolis, MD: Naval Institute Press, 2007.

Ohnuki-Tierney, Emiko. *Kamikaze, Cherry Blossoms, and Nationalisms: The Militarization of Aesthetics in Japanese History*. Chicago: Chicago University Press, 2002.

Overy, Richard. *Why the Allies Won*. New York: Norton, 1995.

Packard, Wyman. *A Century of U.S. Naval Intelligence*. Washington, DC: Office of Naval Intelligence / Naval Historical Center, 1996.

Parillo, Mark. *The Japanese Merchant Marine in World War II*. Annapolis, MD: Naval Institute Press, 1993.

Parshall, Jonathan, and Anthony Tully. *Shattered Sword: The Untold Story of the Battle of Midway*. Washington, DC: Potomac Books, 2005.

Peattie, Mark. *Sunburst: The Rise of Japanese Naval Air Power, 1909–1941*. Annapolis, MD: Naval Institute Press, 2001.

Poolman, Kenneth. *The Winning Edge: Naval Technology in Action, 1939–1945*. Annapolis, MD: Naval Institute Press, 1997.

Potter, Elmer. *Nimitz*. Annapolis, MD: Naval Institute Press, 1976.

Prados, John. *Combined Fleet Decoded: The Secret History of American Intelligence and the Japanese Navy in World War II*. Annapolis, MD: Naval Institute Press, 1995.

Prange, Gordon. *At Dawn We Slept: The Untold Story of Pearl Harbor*. London: Michael Joseph, 1981.

Rearden, Jim. *Cracking the Zero Mystery: How the U.S. Learned to Beat Japan's Vaunted WWII Fighter*. Harrisburg, PA: Stackpole, 1990.

Reynolds, Clark. *Admiral John H. Towers: The Struggle for Naval Air Supremacy*. Annapolis, MD: Naval Institute Press, 1991.

———. *The Fast Carriers: The Forging of an Air Navy*. New York: McGraw Hill, 1968.

———. *On the Warpath in the Pacific: Admiral Jocko Clark and the Fast Carriers*. Annapolis, MD: Naval Institute Press, 2005.

Rielly, Robin. *Kamikazes, Corsairs, and Picket Ships: Okinawa, 1945*. Philadelphia: Casemate, 2008.

Rosen, Philip. "The Treaty Navy, 1919–1937." In *In Peace and War: Interpretations of American Naval History, 1775–1984*, edited by Kenneth Hagan. 2nd ed. London: Greenwood, 1984.

Rosen, Stephen. *Winning the Next War: Innovation and the Modern Military*. Ithaca, NY: Cornell University Press, 1991.

Ross, Steven. *American War Plans, 1941–1945*. London: Frank Cass, 1997.

Sajima, Naoko. "Japan: Strategic Culture at the Crossroads." In *Strategic Cultures in the Asia-Pacific Region*, edited by Ken Booth and Russell Trood. Basingstoke, England: Macmillan, 1999.

Sakaida, Henry. *Imperial Japanese Navy Aces, 1937–1945*. Oxford: Osprey, 1999.

Sauer, Howard. *The Last Big-Gun Naval Battle: The Battle of Surigao Strait*. El Cerrito, CA: Glencannon, 1999.

Scott, Len, and Peter Jackson. "The Study of Intelligence in Theory and Practice." *Intelligence and National Security* 19, no. 2 (2004).

Sherrod, Robert. *History of Marine Corps Aviation in World War II*. Washington, DC: Combat Forces Press, 1952.

Skulski, Janusz. *The Battleship Yamato: Anatomy of the Ship*. London: Conway, 1988.

Smith, Geoffrey. "An Uncertain Passage: The Bureaus Run the Navy, 1842–1861." In *In Peace and War: Interpretations of American Naval History, 1775–1984*, edited by Kenneth Hagan. 2nd ed. London: Greenwood, 1984.

Solberg, Carl. *Decision and Dissent: With Halsey at Leyte Gulf*. Annapolis, MD: Naval Institute Press, 1995.

Spector, Ronald. *At War at Sea: Sailors and Naval Combat in the Twentieth Century*. New York: Viking, 2001.

———. *Eagle against the Sun: The American War with Japan*. New York: Viking, 1985.

———. *Professors of War: The Naval War College and the Development of the Naval Profession*. Newport, RI: Naval War College Press, 1977.

———. "The Triumph of Professional Ideology: The U.S. Navy in the 1890s." In *In Peace and War: Interpretations of American Naval History, 1775–1984*, edited by Kenneth Hagan. 2nd ed. London: Greenwood, 1984.

Stille, Mark. *Imperial Japanese Navy Aircraft Carriers, 1921–45*. Oxford: Osprey, 2005.

———. *U.S. Navy Aircraft Carriers*. Oxford: Osprey, 2007.

Sun Tzu. *The Art of War*. Translated, with a historical introduction by Ralph Sawyer. Boulder, CO: Westview, 1994.

Talbott, J. E. "Weapons Development, War Planning, and Policy: The U.S. Navy and the Submarine, 1917–1941." *Naval War College Review* 37 (May/June 1984).

Taylor, Theodore. *The Magnificent Mitscher*. New York: W. W. Norton, 1991.

Till, Geoffrey. "Adopting the Aircraft Carrier: The British, American, and Japanese Case Studies." In *Military Innovation in the Interwar Period*, edited by Allan Millett and Williamson Murray. Cambridge, England: Cambridge University Press, 1996.

Tillman, Barrett. *Clash of the Carriers: The True Story of the Marianas Turkey Shoot of World War II*. New York: NAL Caliber, 2005.

————. *Corsair: The F4U in World War II and Korea*. Annapolis, MD: Naval Institute Press, 1979.

————. *Hellcat: The F6F in World War II*. Annapolis, MD: Naval Institute Press, 1979.

Tsuzuki, Chushichi. *The Pursuit of Power in Modern Japan, 1825–1995*. Oxford: Oxford University Press, 2000.

Tuleja, Thaddeus. *Statesmen and Admirals: Quest for a Far Eastern Naval Policy*. New York: W. W. Norton, 1963.

————. "Defending the New Empire, 1900–1914." In *In Peace and War: Interpretations of American Naval History, 1775–1984*, edited by Kenneth Hagan. 2nd ed. London: Greenwood, 1984.

Turk, Richard. "Edward Walter Eberle." In *The Chiefs of Naval Operations*, edited by Robert Love. Annapolis, MD: Naval Institute Press, 1980.

Turnbull, Archibald, and Clifford Lord. *History of United States Naval Aviation*. New Haven, CT: Yale University Press, 1949.

Utley, Jonathan. *Going to War with Japan, 1937–1941*, Knoxville: Tennessee University Press, 1985.

Van Creveld, Martin. *Command in War*. Cambridge, MA: Harvard University Press, 1985.

Vandervat, Dan. *The Pacific Campaign*. London: Hodder & Stoughton, 1991.

Vann Woodward, Comer. *The Battle for Leyte Gulf*. New York: Macmillan, 1947.

Vlahos, Michael. *The Blue Sword: The Naval War College and the American Mission, 1919–1941*. Newport, RI: Naval War College Press, 1980.

————. "The Naval War College and the Origins of War Planning against Japan." *Naval War College Review* 33 (July/August 1980).

Von Clausewitz, Carl. *On War*. Indexed edition, edited and translated by Michael Howard and Peter Paret. Princeton, NJ: Princeton University Press, 1984.

Wark, Wesley. "In Search of a Suitable Japan: British Naval Intelligence in the Pacific before the Second World War." *Intelligence and National Security* 1, no. 2 (1986).

————. *The Ultimate Enemy: British Intelligence and Nazi Germany, 1933–1939*. London: I. B. Tauris, 1985.

Warner, Denis, and Peggy Warner. *Disaster in the Pacific: New Light on the Battle of Savo Island*. Annapolis, MD: Naval Institute Press, 1992.

————. *The Sacred Warriors: Japan's Suicide Legions*. New York: Von Nostrand Reinhold, 1982.

Warner, Michael. "Wanted: A Definition of 'Intelligence.'" *Studies in Intelligence* 46, no. 3 (2002).

Watts, Anthony, and Brian Gordon. *The Imperial Japanese Navy*. New York: Doubleday, 1971.

Watts, Barry, and Williamson Murray. "Military Innovation in Peacetime." In *Military Innovation in the Interwar Period*, edited by Allan Millett and Williamson Murray. Cambridge, England: Cambridge University Press, 1996.

Weigley, Russell. *The American Way of War: A History of United States Military Strategy and Policy*. Bloomington: Indiana University Press, 1973.

Weinberg, Gerhard. *A World at Arms: A Global History of World War II*. Cambridge, England: Cambridge University Press, 1994.

Weir, Gary. "Search for an American Submarine Strategy and Design, 1916–1936." *Naval War College Review* 44 (Winter 1991).

Wheeler, Gerald. "Thomas C. Kinkaid: MacArthur's Master of Naval Warfare." In *We Shall Return!: MacArthur's Commanders and the Defeat of Japan, 1942–1945*, edited by William Leary. Lexington: Kentucky University Press, 1988.

Whitley, M. J. *Battleships of World War II: An International Encyclopedia*. London: Arms & Armour, 1998.

Wilford, Timothy. *Pearl Harbor Redefined: U.S. Navy Radio Intelligence in 1941*. Lanham, MD: University Press of America, 2001.

Willmott, Hedley. *The Battle of Leyte Gulf: The Last Fleet Action*. Bloomington: Indiana University Press, 2005.

———. "The Battle of the Philippine Sea." In *Great American Naval Battles*, edited by Jack Sweetman. Annapolis, MD: Naval Institute Press, 1998.

———. *Empires in the Balance: Japanese and Allied Pacific Strategies to April 1942*. Annapolis, MD: Naval Institute Press, 1982.

Winton, John. *ULTRA in the Pacific: How Breaking Japanese Codes and Cyphers Affected Naval Operations against Japan, 1941–45*. London: Leo Cooper, 1993.

Wohlstetter, Roberta. *Pearl Harbor: Warning and Decision*. Stanford, CA: Stanford University Press, 1962.

Wood, James. *Japanese Military Strategy in the Pacific War: Was Defeat Inevitable?* Lanham, MD: Rowman & Littlefield, 2007.

Y'Blood, William. *Red Sun Setting: The Battle of the Philippine Sea*. Annapolis, MD: Naval Institute Press, 1981.

Yoshimura, Akira. *Battleship Musashi: The Making and Sinking of the World's Biggest Battleship*. Translated by V. Murphy. Tokyo: Kodansha, 1991.

———. *Zero Fighter*. Translated by R. Kaiho and M. Gregson. Westport, CT: Praeger, 1996.

Index

About the Author

Dr. Douglas Ford holds MA and PhD degrees in international history from the London School of Economics. He currently teaches the history of warfare and diplomacy at the University of Salford in Manchester, England. He has published over a dozen scholarly works on British and U.S. intelligence during the Pacific War. This is his second book on Allied intelligence in the Asia-Pacific theater during World War II.